PENGUIN

WOMEN WRITE

GEORGE PLIMPTON is perhaps best kn_____ ...s of his experiences as an amateur playing sp_.. at the professional level: *Out of My League* (baseball); *Paper Lion* (football); *The Bogeyman* (golf); *Shadow Box* (boxing); and *Open Net* (hockey). Editor of the literary quarterly *The Paris Review*, he has also co-edited a number of best-selling books: *American Journey: The Times of Robert F. Kennedy*; *Edie: An American Biography*; and *D.V.*. His most recent book is *The Curious Case of Sidd Finch*, a novel.

MARGARET ATWOOD is the author of over twenty volumes of poetry, fiction, and non-fiction. She has received many accolades for the body of her work and individual awards for her six novels, *The Edible Woman*, *Surfacing*, *Lady Oracle*, *Life Before Man*, *Bodily Harm*, and *The Handmaid's Tale*, which was short-listed for the prestigious Booker Prize. A seventh novel, *Cat's Eye*, was published to great acclaim in 1989.

In addition to her literary accomplishments, Ms. Atwood has served as President of International P.E.N. (Canadian-Anglophone chapter), and been awarded honorary degrees from several universities. In 1987, she received the Humanist of the Year award.

Ms. Atwood was born in Ottawa and grew up in northern Ontario, Quebec, and Toronto. She has travelled widely and lived in England, Germany, France, Italy, and the United States. She now lives in Toronto with novelist Graeme Gibson and their daughter Jess.

The Paris Review was founded in 1953 by a group of young Americans including Peter Matthiessen, Harold L. Humes, George Plimpton, Thomas Guinzburg, and Donald Hall. While the emphasis of its editors was on publishing creative work rather than nonfiction (among writers who published their first short stories there were Philip Roth, Terry Southern, Evan S. Connell, and Samuel Beckett), part of the magazine's success can be attributed to its continuing series of interviews on the craft of writing.

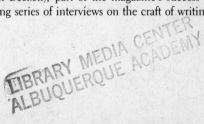

Previously Published

WRITERS AT WORK
The *Paris Review* Interviews

FIRST SERIES

Edited and introduced by MALCOLM COWLEY

E. M. Forster	Frank O'Connor
François Mauriac	Robert Penn Warren
Joyce Cary	Alberto Moravia
Dorothy Parker	Nelson Algren
James Thurber	Angus Wilson
Thornton Wilder	William Styron
William Faulkner	Truman Capote
Georges Simenon	Françoise Sagan

SECOND SERIES

Edited by GEORGE PLIMPTON and introduced by
VAN WYCK BROOKS

Robert Frost	Aldous Huxley
Ezra Pound	Ernest Hemingway
Marianne Moore	S. J. Perelman
T. S. Eliot	Lawrence Durrell
Boris Pasternak	Mary McCarthy
Katherine Anne Porter	Ralph Ellison
Henry Miller	Robert Lowell

THIRD SERIES

Edited by GEORGE PLIMPTON and introduced by ALFRED KAZIN

William Carlos Williams	Saul Bellow
Blaise Cendrars	Arthur Miller
Jean Cocteau	James Jones
Louis-Ferdinand Céline	Norman Mailer
Evelyn Waugh	Allen Ginsberg
Lillian Hellman	Edward Albee
William Burroughs	Harold Pinter

FOURTH SERIES

Edited by GEORGE PLIMPTON and introduced by WILFRID SHEED

Isak Dinesen	John Dos Passos
Conrad Aiken	Vladimir Nabokov
Robert Graves	Jorge Luis Borges
George Seferis	John Berryman
John Steinbeck	Anthony Burgess
Christopher Isherwood	Jack Kerouac
W. H. Auden	Anne Sexton
Eudora Welty	John Updike

FIFTH SERIES

Edited by GEORGE PLIMPTON and introduced by
FRANCINE DU PLESSIX GRAY

P. G. Wodehouse	Joyce Carol Oates
Pablo Neruda	Archibald MacLeish
Henry Green	Isaac Bashevis Singer
Irwin Shaw	John Cheever
James Dickey	Kingsley Amis
William Gass	Joseph Heller
Jerzy Kosinski	Gore Vidal
Joan Didion	

SIXTH SERIES

Edited by GEORGE PLIMPTON and introduced by
FRANK KERMODE

Rebecca West	Kurt Vonnegut, Jr.
Stephen Spender	Nadine Gordimer
Tennessee Williams	James Merrill
Elizabeth Bishop	Gabriel Garcia Márquez
Bernard Malamud	Carlos Fuentes
William Goyen	John Gardner

SEVENTH SERIES

Edited by GEORGE PLIMPTON and introduced by
JOHN UPDIKE

Malcolm Cowley	Arthur Koestler
William Maxwell	May Sarton
Philip Larkin	Eugene Ionesco
Elizabeth Hardwick	John Ashbery
Milan Kundera	John Barth
Edna O'Brien	Philip Roth
Raymond Carver	

EIGHTH SERIES

Edited by GEORGE PLIMPTON and introduced by
JOYCE CAROL OATES

E. B. White	Elie Wiesel
Leon Edel	Derek Walcott
Robert Fitzgerald	E. L. Doctorow
John Hersey	Anita Brookner
James Laughlin	Robert Stone
Cynthia Ozick	Joseph Brodsky
John Irving	

Women Writers at Work

The Paris Review Interviews

Edited by George Plimpton
Introduction by Margaret Atwood

PENGUIN BOOKS

PENGUIN BOOKS
Published by the Penguin Group
Viking Penguin, a division of Penguin Books USA Inc.,
40 West 23rd Street, New York, New York 10010, U.S.A.
Penguin Books Ltd, 27 Wrights Lane,
London W8 5TZ, England
Penguin Books Australia Ltd, Ringwood,
Victoria, Australia
Penguin Books Canada Ltd, 2801 John Street,
Markham, Ontario, Canada L3R 1B4
Penguin Books (N.Z.) Ltd, 182–190 Wairau Road,
Auckland 10, New Zealand

Penguin Books Ltd, Registered Offices:
Harmondsworth, Middlesex, England

First published in simultaneous hardcover and paperback editions by
Viking Penguin Inc., 1989
Published simultaneously in Canada

3 5 7 9 10 8 6 4 2

Copyright © The Paris Review, Inc., 1989
All rights reserved

The interviews in this collection are selected from *Writers at Work*, Series 1–8, published by
Viking Penguin Inc.

LIBRARY OF CONGRESS CATALOGING IN PUBLICATION DATA
Women writers at work: the Paris review interviews / edited by George
Plimpton ; introduction by Margaret Atwood.
p. cm.
ISBN 0 14 01.1790 3
1. Women authors—20th century—Interviews. 2. Literature,
Modern—20th century—History and criticism. 3. Literature, Modern—
Women authors—History and criticism. 4. Authorship.
I. Plimpton, George. II. Paris review.
PN471.W56 1989b
809'.89287—dc19   88-37078

Printed in the United States of America
Set in Electra

Contents

Introduction by Margaret Atwood   xi

1.   ISAK DINESEN   1

2.   MARIANNE MOORE   19

3.   KATHERINE ANNE PORTER   45

4.   REBECCA WEST   71

5.   DOROTHY PARKER   107

6.   LILLIAN HELLMAN   121

7.   EUDORA WELTY   147

8.   MARY McCARTHY   169

9.   ELIZABETH HARDWICK   201

10.   NADINE GORDIMER   225

11.   ANNE SEXTON   263

12.   CYNTHIA OZICK   291

13.   JOAN DIDION   319

14.   EDNA O'BRIEN   337

15.   JOYCE CAROL OATES   361

NOTES ON THE CONTRIBUTORS   385

Introduction

This new volume of the *Paris Review*'s highly praised and praiseworthy series of interviews with writers is a departure from the norm. Previous collections have mixed the genders; this one is unisexual. That the editors have chosen to bring together, within the same covers, fifteen writers as diverse as Dorothy Parker and Nadine Gordimer, Marianne Moore and Rebecca West, Isak Dinesen and Lillian Hellman, Mary McCarthy and Katherine Anne Porter, over what, in some cases, would doubtless be their dead bodies, merely because they share a double-X chromosome, is not due to a sudden mental aberration. Rather it has been the result of readers' requests. Why not a gathering of women writers? the editors were asked. Well, why not? Which is not quite the same thing as *why*.

To some the answer would seem self-evident: women writers belong together because they are different from men, and the writing they do is different as well and cannot be read with the same eyeglasses as those used for the reading of male writers. Nor can writing by women be read in the same way by men as it can by women, and vice versa. For many women, Heathcliff is a romantic hero; for many men, he is a posturing oaf they'd like to punch in the nose. For many men, *The Ginger Man*'s Sebastian Dangerfield is an energy-packed rebel; for many women, he is an immature and tiresome wife-beater. *Paradise Lost* reads differently when viewed by the daughters of Eve, and with Milton's browbeaten secretarial daughters in mind; and so on down through the canon.

Such gender-polarized analyses can reach beyond subject-matter and point of view to encompass matters of structure and style: are women really more subjective? do their novels really end with questions? Especially in this age of semiotics, gender-linked analysis may seek to explore attitudes towards language itself. Is there a distinct female *écriture?* Does the mother-tongue really belong to mothers, or is it yet one more male-shaped institution bent, like foot-binding, on the deformation and hobbling of women? I have had it suggested to me, in all seriousness, that women ought not to write at all, since to do so is to dip one's hand, like Shakespeare's dyer, into a medium both sullied and sullying. (This suggestion was not made telepathically, but in spoken sentences; since, for polemicists as for writers themselves, the alternative to language is silence.)

I was recently on a panel—that polygonal form of discourse so beloved of the democratic twentieth century—consisting entirely of women, including Jan Morris, who used to be James Morris, and Nayantara Sahgal of India. From the audience came the question, "How do you feel about being on a panel of women?" We all prevaricated. Some of us protested that we had been on lots of panels that included men; others said that most panels were male, with a woman dotted here and there for decorative effect, like parsley. Jan Morris said that she was in the process of transcending gender and was aiming at becoming a horse, to which Nayantara Sahgal replied that she hoped it was an English horse, since in some other, poorer countries, horses were not treated very well. Which underlined, for all of us, that there are categories other than male and female worth considering.

I suppose we all should have said, "Why not?" Still, I was intrigued by our collective uneasiness. No woman writer wants to be overlooked and undervalued for being a woman; but few, it seems, wish to be defined solely by gender, or constrained by loyalties to it alone—an attitude which may puzzle, hurt or enrage those whose political priorities cause them to view writing as a tool, a means towards an end, rather than as a Muse who will desert you if you break trust. In the interview which begins this collection, Dorothy Parker articulates the dilemma:

> I'm a feminist, and God knows I'm loyal to my sex, and you must remember that from my very early days, when this city was scarcely safe from buffaloes, I was in the struggle for equal rights for women. But when we paraded through the catcalls of men and when we chained ourselves to lamp posts to try to get our equality—dear child, we didn't foresee *those* female writers. (Pp. 114–115)

Male writers may suffer strains on their single-minded dedication to their art for reasons of class or race or nationality, but so far no male writer is likely to be asked to sit on a panel addressing itself to the special problems of the male writer, or be expected to support another writer simply because he happens to be a man. Such things are asked of women writers all the time, and it makes them jumpy.

Virginia Woolf may have been right about the androgynous nature of the artist, but she was right also about the differences in social situation these androgynous artists are certain to encounter. We may agree with Nadine Gordimer when she says, "By and large, I don't think it matters a damn what sex a writer is, so long as the work is that of a real *writer*" (p. 260), if what she means is that it *shouldn't* matter, in any true assessment of talent or accomplishment; but unfortunately it often has mattered, to other people. When Joyce Carol Oates is asked the "woman" question, phrased in her case as "What are the advantages of being a woman writer?", she makes a virtue of necessity:

> Advantages! Too many to enumerate, probably. Since, being a woman, I can't be taken altogether *seriously* by the sort of male critics who rank writers 1, 2, 3 in the public press, I am free, I suppose, to do as I like. (P. 382)

Joan Didion is asked the same question in its negative form—"disadvantages" instead of "advantages"—and also focuses on social differences, social acceptance and role:

> When I was starting to write—in the late fifties, early sixties—there was a kind of social tradition in which male novelists could operate. Hard drinkers, bad livers. Wives, wars, big fish, Africa, Paris, no second acts. A man who wrote novels had a role in the world, and he could play that role and do whatever he wanted behind it. A woman who wrote novels had no particular role. Women who wrote novels were quite often perceived as invalids. Carson McCullers, Jane Bowles. Flannery O'Connor of course. Novels by women tended to be described, even by their publishers, as sensitive. I'm not sure this is so true anymore, but it certainly was at the time, and I didn't much like it. I dealt with it the same way I deal with everything. I just tended my own garden, didn't pay much attention, behaved—I suppose—deviously. (Pp. 324-325)

I think of Marianne Moore, living decorously with her mother and her "dark" furniture, her height of social rebellion the courageous ignoring of the need for chaperones at Village literary parties, and wonder how many male writers could have lived such a circumscribed life and survived the image.

Not least among perceived social differences is the difficulty women writers have experienced in being taken "altogether *seriously*" as legitimate artists. Ezra Pound, writing in the second decade of this century, spoke for many male authors and critics before and since: "I distrust the 'female artist.' . . . Not wildly anti-feminist we are yet to be convinced that any woman ever invented anything in the arts." (Carpenter, A *Serious Character*, Houghton Mifflin, 1988, p. 239.) Cognate with this view of writing as a male preserve has been the image of women writers as lightweight puffballs, neurotic freaks suffering from what Edna O'Brien calls "a double dose of masochism: the masochism of the woman and that of the artist" (p. 342), or, if approved of, as honorary men. Femininity and excellence, it seemed, were mutually exclusive. Thus Katherine Anne Porter:

> If there is such a thing as a man's mind and a woman's mind—and I'm sure there is—it isn't what most critics mean when they talk about the two. If I show wisdom, they say I have a masculine mind. If I am silly and irrelevant—and Edmund Wilson says I often am—why then they say I have a typically feminine mind! . . . But I haven't ever found it unnatural to be a woman. (P. 65)

The interviewer responds with a question that is asked, in one form or another, not only of almost every woman included in this book, but of almost every woman writer ever interviewed: "But haven't you found that being a woman presented to you, as an artist, certain special problems?"

Katherine Anne Porter's reply—"I think that's very true and very right"—is by no means the only one possible. Some, such as Mary McCarthy, are clearly impatient with the question itself. McCarthy accepts some version of the "masculine" versus the "feminine" sensibility, but aligns herself firmly with the former.

INTERVIEWER: What do you think of women writers, or do you think the category "woman writer" should not be made?

MCCARTHY: Some women writers make it. I mean, there's a certain kind of woman writer who's a capital W, capital W. Virginia Woolf certainly was one, and Katherine Mansfield was one, and Elizabeth Bowen is one. Katherine Anne Porter? Don't think she really is—I mean, her writing is certainly very feminine, but I would say that there wasn't this "WW" business in Katherine Anne Porter. Who else? There's Eudora Welty, who's certainly not a "Woman Writer," though she's become one lately.

INTERVIEWER: What is it that happens to make this change?

MCCARTHY: I think they become interested in décor. You

notice the change in Elizabeth Bowen. Her early work is
much more masculine. Her later work has much more
drapery in it. . . . I was going to write a piece at some point
about this called "Sense and Sensibility," dividing women
writers into these two. I *am* for the ones who represent
sense . . . (Pp. 189–190)

Cynthia Ozick goes much farther; she refuses such dichotomies
altogether:

> INTERVIEWER: . . . you have written about the writer as
> being genderless and living in the world of "as if" rather
> than being restrained by her . . .
> OZICK: Parochial temporary commitments. . . . A writer
> is someone born with a gift. An athlete can run. A painter
> can paint. A writer has a facility with words. A good writer
> can also think. Isn't that enough to define a writer by?
> (P. 304)

Cynthia Ozick also says that the biographers of Wharton and
Woolf "missed the writer" in their subjects, and this is probably
easier to do with women than with men. There is, still, a sort of
trained-dog fascination with the idea of women writers—not that
the thing is done well, but that it is done at all, by a creature
that is not supposed to possess such capabilities. And so a biographer may well focus on the woman, on gossip and sexual detail
and domestic arrangements and political involvement, to the exclusion of the artist. But it is impossible to read any of the interviews in this book and "miss the writer." What these writers
have in common is not their diverse responses to the category
"woman writer," but their shared passion towards the category
"writer."

Reading through these interviews, I was struck again and again
by the intensity of this passion: the commitment to craft, the
informed admiration for the work of other writers from whom
they have learned, the insistence on the importance, not of what
they themselves have done, but on what has been and can be

done through the art itself. In no other art, except painting, perhaps, is the relationship of creation to creator so complex and personal and thus so potentially damaging to self-esteem: if you fail, you fail alone. The dancer realizes someone else's dance, the writer her own. The relationship of any writer towards a vocation so exacting in its specificity, so demanding of love and energy and time, so resistant to all efforts to define its essence or to categorize its best effects, is bound to be an edgy one, and in these conversations the edginess shows through. Some disclaim ego, remarkable in a collection of such strong, assertive, individual voices; others keep secrets; others fence with their considerable intelligence; others protect themselves with wit. Some recommend objectivity, McCarthy's "sense"; others, like Edna O'Brien, speak of necessary demons. It would be a brave person who would try to stuff these wonderful and various talents into one tidy box labelled "WW," and expect that acronym to be definitive. Despite the title of this book, the label should probably read, "WWAAW," Writers Who Are Also Women.

This is not the only collection of such writers that could be made. It is limited in scope by the writers actually interviewed to date by *The Paris Review*. Thus, although there are writers from the United States, Ireland, England, Denmark, and South Africa, there are none here from, for instance, India or Australia or Canada or Latin America: no Alice Munro, no Anita Desai, no Isabel Allende. As this assemblage is unisexual, so is it unicolored: thus far no Toni Morrison, no Alice Walker, no Louise Erdrich. Nor are there many writers who are known for an explicit and self-aware examination of the more colonial features of the relationships between men as a group and women: no Marilyn French, no Marge Piercey, no Fay Weldon, no Adrienne Rich, no Judith Rossner. Some of these omissions may be set down to the slowness characteristic of the mills of the gods and the editors of small magazines, a slowness which may account, too, for the retrospective slant of this volume. But looking back over the territory to see what has been done and, especially, said before, is, in the case of writing, part of the territory.

To write is a solitary and singular act; to do it superbly, as all of these writers have done, is a blessing. Despite everything that gets said about the suffering and panic and horror of being a writer, the final impression left by these remarkable voices is one of thankfulness, of humility in the face of what has been given. From Joyce Carol Oates, one of the youngest writers in this group:

> I take seriously Flaubert's statement that we must love one another in our art as the mystics love one another in God. By honoring one another's creation we honor something that deeply connects us all, and goes beyond us.
>
> (Pp. 383–384)

And from Dorothy Parker, one of the oldest:

> I want so much to write well, though I know I don't . . . But during and at the end of my life, I will adore those who have. (P. 119)

MARGARET ATWOOD, 1988

WOMEN WRITERS AT WORK

1. Isak Dinesen

Isak Dinesen was born Karen Dinesen in 1885 in Rungstedlund, Denmark, and spent her early years in the fashionable world of Copenhagen's upper class. In 1913 she became engaged to her Swedish cousin, Baron Bror von Blixen-Finecke, and they decided to emigrate to Africa and buy a farm. They were married in 1914 in Mombasa and moved onto a large plantation near Nairobi. The marriage was an unhappy one; they were separated after only a few years and divorced in 1921. Karen Blixen continued to live on the coffee plantation, which she developed and ran for seventeen years. When the coffee market collapsed in 1931, she was forced to leave Africa and return to her family home in Rungstedlund. There she dedicated herself to writing under the name of Isak Dinesen.

Seven Gothic Tales was published in England and America in 1934 and established her reputation. *Out of Africa*, a novel about her years in Kenya, was published in 1937. Her later works include *Winter's Tales* (1942), *Last Tales* (1957), *Anecdotes of Destiny* (1958), *Shadows on the Grass* (1960), and *Ehrengard* (1963).

Isak Dinesen continued to live in Denmark for the rest of her life. Her ill health in those years has been attributed to a venereal disease, caught from her husband during the first year of their marriage, which was never properly treated. She spent long periods of time in the hospital, often too ill and weak to sit upright, dictating her later stories to her secretary. She died at the age of seventy-seven on September 7, 1962.

The road to Pisa.

Herman von Spiegelhausen, a young poet of noble birth, was travelling in Italy in the spring of 1822. He was in a way desiring going from place to place in search of peace of mind and happiness which he had not found

One fine May evening he stopped at a little inn on the road to Pisa. - The air was clear as glass and filled with sweet scent and a golden clear light, a lot of swallows were flying about in it. While they made his supper ready Herman walked down the road along which a big row of high poplars grew,

Isak Dinesen manuscript page.

Micheal Batterberry

Isak Dinesen

It was, in a sense, typecasting, when a few years ago a film was planned that would have shown us Garbo playing the role of Isak Dinesen in a screen version of Out of Africa . . . for the writer was, like the actress, a "Mysterious Creature of the North." Isak Dinesen was really the Danish Baroness Karen Christentze Blixen-Finecke and was the daughter of Wilhelm Dinesen, author of a classic nineteenth-century work, Boganis' Jagtbreve (A Hunter's— or Sportsman's—Letters). Baroness Blixen published under different names in various countries: usually Isak Dinesen, but also Tania Blixen and Karen Blixen. Old friends called her Tanne, Tanya, and Tania. Then there was a delightful novel she preferred not to acknowledge for a while, though any reader with half an eye could guess the baroness hiding behind the second pseudonym, Pierre Andrézel. Literary circles have buzzed with legends about her: she is really a man, he is really a woman; "Isak Dinesen" is really a brother-and-sister collaboration; "Isak Dinesen" came to

America in the 1870s; she is really a Parisienne; he lives at Elsinore; she stays mostly in London; she is a nun; he is very hospitable and receives young writers; she is difficult to see and lives a recluse; she writes in French; no, in English; no, in Danish; she is really— and so the buzzing never stopped.

In 1934 the house of Haas and Smith (later absorbed by Random House) brought out a book called Seven Gothic Tales which Mr. Haas accepted on first reading. It became a best-seller. A favorite among writers and painters, the book was discussed from first appearance as of some permanence.

Outside the canon of modern literature, like an oriole outside a cage of moulting linnets, "Isak Dinesen" offered to her readers the unending satisfaction of the tale told: "And then what happened? . . . Well, then . . ." Her storyteller's, or ballad maker's, instinct, coupled with an individual style of well-ornamented clarity, led Hemingway, accepting the Nobel Prize, to protest it should have gone to Dinesen.

SCENE ONE

Rome, Early Summer, 1956. *The first dialogue took place in a sidewalk restaurant in the Piazza Navona, that long space, once flooded, where mock naval battles raged. The twilight darkened the sky to an iris color; against it the obelisk that stands amidst Bernini's figures seemed pale and weightless. At a café table sat Baroness Blixen, her secretary-traveling companion, Clara Svendsen, and the interviewer. The baroness was like a personage from one of her own tales. Slim, straight, chic, she was dressed in black, with long black gloves and a black Parisian hat that came forward to shadow her remarkable eyes that were lighter in color at the top than at the bottom. Her face was slender and distinguished; around her mouth and eyes played the faint ghosts of smiles, changing constantly. Her voice was pleasing, soft but with enough force and timbre for one to hear at once that this was a lady with opinions of both grave profundity and of the most enchanting frivolity. Her companion, Miss Svendsen, was a fresh-faced young person with a charming smile.*

ISAK DINESEN: Interview? Oh, dear. . . . Well, yes, I suppose so . . . but not a list of questions or a third degree, I hope. . . . I was interviewed a short time ago. . . . Terrible. . . .

MISS SVENDSEN: Yes, there was a man who came for a documentary film. . . . It was like a catechism lesson. . . .

ISAK DINESEN: Couldn't we just talk together as we've been doing, you could write down what you like? ·

INTERVIEWER: Yes, then you could scratch out some things and scribble in others.

ISAK DINESEN: Yes. I ought not to undertake too much. I've been ill for over a year and in a nursing home. I really thought I should die. I planned to die, that is, I made preparations. I expected to.

MISS SVENDSEN: The doctor in Copenhagen told me: "Tania Blixen is very clever, but the cleverest thing she's ever done is to survive these two operations."

ISAK DINESEN: I even planned a last radio talk. . . . I have made a number of radio talks on all kinds of subjects, in Denmark. . . . They seem to enjoy me as a radio speaker there. . . . I planned a talk on how easy it was to die. . . . Not a morbid message, I don't mean that, but a message of, well, cheer . . . that it was a great and lovely experience to die. But I was too ill, you know, to get it done. Now, after being so long in the nursing home and so ill, I don't feel I do really belong to this life. I am hovering like a seagull. I feel that the world is happy and splendid and goes on but that I'm not part of it. I've come to Rome to try and get into the world again. Oh, look at the sky now!

INTERVIEWER: Do you know Rome well? How long since you've been here?

ISAK DINESEN: A few years ago, when I had an audience with the Pope. I first came in 1912 as a young girl, staying with my cousin and best friend, who was married to our Danish ambassador to Rome. We rode in the Borghese Gardens then, every day. There were carriages with all the great beauties of the day in them, and one stopped and chatted. It was delightful. Now look at these motors and motor-bicycles and noise and rushing about. It's what the young today want, though: Speed is the greatest thing for them. But when I think of riding my horse—I always had a horse when I was a girl—I feel that something very precious is lost to them today. Children of my day lived differently. We had little in the way of toys, even in great houses. Modern mechanical playthings, which furnish their own motion, had hardly come into existence. We had simpler toys and had to animate them. My love of marionettes springs from this, I think. I've tried my hand at writing marionette plays. One might, of course, buy a hobbyhorse, but we loved better a knotted stick personally chosen in the woods, which our imagination could turn into Bucephalus or Pegasus. Unlike children of today, who are content from birth to be observers . . . we were creators. Young people today are not acquainted with the elements or in touch with them. Everything is mechanical and urban: Children are raised up without knowing live fire, living water, the earth. Young people want to break with the past, they hate the past, they don't want to even hear of it, and one can partly understand it. The near past to them is nothing but a long history of wars, which to them is without interest. It may be the end of something, of a kind of civilization.

INTERVIEWER: But loathe leads to love: They may be led in a circle back to a tradition. I should be frightened of indifference more.

ISAK DINESEN: Perhaps. And I myself, you know, I should like to love what they love. Now, I love jazz. I think it's the only new thing in music in my lifetime. I don't prefer it to the old music, but I enjoy it very much.

INTERVIEWER: Much of your work seems to belong to the last century. For instance, *The Angelic Avengers*.

ISAK DINESEN (*laughing*): Oh, that's my illegitimate child! During the German occupation of Denmark I thought I should go mad with boredom and dullness. I wanted so to be amused, to amuse myself, and besides I was short of money, so I went to my publisher in Copenhagen and said, Look here, will you give me an advance on a novel and send me a stenographer to dictate it to? They said they would, and she appeared, and I started dictating. I had no idea at all of what the story would be about when

I began. I added a little every day, improvising. It was very baffling to the poor stenographer.

MISS SVENDSEN: Yes, she was used to business letters, and when she'd type the story from her shorthand notes, she'd put numbers sometimes like "the 2 terrified girls" or "his 1 love."

ISAK DINESEN: I'd start one day by saying, "Then Mr. So-and-so entered the room," and the stenographer would cry out, "Oh dear, but he can't! He died yesterday in Chapter Seventeen." No, I prefer to keep *The Angelic Avengers* my secret.

INTERVIEWER: I loved it, and I remember it had excellent notices. Did many people guess that you had written it?

ISAK DINESEN: A few.

INTERVIEWER: And what about *Winter's Tales*? That came out in the midst of the war—how did you get the book to America?

ISAK DINESEN: I went to Stockholm—not in itself an easy thing to accomplish—and what was even more difficult took the manuscript with me. I went to the American embassy and asked them if they didn't have planes going to the United States every day, and if they couldn't take the manuscript, but they said they only carried strictly political or diplomatic papers, so I went to the British embassy and asked them, and they asked could I supply references in England, and I could (I had many friends in the Cabinet, among them Anthony Eden), so they cabled to check this then said yes they could, so started the manuscript on its way to America.

INTERVIEWER: I'm ashamed of the American embassy. They surely could have taken it.

ISAK DINESEN: Oh, don't be too hard on them. I owe a lot to my American public. Anyway, with the manuscript I sent a letter to my American publishers just telling them that everything was in their hands, and that I couldn't communicate with them at all, and I never knew anything of how *Winter's Tales* was received until after the war ended, when suddenly I received dozens of charming letters from American soldiers and sailors all over the world: The book had been put into *Armed Forces Editions*—little paper books to fit a soldier's pocket. I was very touched. They sent me two copies of it; I gave one to the King of Denmark and he was pleased to see that, after all, some voice had spoken from his silent country during that dark time.

INTERVIEWER: And you were saying about your American public?

ISAK DINESEN: Yes, I shall never forget that they took me in at once. When I came back from Africa in 1931, after living there since 1914, I had lost all the money I had when I married because the coffee plantation didn't pay, you know; I asked my brother to finance me for two years while I prepared *Seven Gothic Tales*, and I told him that at the end of two years I'd be on my own. When the manuscript was ready, I went to England, and one day at luncheon there was the publisher Huntington and I said, "Please, I have a manuscript and I wish you'd look at it." He said, "What is it?" and when I replied, "A book of short stories," he threw up his hands and cried, "No!" and I begged, "Won't you even look at it?" and he said, "A book of short stories by an unknown writer? No hope!" Then I sent it to America, and it was taken right away by Robert Haas, who published it, and the general public took it and liked it, and they have always been faithful. No, thank you, no more coffee. I'll have a cigarette.

INTERVIEWER: Publishers everywhere are bone-headed. It's the traditional lament of the author.

ISAK DINESEN: The amusing thing is that after the book was published in America, Huntington wrote to Robert Haas praising it and begging for the address of the author, saying he must have the book for England. He had met me as Baroness Blixen, while Mr. Haas and I had never seen one another. Huntington never connected me with Isak Dinesen. Later he did publish the book in England.

INTERVIEWER: That's delightful; it's like something from one of the tales.

ISAK DINESEN: How lovely to sit here in the open, but we must be going, I think. Shall we continue our discussion on Sunday? I should like to see the Etruscan things at the Villa Giulia: We might chat a little then. Oh, look at the moon!

INTERVIEWER: Splendid. I'll find a taxi.

SCENE TWO

Rainy, warm Sunday noon. The Etruscan Collection in the Villa Giulia was not too crowded because of the weather. The Baroness Blixen was now attired in a suit of reddish-brown wool and a conical ochre-colored straw hat that again shadowed her extraordinary eyes. As she strolled through the newly arranged Etruscan figures, pottery, and jewelry, she seemed as remote as they from the ordinary gallery-goers who were pattering through. She walked slowly, very erect, stopping to gaze lingeringly at those details that pleased her.

ISAK DINESEN: How could they get that blue, do you suppose? Powdered lazuli? Look at that pig! In the North we give a great mythological importance to the pig. He's a kind of minion of the sun. I suppose because his sweet fat helps to keep us warm in the darkest and coldest time. Very intelligent animal. . . . I love all animals. I have a huge dog in Denmark, an Alsatian; he's enormous. I take him walking. If I survive him, I think I shall get a very small dog—a pug. Though I wonder if it's possible to get a pug now. They used to be very fashionable. Look at the lions on that sarcophagus. How could the Etruscans have known the lion? In Africa it was the animal that I loved the most.

INTERVIEWER: You must have known Africa at its best. What made you decide to go?

ISAK DINESEN: When I was a young girl, it was very far from my thoughts to go to Africa, nor did I dream then that an African farm should be the place in which I should be perfectly happy. That goes to prove that God has a greater and finer power of imagination than we have. But at the time when I was engaged to be married to my cousin Bror Blixen, an uncle of ours went out to Africa big-game hunting and came back all filled with praise of the country. Theodore Roosevelt had been hunting there then, too; East Africa was in the news. So Bror and I made up our minds to try our luck there, and our relations on both sides financed us in buying the farm, which was in the highlands of

Kenya, not far from Nairobi. The first day I arrived there, I loved the country and felt at home, even among unfamiliar flowers, trees, and animals, and changing clouds over the Ngong hills, unlike any clouds I had ever known. East Africa then was really a paradise, what the Red Indians called "happy hunting-grounds." I was very keen on shooting in my young days, but my great interest all through my many years in Africa was the African natives of all tribes, in particular the Somali and the Masai. They were beautiful, noble, fearless, and wise people. Life was not easy running a coffee plantation. Ten thousand acres of farmland, and locusts and drought . . . and too late we realized that the table land where we were located was really too high for raising coffee successfully. Life out there was, I believe, rather like eighteenth-century England: one might often be hard up for cash, but life was still rich in many ways, with the lovely landscape, dozens of horses and dogs, and a multitude of servants.

INTERVIEWER: I suppose that you began to write seriously there?

ISAK DINESEN: No, I really began writing before I went to Africa, but I never once wanted to be a writer. I published a few short stories in literary reviews in Denmark when I was twenty years old, and the reviews encouraged me, but I didn't go on—I don't know, I think I had an intuitive fear of being trapped. Also, when I was quite young, for a while I studied painting at the Danish Royal Academy; then I went to Paris in 1910 to study with Simon and Menard, but (*she chuckles*) . . . but I did little work. The impact of Paris was too great; I felt it was more important to go about and see pictures, to see Paris, in fact. I painted a little in Africa, portraits of the natives mostly, but every time I'd get to work, someone would come up and say an ox has died or something, and I'd have to go out in the fields. Later, when I knew in my heart I should have to sell the farm and go back to Denmark, I did begin to write. To put my mind to other things I began to write tales. Two of the *Gothic Tales* were written there. But earlier, I learned how to tell tales. For, you see, I had the perfect audience. White people can no longer listen to a tale recited. They fidget or become drowsy. But the natives have an ear still. I told stories constantly to them, all kinds. And all kinds of nonsense. I'd say, "Once there was a man who had an elephant with two heads" . . . and at once they were eager to hear more. "Oh? Yes, but Mem-Sahib, how did he find it, and how did he manage to feed it?" or whatever. They loved such invention. I delighted my people there by speaking in rhyme for them; they have no rhyme, you know, had never discovered it. I'd say things like "Wakamba na kula mamba" ("The Wakamba tribe eats snakes"), which in prose would have infuriated them, but which amused them mightily in rhyme. Afterwards they'd say, "Please, Mem-Sahib, talk like rain," so then I knew they had liked it, for rain was very precious to us there. Oh, here's Miss Svendsen. She's Catholic, so she went off today to hear a special cardinal. Now we'll go buy some post cards. Hope there is one of the lions.

MISS SVENDSEN: Good morning.

ISAK DINESEN: Clara, you must see the delightful lions; then we'll get some post cards and go for lunch.

Post cards are found, a taxi is summoned, umbrellas opened, the party runs for taxi, drives off through the rainy Borghese Gardens.

SCENE THREE

The Casino Valadier was a fashionable restaurant in the Gardens, just above the Piazza del Popolo, which commanded a fine view of Rome. After a brief glimpse of the rain-grayed city from the flooded terrace, the party went into a brocaded room, with considerately shaded girandoles, brightly colored carpets, and pictures.

ISAK DINESEN: I'll sit here so I can see everything. (*Lights cigarette*)

INTERVIEWER: Pleasant place, isn't it?

ISAK DINESEN: Yes, very pleasant, and I recognize it. I was here in 1912. Every now and again here in Rome I recognize very vividly a place I've visited then. (*Pause*) Oh, I shall go mad!

INTERVIEWER (*startled*): What is it?

ISAK DINESEN: Look how crooked that picture is! (*Indicates blackened portrait across room*)

INTERVIEWER: I'll straighten it. *(Goes to it)*

ISAK DINESEN: No, more to the right.

INTERVIEWER: Like this?

ISAK DINESEN: That's better. *(Two solemn gentlemen at table beneath portrait indicate bewilderment.)*

MISS SVENDSEN: It's like that at home. So much traffic passes, and I have always to straighten the pictures.

ISAK DINESEN: I live on the North Sea, halfway between Copenhagen and Elsinore.

INTERVIEWER: Perhaps halfway between Shiraz and Atlantis?

ISAK DINESEN: . . . Halfway between that island in *The Tempest* and wherever I am.

(Waiter takes order; luncheon is served.)

ISAK DINESEN: I'll have a cigarette now. Do you mind if we just stay here for a while? I hate to change once I'm installed in a décor I like. People are always telling me to hurry up or come on and do this or do that. Once when I was sailing around the Cape of Good Hope and there were albatrosses, people kept saying, "Why do you stay on deck? Come on in." They said, "It's time for lunch," and I said, "Damn lunch." I said, "I can eat lunch any day, but I shan't see albatrosses again." Such wingspread!

INTERVIEWER: Tell me about your father.

ISAK DINESEN: He was in the French army, as was my grandfather. After the Franco-Prussian War, he went to America and lived with the Plains Indians in the great middle part of your country. He built himself a little hut and named it after a place in Denmark where he had been very happy as a young man—Frydenlund ("Happy Grove"). He hunted animals for their skins and became a fur trader. He sold his skins mostly to the Indians, then used his profits to buy them gifts. A little community grew up around him, and now Frydenlund is, I believe, the name of a locality in the state of Wisconsin. When he returned to Denmark, he wrote his books. So you see, it was natural for me, his daughter, to go off to Africa and live with the natives and after return home to write about it. He also, incidentally, wrote a volume of his war experiences called *Paris Under the Commune*.

INTERVIEWER: And how is it that you write in English?

ISAK DINESEN: It was quite natural to do so. I was partly schooled in England after being taught always by governesses at home. Because of that, I lack knowledge of plain facts which are common coinage for others. But those governesses were ambitious: They did teach languages, and one of them put me to translating *The Lady of the Lake* into Danish. Then, in Africa, I had been seeing only English people, really. I had spoken English or Swahili for twenty years. And I read the English poets and English novelists. I prefer the older writers, but I remember when I first read Huxley's *Crome Yellow*, it was like biting into an unknown and refreshing fruit.

INTERVIEWER: Most of your tales are laid in the last century, aren't they? You never write about modern times.

ISAK DINESEN: I do, if you consider that the time of our grandparents, that just-out-of-reach time, is so much a part of *us*. We absorb so much without being aware. Also, I write about characters who together *are* the tale. I begin, you see, with a flavor of the tale. Then I find the characters, and they take over. They make the design, I simply permit them their liberty. Now, in modern life and in modern fiction there is a kind of atmosphere and above all an interior movement—inside the characters— which is something else again. I feel that in life and in art people have drawn a little apart in this century. Solitude is now the universal theme. But I write about characters within a design, how they act upon one another. Relation with others is important to me, you see, friendship is precious to me, and I have been blessed with heroic friendships. But time in my tales is flexible. I may begin in the eighteenth century and come right up to World War I. Those times have been sorted out, they are clearly visible. Besides, so many novels that we think are contemporary in subject with their date of publication—think of Dickens or Faulkner or Tolstoy or Turgenev—are really set in an earlier period, a generation or so back. The present is always unsettled, no one has had time to contemplate it in tranquillity . . . I was a painter before I was a writer . . . and a painter never wants the subject right under his nose; he wants to stand back and study a landscape with half-closed eyes.

INTERVIEWER: Have you written poetry?

ISAK DINESEN: I did as a young girl.

INTERVIEWER: What is your favorite fruit?

ISAK DINESEN: Strawberries.

INTERVIEWER: Do you like monkeys?

ISAK DINESEN: Yes, I love them in art: in pictures, in stories, in porcelain, but not in life, they somehow look so sad. They make me nervous. I like lions and gazelles. . . . Do you think I look like a monkey?

(The baroness refers to an earlier conversation where someone had suggested that if the tale "The Monkey" were ever filmed, she should play the character of the Chanoiness who turns into a monkey.)

INTERVIEWER: Of course. But you must understand that there are many kinds of monkeys.

(The Interviewer has copied out a passage from Ivan Sanderson's The Monkey Kingdom *for the baroness's delectation and now reads it.)*

INTERVIEWER: "The definition of 'monkey' has not, however, been satisfactorily resolved. This apparently simple question, moreover, requires careful examination before we may proceed in our story, for, although we are not solely or even primarily interested in mere monkeys, we cannot, without its resolution, attempt the greater galaxy of life-forms to which they belong."

ISAK DINESEN *(laughs delightedly)*: But no tale can proceed without examining apparently simple questions. And no tail, either.

SCENE FOUR

We moved to the parapets of the central tower of the Castle of Sermonetta, perched on a hill amidst a clustering town, about an hour and a half south of Rome. We crossed a moated drawbridge, climbed a rickety ladder-stair. We saw remains of fourteenth-

century frescoes, and in the tower stronghold saw scrawled phrases and drawings on the wall, fresh as new, from when Napoleonic soldiers were incarcerated here. The party emerged, shading their eyes. Below, the Pontine plain stretched green and gold to the sea, bathed in bright afternoon sunlight. Tiny figures were visible miles below working amidst the bean fields and the peach orchards.

INTERVIEWER: I think it is curious that practically no critic nor reviewer in either America or England has pointed out the great comic element in your works. I hope we might speak a little of the comic spirit in your tales.

ISAK DINESEN: Oh, I'm glad you mentioned that! People are always asking me what is the significance of this or that in the tales—"What does this symbolize? What does that stand for?" And I always have a difficult time making them believe that I intend everything as it's stated. It would be terrible if the explanation of the work were outside the work itself. And I do often intend a comic sense, I love a joke, I love the humorous. The name "Isak" means "laughter." I often think that what we most need now is a great humorist.

INTERVIEWER: What humorists in the English language please you?

ISAK DINESEN: Well, Mark Twain, for example. But then all the writers I admire usually have a vein of comic spirit. Writers of tales always do, at least.

INTERVIEWER: Who are writers of tales that appeal to you, or with whom you feel a kinship?

ISAK DINESEN: E. T. A. Hoffman, Hans Andersen, Barbey D'Aurevilly, La Motte Fouqué, Chamisso, Turgenev, Hemingway, Maupassant, Stendhal, Chekhov, Conrad, Voltaire . . .

MISS SVENDSEN: Don't forget Melville! She calls me Babu after the character in *Benito Cereno*, when she doesn't refer to me as Sancho Panza.

INTERVIEWER: Heavens, you've read them all!

ISAK DINESEN: I am really three thousand years old and have dined with Socrates.

INTERVIEWER: Pardon?

ISAK DINESEN *(laughing and lighting a cigarette)*: Because I was never told what I must read or what I mustn't read. I did read everything that fell into my hands. I discovered Shakespeare very early in life, and now I feel that life would be nothing without him. One of my new stories is about a company of actors playing *The Tempest*, incidentally. I love some of the Victorian novelists no one reads anymore: Walter Scott, for instance. Oh, and I like Melville very much, and the *Odyssey*, the Norse Sagas—Have you read the Norse Sagas? I love Racine, too.

INTERVIEWER: I remember your observation on the Norse mythology in one of the *Winter's Tales*.* It's very interesting to me, incidentally, how you have chosen the tale for your form.

ISAK DINESEN: It came naturally to me. My literary friends at home tell me that the heart of my work is not in the idea but in the line of the tale. Something you can tell, like one can TELL *Ali Baba and the Forty Thieves* but one could not TELL *Anna Karenina*.

INTERVIEWER: But there are some who find your tales "artificial" . . .

ISAK DINESEN *(smiling)*: Artificial? Of course, they are artificial. They were meant to be, for such is the essence of the tale-telling art. And I felt I acknowledged that . . . or rather, pointed it out . . . by calling my first tales "Gothic." . . . When I used the word Gothic, I didn't mean the real Gothic, but the imitation of the Gothic, the Romantic age of Byron, the age of Horace Walpole, who built Strawberry Hill, the age of the Gothic Revival . . . you know Walpole's *Castle of Otranto*, of course?

---

* "And I have wondered, while I read," says the young nobleman in "Sorrow-Acre," "that we have not till now understood how much our Nordic mythology in moral greatness surpasses that of Greece and Rome. If it had not been for the physical beauty of the ancient gods, which has come down to us in marble, no modern mind could hold them worthy of worship. They were mean, capricious and treacherous. The gods of our Danish forefathers are as much more divine than they as the Druid is nobler than the Augur."

INTERVIEWER: Yes, indeed. In a tale, the plot is all important, isn't it?

ISAK DINESEN: Yes, it is. I start with a tingle, a kind of feeling of the story I will write. Then come the characters, and they take over, they make the story. But all this ends by being a plot. For other writers, that seems an unnatural thing. But a proper tale has a shape and an outline. In a painting the frame is important. Where does the picture end? What details should one include? Or omit! Where does the line go that cuts off the picture? People always ask me, they say, "In 'The Deluge at Norderney,' were those characters drowned or saved at the end?" (You remember they are trapped in a loft during a flood and spend the night recounting their stories while awaiting rescue.) Well, what can I reply? How can I tell them? That's outside the story. I really don't know!

INTERVIEWER: Do you rewrite your tales very much?

ISAK DINESEN: Oh, I do, I do. It's hellish. Over and over again. Then when I think I'm finished, and Clara copies them out to send to the publishers, I look over them, and have a fit, and rewrite again.

MISS SVENDSEN: In one tale there was a lesser character called "Mariana the Rat" who ran an inn called The Lousing-Comb. The publishers mentioned her in the text for the book jacket, but by the time they had the final proofs, she had been removed from the tale. It must have caused mystification.

INTERVIEWER: Many people are mystified by the tale "The Monkey."

ISAK DINESEN: Yes, I grow weary from the questions people ask me about that particular tale. But that is a fantastic story; it should be interpreted that way. The principle is this: Let the monkey resolve the mess when the plot has got too complicated for the human characters. But people say, "What does it mean?" *That's* what it means. . . . *(She pauses, with a little laugh.)* It would be a bad thing if I could explain the tale better than what I have already said in the tale. As I never tire of pointing out, the story should be *all*.

INTERVIEWER: Everyone would be interested to know just how one of your tales takes shape. Especially those with tales within the tale. Take "The Deluge at Norderney," for instance . . . it seems so inevitable and ordered, but if one studies it, the design is amazing . . . How did . . . ?

ISAK DINESEN *(interrupting, smiling mischievously)*: Read it, read it, and you'll see how it's written!

For Epilogue here, I append a passage from the Baroness Blixen's Albondocani, *a long series of connected tales still unfinished at the time of the author's death in 1962. This excerpt is from "The Blank Page," published in* Last Tales *(1957). An old woman who earns her living by storytelling is speaking*:

"With my grandmother," she said, "I went through a hard school. 'Be loyal to the story,' the old hag would say to me, 'Be eternally and unswervingly loyal to the story.' 'Why must I be that, Grandmother,' I asked her. 'Am I to furnish you with reasons, baggage?' she cried. 'And you mean to be a story-teller! Why, you are to become a story-teller, and I shall give you the reasons! Hear then: Where the story-teller is loyal, eternally and unswervingly loyal to the story, there, in the end, silence will speak. Where the story has been betrayed, silence is but emptiness. But we, the faithful, when we have spoken our last word, will hear the voice of silence. Whether a small snotty lass understands it or not.'

"Who then," she continues, "tells a finer tale than any of us? Silence does. And where does one read a deeper tale than upon the most perfectly printed page of the most precious book? Upon the blank page. When a royal, and gallant pen, in the moment of its highest inspiration, has written down its tale with the rarest ink of all—where, then, may one read a still deeper, sweeter, merrier, and more cruel tale than that? Upon the blank page."

—EUGENE WALTER
1956

2. Marianne Moore

Marianne Craig Moore was born in St. Louis, Missouri, on November 15, 1887. She attended Metzger Institute in Carlisle, Pennsylvania, then Bryn Mawr, from which she was graduated in 1909. The following year she was graduated from Carlisle Commercial College.

Miss Moore's first poems appeared in Bryn Mawr College publications; in 1917 some of her work was published in *The Egoist*, London, and later in Harriet Monroe's *Poetry*. In 1921 Winifred Ellerman (Bryher) and the poet Hilda Doolittle (H.D.), without the knowledge of Miss Moore, brought out *Poems* (The Egoist Press). Four years later *Observations* appeared in the United States and won the Dial Award as an outstanding contribution to American literature. In 1925, Miss Moore joined the editorial staff of *The Dial* and continued work with that magazine until its demise. She took up residence in Brooklyn, where she lived until her death in 1972.

In her lifetime, Marianne Moore won nearly all the prizes for poetry which are presented in this country, and in 1947 she was elected a member of the National Institute of Arts and Letters. Her published work includes *Observations* (1924), *Selected Poems* (1935), *The Pangolin and Other Verse* (1936), *What Are Years* (1941), *Nevertheless* (1944), *Collected Poems* (1951), which was awarded the Bollingen and Pulitzer prizes, *The Fables of La Fontaine* (translation, 1954), *Predilections* (essays, 1955), *Like a Bulwark* (1956), *O to Be a Dragon* (1959), *A Marianne Moore Reader* (1961), and *The Complete Poems of Marianne Moore* (1967).

T. S. Eliot wrote in 1935: "My conviction has remained unchanged for the last fourteen years—that Miss Moore's poems form part of the small body of durable poetry written in our time . . . in which an original sensibility and alert intelligence and deep feeling have been engaged in maintaining the life of the English language."

RESCUE WITH YUL BRYNNER
(appointed by President Eisenhower, consultant
to the United Nations commission on Refugees,
1959-1960)

with Dances Galanta by Zoltán Kodály
favorites of Budapest Symphony Orchestra
now refugee Symphonia Hungarica in Marl
CBS; December 10, 1960

Head, down low over the guitar,
he barely seemed to hum, ending "all come home";
did not smile; came by air;
did not have to come.
    The guitar's an event.
    Guests of honor is old, doesn't dance; can't smile.
    "Have a home?" a boy asks. "Shall we live in a tent?"
    "In a house", Yul answers. His neat cloth hat
has nothing like the glitter reflected on the face
of milkweed-seed brown dominating a palace place
in those hells devoid of solace
where he is now. His deliberate pace
is a king's however, "You'll have plenty of space."
    "Recital"? 'concert is the word.'
in Marl Austria's Marl, by the Budapest Symphonia Symphony —
    displaced but not deterred —
listened to by me —
    detachedly then —
    like a frog or grasshopper that did not
    know it had missed the mower, a pigmy citizen;
    in any case, too slow a grower.
There were thirty million; there are thirteen still —
healthy to begin with, kept waiting till they're ill/
History judges. It certainly will
remember Winnipeg's incredible
conditions: "Ill; no p sponsor; and no kind of skill."
    Odd - a reporter with small guitar - a puzzle.
Mysterious Yul did not come to dazzle.

    Magic bird with multiple tongue -
five tongues - embarked on a crazy twelve-month tramp
or plod), he flew among
the damned, found each camp
    where hope had slowly died
    & came to end that sort of death;
Instead did not feather himself,
    "Two small fishes and five loaves of bread.
    Nourished seeds of dignity. All were fed.
He said, You may feel strange; not dressed the way they dress.
Nobody notices; you'll find some happiness.
No new "big fear"; no distress."
He can sing - twinned with an enchantress -
elephant-borne fairy with blue sequinned-spangled dress -
    aloft by trunk, with star-tipped wand,
    truer to the beat than Symphonia Hungaria.

Marianne Moore

American poetry is a great literature, and it has come to its maturity only in the last sixty years; Walt Whitman and Emily Dickinson in the last century were rare examples of genius in a hostile environment. One decade gave America the major figures of our modern poetry: Wallace Stevens was born in 1879, and T. S. Eliot in 1888. To the ten years which these dates enclose belong H.D., Robinson Jeffers, John Crowe Ransom, William Carlos Williams, Ezra Pound, and Marianne Moore.

Marianne Moore began to publish during the First World War. She was printed and praised in Europe by the expatriates T. S. Eliot and Ezra Pound. In Chicago, Harriet Monroe's magazine Poetry, *which provided the enduring showcase for the new poetry, published her too. But she was mainly a poet of New York, of the Greenwich Village group which created magazines called* Others *and* Broom. *The poets with whom she was mostly associated were*

Alfred Kreymborg, William Carlos Williams, and Wallace Ste-
vens—stateside representatives of the miraculous generation.

Marianne Moore settled not in Bloomsbury or Rapallo but in
Brooklyn. She moved there from the Village in 1929, into an
apartment house. To visit her you had to cross the Brooklyn Bridge,
turn left at Myrtle Avenue, follow the elevated for a mile or two,
and then turn right onto her street. It was pleasantly lined with
a few trees, and Miss Moore's apartment was conveniently near
a grocery store and the Presbyterian church which she attended.

The interview took place in November 1960, the day before the
presidential election. The front door of Miss Moore's apartment
opened onto a long narrow corridor. Rooms led off to the right,
and at the end of the corridor was a large sitting room which
overlooked the street. On top of a bookcase which ran the length
of the corridor was a Nixon button.

Miss Moore and the interviewer sat in her sitting room, a mi-
crophone between them. Piles of books stood everywhere. On the
walls hung a variety of paintings. One came from Mexico, a gift
of Mabel Dodge; others were examples of the heavy, tea-colored
oils which Americans hung in the years before 1914. The furniture
was old-fashioned and dark.

Miss Moore spoke with an accustomed scrupulosity, and with
a humor which her readers will recognize. When she ended a
sentence with a phrase which was particularly telling, or even tart,
she glanced quickly at the interviewer to see if he was amused,
and then snickered gently. Later Miss Moore took the interviewer
to an admirable lunch at a nearby restaurant. She decided not
to wear her Nixon button because it clashed with her coat and
hat.

INTERVIEWER: Miss Moore, I understand that you were born
in St. Louis only about ten months before T. S. Eliot. Did your
families know each other?

MOORE: No, we did not know the Eliots. We lived in Kirkwood,
Missouri, where my grandfather was pastor of the First Presbyterian Church. T. S. Eliot's grandfather—Dr. William Eliot—
was a Unitarian. We left when I was about seven, my grandfather

having died in 1894, February 20th. My grandfather like Dr. Eliot had attended ministerial meetings in St. Louis. Also, at stated intervals, various ministers met for luncheon. After one of these luncheons my grandfather said, "When Dr. William Eliot asks the blessing and says, 'and this we ask in the name of our Lord Jesus Christ,' he is Trinitarian enough for me." The Mary Institute, for girls, was endowed by him as a memorial to his daughter Mary, who had died.

INTERVIEWER: How old were you when you started to write poems?

MOORE: Well, let me see, in Bryn Mawr. I think I was eighteen when I entered Bryn Mawr. I was born in 1887, I entered college in 1906. Now how old would I have been? Can you deduce my probable age?

INTERVIEWER: Eighteen or nineteen.

MOORE: I had no literary plans, but I was interested in the undergraduate monthly magazine, and to my surprise (I wrote one or two little things for it) the editors elected me to the board. It was my sophomore year—I am sure it was—and I stayed on, I believe. And then when I had left college I offered contributions (we weren't paid) to the *Lantern*, the alumnae magazine. But I didn't feel that my product was anything to shake the world.

INTERVIEWER: At what point did poetry become world-shaking for you?

MOORE: Never! I believe I was interested in painting then. At least I said so. I remember Mrs. Otis Skinner asking at commencement time, the year I was graduated, "What would you like to be?"

"A painter," I said.

"Well, I'm not surprised," Mrs. Skinner answered. I had something on that she liked, some kind of summer dress. She commended it—said, "I'm not at all surprised."

I like stories. I like fiction. And—this sounds rather pathetic, bizarre as well—I think verse perhaps was for me the next best thing to it. Didn't I write something one time, "Part of a Poem, Part of a Novel, Part of a Play"? I think I was all too truthful. I could visualize scenes, and deplored the fact that Henry James had to do it unchallenged. Now, if I couldn't write fiction, I'd like to write plays. To me the theater is the most pleasant, in fact my favorite, form of recreation.

INTERVIEWER: Do you go often?

MOORE: No. Never. Unless someone invites me. Lillian Hellman invited me to *Toys in the Attic*, and I am very happy that she did. I would have had no notion of the vitality of the thing, have lost sight of her skill as a writer if I hadn't seen the play; would like to go again. The accuracy of the vernacular! That's the kind of thing I am interested in, am always taking down little local expressions and accents. I think I should be in some philological operation or enterprise, am really much interested in dialect and intonations. I scarcely think of any that comes into my so-called poems at all.

INTERVIEWER: I wonder what Bryn Mawr meant for you as a poet. You write that most of your time there was spent in the biological laboratory. Did you like biology better than literature as a subject for study? Did the training possibly affect your poetry?

MOORE: I had hoped to make French and English my major studies, and took the required two-year English course—five hours a week—but was not able to elect a course until my junior year. I did not attain the requisite academic stand of eighty until that year. I then elected seventeenth-century imitative writing—Fuller, Hooker, Bacon, Bishop Andrewes, and others. Lectures in French were in French, and I had had no spoken French.

Did laboratory studies affect my poetry? I am sure they did. I found the biology courses—minor, major, and histology—exhilarating. I thought, in fact, of studying medicine. Precision, economy of statement, logic employed to ends that are disinterested, drawing and identifying, liberate—at least have some bearing on—the imagination, it seems to me.

INTERVIEWER: Whom did you know in the literary world, before you came to New York? Did you know Bryher and H.D.?

MOORE: It's very hard to get these things seriatim. I met Bryher in 1921 in New York. H.D. was my classmate at Bryn Mawr. She was there, I think, only two years. She was a non-resident and I did not realize that she was interested in writing.

INTERVIEWER: Did you know Ezra Pound and William Carlos Williams through her? Didn't she know them at the University of Pennsylvania?

MOORE: Yes. She did. I didn't meet them. I had met no writers until 1916 when I visited New York, when a friend in Carlisle wanted me to accompany her.

INTERVIEWER: So you were isolated really from modern poetry until 1916?

MOORE: Yes.

INTERVIEWER: Was that your first trip to New York, when you went there for six days and decided that you wanted to live there?

MOORE: Oh, no. Several times my mother had taken my brother and me sightseeing and to shop; on the way to Boston, or Maine, and to Washington and Florida. My senior year in college in 1909, I visited Dr. Charles Spraguesmith's daughter, Hilda, at Christmas time in New York. And Louis Anspacher lectured in a very ornamental way at Cooper Union. There was plenty of music at Carnegie Hall, and I got a sense of what was going on in New York.

INTERVIEWER: And what was going on made you want to come back?

MOORE: It probably did, when Miss Cowdrey in Carlisle invited me to come with her for a week. It was the visit in 1916 that made me want to live there. I don't know what put it into her head to do it, or why she wasn't likely to have a better time without me. She was most skeptical of my venturing forth to bohemian parties. But I was fearless about that. In the first place, I didn't think anyone would try to harm me, but if they did I felt impervious. It never occurred to me that chaperones were important.

INTERVIEWER: Do you suppose that moving to New York, and the stimulation of the writers whom you found there, led you to write more poems than you would otherwise have written?

MOORE: I'm sure it did—seeing what others wrote, liking this or that. With me it's always some fortuity that traps me. I certainly never intended to write poetry. That never came into my head. And now, too, I think each time I write that it may be the last time; then I'm charmed by something and seem to have to say something. Everything I have written is the result of reading or of interest in people, I'm sure of that. I had no ambition to be a writer.

INTERVIEWER: Let me see. You taught at the Carlisle Indian School, after Bryn Mawr. Then after you moved to New York in 1918 you taught at a private school and worked in a library. Did these occupations have anything to do with you as a writer?

MOORE: I think they hardened my muscles considerably, my mental approach to things. Working as a librarian was a big help, a tremendous help. Miss Leonard of the Hudson Park branch of the New York Public Library opposite our house came to see me one day. I wasn't in, and she asked my mother did she think I would care to be on the staff, work in the library, because I was so fond of books and liked to talk about them to people. My mother said no, she thought not; the shoemaker's children never have shoes, I probably would feel if I joined the staff that I'd have no time to read. When I came home she told me, and I said, "Why, certainly. Ideal. I'll tell her. Only I couldn't work more than half a day." If I had worked all day and maybe evenings or overtime, like the mechanics, why, it would *not* have been ideal.

As a free service we were assigned books to review and I did like that. We didn't get paid but we had the chance to diagnose. I reveled in it. Somewhere I believe I have carbon copies of those "P-slip" summaries. They were the kind of things that brought the worst-best out. I was always wondering why they didn't honor me with an art book or medical book or even a history, or criticism. But no, it was fiction, silent-movie fiction.

INTERVIEWER: Did you travel at this time? Did you go to Europe at all?

MOORE: In 1911. My mother and I went to England for about two months, July and August probably. We went to Paris and we stayed on the left bank, in a pension in the rue Valette, where Calvin wrote his *Institutes*, I believe. Not far from the Panthéon and the Luxembourg Gardens. I have been much interested in Sylvia Beach's book—reading about Ezra Pound and his Paris days. Where was I and what was I doing? I think, with the objective, an evening stroll—it was one of the hottest summers the world has ever known, 1911—we walked along to 12, rue de l'Odéon, to see Sylvia Beach's shop. It wouldn't occur to me to say, "Here am I, I'm a writer, would you talk to me a while?" I had no feeling at all like that. I wanted to observe things. And we went to every museum in Paris, I think, except two.

INTERVIEWER: Have you been back since?

MOORE: Not to Paris. Only to England in 1935 or 1936. I like England.

INTERVIEWER: You have mostly stayed put in Brooklyn, then, since you moved here in 1929?

MOORE: Except for four trips to the West: Los Angeles, San Francisco, Puget Sound, and British Columbia. My mother and I went through the canal previously, to San Francisco, and by rail to Seattle.

INTERVIEWER: Have you missed the Dodgers here, since *they* went West?

MOORE: Very much, and I am told that they miss us.

INTERVIEWER: I am still interested in those early years in New York. William Carlos Williams, in his *Autobiography*, says that you were "a rafter holding up the superstructure of our uncompleted building," when he talks about the Greenwich Village group of writers. I guess these were people who contributed to *Others*.

MOORE: I never was a rafter holding up anyone! I have his *Autobiography* and took him to task for his misinformed statements about Robert McAlmon and Bryher. In my indignation I missed some things I ought to have seen.

INTERVIEWER: To what extent did the *Others* contributors form a group?

MOORE: We did foregather a little. Alfred Kreymborg was editor, and was married to Gertrude Lord at the time, one of the loveliest persons you could ever meet. And they had a little apartment somewhere in the village. There was considerable unanimity about the group.

INTERVIEWER: Someone called Alfred Kreymborg your American discoverer. Do you suppose this is true?

MOORE: It could be said, perhaps; he did all he could to promote me. Miss Monroe and the Aldingtons had asked me simultaneously to contribute to *Poetry* and the *Egoist* in 1917 at the same time. Alfred Kreymborg was not inhibited. I was a little different from the others. He thought I might pass as a novelty, I guess.

INTERVIEWER: What was your reaction when H.D. and Bryher brought out your first collection, which they called *Poems*, in 1921 without your knowledge? Why had you delayed to do it yourself?

MOORE: To issue my slight product—conspicuously tentative—seemed to me premature. I disliked the term "poetry" for any but Chaucer's or Shakespeare's or Dante's. I do not now feel quite my original hostility to the word, since it is a convenient almost unavoidable term for the thing (although hardly for me—my observations, experiments in rhythm, or exercises in composition). What I write, as I have said before, could only be called poetry because there is no other category in which to put it. For the chivalry of the undertaking—issuing my verse for me in 1921, certainly in format choicer than the content—I am intensely grateful. Again, in 1925, it seemed to me not very self-interested of Faber and Faber, and simultaneously of the Macmillan Company, to propose a *Selected Poems* for me. Desultory occasional magazine publications seemed to me sufficient, conspicuous enough.

INTERVIEWER: Had you been sending poems to magazines before the *Egoist* printed your first poem?

MOORE: I must have. I have a little curio, a little wee book about two by three inches, or two and a half by three inches, in which I systematically entered everything sent out, when I got it back, if they took it, and how much I got for it. That lasted about a year, I think. I can't care as much as all that. I don't know that I submitted anything that wasn't extorted from me.

I have at present three onerous tasks, and each interferes with the others, and I don't know how I am going to write anything. If I get a promising idea I set it down, and it stays there. I don't make myself do anything with it. I've had several things in the *New Yorker*. And I said to them, "I might never write again," and not to expect me to. I never knew anyone who had a passion for words who had as much difficulty in saying things as I do and I very seldom say them in a manner I like. If I do it's because I don't know I'm trying. I've written several things for the *New Yorker*—and I did want to write *them*.

INTERVIEWER: When did you last write a poem?

MOORE: It appeared in August. What was it about? Oh . . . Carnegie Hall. You see, anything that really rouses me . . .

INTERVIEWER: How does a poem start for you?

MOORE: A felicitous phrase springs to mind—a word or two, say—simultaneous usually with some thought or object of equal attraction: "Its leaps should be *set*/to the flage*olet*"; "Katydidwing subdivided by *sun*/till the nettings are *legion*." I like light rhymes, inconspicuous rhymes and un-pompous conspicuous rhymes: Gilbert and Sullivan:

> Yet, *when the danger's near*,
> We *manage to appear*
> As *insensible to fear*
> As *anybody here*.

I have a passion for rhythm and accent, so blundered into versifying. Considering the stanza the unit, I came to hazard hyphens at the end of the line, but found that readers are distracted from the content by hyphens, so I try not to use them. My interest in La Fontaine originated entirely independent of content. I then fell a prey to that surgical kind of courtesy of his.

> *I fear that appearances are worshiped throughout France*
> *Whereas pre-eminence perchance*
> *Merely means a pushing person*.

I like the unaccented syllable and accented near-rhyme:

> *By love and his blindness*
> *Possibly a service was done,*
> *Let lovers say. A lonely man has no criterion.*

INTERVIEWER: What in your reading or your background led you to write the way you do write? Was imagism a help to you?

MOORE: No. I wondered why anyone would adopt the term.

INTERVIEWER: The descriptiveness of your poems has nothing to do with them, you think?

MOORE: No; I really don't. I was rather sorry to be a pariah, or at least that I had no connection with anything. But I *did* feel gratitude to *Others*.

INTERVIEWER: Where do you think your style of writing came from? Was it a gradual accumulation, out of your character? Or does it have literary antecedents?

MOORE: Not so far as I know. Ezra Pound said, "Someone has been reading Laforgue, and French authors." Well, sad to say, I had not read any of them until fairly recently. Retroactively I see that Francis Jammes' titles and treatment are a good deal like my own. I seem almost a plagiarist.

INTERVIEWER: And the extensive use of quotations?

MOORE: I was just trying to be honorable and not to steal things. I've always felt that if a thing had been said in the *best* way, how can you say it better? If I wanted to say something and somebody had said it ideally, then I'd take it but give the person credit for it. That's all there is to it. If you are charmed by an author, I think it's a very strange and invalid imagination that doesn't long to share it. Somebody else should read it, don't you think?

INTERVIEWER: Did any prose stylists help you in finding your poetic style? Elizabeth Bishop mentions Poe's prose in connection with your writing, and you have always made people think of Henry James.

MOORE: Prose stylists, very much. Doctor Johnson on Richard Savage: "He was in two months illegitimated by the Parliament, and disowned by his mother, doomed to poverty and obscurity, and launched upon the ocean of life only that he might be swallowed by its quicksands, or dashed upon its rocks. . . . It was his peculiar happiness that he scarcely ever found a stranger whom he did not leave a friend; but it must likewise be added, that he had not often a friend long without obliging him to become a stranger." Or Edmund Burke on the colonies: "You can shear a wolf; but will he comply?" Or Sir Thomas Browne: "States are not governed by Ergotisms." He calls a bee "that industrious flie," and his home his "hive." His manner is a kind of erudition-proof sweetness. Or Sir Francis Bacon: "Civil War is like the heat of fever; a foreign war is like the heat of exercise." Or Cellini: "I had by me a dog black as a mulberry. . . . I swelled up in my rage like an asp." Or Caesar's *Commentaries*, and Xenophon's *Cynegeticus*: the gusto and interest in every detail! In Henry James it is the essays and letters especially that affect me. In Ezra Pound, *The Spirit of Romance*: his definiteness, his indigenously unmistakable accent. Charles Norman says in his biography of Ezra Pound that he said to a poet, "Nothing, *nothing*, that you couldn't in some circumstance, under stress of some emotion, *actually say*." And Ezra said of Shakespeare and Dante, "Here we are with the masters; of neither can we say, 'He is the greater'; of each we must say, 'He is unexcelled.' "

INTERVIEWER: Do you have in your own work any favorites and unfavorites?

MOORE: Indeed, I do. I think the most difficult thing for me is to be satisfactorily lucid, yet have enough implication in it to suit myself. That's a problem. And I don't approve of my "enigmas," or as somebody said, "the not ungreen grass." I said to my mother one time, "How did you ever permit me to let this be printed?" And she said, "You didn't ask my advice."

INTERVIEWER: One time I heard you give a reading, and I think you said that you didn't like "In Distrust of Merits," which is one of your most popular poems.

MOORE: I do like it; it is sincere but I wouldn't call it a poem. It's truthful; it is testimony—to the fact that war is intolerable, and unjust.

INTERVIEWER: How can you call it not a poem, on what basis?

MOORE: Haphazard; as form, what has it? It is just a protest—disjointed, exclamatory. Emotion overpowered me. First this thought and then that.

INTERVIEWER: Your mother said that you hadn't asked her advice. Did you ever? Do you go for criticism to your family or friends?

MOORE: Well, not friends, but my brother if I get a chance. When my mother said "You didn't ask my advice" must have

been years ago, because when I wrote "A Face," I had written
something first about "the adder and the child with a bowl of
porridge," and she said "It won't do." "All right," I said, "but I
have to produce something." Cyril Connolly had asked me for
something for *Horizon*. So I wrote "A Face." That is one of the
few things I ever set down that didn't give me any trouble. She
said, "I like it." I remember that.

Then, much before that, I wrote "The Buffalo." I thought it
would probably outrage a number of persons because it had to
me a kind of pleasing jerky progress. I thought, "Well, if it seems
bad my brother will tell me, and if it has a point he'll detect it."
And he said, with considerable gusto, "It takes my fancy." I was
happy as could be.

INTERVIEWER: Did you ever suppress anything because of family
objections?

MOORE: Yes, "the adder and the child with a bowl of porridge."
I never even wanted to improve it. You know, Mr. Saintsbury
said that Andrew Lang wanted him to contribute something on
Poe, and he did, and Lang returned it. Mr. Saintsbury said,
"Once a thing has been rejected, I would not offer it to the most
different of editors." That shocked me. I have offered a thing,
submitted it thirty-five times. Not simultaneously, of course.

INTERVIEWER: A poem?

MOORE: Yes. I am very tenacious.

INTERVIEWER: Do people ever ask you to write poems for them?

MOORE: Continually. Everything from on the death of a dog
to a little item for an album.

INTERVIEWER: Do you ever write them?

MOORE: Oh, perhaps; usually quote something. Once when I
was in the library we gave a party for Miss Leonard, and I wrote
a line or two of doggerel about a bouquet of violets we gave her.
It has no life or point. It was meant well but didn't amount to
anything. Then in college, I had a sonnet as an assignment. The
epitome of weakness.

INTERVIEWER: I'm interested in asking about the principles, and
the methods, of your way of writing. What is the rationale behind

syllabic verse? How does it differ from free verse in which the line length is controlled visually but not arithmetically?

MOORE: It never occurred to me that what I wrote was something to define. I am governed by the pull of the sentence as the pull of a fabric is governed by gravity. I like the end-stopped line and dislike the reversed order of words; like symmetry.

INTERVIEWER: How do you plan the shape of your stanzas? I am thinking of the poems, usually syllabic, which employ a repeated stanza form. Do you ever experiment with shapes before you write, by drawing lines on a page?

MOORE: Never, I never "plan" a stanza. Words cluster like chromosomes, determining the procedure. I may influence an arrangement or thin it, then try to have successive stanzas identical with the first. Spontaneous initial originality—say, impetus—seems difficult to reproduce consciously later. As Stravinsky said about pitch, "If I transpose it for some reason, I am in danger of losing the freshness of first contact and will have difficulty in recapturing its attractiveness."

No, I never "draw lines." I make a rhyme conspicuous, to me at a glance, by underlining with red, blue, or other pencil—as many colors as I have rhymes to differentiate. However, if the phrases recur in too incoherent an architecture—as print—I notice that the words as a tune do not sound right. I may start a piece, find it obstructive, lack a way out, and not complete the thing for a year, or years, am thrifty. I salvage anything promising and set it down in a small notebook.

INTERVIEWER: I wonder if the act of translating La Fontaine's *Fables* helped you as a writer.

MOORE: Indeed it did. It was the best help I've ever had. I suffered frustration. I'm so naïve, so docile, I *tend* to take anybody's word for anything the person says, even in matters of art. The publisher who had commissioned the *Fables* died. I had no publisher. Well, I struggled on for a time and it didn't go very well. I thought, I'd better ask if they don't want to terminate the contract; then I could offer it elsewhere. I thought Macmillan, who took an interest in me, might like it. *Might*. The editor in charge of translations said, "Well, I studied French at Cornell, took a degree in French, I love French, and . . . well, I think you'd better put it away for a while." "How long?" I said. "About ten years; besides, it will hurt your own work. You won't write so well afterward."

"Oh," I said, "that's one reason I was undertaking it; I thought it would train me and give me momentum." Much dejected, I asked, "What is wrong? Have I not a good ear? Are the meanings not sound?"

"Well, there are conflicts," the editor reiterated, as it seemed to me, countless times. I don't know yet what they are or were. (A little "editorial.")

I said, "Don't write me an extenuating letter, please. Just send back the material in the envelope I put with it." I had submitted it in January and this was May. I had had a kind of uneasy hope that all would be well; meanwhile had volumes, hours, and years of work yet to do and might as well go on and do it, I had thought. The ultimatum was devastating.

At the same time Monroe Engel of the Viking Press wrote to me and said that he had supposed I had a commitment for my *Fables*, but if I hadn't would I let the Viking Press see them? I feel an everlasting gratitude to him.

However, I said, "I can't offer you something which somebody else thinks isn't fit to print. I would have to have someone to stabilize it and guarantee that the meanings are sound."

Mr. Engel said, "Who do you think could do that? Whom would you like?"

I said, "Harry Levin," because he had written a cogent, very shrewd review of Edna St. Vincent Millay's and George Dillon's translation of Baudelaire. I admired its finesse.

Mr. Engel said, "I'll ask him. But you won't hear for a long time. He's very busy. And how much do you think we ought to offer him?"

"Well," I said, "not less than ten dollars a Book; there would be no incentive in undertaking the bother of it, if it weren't twenty."

He said, "That would reduce your royalties too much on an advance."

I said, "I don't want an advance, wouldn't even consider one."

And then Harry Levin said, quite soon, that he would be glad to do it as a "refreshment against the chores of the term," but of course he would accept no remuneration. It was a very dubious refreshment, let me tell you. (He is precise, and not abusive, and did not "resign.")

INTERVIEWER: I've been asking you about your poems, which is of course what interests me most. But you were editor of *The Dial*, too, and I want to ask you a few things about that. You were editor from 1925 until it ended in 1929, I think. How did you first come to be associated with it?

MOORE: Let me see. I think I took the initiative. I sent the editors a couple of things and they sent them back. And Lola Ridge had a party—she had a large apartment on a ground floor somewhere—and John Reed and Marsden Hartley, who was very confident with the brush, and Scofield Thayer, editor of *The Dial*, were there. And much to my disgust, we were induced each to read something we had written. And Scofield Thayer said of my piece, "Would you send that to us at *The Dial?*"

"I did send it," I said.

And he said, "Well, send it again." That is how it began, I think. Then he said, one time, "I'd like you to meet my partner, Sibley Watson," and invited me to tea at 152 W. 13th St. I was impressed. Doctor Watson is rare. He said nothing, but what he did say was striking and the significance would creep over you because unanticipated. And they asked me to join the staff, at *The Dial*.

INTERVIEWER: I have just been looking at that magazine, the years when you edited it. It's an incredible magazine.

MOORE: *The Dial?* There *were* good things in it, weren't there?

INTERVIEWER: Yes. It combined George Saintsbury and Ezra Pound in the same issue. How do you account for it? What made it so good?

MOORE: Lack of fear, for one thing. We didn't care what other people said. I never knew a magazine which was so self-propulsive. Everybody liked what he was doing, and when we made grievous mistakes we were sorry but we laughed over them.

INTERVIEWER: Louise Bogan said that *The Dial* made clear "the obvious division between American *avant-garde* and American conventional writing." Do you think this kind of division continues or has continued? Was this in any way a deliberate policy?

MOORE: I think that individuality was the great thing. We were not conforming to anything. We certainly didn't have a policy, except I remember hearing the word "intensity" very often. A thing must have "intensity." That seemed to be the criterion.

The thing applied to it, I think, that should apply to your own writing. As George Grosz said, at that last meeting he attended at the National Institute, "How did I come to be an artist? Endless curiosity, observation, research—and a great amount of joy in the thing." It was a matter of taking a liking to things. Things that were in accordance with your taste. I think that was it. And we didn't care how unhomogeneous they might seem. Didn't Aristotle say that it is the mark of a poet to see resemblances between apparently incongruous things? There was any amount of attraction about it.

INTERVIEWER: Do you think there is anything in the change of literary life in America that would make *The Dial* different if it existed today under the same editors? Were there any special conditions in the twenties that made the literary life of America different?

MOORE: I think it is always about the same.

INTERVIEWER: I wonder, if it had survived into the thirties, if it might have made that rather dry literary decade a little better.

MOORE: I think so. Because we weren't in captivity to anything.

INTERVIEWER: Was it just finances that made it stop?

MOORE: No, it wasn't the depression. Conditions changed. Scofield Thayer had a nervous breakdown, and he didn't come to meetings. Doctor Watson was interested in photography—was studying medicine; is a doctor of medicine, and lived in Rochester. I was alone. I didn't know that Rochester was about a night's journey away, and I would say to Doctor Watson, "Couldn't you come in for a make-up meeting, or send us these manuscripts and say what you think of them?" I may, as usual, have exaggerated my enslavement and my preoccupation with tasks—writing letters and reading manuscripts. Originally I had said I would come if I didn't have to write letters and didn't have to see contributors. And presently I was doing both. I think it was largely chivalry—the decision to discontinue the magazine—because I didn't have time for work of my own.

INTERVIEWER: I wonder how you worked as an editor. Hart Crane complains, in one of his letters, that you rearranged "The Wine Menagerie" and changed the title. Do you feel that you were justified? Did you ask for revisions from many poets?

MOORE: No. We had an inflexible rule: do not ask changes of so much as a comma. Accept it or reject it. But in that instance I felt that in compassion I should disregard the rule. Hart Crane complains of me? Well, I complain of *him*. He liked *The Dial* and we liked him—friends, and with certain tastes in common. He was in dire need of money. It seemed careless not to so much as ask if he might like to make some changes ("like" in quotations). His gratitude was ardent and later his repudiation of it commensurate—he perhaps being in both instances under a disability with which I was not familiar. (Penalizing us for compassion?) I say "us," and should say "me." Really I am not used to having people in that bemused state. He was so *anxious* to have us take that thing, and so *delighted*. "Well, if you would modify it a little," I said, "we would like it better." I never attended "their" wild parties, as Lachaise once said. It was lawless of me to suggest changes; I disobeyed.

INTERVIEWER: Have you had editors suggest changes to you? Changes in your own poems, I mean?

MOORE: No, but my ardor to be helped being sincere, I sometimes *induce* assistance: the *Times*, the *Herald Tribune*, the *New Yorker*, have a number of times had to patch and piece me out. If you have a genius of an editor, you are blessed: e.g., T. S. Eliot and Ezra Pound, Harry Levin, and others; Irita Van Doren and Miss Belle Rosenbaum.

Have I found "help" helpful? I certainly have; and in three

instances when I was at *The Dial*, I hazarded suggestions the results of which were to me drama. Excoriated by Herman George Scheffauer for offering to suggest a verbal change or two in his translation of Thomas Mann's *Disorder and Early Sorrow*, I must have posted the suggestions before I was able to withdraw them. In any case, his joyous subsequent retraction of abuse, and his pleasure in the narrative, were not unwelcome. Gilbert Seldes strongly commended me for excisions proposed by me in his "Jonathan Edwards" (for *The Dial*); and I have not ceased to marvel at the overrating by Mark Van Doren of editorial conscience on my reverting (after an interval) to keeping some final lines I had wished he would omit. (Verse! but not a sonnet.)

We should try to judge the work of others by the most that it is, and our own, if not by the least that it is, take the least into consideration. I feel that I would not be worth a button if not grateful to be preserved from myself, and informed if what I have written is not to the point. I think we should feel free, like La Fontaine's captious critic, to say, if asked, "Your phrases are too long, and the content is not good. Break up the type and put it in the font." As Kenneth Burke says in *Counter-Statement*: "[Great] artists feel as opportunity what others feel as a menace. This ability does not, I believe, derive from exceptional strength, it probably arises purely from professional interest the artist may take in his difficulties."

Lew Sarett says, in the *Poetry Society Bulletin*, we ask of a poet: Does this mean something? Does the poet say what he has to say and in his own manner? Does it stir the reader?

Shouldn't we replace vanity with honesty, as Robert Frost recommends? Annoyances abound. We should not find them lethal—a baffled printer's emendations for instance (my "elephant with frog-colored skin" instead of "fog-colored skin," and "the power of the invisible is the invisible," instead of "the power of the visible is the invisible") sounding like a parody on my meticulousness; a "glasshopper" instead of a "grasshopper."

INTERVIEWER: Editing *The Dial* must have acquainted you with the writers of the day whom you did not know already. Had you known Hart Crane earlier?

MOORE: Yes, I did. You remember *Broom*? Toward at the beginning of that magazine, in 1921, Lola Ridge was very hospitable, and she invited to a party—previous to my work on *The Dial*—Kay Boyle and her husband, a French soldier, and Hart Crane, Elinor Wylie, and some others. I took a great liking to Hart Crane. We talked about French bindings, and he was diffident and modest and seemed to have so much intuition, such a feel for things, for books—really a bibliophile—that I took special interest in him. And Doctor Watson and Scofield Thayer liked him—felt that he was one of our talents, that he couldn't fit himself into an IBM position to find a livelihood; that we ought to, whenever we could, take anything he sent us.

I know a cousin of his, Joe Nowak, who is rather proud of him. He lives here in Brooklyn, and is* at the Dry Dock Savings Bank and used to work in antiques. Joe was very convinced of Hart's sincerity and his innate love of all that I have specified. Anyhow, *The Bridge* is a grand theme. Here and there I think he could have firmed it up. A writer is unfair to himself when he is unable to be hard on himself.

INTERVIEWER: Did Crane have anything to do with *Others*?

MOORE: *Others* antedated *Broom*. *Others* was Alfred Kreymborg and Skipwith Cannéll, Wallace Stevens, William Carlos Williams. Wallace Stevens—odd; I nearly met him a dozen times before I did meet him in 1941 at Mount Holyoke, at the college's *Entretiens de Pontigny* of which Professor Gustav Cohen was chairman. Wallace Stevens was Henry Church's favorite American poet. Mr. Church had published him and some others, and me, in *Mésure*, in Paris. Raymond Queneau translated us.

During the French program at Mount Holyoke one afternoon Wallace Stevens had a discourse, the one about Goethe dancing, on a packet-boat in black wool stockings. My mother and I were there; and I gave a reading with commentary. Henry Church had an astoundingly beautiful Panama hat—a sort of pork-pie with a wide brim, a little like Bernard Berenson's hats. I have never seen as fine a weave, and he had a pepper-and-salt

---

* *Was*; killed; his car run into by a reckless driver in April 1961.—M.M.

shawl which he draped about himself. This lecture was on the lawn.

Wallace Stevens was extremely friendly. We should have had a tape recorder on that occasion, for at lunch they seated us all at a kind of refectory table and a girl kept asking him questions such as, "Mr. Stevens have you read the—*Four—Quartets?*"

"Of course, but I can't read much of Eliot or I wouldn't have any individuality of my own."

INTERVIEWER: Do you read new poetry now? Do you try to keep up?

MOORE: I am always seeing it—am sent some every day. Some, good. But it does interfere with my work. I can't get much done. Yet I would be a monster if I tossed everything away without looking at it; I write more notes, letters, cards in an hour than is sane.

Although everyone is penalized by being quoted inexactly, I wonder if there is anybody alive whose remarks are so often paraphrased as mine—printed as verbatim. It is really martyrdom. In his book *Ezra Pound*, Charles Norman was very scrupulous. He got several things exactly right. The first time I met Ezra Pound, when he came here to see my mother and me, I said that Henry Eliot seemed to me more nearly the artist than anyone I had ever met. "Now, now," said Ezra. "Be careful." Maybe that isn't exact, but he quotes it just the way I said it.

INTERVIEWER: Do you mean Henry Ware Eliot, T. S. Eliot's brother?

MOORE: Yes. After the Henry Eliots moved from Chicago to New York to—is it 68th Street? It's the street on which Hunter College is—to an apartment there, they invited me to dinner, I should think at T. S. Eliot's suggestion, and I took to them immediately. I felt as if I'd known them a great while. It was some time before I felt that way about T. S. Eliot.

About inaccuracies—when I went to see Ezra Pound at St. Elizabeths, about the third time I went, the official who escorted me to the grounds said, "Good of you to come to see him," and I said, "Good? You have no idea how much he has done for me, and others." This pertains to an early rather than final visit.

I was not in the habit of asking experts or anybody else to help me with things that I was doing, unless it was a librarian or someone whose business it was to help applicants; or a teacher. But I was desperate when Macmillan declined my *Fables*. I had worked about four years on them and sent Ezra Pound several— although I hesitated. I didn't like to bother him. He had enough trouble without that; but finally I said, "Would you have time to tell me if the rhythms grate on you? Is my ear not good?"

INTERVIEWER: He replied?

MOORE: Yes, said, "The least touch of merit upsets these blighters."

INTERVIEWER: When you first read Pound in 1916, did you recognize him as one of the great ones?

MOORE: Surely did. *The Spirit of Romance*. I don't think anybody could read that book and feel that a flounderer was writing.

INTERVIEWER: What about the early poems?

MOORE: Yes. They seemed a little didactic, but I liked them.

INTERVIEWER: I wanted to ask you a few questions about poetry in general. Somewhere you have said that originality is a by-product of sincerity. You often use moral terms in your criticism. Is the necessary morality specifically literary, a moral use of words, or is it larger? In what way must a man be good if he is to write good poems?

MOORE: If emotion is strong enough, the words are unambiguous. Someone asked Robert Frost (is this right?) if he was selective. He said, "Call it passionate preference." Must a man be good to write good poems? The villains in Shakespeare are not illiterate, are they? But rectitude *has* a ring that is implicative, I would say. And with *no* integrity, a man is not likely to write the kind of book I read.

INTERVIEWER: Eliot, in his introduction to your *Selected Poems*, talks about your function as poet relative to the living language, as he calls it. Do you agree that this is a function of a poet? How does the poetry have the effect on the living language? What's the mechanics of it?

MOORE: You accept certain modes of saying a thing. Or strongly repudiate things. You do something of your own, you modify, invent a variant or revive a root meaning. Any doubt about that?

INTERVIEWER: I want to ask you a question about your correspondence with the Ford Motor Company, those letters which
were printed in the *New Yorker*. They were looking for a name
for the car they eventually called the Edsel, and they asked you
to think of a name that would make people admire the car—

MOORE: Elegance and grace, they said it would have—

INTERVIEWER: ". . . some visceral feeling of elegance, fleetness,
advanced features and design. A name, in short, which flashes a
dramatically desirable picture in people's minds."

MOORE: Really?

INTERVIEWER: That's what they said, in their first letter to you.
I was thinking about this in connection with my question about
language. Do you remember Pound's talk about expression and
meaning? He says that when expression and meaning are far apart,
the culture is in a bad way. I was wondering if this request doesn't
ask you to remove expression a bit further from meaning.

MOORE: No, I don't think so. At least, to exposit the irresisti-
bleness of the car. I got deep in motors and turbines and recessed
wheels. No. That seemed to me a very worthy pursuit. I was
more interested in the mechanics. I am interested in mechanisms,
mechanics in general. And I enjoyed the assignment, for all that
it was abortive. Dr. Pick at Marquette University procured a young
demonstrator of the Edsel to call for me in a black one, to convey
me to the auditorium. Nothing was wrong with that Edsel! I
thought it was a very handsome car. It came out the wrong year.

INTERVIEWER: Another thing: in your criticism you make frequent analogies between the poet and the scientist. Do you think
this analogy is helpful to the modern poet? Most people would
consider the comparison a paradox, and assume that the poet and
the scientist are opposed.

MOORE: Do the poet and scientist not work analogously? Both
are willing to waste effort. To be hard on himself is one of the
main strengths of each. Each is attentive to clues, each must
narrow the choice, must strive for precision. As George Grosz
says, "In art there is no place for gossip and but a small place for
the satirist." The objective is fertile procedure. Is it not? Jacob

Bronowski says in the *Saturday Evening Post* that science is not a mere collection of discoveries, but that science is the process of discovering. In any case it's not established once and for all; it's evolving.

INTERVIEWER: One last question. I was intrigued when you wrote that "America has in Wallace Stevens at least one artist whom professionalism will not demolish." What sort of literary professionalism did you have in mind? And do you find this a feature of America still?

MOORE: Yes. I think that writers sometimes lose verve and pugnacity, and he never would say "frame of reference" or "I wouldn't know." A question I am often asked is: "What work can I find that will enable me to spend my whole time writing?" Charles Ives, the composer, says, "You cannot set art off in a corner and hope for it to have vitality, reality, and substance. The fabric weaves itself whole. My work in music helped my business and my work in business helped my music." I am like Charles Ives. I guess Lawrence Durrell and Henry Miller would not agree with me.

INTERVIEWER: But how does professionalism make a writer lose his verve and pugnacity?

MOORE: Money may have something to do with it, and being regarded as a pundit; Wallace Stevens was really very much annoyed at being catalogued, categorized, and compelled to be scientific about what he was doing—to give satisfaction, to answer the teachers. He wouldn't do that. I think the same of William Carlos Williams. I think he wouldn't make so much of the great American language if he were plausible; and tractable. That's the beauty of it; he is willing to be reckless; if you can't be that, what's the point of the whole thing?

—DONALD HALL
1960

3. Katherine Anne Porter

Katherine Anne Porter was born May 15, 1890, at Indian Creek, Texas. She spent her early youth in Texas and Louisiana, and received her education from small convent schools in that area. She began writing, she once said, almost as soon as she could put words on paper. "I did not choose this vocation, and if I had any say in the matter, I would not have chosen it . . . yet for this vocation I was and am willing to live and die, and I consider very few other things of the slightest importance."

Supporting herself by book reviewing, political articles, hack writing, and editing, she worked continually at her own stories, although she did not publish until she was in her thirties. Her first collection of short stories, *Flowering Judas*, appeared in 1930 and earned her an immediate reputation. In 1931 she was awarded a Guggenheim Fellowship and went abroad to study and write—in Berlin, Basel, and Madrid.

When she returned to America she received a Book-of-the-Month Club Fellowship, and in 1938 another Guggenheim grant. In 1949 Miss Porter was given an honorary Doctorate in Literature from the Woman's College of the University of North Carolina. She was a vice-president of the National Institute of Arts and Letters, a fellow in the Library of Congress, and in 1952 was the only woman writer in the United States delegation to the Cultural Exposition in Paris sponsored by the Congress for Cultural Freedom.

Her published work includes: *Hacienda* (1934), *Noon Wine* (1937), *Pale Horse, Pale Rider* (1939), *The Leaning Tower and Other Stories* (1944), *The Days Before* (essays, 1952), *Ship of Fools* (1962), and *Collected Stories* (1965), which won both the Pulitzer Prize and the National Book Award. In 1970 an augmented version of her *Collected Essays and Occasional Writings* was published. She died in 1980.

er ~~such~~ greeting for any one. She sat there alone reading stale magazines until the luncheon bugle sounded. The exact vision of the Baumgartner's faces ~~haunted them~~, would not leave her. It was plain they too had ~~had~~ *suffered* some sort of shabby little incident during the night— no matter what. Mrs. Treadwell did not even wish to guess what it might have been, but that sad dull display ~~of~~ high ~~manners~~ *manner* after they had behaved *was intended no doubt* no doubt disgracefully to each other and their child— ~~seeking~~ to prove ~~as could~~ that they were not so base as they had caused each other to seem. That dreadful little door-holding,bowing scene had meant to say You can see, can't you,that in another time or place,or another society, I might have been very different, much better than you have ever seen me? Mrs. Treadwell leaned back and closed her eyes. What they were saying to each other was only <u>Love me, love me in spite of all!</u> Whether or not <u>I love you, whether</u> <u>I</u> <u>am fit to love, whether you are able to love, even if there</u> <u>is no such thing as love. Love me!</u>

A small deep wandering sensation of disgust, self-distaste came with these straying thoughts. She remembered as in a dream again her despairs, her long weeping, her incurable grief over the failure of love or what she had been told was love, and the ruin of her hopes— what hopes? she could not remember— and what had it been but the childish refusal to admit an accept on some term or other the difference between what one had hoped was true and what one discovers to be the *mere* ~~decay of the human condition~~ *farce of the human condition* She had been hurt, she had recovered, and what had it all been but a foolish piece of romantic carelessness? She stood up to take a deep breath and walk around the stuffy room. All morning long she had been trying in the back of her mind to piece together exactly what had happened last night to her, and what she had done. The scene with that young officer was clear enough. She remembered Herr Baumgartner hanging over the rail looking sick. Lizzi delivered to her hands later, when she had been amusing herself painting her face; and then—

No good putting it off any longer. She could not find her gilded sandals when she was putting her things in order. There were small random bloodspots on the lower front of her night gown. And as she walked, she remembered, and stopped clutching a chairback feeling faint; walked again, then left the room and set out to look for Jenny Brown. She should know everything about it, being the "girl" of that rather self-absorbed young man, Denny's *cabin* mate... Mrs.Treadwell remembered very well what had happened, what she had done; she wanted a few particulars of the damage she had done, and above all to learn whether her *enemy* ~~victim~~ had recognized her.

Jenny Brown was reading the bulletin board. A ragged-edged imitation of an ancient proclamation announced:" The victims of last night's violence and bloodshed are resting quietly. The suspected criminals are under surveillance, not yet ~~identified~~ *under arrest*, ~~but several possible suspects have been several interesting personages is empty.~~"

but an early disclosure of several interesting identities is expected.
Signed The Camelots de la Cucaracha.

Manuscript page from Katherine Anne Porter's novel Ship of Fools.

WILLIAM WALTON

Katherine Anne Porter

The Victorian house in which Katherine Anne Porter lived was narrow and white, reached by an iron-railed stairway curving up from the shady brick-walked Georgetown street. The parlor to which a maid admitted the caller was an elegant mélange of several aspects of the past, both American and European. Dim and cool after the midsummer glare, the high-ceilinged room was dominated by a bottle-green settee from the period of Napoleon III. Outside the alcove of windows there was a rustle of wind through ginkgo trees, then a hush.

Finally, a voice in the upper hallway: its tone that of someone talking to a bird, or coquetting with an old beau—light and feathery, with a slight flutter. A few moments later, moving as lightly as her voice, Miss Porter hurried through the wide doorway, unexpectedly modern in a soft green suit of woven Italian silk. Small and elegant, she explained her tardiness, related an anecdote

47

from the morning's mail, offered a minted ice tea, and speculated aloud on where we might best conduct our conversation.

She decided on the dining room, a quiet, austere place over-looking the small enclosed garden. Here the aspect was a different one. "I want to live in a world capital or the howling wilderness," she said once, and did. The drawing room was filled with pieces that had once been part of the house on rue Notre-Dame des Champs; this one was bright with Mexican folk art—whistles and toy animals collected during a recent tour for the Department of State—against simpler, heavier pieces of furniture. The round table at which we sat was of Vermont marble, mottled and colored like milk glass, on a wrought-iron base of her own design. There was a sixteenth-century cupboard from Avila, and a refectory table of the early Renaissance from a convent in Fiesole. Here we settled the tape recorder, under an image of the great god Horus.

We tried to make a beginning. She was an experienced lecturer, familiar with microphone and tape recorder, but now she was to talk about herself as well as her work, the link between, and the inexorable winding of the tape from one spool to the other acted almost as a hypnotic. Finally we turned it off and talked for a while of other things, more frivolous and more autobiographical, hoping to surprise an easier revelation. . . .

INTERVIEWER: You were saying that you had never intended to make a career of writing.

PORTER: I've never made a career of anything, you know, not even of writing. I started out with nothing in the world but a kind of passion, a driving desire. I don't know where it came from, and I don't know why—or why I have been so stubborn about it that nothing could deflect me. But this thing between me and my writing is the strongest bond I have ever had—stronger than any bond or any engagement with any human being or with any other work I've ever done. I really started writing when I was six or seven years old. But I had such a multiplicity of half-talents, too: I wanted to dance, I wanted to play the piano, I sang, I drew. It wasn't really dabbling—I was investigating everything, experimenting in everything. And then, for one thing, there weren't very many amusements in those days. If you wanted music, you had to play the piano and sing yourself. Oh, we saw all the great things that came during the season, but after all, there would only be a dozen or so of those occasions a year. The rest of the time we depended upon our own resources: our own music and books. All the old houses that I knew when I was a child were full of books, bought generation after generation by members of the family. Everyone was literate as a matter of course. Nobody told you to read this or not to read that. It was there to read, and we read.

INTERVIEWER: Which books influenced you most?

PORTER: That's hard to say, because I grew up in a sort of mélange. I was reading Shakespeare's sonnets when I was thirteen years old, and I'm perfectly certain that they made the most profound impression upon me of anything I ever read. For a time I knew the whole sequence by heart; now I can only remember two or three of them. That was the turning point of my life, when I read the Shakespeare sonnets, and then all at one blow, all of Dante—in that great big book illustrated by Gustave Doré. The plays I saw on the stage, but I don't remember reading them with any interest at all. Oh, and I read all kinds of poetry—Homer, Ronsard, all the old French poets in translation. We also had a very good library of—well, you might say secular philosophers. I was incredibly influenced by Montaigne when I was very young. And one day when I was about fourteen, my father led me up to a great big line of books and said, "Why don't you read this? It'll knock some of the nonsense out of you!" It happened to be the entire set of Voltaire's philosophical dictionary with notes by Smollett. And I plowed through it; it took me about five years.

And of course we read all the eighteenth-century novelists, though Jane Austen, like Turgenev, didn't really engage me until I was quite mature. I read them both when I was very young, but I was grown up before I really took them in. And I discovered for myself *Wuthering Heights*; I think I read that book every year of my life for fifteen years. I simply adored it. Henry James and Thomas Hardy were really my introduction to modern literature; Grandmother didn't much approve of it. She thought Dickens might do, but she was a little against Mr. Thackeray; she thought he was too trivial. So that was as far as I got into the modern world until I left home!

INTERVIEWER: Don't you think this background—the comparative isolation of Southern rural life, and the atmosphere of literary interest—helped to shape you as a writer?

PORTER: I think it's something in the blood. We've always had great letter writers, readers, great storytellers in our family. I've listened all my life to articulate people. They were all great storytellers, and every story had shape and meaning and point.

INTERVIEWER: Were any of them known as writers?

PORTER: Well, there was my sixth or seventh cousin once removed, poor William Sidney. O. Henry, you know. He was my father's second cousin—I don't know what that makes him to me. And he was more known in the family for being a bank robber. He worked in a bank, you know, and he just didn't seem to find a talent for making money; no Porter ever did. But he had a wife who was dying of TB and he couldn't keep up with the doctor's bills. So he took a pitiful little sum—oh, about three hundred and fifty dollars—and ran away when he was accused. But he came back, because his wife was dying, and went to prison. And there was Horace Porter, who spent his whole eight years as ambassador to France looking for the bones of John Paul Jones. And when he found them, and brought them back, he wrote a book about them.

INTERVIEWER: It seems to me that your work is pervaded by a sense of history. Is that part of the family legacy?

PORTER: We were brought up with a sense of our own history, you know. My mother's family came to this country in 1648 and went to the John Randolph territory of Virginia. And one of my great great grandfathers was Jonathan Boone, the brother of Daniel. On my father's side I'm descended from Colonel Andrew Porter, whose father came to Montgomery County, Pennsylvania, in 1720. He was one of the circle of George Washington during the Revolution, a friend of Lafayette, and one of the founders of the Society of the Cincinnati—oh, he really took it seriously!—and when he died in 1809—well, just a few years before that he was offered the post of Secretary of War, but he declined. We were never very ambitious people. We never had a President, though we had two governors and some in the Army and the Navy. I suppose we did have a desire to excel but not to push our way to higher places. We thought we'd *already* arrived!

INTERVIEWER: The "we" of family is very strong, isn't it? I remember that you once wrote of the ties of blood as the "absolute point of all departure and return." And the central character in many of your stories is defined, is defining herself often, in relation to a family organization. Even the measure of time is human—expressed in terms of the very old and the very young, and how much of human experience they have absorbed.

PORTER: Yes, but it wasn't a conscious made-up affair, you know. In those days you belonged together, you lived together, because you were a family. The head of our house was a grandmother, an old matriarch, you know, and a really lovely and beautiful woman, a good soul, and so she didn't do us any harm. But the point is that we did live like that, with Grandmother's friends, all reverend old gentlemen with frock coats, and old ladies with jet breastplates. Then there were the younger people, the beautiful girls and the handsome young boys, who were all ahead of me; when I was a little girl, eight or nine years old, they were eighteen to twenty-two, and they represented all glamour, all beauty, all joy and freedom to me. Then there was my own age, and then there were the babies. And the servants, the Negroes. We simply lived that way; to have four generations in one house, under one roof, there was nothing unusual about that. That was just my experience, and this is just the way I've reacted to it. Many other people didn't react, who were brought up in very much the same way.

I remember when I was very young, my older sister wanted to buy some old furniture. It was in Louisiana, and she had just been married. And I went with her to a wonderful old house in the country where we'd been told there was a very old gentleman who probably had some things to sell. His wife had died, and he was living there alone. So we went to this lovely old house, and, sure enough, there was this lonely beautiful old man, eighty-seven or -eight, surrounded by devoted Negro servants. But his wife was dead and his children were married and gone. He said, yes, he had a few things he wanted to sell. So he showed us through the house. And finally he opened a door, and showed us a bedroom with a beautiful four-poster bed, with a wonderful satin coverlet: the most wonderful, classical-looking bed you ever saw. And my sister said, "Oh, that's what I want." And he said, "Oh, madame, that is my marriage bed. That is the bed that my wife brought with her as a bride. We slept together in that bed for nearly sixty years. All our children were born there. Oh," he said, "I shall die in that bed, and then they can dispose of it as they like."

I remember that I felt a little suffocated and frightened. I felt a little trapped. But why? Only because I understood that. I was brought up in that. And I was at the age of rebellion then, and it really scared me. But I look back on it now and think how perfectly wonderful, what a tremendously beautiful life it was. Everything in it had meaning.

INTERVIEWER: But it seems to me that your work suggests someone who was searching for new—perhaps broader—meanings . . . that while you've retained the South of your childhood as a point of reference, you've ranged far from that environment itself. You seem to have felt little of the peculiarly Southern preoccupation with racial guilt and the death of the old agrarian life.

PORTER: I'm a Southerner by tradition and inheritance, and I have a very profound feeling for the South. And, of course, I belong to the guilt-ridden white-pillar crowd myself, but it just didn't rub off on me. Maybe I'm just not Jewish enough, or Puritan enough, to feel that the sins of the father are visited on the third and fourth generations. Or maybe it's because of my European influences—in Texas and Louisiana. The Europeans didn't have slaves themselves as late as my family did, but they *still* thought slavery was quite natural. . . . But, you know, I was always restless, always a roving spirit. When I was a little child I was always running away. I never got very far, but they were always having to come and fetch me. Once when I was about six, my father came to get me somewhere I'd gone, and he told me later he'd asked me, "Why are you so restless? Why can't you stay here with us?" and I said to him, "I want to go and see the world. I want to know the world like the palm of my hand."

INTERVIEWER: And at sixteen you made it final.

PORTER: At sixteen I ran away from New Orleans and got married. And at twenty-one I bolted again, went to Chicago, got a newspaper job, and went into the movies.

INTERVIEWER: The movies?

PORTER: The newspaper sent me over to the old S. and A. movie studio to do a story. But I got into the wrong line, and then was too timid to get out. "Right over this way, Little Boy Blue," the man said, and I found myself in a courtroom scene with Francis X. Bushman. I was horrified by what had happened to me, but they paid me five dollars for that first day's work, so I stayed on. It was about a week before I remembered what I had been sent to do; and when I went back to the newspaper they gave me eighteen dollars for my week's non-work and fired me!

I stayed on for six months—I finally got to nearly ten dollars a day—until one day they came in and said, "We're moving to the coast." "Well, I'm not," I said. "Don't you want to be a movie actress?" "Oh, no!" I said. "Well, be a fool!" they said, and they left. That was 1914 and World War had broken out, so in September I went home.

INTERVIEWER: And then?

PORTER: Oh, I sang old Scottish ballads in costume—I made it myself—all around Texas and Louisiana. And then I was supposed to have TB, and spent about six weeks in a sanitarium. It was just bronchitis, but I was in Denver, so I got a newspaper job.

INTERVIEWER: I remember that you once warned me to avoid that at all costs—to get a job "hashing" in a restaurant in preference.

PORTER: Anything, anything at all. I did it for a year and that is what confirmed me that it wasn't doing me any good. After that I always took little dull jobs that didn't take my mind and wouldn't take all of my time, and that, on the other hand, paid me just enough to subsist. I think I've only spent about ten per cent of my energies on writing. The other ninety per cent went to keeping my head above water.

And I think that's all wrong. Even Saint Teresa said, "I can pray better when I'm comfortable," and she refused to wear her haircloth shirt or starve herself. I don't think living in cellars and starving is any better for an artist than it is for anybody else; the only thing is that sometimes the artist has to take it, because it is the only possible way of salvation, if you'll forgive that old-fashioned word. So I took it rather instinctively. I was inexperienced in the world, and likewise I hadn't been trained to do anything, you know, so I took all kinds of laborious jobs. But, you know, I think I could probably have written better if I'd been a little more comfortable.

INTERVIEWER: Then you were writing all this time?

PORTER: All this time I was writing, writing no matter what else I was doing; no matter what I *thought* I was doing, in fact. I was living almost as instinctively as a little animal, but I realize now that all that time a part of me was getting ready to be an artist. That my mind was working even when I didn't know it, and didn't care if it was working or not. It is my firm belief that all our lives we are preparing to be somebody or something, even if we don't do it consciously. And the time comes one morning when you wake up and find that you have become irrevocably what you were preparing all this time to be. Lord, that could be a sticky moment, if you had been doing the wrong things, something against your grain. And, mind you, I know that can happen. I have no patience with this dreadful idea that whatever you have in you has to come out, that you can't suppress true talent. People *can* be destroyed; they can be bent, distorted, and completely crippled. To say that you can't destroy yourself is just as foolish as to say of a young man killed in war at twenty-one or twenty-two that that was his fate, that he wasn't going to have anything anyhow.

I have a very firm belief that the life of no man can be explained in terms of his experiences, of what has happened to him, because in spite of all the poetry, all the philosophy to the contrary, we are not really masters of our fate. We don't really direct our lives unaided and unobstructed. Our being is subject to all the chances of life. There are so many things we are capable of, that we could be or do. The potentialities are so great that we never, any of us, are more than one-fourth fulfilled. Except that there may be one powerful motivating force that simply carries you along, and I think that was true of me. . . . When I was a very little girl I wrote a letter to my sister saying I wanted glory. I don't know quite what I meant by that now, but it was something different from fame or success or wealth. I know that I wanted to be a good writer, a good artist.

INTERVIEWER: But weren't there certain specific events that crystallized that desire for you—something comparable to the experience of Miranda in *Pale Horse, Pale Rider*?

PORTER: Yes, that was the plague of influenza, at the end of the First World War, in which I almost died. It just simply divided my life, cut across it like that. So that everything before that was just getting ready, and after that I was in some strange way altered, ready. It took me a long time to go out and live in the world again. I was really "alienated," in the pure sense. It was, I think, the fact that I really had participated in death, that I knew what death was, and had almost experienced it. I had what the Christians call the "beatific vision," and the Greeks called the "happy day," the happy vision just before death. Now if you have had that, and survived it, come back from it, you are no longer like other people, and there's no use deceiving yourself that you are. But you see, I did: I made the mistake of thinking I was quite like anybody else, of trying to live like other people. It took me a long time to realize that that simply wasn't true, that I had my own needs and that I had to live like me.

INTERVIEWER: And that freed you?

PORTER: I just got up and bolted. I went running off on that wild escapade to Mexico, where I attended, you might say, and assisted at, in my own modest way, a revolution.

INTERVIEWER: That was the Obregón Revolution of 1921?

PORTER: Yes—though actually I went to Mexico to study the Aztec and Mayan art designs. I had been in New York, and was getting ready to go to Europe. Now, New York was full of Mexican artists at that time, all talking about the renaissance, as they called it, in Mexico. And they said, "Don't go to Europe, go to Mexico. That's where the exciting things are going to happen." And they were right! I ran smack into the Obregón Revolution, and had, in the midst of it, the most marvelous, natural, spontaneous experience of my life. It was a terribly exciting time. It was alive, but death was in it. But nobody seemed to think of that: life was in it, too.

INTERVIEWER: What do you think are the best conditions for a writer, then? Something like your Mexican experience, or—

PORTER: Oh, I can't say what they are. It would be such an individual matter. Everyone needs something different. . . . But what I find most dreadful among the young artists is this tendency toward middle-classness—this idea that they have to get married and have lots of children and live just like everybody else, you know? Now, I am all for human life, and I am all for marriage and children and all that sort of thing, but quite often you can't have that and do what you were supposed to do, too. Art is a vocation, as much as anything in this world. For the real artist, it is the most natural thing in the world, not as necessary as air and water, perhaps, but as food and water. But we really do lead almost a monastic life, you know; to follow it you very often have to give up something.

INTERVIEWER: But for the unproven artist that is a very great act of faith.

PORTER: It *is* an act of faith. But one of the marks of a gift is to have the courage of it. If they haven't got the courage, it's just too bad. They'll fail, just as people with lack of courage in other vocations and walks of life fail. Courage is the first essential.

INTERVIEWER: In choosing a pattern of life compatible with the vocation?

PORTER: The thing is not to follow a pattern. Follow your own pattern of feeling and thought. The thing is, to accept your own life and not try to live someone else's life. Look, the thumbprint is not like any other, and the thumbprint is what you must go by.

INTERVIEWER: In the current vernacular then, you think it's

necessary for an artist to be a "loner"—not to belong to any literary movement?

PORTER: I've never belonged to any group or huddle of any kind. You cannot be an artist and work collectively. Even the fact that I went to Mexico when everybody else was going to Europe—I went to Mexico because I felt I had business there. And there I found friends and ideas that were sympathetic to me. That was my entire milieu. I don't think anyone even knew I was a writer. I didn't show my work to anybody or talk about it, because—well, no one was particularly interested in that. It was a time of revolution, and I was running with almost pure revolutionaries!

INTERVIEWER: And you think that was a more wholesome environment for a writer than, say, the milieu of the expatriated artist in Europe at the same time?

PORTER: Well, I know it was good for me. I would have been completely smothered—completely disgusted and revolted—by the goings-on in Europe. Even now when I think of the twenties and the legend that has grown up about them, I think it was a horrible time: shallow and trivial and silly. The remarkable thing is that anybody survived in such an atmosphere—in a place where they could call F. Scott Fitzgerald a great writer!

INTERVIEWER: You don't agree?

PORTER: Of course I don't agree. I couldn't read him then and I can't read him now. There was just one passage in a book called *Tender Is the Night*—I read that and thought, "Now I will read this again," because I couldn't be sure. Not only didn't I like his writing, but I didn't like the people he wrote about. I thought they weren't worth thinking about, and I still think so. It seems to me that your human beings have to have some kind of meaning. I just can't be interested in those perfectly stupid meaningless lives. And I don't like the same thing going on now—the way the artist simply will not face up to the final reckoning of things.

INTERVIEWER: In a philosophical sense?

PORTER: I'm thinking of it now in just the artistic sense—in the sense of an artist facing up to his own end meanings. I suppose I shouldn't be mentioning names, but I read a story some time

ago, I think it was in the *Paris Review*, called "The McCabes."*
Now I think William Styron is an extremely gifted man: he's very
ripe and lush and with a kind of Niagara Falls of energy, and a
kind of power. But he depends so on violence and a kind of
exaggerated heat—at least it looks like heat, but just turns out to
be summer lightning. Because there is nothing in the world more
meaningless than that whole escapade of this man going off and
winding up in the gutter. You sit back and think, "Well, let's
see, where are we now?" All right, it's possible that that's just
what Styron meant—the whole wicked pointlessness of things.
But I tell you, nothing is pointless, and nothing is meaningless
if the artist will face it. And it's his business to face it. He hasn't
got the right to sidestep it like that. Human life itself may be
almost pure chaos, but the work of the artist—the only thing he's
good for—is to take these handfuls of confusion and disparate
things, things that seem to be irreconcilable, and put them together in a frame to give them some kind of shape and meaning.
Even if it's only his view of a meaning. That's what he's for—to
give his view of life. Surely, we understand very little of what is
happening to us at any given moment. But by remembering,
comparing, waiting to know the consequences, we can sometimes
see what an event really meant, what it was trying to teach us.

INTERVIEWER: You once said that every story begins with an
ending, that until the end is known there is no story.

PORTER: That is where the artist begins to work: With the
consequences of acts, not the acts themselves. Or the events. The
event is important only as it affects your life and the lives of those
around you. The reverberations, you might say, the overtones:
that is where the artist works. In that sense it has sometimes taken
me ten years to understand even a little of some important event
that had happened to me. Oh, I could have given a perfectly
factual account of what had happened, but I didn't know what
it meant until I knew the consequences. If I didn't know the

* "The McCabes" was mistakenly not identified as a section from Styron's novel *Set This House on Fire*.

ending of a story, I wouldn't begin. I always write my last lines, my last paragraph, my last page first, and then I go back and work towards it. I know where I'm going. I know what my goal is. And how I get there is God's grace.

INTERVIEWER: That's a very classical view of the work of art—that it must end in resolution.

PORTER: Any true work of art has got to give you the feeling of reconciliation—what the Greeks would call catharsis, the purification of your mind and imagination—through an ending that is endurable because it is right and true. Oh, not in any pawky individual idea of morality or some parochial idea of right and wrong. Sometimes the end is very tragic, because it needs to be. One of the most perfect and marvelous endings in literature—it raises my hair now—is the little boy at the end of *Wuthering Heights*, crying that he's afraid to go across the moor because there's a man and woman walking there.

And there are three novels that I reread with pleasure and delight—three almost perfect novels, if we're talking about form, you know. One is *A High Wind in Jamaica* by Richard Hughes, one is *A Passage to India* by E. M. Forster, and the other is *To the Lighthouse* by Virginia Woolf. Every one of them begins with an apparently insoluble problem, and every one of them works out of confusion into order. The material is all used so that you are going toward a goal. And that goal is the clearing up of disorder and confusion and wrong, to a logical and human end. I don't mean a happy ending, because after all at the end of *A High Wind in Jamaica* the pirates are all hanged and the children are all marked for life by their experience, but it comes out to an orderly end. The threads are all drawn up. I have had people object to Mr. Thompson's suicide at the end of *Noon Wine*, and I'd say, "All right, where was he going? Given what he was, his own situation, what else could he do?" Every once in a while when I see a character of mine just going towards perdition, I think, "Stop, stop, you can always stop and choose, you know." But no, being what he was, he already *has* chosen, and he can't go back on it now. I suppose the first idea that man had was the idea of fate, of the servile will, of a deity who destroyed as he would, without regard for the creature. But I think the idea of free will was the second idea.

INTERVIEWER: Has a story never surprised you in the writing? A character suddenly taken a different turn?

PORTER: Well, in the vision of death at the end of "Flowering Judas" I knew the real ending—that she was not going to be able to face her life, what she'd done. And I knew that the vengeful spirit was going to come in a dream to tow her away into death, but I didn't know until I'd written it that she was going to wake up saying, "No!" and be afraid to go to sleep again.

INTERVIEWER: That was, in a fairly literal sense, a "true" story, wasn't it?

PORTER: The truth is, I have never written a story in my life that didn't have a very firm foundation in actual human experience—somebody else's experience quite often, but an experience that became my own by hearing the story, by witnessing the thing, by hearing just a word perhaps. It doesn't matter, it just takes a little—a tiny seed. Then it takes root, and it grows. It's an organic thing. That story had been on my mind for years, growing out of this one little thing that happened in Mexico. It was forming and forming in my mind, until one night I was quite desperate. People are always so sociable, and I'm sociable too, and if I live around friends. . . . Well, they were insisting that I come and play bridge. But I was very firm, because I knew the time had come to write that story, and I had to write it.

INTERVIEWER: What was that "little thing" from which the story grew?

PORTER: Something I saw as I passed a window one evening. A girl I knew had asked me to come and sit with her, because a man was coming to see her, and she was a little afraid of him. And as I went through the courtyard, past the flowering judas tree, I glanced in the window and there she was sitting with an open book on her lap, and there was this great big fat man sitting beside her. Now Mary and I were friends, both American girls living in this revolutionary situation. She was teaching at an Indian school, and I was teaching dancing at a girls' technical school in Mexico City. And we were having a very strange time of it. I was more skeptical, and so I had already begun to look with a skeptical eye on a great many of the revolutionary leaders. Oh, the idea was all right, but a lot of men were misapplying it.

And when I looked through that window that evening, I saw something in Mary's face, something in her pose, something in the whole situation, that set up a commotion in my mind. Because until that moment I hadn't really understood that she was not able to take care of herself, because she was not able to face her own nature and was afraid of everything. I don't know why I saw it. I don't believe in intuition. When you get sudden flashes of perception, it is just the brain working faster than usual. But you've been getting ready to know it for a long time, and when it comes, you feel you've known it always.

INTERVIEWER: You speak of a story "forming" in your mind. Does it begin as a visual impression, growing to a narrative? Or how?

PORTER: All my senses were very keen; things came to me through my eyes, through all my pores. Everything hit me at once, you know. That makes it very difficult to describe just exactly what is happening. And then, I think the mind works in such a variety of ways. Sometimes an idea starts completely inarticulately. You're not thinking in images or words or—well, it's exactly like a dark cloud moving in your head. You keep wondering what will come out of this, and then it will dissolve itself into a set of—well, not images exactly, but really thoughts. You begin to think directly in words. Abstractly. Then the words transform themselves into images. By the time I write the story my people are up and alive and walking around and taking things into their own hands. They exist as independently inside my head as you do before me now. I have been criticized for not enough detail in describing my characters, and not enough furniture in the house. And the odd thing is that I see it all so clearly.

INTERVIEWER: What about the technical problems a story presents—its formal structure? How deliberate are you in matters of technique? For example, the use of the historical present in "Flowering Judas"?

PORTER: The first time someone said to me, "Why did you write 'Flowering Judas' in the historical present?" I thought for a moment and said, "Did I?" I'd never noticed it. Because I didn't *plan* to write it any way. A story forms in my mind and forms and forms, and when it's ready to go, I strike it down—it takes just the time I sit at the typewriter. I never think about form at all. In fact, I would say that I've never been interested in anything about writing after having learned, I hope, to write. That is, I mastered my craft as well as I could. There is a technique, there is a craft, and you have to learn it. Well, I did as well as I could with that, but now all in the world I am interested in is telling a story. I have something to tell you that I, for some reason, think is worth telling, and so I want to tell it as clearly and purely and simply as I can. But I had spent fifteen years at least learning to write. I practiced writing in every possible way that I could. I wrote a pastiche of other people, imitating Dr. Johnson and Laurence Sterne, and Petrarch and Shakespeare's sonnets, and then I tried writing my own way. I spent fifteen years learning to trust myself: that's what it comes to. Just as a pianist runs his scales for ten years before he gives his concert: because when he gives that concert, he can't be thinking of his fingering or of his hands; he has to be thinking of his interpretation, of the music he's playing. He's thinking of what he's trying to communicate. And if he hasn't got his technique perfected by then, he needn't give the concert at all.

INTERVIEWER: From whom would you say you learned most during this period of apprenticeship?

PORTER: The person who influenced me most, the real revelation in my life as a writer—though I don't write in the least like him—was Laurence Sterne, in *Tristram Shandy*. Why? Because, you know, I loved the grand style, and he made it look easy. The others, the great ones, really frightened me; they were so grand and magnificent they overawed me completely. But Laurence Sterne—well, it was just exactly as if he said, "Oh, come on, do it this way. It's so easy." So I tried to do it that way, and that taught me something, that taught me more than anybody else had. Because Laurence Sterne is a most complex and subtle man.

INTERVIEWER: What about your contemporaries? Did any of them contribute significantly to your development as a writer?

PORTER: I don't think I learned very much from my contemporaries. To begin with, we were all such individuals, and we were all so argumentative and so bent on our own courses that although I got a kind of support and personal friendship from my contemporaries, I didn't get very much help. I didn't show my work to anybody. I didn't hand it around among my friends for criticism, because, well, it just didn't occur to me to do it. Just as I didn't even try to publish anything until quite late because I didn't think I was ready. I published my first story in 1923. That was "María Concepción," the first story I ever finished. I rewrote "María Concepción" fifteen or sixteen times. That was a real battle, and I was thirty-three years old. I think it is the most curious lack of judgment to publish before you are ready. If there are echoes of other people in your work, you're not ready. If anybody has to help you rewrite your story, you're not ready. A story should be a finished work before it is shown. And after that, I will not allow anyone to change anything, and I will not change anything on anyone's advice. "Here is my story. It's a finished story. Take it or leave it!"

INTERVIEWER: You are frequently spoken of as a stylist. Do you think a style can be cultivated, or at least refined?

PORTER: I've been called a stylist until I really could tear my hair out. And I simply don't believe in style. The style is you. Oh, you can cultivate a style, I suppose, if you like. But I should say it remains a cultivated style. It remains artificial and imposed, and I don't think it deceives anyone. A cultivated style would be like a mask. Everybody knows it's a mask, and sooner or later you must show yourself—or at least, you show yourself as someone who could not afford to show himself, and so created something to hide behind. Style is the man. Aristotle said it first, as far as I know, and everybody has said it since, because it is one of those unarguable truths. You do not create a style. You work, and develop yourself; your style is an emanation from your own being. Symbolism is the same way. I never consciously took or adopted a symbol in my life. I certainly did not say, "This blooming tree upon which Judas is supposed to have hanged himself is going to be the center of my story." I named "Flowering Judas" after it was written, because when reading back over it I suddenly saw the whole symbolic plan and pattern of which I was totally unconscious while I was writing. There's a pox of symbolist theory going the rounds these days in American colleges in the writing courses. Miss Mary McCarthy, who is one of the wittiest and most acute and in some ways the worst-tempered woman in American letters, tells about a little girl who came to her with a story. Now Miss McCarthy is an extremely good critic, and she found this to be a good story, and she told the girl that it was—that she considered it a finished work, and that she could with a clear conscience go on to something else. And the little girl said, "But Miss McCarthy, my writing teacher said, 'Yes, it's a good piece of work, but now we must go back and put in the symbols!' " I think that's an amusing story, and it makes my blood run cold.

INTERVIEWER: But certainly one's command of the language can be developed and refined?

PORTER: I love the purity of language. I keep cautioning my students and anyone who will listen to me not to use the jargon of trades, not to use scientific language, because they're going to be out of date the day after tomorrow. The scientists change their vocabulary, their jargon, every day. So do the doctors, and the politicians, and the theologians—every body, every profession, every trade changes its vocabulary all of the time. But there is a basic pure human speech that exists in every language. And that is the language of the poet and the writer. So many words that had good meanings once upon a time have come to have meanings almost evil—certainly shabby, certainly inaccurate. And "psychology" is one of them. It has been so abused. This awful way a whole segment, not a generation but too many of the young writers, have got so soaked in the Freudian and post-Freudian vocabulary that they can't speak—not only can't speak English, but they can't speak *any* human language anymore. You can't write about people out of textbooks, and you can't use a jargon. You have to speak clearly and simply and purely in a language that a six-year-old child can understand; and yet have the meanings and the overtones of language, and the implications, that appeal to the highest intelligence—that is, the highest intelligence that one is able to reach. I'm not sure that I'm able to appeal to the highest intelligence, but I'm willing to try.

INTERVIEWER: You speak of the necessity of writing out of your own understanding rather than out of textbooks, and I'm sure any writer would agree. But what about the creation of masculine characters then? Most women writers, even the best of them like George Eliot, have run aground there. What about you? Was Mr. Thompson, say, a more difficult imaginative problem than Miranda?

PORTER: I never did make a profession of understanding people, man or woman or child, and the only thing I know about people is exactly what I have learned from the people right next to me. I have always lived in my immediate circumstances, from day to day. And when men ask me how I know so much about men, I've got a simple answer: everything I know about men, I've learned from men. If there is such a thing as a man's mind and a woman's mind—and I'm sure there is—it isn't what most critics mean when they talk about the two. If I show wisdom, they say I have a masculine mind. If I am silly and irrelevant—and Edmund Wilson says I often am—why then they say I have a typically feminine mind! (That's one thing about reaching my age: you can always quote the authorities about what you are.) But I haven't ever found it unnatural to be a woman.

INTERVIEWER: But haven't you found that being a woman presented to you, as an artist, certain special problems? It seems to me that a great deal of the upbringing of women encourages the dispersion of the self in many small bits, and that the practice of any kind of art demands a corralling and concentrating of that self and its always insufficient energies.

PORTER: I think that's very true and very right. You're brought up with the notion of feminine chastity and inaccessibility, yet with the curious idea of feminine availability in all spiritual ways, and in giving service to anyone who demands it. And I suppose that's why it has taken me twenty years to write this novel; it's been interrupted by just anyone who could jimmy his way into my life.

INTERVIEWER: Hemingway said once that a writer writes best when he's in love.

PORTER: I don't know whether you write better, but you feel so good you *think* you're writing better! And certainly love does create a rising of the spirit that makes everything you do seem easier and happier. But there must come a time when you no longer depend upon it, when the mind—not the will, really, either—takes over.

INTERVIEWER: In judging that the story is ready? You said a moment ago that the actual writing of a story is always done in a single spurt of energy—

PORTER: I always write a story in one sitting. I started "Flowering Judas" at seven p.m. and at one-thirty I was standing on a snowy windy corner putting it in the mailbox. And when I wrote my short novels, two of them, I just simply took the manuscript, packed a suitcase and departed to an inn in Georgetown, Pennsylvania, without leaving any forwarding address! Fourteen days later I had finished *Old Mortality* and *Noon Wine*.

INTERVIEWER: But the new novel *Ship of Fools* has been in the writing since 1942. The regime for writing this must have been a good deal different.

PORTER: Oh, it was. I went up and sat nearly three years in the country, and while I was writing it I worked every day, anywhere from three to five hours. Oh, it's true I used to do an awful lot of just sitting there thinking what comes next, because this is a great big unwieldy book with an enormous cast of characters—it's four hundred of my manuscript pages, and I can get four hundred and fifty words on a page. But all that time in Connecticut, I kept myself free for work; no telephone, no visitors—oh, I really lived like a hermit, everything but being fed through a grate! But it is, as Yeats said, a "solitary sedentary trade." And I did a lot of gardening, and cooked my own food, and listened to music, and of course I would read. I was really very happy. I can live a solitary life for months at a time, and it does me good, because I'm working. I just get up bright and early—sometimes at five o'clock—have my black coffee, and go to work.

INTERVIEWER: You work best in the morning, then?

PORTER: I work whenever I'm let. In the days when I was taken up with everything else, I used to do a day's work, or housework, or whatever I was doing, and then work at night. I worked when I could. But I prefer to get up very early in the morning and work. I don't want to speak to anybody or see anybody. Perfect silence. I work until the vein is out. There's something about the way you feel, you know when the well is dry, that you'll have to wait till tomorrow and it'll be full up again.

INTERVIEWER: The important thing, then, is to avoid any breaks or distractions while you're writing?

PORTER: To keep at a boiling point. So that I can get up in the morning with my mind still working where it was yesterday. Then I can stop in the middle of a paragraph and finish it the next day. I began writing *Ship of Fools* twenty years ago, and I've been away from it for several years at a time and stopped in the middle of a paragraph—but, you know, I can't tell where the crack is mended, and I hope nobody else can.

INTERVIEWER: You find no change in style, or in attitudes, over the years?

PORTER: It's astonishing how little I've changed: nothing in my point of view or my way of feeling. I'm going back now to finish some of the great many short stories that I have begun and not been able to finish for one reason or another. I've found one that I think I can finish. I have three versions of it: I started it in 1923, and it's based on an episode in my life that took place when I was twenty. Now here I am, seventy, and it's astonishing how much it's like me now. Oh, there are certain things, certain turns of sentence, certain phrases that I think I can sharpen and make more clear, more simple and direct, but my point of view, my being, is strangely unchanged. We change, of course, every day; we are not the same people who sat down at this table, yet there is a basic and innate being that is unchanged.

INTERVIEWER: *Ship of Fools* too is based upon an event that took place ten years or more before the first writing, isn't it? A sea voyage just before the beginning of the European war.

PORTER: It is the story of my first voyage to Europe in 1931. We embarked on an old German ship at Vera Cruz and we landed in Bremerhaven twenty-eight days later. It was a crowded ship, a great mixture of nationalities, religions, political beliefs—all that sort of thing. I don't think I spoke a half-dozen words to anybody. I just sat there and watched—not deliberately, though. I kept a diary in the form of a letter to a friend, and after I got home the friend sent it back. And, you know, it is astonishing what happened on that boat, and what happened in my mind afterwards. Because it is fiction now.

INTERVIEWER: The title—isn't it from a medieval emblem?—suggests that it might also be an allegory.

PORTER: It's just exactly what it seems to be. It's an allegory if you like, though I don't think much of the allegorical as a standard. It's a parable, if you like, of the ship of this world on its voyage to eternity.

INTERVIEWER: I remember your writing once—I think in the preface to "Flowering Judas"—of an effort to understand what you called the "majestic and terrible failure" of Western man. You were speaking then of the World War and what it signified of human folly. It seems to me that *Ship of Fools* properly belongs to that investigation of betrayal and self-delusion—

PORTER: Betrayal and treachery, but also self-betrayal and self-deception—the way that all human beings deceive themselves about the way they operate. . . . There seems to be a kind of order in the universe, in the movement of the stars and the turning of the earth and the changing of the seasons, and even in the cycle of human life. But human life itself is almost pure chaos. Everyone takes his stance, asserts his own rights and feelings, mistaking the motives of others, and his own. . . . Now, nobody knows the end of the life he's living, and neither do I. Don't forget I am a passenger on that ship; it's not the other people altogether who are the fools! We don't really know what is going to happen to us, and we don't know why. Quite often the best we can do is to keep our heads, and try to keep at least one line unbroken and unobstructed. Misunderstanding and separation are the natural conditions of man. We come together only at these pre-arranged meeting grounds; we were all passengers on that ship, yet at his destination, each one was alone.

INTERVIEWER: Did you find that the writing of *Ship of Fools* differed from the writing of shorter fiction?

PORTER: It's just a longer voyage, that's all. It was the question of keeping everything moving at once. There are about forty-five main characters, all taking part in each others' lives, and then there was a steerage of sugar workers, deportees. It was all a matter of deciding which should come first, in order to keep the harmonious moving forward. A novel is really like a symphony, you know, where instrument after instrument has to come in at its own time, and no other. I tried to write it as a short novel, you know, but it just wouldn't confine itself. I wrote notes and sketches. And finally I gave in. "Oh, no, this is simply going to have to be a novel," I thought. That was a real horror. But it needed a book to contain its full movement: of the sea, and the ship on the sea, and the people going around the deck, and into the ship, and up from it. That whole movement, felt as one forward motion: I can feel it while I'm reading it. I didn't "intend" it, but it took hold of me.

INTERVIEWER: As writing itself, perhaps, "took hold" of you— we began by your saying that you had never intended to be a professional anything, even a professional writer.

PORTER: I look upon literature as an art, and I practice it as an art. Of course, it is also a vocation, and a trade, and a profession, and all kinds of things; but first it's an art, and you should practice it as that, I think. I know a great many people disagree, and they are welcome to it. I think probably the important thing is to get your work done, in the way you can—and we all have our different and separate ways. But I look upon literature as an art, and I believe that if you misuse it or abuse it, it will leave you. It is not a thing that you can nail down and use as you want. You have to let it use you, too.

—BARBARA THOMPSON
1963

4. Rebecca West

A literary presence for more than half a century, Rebecca West was born Cicily Isabel Fairfield in County Kerry, Ireland, in December 1892. She changed her name to that of the heroine of Ibsen's play *Rosmersholm*, who is characterized by a passionate will. As "Rebecca West" she began in journalism and literary criticism, and continued to write throughout the traumatic years when she was alone bringing up her only child, Anthony Panther West, born to her and H. G. Wells in 1914. She published her first book in 1916 and her first novel, *The Return of the Soldier*, in 1918. She wrote novels throughout the twenties (*The Judge*, 1922; *Harriet Hume*, A *London Fantasy*, 1929), and in 1928 collected her criticism in *The Strange Necessity*. The subject of the title essay is the touchstone of Rebecca West's philosophy: the unquenchable and healing need of human beings for art and literature. More essays followed in *Ending in Earnest: A Literary Log* (1931), in which, notably, she acclaimed the genius of D. H. Lawrence. Two years later, she published her biographical masterwork, *St. Augustine*.

In the late thirties, she travelled widely with her husband, Henry Maxwell Andrews, in the Balkans, and from these experiences she built her formidable analysis of the origins of World War II, *Black Lamb and Grey Falcon* (1941), the book generally considered her masterpiece. The marked political and historical character of this work led naturally to *The New Meaning of Treason* (1947), and *A Train of Powder* (1955), West's matchless account of the Nuremburg trials.

Honored with the French Legion of Honor and an award from the Women's Press Club for Journalism, Dame Rebecca West was still writing book reviews up until her death on March 16, 1983.

Since sunrise it had died and been reborn.

Its rebirth, I calculated rapidly, was likely to be followed by an agonising existence. I knew at once, as everybody must who had any knowledge of international affairs, what foreign powers had combined to kill this man. It appeared to me ~~then~~, as I lay in bed in the nursing-home, inevitable that war must follow; and indeed it must have done, had not the Yugoslavian Government exercised an iron control over its population, then and thereafter, and abstained from the smallest provocative action against its enemies. On that forbearance, which is indeed one of the most extraordinary feats of statesmanship performed in post-war Europe, I could not be expected to rely. So I saw myself widowed and childless, which was another instance of the archaic outlook of the back of the mind; for in the next war we women will have hardly any reason to fear bereavement, as bombardments unpreceded by declarations of war will send us and our loved ones to the next world in the breathless unity of scrambled eggs. That thought did not then occur to me, so I rang for my nurse, and when she came I cried to her, "Get me a telephone quickly! I must speak to my husband at once. A most terrible thing has happened. The King of Yugoslavia has been assassinated." "Oh, dear!" she replied. "Did you know him?" "No," I said. "Then why," she said, "do you think it is so terrible?"

Her words made me realise that the word 'idiot' comes from a Greek root meaning a private person. She was certainly intelligent in her work and was probably so in her ~~personal~~ life, but her unawareness of the bonds that linked her to strangers made her <ins>follow her fate in a</ins> ~~life ... .~~ darkness deep as that cast by malformed cells in the brain. It might be argued that she was happier so; but that is true only in the most limited sense. She would not be happy long. A population which does not know that the assassination of the King of Yugoslavia might precipitate a European war is a perpetual temptation to its governors; it will believe any lies, it can be seduced into supporting unnecessary wars and peace treaties that favour class interests. But it might be

Rebecca West

In Rebecca West's hallway hung a drawing of her by Wyndham Lewis done in the thirties, "before the ruin," as she put it. In fact, in person, there was no ruin, not of her brilliant, penetrating brown eyes, the energy of her voice, and her attention to all things. She was wearing a bright and patterned caftan when we first met, a loose blouse over trousers the second time. Cataracts meant she had two pairs of spectacles, on chains like necklaces; arthritis had made a stick necessary. Her hair was white and short; she wore beautiful rings. Her voice had kept some of the vowel sounds of the Edwardian period, and some of its turns of phrase: "I can't see someone or something" meant "I can't tolerate." She said words of foreign derivation, like "memoirs," with the accent of the parent language. We had sat in her sitting room, a room filled with drawings and paintings with a wide bay window on to some of London's tall trees. Their leaves, which were turning when we met, almost brushed against the window panes.

INTERVIEWER: In your novel, *The Fountain Overflows*, you describe the poverty of the educated class very beautifully. Was that your background?

WEST: Oh, yes. I'll tell you what the position was. We had lots of pleasant furniture that had belonged to my father's family, none that had belonged to my mother's family, because they didn't die—the whole family all went on to their eighties, nineties—but we had furniture and we had masses of books, and we had a very good piano my mother played on. We were poor because my father's father died, when he and his three brothers were schoolboys. Their mother was a member of the Plymouth Brethren and a religious fanatic with a conscience that should have been held down and, you know, been eunuchized or castrated. She refused to keep on, to accept any longer, an annuity, which she was given by the Royal Family. And nobody knows why she was given it, and she found out the reason and she didn't approve of it, and she refused it, and they were poor forever after. The maddening thing was nobody ever knew why she said to Queen Victoria, "I cannot accept this allowance." It was hard on my father, who was in the army, because you needed money to be an officer. He was a ballistics expert. He did quite well in various things.

INTERVIEWER: He was a professional soldier?

WEST: No. Not all his life. He left the army after he got his captaincy. He went out to America and he ran a mine and wrote a certain amount, mostly on political science. He wrote well. He had a great mechanical mind and he drew very well. He did all sorts of things, and he'd had a fairly good training at Woolwich, a military academy. We were the children of his second marriage and he could no longer make much money. He went out to Africa and just got ill there. He came back and died in Liverpool when I was twelve or thirteen.

INTERVIEWER: Was he a remote and admirable figure, as the father is in *The Fountain Overflows*?

WEST: Oh, he wasn't so cracked as the father and he didn't sell furniture that didn't belong to him and all that sort of thing. That was rather a remembrance of another strange character.

INTERVIEWER: You've written very movingly, in several of your books, on how cruel natural death is, how it is the greatest hardship as opposed to some of the more violent deaths that you've also written about. Was it a very traumatic experience for you, as a child, when you lost your father?

WEST: Oh, yes, it was terrible. . . . The whole of life was extremely uncomfortable for us at that time. We had really got into terrible financial straits, not through anybody's fault. My mother had had to work very hard, and though she was a very good pianist, she was out of the running by then, and when she realized that my father was old and wasn't going to be able to go on with things, she very nobly went and learnt typewriting. Do you know people are always writing in the papers and saying that typists started in the last war, but they've been going on since the eighties and the nineties and 1900. Well, my mother did some typing for American evangelists called Torry and Alexander and she took over their music. They toured in England and my mother whacked the "Glory Song," a famous hymn—you still hear it whistled in the streets—out on the grand piano on the platform. It was a very noble thing to do. She wasn't well and she wasn't young, and then we came up to Scotland. My sister was studying medicine. My other sister had a scholarship at Cheltenham, which was rather useless to her; she was very brilliant indeed, and amusing as well.

INTERVIEWER: Which sister was that?

WEST: That's Winifred, who was more or less like Mary in *The Fountain Overflows*. Then there was myself, who had to go and try to get scholarships, which I usually did, at the local school. My mother ran a typing business, and I assisted her, which was amusing and which gave me a quickness of eye, which has been quite useful. She used to type manuscripts, particularly for the music faculty in Edinburgh. There was a German professor she'd known all her life. He used to send along pieces and I remember still with horror and amusement an enormous German book of his on program music with sentences like, "If the hearer turns his attention to the flutes and the piccolos, surely there will come to his mind the dawn rising over the bronze horses of Venice."

There is a lot of rather good idiom of writing I can summon up, if necessary, about music in the post-Wagnerian period, which was very, very lush.

INTERVIEWER: Were you brought up to play yourself?

WEST: I played, but not well. From an early age—but it was not detected for many, many years—I've had difficulty about hearing. Finally, I lost my hearing almost entirely in this ear. I got pneumonia in it, which I think is rather chic. Then I thought I'd got my hearing back slowly, but really I'd learnt to lip-read and, it's an extraordinary thing, young people—if they lose their hearing young—learn lip-reading unconsciously, lots of them. It's quite common. I did that without knowing when I got double cataracts, I suddenly found my hearing going and I said, "Goodness, I've gone deaf at the same time as my eyes are going wrong," but my aurist, who's a very nice man, said, "No, you haven't. Your lip-reading power is breaking down," which was very disappointing, but, on the other hand, I was amazed at the ingenuity of the human animal. It did strike me as an extraordinary thing.

INTERVIEWER: In your home, was the atmosphere for women very emancipated because you were left alone?

WEST: Oh, yes. We were left alone. We had an uncle, who was very preoccupied. He was president of the Royal Academy of Music, Sir Alexander MacKenzie, and he didn't really think anything of any woman but his wife. He was very thoughtless about his own daughter, who was an actress who acted very well in the early Chekhov plays. He treated her very inconsiderately and made her come back and nurse her mother and leave her husband in Paris, and the husband, after six years, lost heart and went off with someone else. We were very feminist altogether, and it was a very inspiring thing. Who is that man, David Mitchell, who writes silly hysterical books about Christabel Pankhurst? What is he? Who is he?

INTERVIEWER: He's now writing a book about the Jesuits.

WEST: The Jesuits? How does he know about the Jesuits?

INTERVIEWER: You thought his book on Christabel was hysterical, did you?

WEST: Absolute rubbish and nonsense. He writes about how

she went to Paris and how she didn't go down to the cafés and meet the young revolutionaries. But how on earth was she to find out where they were? Because, you see, the Bolshevik generation was not yet identifiable. How would she find out any of the people, who hadn't really made their mark? It was an obscure time in the history of revolution. It was a time when very remarkable people were coming up, but they weren't visible yet. She did know the people like Henri de Rochefort very well. Mitchell also says she took a flat and had a housekeeper, who was also a very good cook, and didn't that show great luxury? Well, if he'd asked anybody, he would have found that, in those days, you couldn't take a furnished flat or house in Paris, nor, so far as I know, in most parts of France, unless you took a servant, who was left by the owner. All the furnished houses I ever had in France, modest as they were, had somebody that I had to take with the house.

INTERVIEWER: But you yourself broke with the suffragette movement.

WEST: I was too young and unimportant for that to mean much. I admired them enormously, but all that business about venereal disease, which was supposed to be round every corner, seemed to me excessive. I wasn't in a position to judge, but it did seem a bit silly. [Christabel Pankhurst headed a chastity campaign for women.]

INTERVIEWER: Christabel, in her later phase, became the equivalent of a misogynist. She became very, what would the word be, misanthropic against men only, didn't she?

WEST: It wasn't quite that. She fell curiously into a sort of transatlantic form of mysticism, where there is a sort of repudiation of sex. Do you ever read anything about Thomas Lake Harris? He was an American mystic. Curious thing—you repudiated sex but you had a "counterpart," and you usually could get a counterpart by getting into bed with somebody else, with whom your relations were supposed to be chaste, but when you lay in his arms, you were really lying in the counterpart's arms, and . . . isn't it a convenient arrangement? That was one sort of pattern of American mysticism and dottyism. Christabel got caught up with that vagueness—though not with counterparts. If you read

Harris's sermons—somebody took them down and I had a look at them—they were all very queer like that, disguised sexuality, but I wouldn't say the worse for that.

INTERVIEWER: You have written that there is a great difference between a male sensibility and a female sensibility, and you have a marvelous phrase for it in *Black Lamb and Grey Falcon.*

WEST: Idiots and lunatics. It's a perfectly good division. [The Greek root of "idiot" means "private person"; men "see the world as if by moonlight, which shows the outlines of every object but not the details indicative of their nature."] It seems to me in any assembly where you get people, who are male and female, in a crisis, the women are apt to get up and, with a big wave of the hand, say: "It's all very well talking about the defenses of the country, but there are thirty-six thousand houses in whatever— wherever they're living—that have no bathrooms. Surely it's more important to have clean children for the future." Silly stuff, when the enemy's at the gate. But men are just as silly. Even when there are no enemies at the gate, they won't attend to the bathrooms, because they say defense is more important. It's mental deficiency in both cases.

INTERVIEWER: But do you think it's innate or do you think it's produced by culture?

WEST: Oh, I really can't tell you that. It's awfully hard. You can't imagine what maleness and femaleness would be if you got back to them in pure laboratory state, can you? I suspect the political imbecility is very great on both sides.

I've never gone anywhere where the men have come up to my infantile expectations. I always have gone through life constantly being surprised by the extreme, marvelous qualities of a small minority of men. But I can't see the rest of them. They seem awful rubbish.

INTERVIEWER: In many of the political things that you've written, it would be impossible to tell that you were a woman, except that here and there you sometimes produce a comparison to do with a child or something, which may betray a certain feminine stance, but, in fact, you have overcome completely this division between idiot and lunatic. You're not an "idiot" at all. You don't only think of the personal angle.

WEST: I think that probably comes of isolation, that I grew up just as I was without much interference from social images except at my school.

INTERVIEWER: What were they at school?

WEST: We had large classes, which was an ineffable benefit, because the teachers really hadn't time to muck about with our characters. You see, the people who wanted to learn, sat and learnt, and the people who didn't, didn't learn, but there was no time, you know, for bringing out the best in us, thank God. I had some magnificent teachers, actually, a Miss MacDonald, who taught me Latin irregular verbs.

INTERVIEWER: Did you have a classical training?

WEST: No, no. I had no Greek. They didn't teach any Greek for the reason that our school took on from a very early school, at which they had followed Madame de Maintenon's school at St. Cyr, where the children were taught Latin but not Greek. Why do you think I wasn't taught Greek?—Because Madame de Maintenon thought girls shouldn't learn Greek in case they fell into the toils of the heretical Eastern Orthodox Church, which is rather funny, considering we were all good girls at Edinburgh. Very curious bit of history, that.

INTERVIEWER: And this tradition reached as far as Scotland?

WEST: Well, you see, the man who was the begetter of our school had been to St. Cyr, and he just took the whole thing on.

INTERVIEWER: What did your mother expect you to be? What images did she set up for you?

WEST: There was a great idea that I should be an actress because a woman called Rosina Fillipi had seen me act in a play and she thought I was terribly good as a comedian, as a sort of low-comedy character, and she said, "If you come to the Royal Academy of Dramatic Art, I will look after you and you can get a job." I'm the only person I ever heard of who wanted to go on the stage not because I was stagestruck but it just seemed to be the thing to do. I loved the theatre. I still love it, but I had no stagestruck feeling. I felt how nice if people would give me a part. I went to the Royal Academy of Art, where there was a man called Kenneth Barnes, who ran it, who had got his job because he was the brother of the Vanbrughs, Irene and Violet Vanbrugh, if that means anything to you. He couldn't understand what Rosina Fillipi had seen in me and he made me very uncomfortable. I didn't stay out the course.

INTERVIEWER: But you chose the name of a dramatic character—Rebecca West.

WEST: Yes. Not really for any profound reason. It was just to get a pseudonym.

INTERVIEWER: It really wasn't profound? You don't think unconsciously it was?

WEST: People have always been putting me down in any role that was convenient but it would not, I think, naturally have been my own idea. I've aroused hostility in an extraordinary lot of people. I've never known why. I don't think I'm formidable.

INTERVIEWER: I think that your hallmark is that you have always disliked people who wanted approval. You like the heterodox.

WEST: I should like to be approved of. Oh, yes. I blench. I hate being disapproved of. I've had rather a lot of it.

INTERVIEWER: And yet, in your writing, there is quite a strong strain of impatience with people who do things because society approves of it.

WEST: Oh, yes. I think I see what you mean. Oh, that's Scotch, I think, yes, Scotch, because . . . oh, yes, and it's also a bit of my mother and my father. My father was educated by Elisée and Eli Reclus, two famous French brothers, early geographers; my cracked grandmother, the religious maniac who refused the family fortune, had hired them because they were refugees in England; she thought that, as young Frenchmen in England, they must be Protestants who had escaped from the wicked Catholics' persecution. They were actually anarchists and they'd escaped, run away from France because they'd seized the town hall—I can't remember which town it was—in the course of an émeute against Louis Napoleon. They were very sweet. They said, when they found out the mistake, "Oh, well, we must be careful about teaching the children." They taught them awfully well. My father was a very, very well educated man, and so were all his brothers.

INTERVIEWER: What did you read at home as a child? Who were the early formative influences?

WEST: Oh, pretty well everything. We read a terrific lot of Shakespeare, which my mother knew by heart and so did my father . . . and a lot of George Borrow. Funny thing to read, but . . . really early Victorian England was quite familiar to me because of that. Oh, lots . . . I can't think. My mother and my sister, Winifred, who was much the cleverest of us, she read frightfully good poetry. She taught me a lot of poetry, which I've all forgotten now, but you know, if I see the first line, I can go on.

INTERVIEWER: Would you acknowledge Conrad or anyone else as an influence on you?

WEST: Well, I longed, when I was young, to write as well as Mark Twain. It's beautiful stuff and I always liked him. If I wanted to write anything that attacked anybody, I used to have a look at his attack on Christian Science, which is beautifully written. He was a man of very great shrewdness. The earliest article on the Nazis, on Nazism, a sort of first foretaste, a prophetic view of the war, was an article by Mark Twain in *Harper's* in, I should think, the nineties. He went to listen to the Parliament in Vienna and he describes an awful row and what the point of view of Luger, the Lord Mayor, was, and the man called George Schwartz, I think, who started the first Nazi paper, and what it must all lead to. It's beautifully done. It's the very first notice that I've ever found of the Austrian Nazi Party, that started it all.

INTERVIEWER: What was your first conscious encounter with fascism?

WEST: A lot of boys, who stopped my sister and myself and took her hockey stick away from her. The thing was they weren't doing it as robbery but it was fun and good fellowship, and they were the boys together. That was the first. They were just street children. We had a brick wall and an alley behind it and we used to come up half the alley, if we were going into the house of some neighbors, and there these boys caught us in the alley and they took it away; but we fought them and screamed and shouted and got back the hockey stick.

INTERVIEWER: That was when?

WEST: That must have been—I was born in 1892—about 1903, or, no earlier than that, just in this century perhaps.

INTERVIEWER: Yes, so, before the First World War, you saw the seeds of fascism.

WEST: No, no. I just saw violence. There was the race thing and sacred Germanism and all that, but the enemy before the First World War you can't really compare with fascism. It was the imperialism of Germany and the supremacy of the army, but that isn't exactly fascism. I think you could say, there was more fascism, but of an intellectualized kind, in France. The crux of the Dreyfus case was that it didn't matter whether Dreyfus was guilty or not, you mustn't spoil the image of the army. That was more or less fascist.

INTERVIEWER: But do you feel, with your strong sense of justice and of pity, that our wars have remained as terrible, or do you feel that we have learned?

WEST: I don't know what *you've* learnt. I'll tell you I think the Second World War was much more comfortable because in the First World War women's position was so terrible, because there you were, not in danger. Men were going out and getting killed for you and you'd much prefer they weren't. My father was always very tender about armies, having been a soldier. The awful feeling for a small professional army was that they were recruited from poor people who went out and got killed. That was, do you know, very disagreeable. There was a genuine humanitarian feeling of guilt about that in the first war. It was very curious, you see. There I sat on my balcony in Leigh-on-Sea and heard guns going in France. It was a most peculiar war. It was really better, in the Second World War, when the people at home got bombed. I found it a relief. You were taking your chance and you might be killed and you weren't in that pampered sort of unnatural state. I find the whole idea of a professional army very disgusting still. Lacking a normal life, they turn into scoundrels. As Wellington said, they're despised for being scoundrels and it's not their fault and they die like flies and have the worst discomforts.

INTERVIEWER: And yet a conscripted army, as fought in Vietnam . . . You laugh?

WEST: Well, I can't help thinking that the whole of the Vietnam War was the blackest comedy that ever was, because it showed the way you can't teach humanity anything. We'd all learnt in the rest of the world that you can't now go round and put out your hand and, across seas, exercise power; but the poor Americans had not learned that and they tried to do it. The remoteness of America from German attack had made them feel confident. They didn't really believe that anything could reach out and kill them. Americans are quite unconscious now that we look on them as just as much beaten as we are. They're quite unconscious of that. They always have talked of Vietnam as if by getting out they were surrendering the prospect of victory, as if they were being noble by renouncing the possibility of victory. But they couldn't have had a victory. They couldn't possibly have won.

INTERVIEWER: But when you say they're beaten as we are, in what way do you mean we are beaten?

WEST: Only as regards world power. We can't put our hands out and order things to happen a long way away. Oh, I think we're also beaten in other ways—in industry. I think the war between the public and the unions is very difficult and I don't see where its solution lies.

INTERVIEWER: Have you ever seen a society about which you really felt: Here is society that works for the benefit of its citizens without harming others?

WEST: No, I think the earth itself is slightly resistant to routine. You might come to a place which was favorable, because of a discovery of minerals that could be mined more easily, you know, "place mines," as they call the ones on the surface, and you'd think that was very nice and they would get on with it. Then round the corner you'd find there was a dispute about water rights. Humanity wasn't obviously a made-to-order thing. It's a continual struggle, isn't it?

INTERVIEWER: Have you ever been tempted at all to any religious belief?

WEST: Oh, yes. It all seems so damned silly and incomprehensible, there might as well be a silly and incomprehensible solution, don't you think? I'd be quite prepared for anything to happen, but not very respectfully, I think.

INTERVIEWER: I think you might stand up to God.

WEST: No, not exactly that, but I don't think there would be a God who would really demand it. If there is a God, I don't think He would demand that anybody bow down or stand up to Him. I have often a suspicion God is still trying to work things out and hasn't finished.

INTERVIEWER: Were your parents at all believing?

WEST: My mother was, in a sort of musical way, and I think my father accepted it as part of the structure, but didn't do anything. We always went to church and enjoyed it. I don't feel the slightest resistance to the church except when it's a bad landlord or something like that. I don't see why people feel any *écrasez l'infâme*. I know much infâm-er things than religion, much more worthy of being écraséd.

INTERVIEWER: What can you remember as being a moment of great happiness?

WEST: Extremely few. I had a very unhappy time with H. G. Wells, because I was a victim of a sort of sadistic situation. Partly people disapproved of H. G. so much less than they did of me, and they were very horrible to me, and it was very hard. It was particularly hard later, people being horrid to me because I was living with H. G., when I was trying as hard as I could to leave him. It was really absurd, and now I think it's rather funny, but it wasn't funny at the time. Then I had a short time of happiness on my own and a time of happiness with my marriage [R. W. married Henry Andrews in 1930], but then my husband got ill, very ill. He had meningitis, this thing that's always struck at people near me, when he was young and then he got cerebral arteriosclerosis, and after years it came down on him. He was in a very unhappy state of illness for a good many years before he died, but we had a great many good years together. I was very happy.

INTERVIEWER: Have any of the men you've known helped you?

WEST: The men near you always hinder you because they always want you to do the traditional female things and they take a lot of time. My mother helped me to work because she always talked to me as if I were grown-up.

INTERVIEWER: Do you feel men did not want to help you as a writer?

WEST: Oh, yes! So many men hate you. When my husband was dying I had some very strange dialogues. People were very rude just because they'd heard I was a woman writer. That kind of rudeness is as bad as ever.

INTERVIEWER: Would it have been easier to have been a man?

WEST: It certainly would have been.

INTERVIEWER: Are there any advantages at all in being a woman and a writer?

WEST: None whatsoever. You could have a good time as a woman, but you'd have a much better time as a man. If in the course of some process, people turn up a card with a man's name on it and then a card with a woman's, they feel much softer towards the man, even though he might be a convicted criminal. They'd treat the man's card with greater tenderness.

INTERVIEWER: You don't think there's been an improvement?

WEST: Not very much.

INTERVIEWER: Everyone is still very curious about your love affair with H. G. Wells.

WEST: Why, I can't see why. It was a very long time ago, and it wasn't interesting. Why would I have brought it to an end if it had been interesting? It wasn't.

INTERVIEWER: What did your husband, Henry Andrews, do?

WEST: He was unfortunately put into a bank. He should have been an art historian. He got out of the bank in the end because he was too ill. He did a bit in the war where he was in the Ministry of Economic Warfare and very good. He was a delightfully funny man. He said very funny things, and he was very scholarly and he was very generous and he was very kind. There were all sorts of pleasant things about him.

INTERVIEWER: You could talk to him.

WEST: We talked a very great deal, but it's extraordinary the really tragic and dreadful things there are in marriage which are funny. I've never known anybody to write about this. My husband would insist on going and driving a car, and he'd never been a good driver. Like all bad drivers, he thought he was the best driver in the world and he couldn't drive at all at the end and it was terrible. I'm one of the few women who has been driven on the left side of a bus queue, on the *near* side of the pavement. It was awful. Well, that really made my life poisoned for years. All the time I never thought I would live to the end of the year. I thought he would be sure to kill me here or there. And he meant no harm.

INTERVIEWER: You weren't able to tell him this?

WEST: I told him and he wouldn't believe me. Two doctors said to me it could be so bad for his ego values, if he was not allowed to drive a car. Doctors tend to be chumps. I have had two or three marvelous doctors. I have a marvelous doctor now, who's very nice, very funny and very clever, but some of my worst enemies have been doctors, I can assure you.

INTERVIEWER: You have actually been quite ill yourself, haven't you?

WEST: Well, I had an attack of TB when I was a schoolgirl. Everybody did in those days. It simply meant that you got a shot of TB in your youth and you didn't get it later on. It was rather dramatic. What was awful was that I got it at the same time as my great friend, Flora Duncan, who was at school with me and whom I liked enormously; she died of it years afterwards in the most dreary way. She went with her aunt to stay in a hotel from which she was coming to lunch with me—this was just after I was married—and she pulled down the window and the bit where her left lung had gone thin started to hemorrhage; and she was dead in a few hours. They couldn't stop the hemorrhage. It has sometimes inconvenienced me, but as I've lived to be eighty-eight, I can't say I've really suffered very much from it. At the time it gave me a lot of time to read.

INTERVIEWER: When you look back on all the books that you've written, is there one that you like best?

WEST: Oh, no. They don't seem to me as good as they might be. But I really write to find out what I know about something and what is to be known about something. And I'm more or less experimental. I wish I could have written very much more but, to be absolutely frank, for twenty-five years, you see, I've had this disastrous personal trouble. You don't easily get over it if someone near to you is constantly attacking you in public. Do you know Anthony [West]?

INTERVIEWER: I've met him once. He's writing about Joan of Arc, he told me.

WEST: What on earth about Joan of Arc?

INTERVIEWER: He believes that she was a princess, a bastard princess.

WEST: Why? What an extraordinary idea.

INTERVIEWER: A lot of people do.

WEST: What! This is new to me. Who might she be?

INTERVIEWER: She's meant to be the result of an incestuous adulterous match, the Queen and the Queen's brother-in-law, Louis d'Orléans.

WEST: I wish he'd turn his mind to other problems than bastardy. Alas. He's writing about six books, he told me. But I wonder why this. Whose theory is this? I never heard of it.

INTERVIEWER: Oh, it's a very old one. It was produced in 1810 by Pierre Caze in a play. Instead of accepting that Joan of Arc was exciting for spiritual reasons, you say she was exciting because she was a royal princess—which is a practical solution.

WEST: Nonsense. Have you seen Princess Anne? Can you imagine, if she appeared and said, "Save England," or whatever, that it would work? What a wonderful idea.

INTERVIEWER: What are you working on now?

WEST: I've been looking at old photographs . . . Rangoon in the last century. Goodness, some are absolutely beautiful. It's funny how photographs were better in the past than they are now.

INTERVIEWER: Why are you looking at Rangoon?

WEST: In what I'm writing now, I'm describing my husband's mother's life. She went out to Rangoon and lived there in vast, great big rooms each the size of a gymnasium, and full of cluttered little tables.

INTERVIEWER: She was the wife of an official, was she?

WEST: No, she was the wife of a man who had a job in Wallace Export-Import. They exported Burmese teak and they imported machinery. I've got masses of photographs I have to give to the Institute of Machinery but I never get round to it, showing the machines, as they came in. They had the largest army of elephants ever. There are beautiful photographs in this book of things like a lot of elephants crossing a wide river in a sort of floating island. She was a lady of very mixed ancestry, my husband's mother, and after Rangoon, she came back to Hamburg. Her mother was a Miss Chapman, who was related to the Chapman family that T. E. Lawrence belonged to. They lived in Lancashire, and then she married a local alien, a member of the hereditary Teutonic knights of Lithuania. She had various children in Lithuania, and then her daughter came to live in Hamburg and married Lewis Andrews, who was working in this firm in Rangoon, and ultimately became my mother-in-law.

INTERVIEWER: What are you writing about her?

WEST: It comes into my memoirs. Poor widow. She took her son [Henry Andrews] out with her to Hamburg and kept him too long. It was 1914 and the war came. Eventually she was sent back to England, but he was sent into a camp. He was there all through the war, in Rubleden [the civilian POW camp at Spandau]. It was very sad. It did spoil his life, really. He was nineteen. It was very tough. But these young creatures were highly educated; he wrote quite clever letters to Romain Rolland.

INTERVIEWER: How far have you got with your memoirs?

WEST: I've nearly got my father and mother to the end of their respective careers. It's been supernatural, which is always encouraging. Do you know, my mother was always saying that the scenery in Australia was so extraordinarily beautiful, and my father did some very nice pictures of Australian landscapes. Suddenly, a man started sending me picture books of Australia. He said, "I've always liked your books, and I wanted to send these to you." So extraordinarily dead-on: pictures of what Australia was like when my parents were there in the last century.

INTERVIEWER: Are you taking only a section of your life in your memoirs?

WEST: Well, I hope to cover most of it, but still, I've only just begun it really and I must really get on with it. I haven't read anybody's memoirs for ages except Coulton's [medieval historian, author of *Five Centuries of Religion*], which I liked very much. He wrote a life called *Four Score*. Hated Catholics. When did you read him?

INTERVIEWER: I read him on the Virgin Mary.

WEST: You know, I don't really appreciate the Virgin Mary. She always looks so dull. I particularly hate Raphael, Raphael's Madonnas. They are awful, aren't they?

INTERVIEWER: Are you working on anything else?

WEST: I'm doing a book for Weidenfeld on the 1900s, but it's not a long book. I'm not approaching the 1900s chronologically. I've started by doing a lot with the paintings of Sargent, and with some beautiful photographs. But that period in America has been done and done and done, and it's hard to be fresh. They've really dealt with nostalgia too fiercely. I begin with the death of Gladstone in 1898, and more I cannot tell you.

INTERVIEWER: You have lots of paintings. Have you written about them?

WEST: To a certain extent, yes. My husband bought the ones over there, but these I bought. It was lovely that I could buy them when they were cheap. They didn't cost me very much, even the Bonnard, and I think that's the best picture that Dufy ever painted. I have a passion, too, for Carol Weight, the man who painted this one, because I think he paints the contours of the land so beautifully. And that's by Vuillard, the woman over there, Madame Marchand. She committed suicide in the war, alas. She was a Polish Jewess, a friend of Colette's and a lot of other people.

INTERVIEWER: You have a high opinion of Colette, don't you?

WEST: Yes. I didn't like her very much as a person and I think she was repetitive and I hate all her knowing nudges about men, but I think she was a good writer on the whole and she was very good on landscape. She did a wonderful book called *Trio*. She was really more egotistical than you could possibly imagine, and she was outside a lot of experiences in a most curious way. I was taken to see her in Paris with a man who was a judge at Nuremburg. She didn't pick it up at all.

INTERVIEWER: You were in Paris again recently, I believe?

WEST: To film *The Birds Fall Down*, yes, for the B.B.C. It was quite fun. It was uncomfortable in many ways and I was so horrified by the cheap food in Paris. It was so bad. Terribly bad. The film turned out to be visually very beautiful. Sometimes it seemed to me a little slow. Some of the dresses are lovely.

INTERVIEWER: Have you had other books adapted?

WEST: No, people always buy them and then find they can't do them, so that I've gained financially but otherwise hardly ever. A man called Van Druten, who's forgotten now, did *The Return of the Soldier* as a play and it wasn't really good, though some of his plays were. I can't remember who acted it, or indeed anything about it.

INTERVIEWER: You've never written for the stage yourself?

WEST: I've had so little time to write. Also, theatrical people can't be bothered with me. I wrote a play in the twenties which I think had lovely stuff in it, *Goodbye Nicholas*, and fourteen copies were lost by managers, fourteen, that's really true, and I just gave up. One of them, who lost three, was a man called Barry Jackson, who was at the Birmingham Repertory Theatre; after we'd had a terrific apologies and that kind of thing, about a year later he met me in the bar of some theatre and said, Rebecca, why have you never written a play? They are like that.

INTERVIEWER: What was the play about?

WEST: Oh, it was about Kruger, the financier, who committed suicide. It just showed you how they did the fraud and what they thought about it. It was sound enough, but nobody was interested in it at all. Then I lent it to an old friend of mine. I'm sorry to say he used a lot of it, without acknowledgement, in a play of his, an American man.

INTERVIEWER: Who was that?

WEST: I won't tell you, but it was very naughty. But never mind. His play died a death too. I would like to write old-fashioned plays like de Musset's. I think they're lovely. I think de Musset's essay on Rachel and Malibran is one of the loveliest things in the world. It's lovely about acting and romanticism. It's beautifully written and it's quite wonderful.

INTERVIEWER: Rachel is quite important to you, because you wrote a beautiful thing in your lecture on McLuhan about her.

WEST: Oh, not *my* beauty, not *my* beauty, it's Valéry's, who wrote the beautiful thing and who loved Rachel. Isn't it a beautiful thing? The ear of the lover took down what his beloved Rachel was saying and commemorated the secret of it. It's really wonderful. It's about as nice a form of immortality as anyone could have, isn't it? I fell on the essay, when I was quite young, and then I read it again because Malibran [Maria-Felicia García, d. 1836] was the sister of Madame Viardot [Pauline García, d. 1910] who is, you know, the lady who is supposed to have been the mistress—but I think the duties were light—of Turgenev. Turgenev lived in the house of Madame Viardot nearly all his life, and she brought up his illegitimate daughter. She was an opera singer but she had a dreadful time getting jobs at the opera because she and her husband were anti-Bonapartist and the Bonapartists had command of the opera. She was a great girl, and it's a very terrible thing: all her life she wrote compositions but nobody has ever played them. She was terribly busy. There's a description of her as "*too* busy" in the letters of Brahms and Clara Schumann. The Garcías were people who had two odd genetic streaks: one was for longevity, the other was for music. The first García bumped his family all over the Americas and all over Europe as a musical troupe. There were several in the family; the brother taught at the Royal Academy of Music in London, where my uncle was principal, and he used to give children's parties. I remember going to a children's party and being kissed by the old gentleman who was the brother of Malibran. He lived to be a hundred and one. I think his descendants transplanted themselves to somewhere in the north of England. The life of the family has all sorts of odd things embedded in it. You know how in du

Maurier's books, how in *Trilby*, she vocalised to the music of Chopin's Nocturnes and people say that's so absurd. But Viardot did it and it apparently came off and Chopin himself liked it.

INTERVIEWER: Did you used to go to concerts a lot?

WEST: Yes, I used to and I used to listen on the radio. I can't do even the radio any longer. It doesn't seem to *respond*, as the Americans say.

INTERVIEWER: You said once that all your intelligence is in your hands.

WEST: Yes, a lot, I think. Isn't yours? My memory is certainly in my hands. I can remember things only if I have a pencil and I can write with it and I can play with it.

INTERVIEWER: You use a pencil, do you, when you write?

WEST: When anything important has to be written, yes. I think your hand concentrates for you. I don't know why it should be so.

INTERVIEWER: You never typed?

WEST: I did, but not now. I can't see in front and behind a typewriter now with cataract-operated eyes. If you have the spectacles for the front thing, you can't see the back, and I can't do with bifocals. I just get like a distracted hen. I can't do it. Hens must wear bifocals, if one looks closely. It explains it all. It's so difficult dealing with ribbons too. I can only write by hand now. I used to do a rough draft longhand and then another on the typewriter. I'm a very quick typist. When I had mumps I was shut up in a bedroom, because both my sisters had to sit examinations. When I came out, I could type.

INTERVIEWER: Do you do many drafts?

WEST: I fiddle away a lot at them. Particularly if it's a fairly elaborate thing. I've never been able to do just one draft. That seems a wonderful thing. Do you know anyone who can?

INTERVIEWER: I think D. H. Lawrence did.

WEST: You could often tell.

INTERVIEWER: How many hours a day do you write?

WEST: I don't manage much. When I write uninterrupted, I *can* write all day, straight through.

INTERVIEWER: Did you find any of your books especially easy to write?

WEST: No. It's a nauseous process. They're none of them easy.

INTERVIEWER: Have you ever abandoned a book before it was finished?

WEST: I've abandoned work because I've not had time. I've had a worrisome family thinking up monkey tricks to prevent me finishing books, and I had a terrible time when I was young and in the country, because I had no money, and no reference books, and I couldn't get up to London and to the London Library, where I had a subscription.

INTERVIEWER: There is a great diversity in your work. Did you find it difficult to combine criticism and journalism and history and fiction?

WEST: I did, really. My life has been dictated to and broken up by forces beyond my control. I couldn't control the two wars! The second war had a lot of personal consequences for me, both before and after. But I had enough money at that time, because I had a large herd of cows and a milk contract. I had to take some part in looking after the cows, but the dear things worked for me industriously. At one time I had to write articles because I had to put up a lot of money for family reasons. Everyone has to pay for their families every now and then.

INTERVIEWER: Who are the writers you admire? You commented recently that Tolstoy was most overrated.

WEST: I'm a heretic about Tolstoy. I really don't see *War and Peace* as a great novel because it seems constantly to be trying to prove that nobody who was in the war knew what was going on. Well, I don't know whoever thought they would . . . that if you put somebody down in the wildest sort of mess they understand what's happening. The point's very much better done, I think, by Joseph de Maistre. He wrote a very interesting essay in the late eighteenth century, saying how more and more people would not be able to know what was happening to them in wartime because it was all too complicated. He was in a very complicated state himself because he came from Aspramonte, which is a village on a hill near Nice. The people of Aspramonte were of the original Mediterranean population. They wore long hair all through the centuries, the conservative hippies. He was descended from a family who went round getting mulberry leaves for the silk worms. He got into the service of the King of Sardinia. He was sent as an ambassador to St. Petersburg. He wrote *Les Soirées de St.-Pétersbourg*, which is marvelous descriptive writing. He did a very good thing about hanging. He was for it, but his essay demonstrates the painfulness of ever considering whether you do hang people or not. I don't know how he became a diplomat for the King of Sardinia. I'm very often curious about people in history; they turn up in the oddest places. They strayed like goats in a road, but from class to class.

INTERVIEWER: Do you admire E. M. Forster?

WEST: No. I think the Indian one [A *Passage to India*] is very funny because it's all about people making a fuss about nothing, which isn't really enough. I can never understand how people read Proust at the same time. But they did. You can read Proust all the time. There is a book of that period that I do like very much, and that is *They Went* by Norman Douglas. It's about the king of a legendary country. I've read it several times and I've always found it beautiful.

INTERVIEWER: Are you interested in T. S. Eliot's writing?

WEST: Goodness! T. S. Eliot, whom I didn't like a bit? He was a poseur. He was married to this woman who was very pretty. My husband and I were asked to see them, and my husband roamed around the flat and there were endless photographs of T. S. Eliot and bits of his poetry done in embroidery by pious American ladies, and only one picture of his wife, and that was when she was getting married. Henry pointed it out to me and said, "I don't think I like that man."

INTERVIEWER: What about the work of Somerset Maugham, whom you also knew?

WEST: He couldn't write for toffee, bless his heart. He wrote conventional short stories, much inferior to the work of other people. But they were much better than his plays, which were too frightful. He was an extremely interesting man, though, not a bit clever or cold or cynical. I know of many affectionate things he did. He had a great capacity for falling in love with the wrong people. His taste seemed to give way under him so extraordinarily sometimes. He fascinated me by his appearance; he was so neatly made, like a swordstick that fits just so. Occasionally his conversation was beautifully funny and quite unmalicious. I object strongly to pictures of Maugham as if he were a second-rate Hollywood producer in the lavish age. His house was very pleasant and quiet and agreeable.

INTERVIEWER: Some critics think that sex is still written about with great awkwardness. Why is this?

WEST: I would have thought that was completely true of Kafka, who couldn't write about sex or value its place in life. I think there's an awful lot of nonsense in Lawrence when he writes about Mexican sacrifices and sexual violence. Their only relevance was to the Mexicans' lack of protein, as in the South Sea Islands. Funny, that's a wonderful thing. I don't know why more people don't write about it: how the whole of life must have been different when four-footed animals came in. They had just a few deer before, but not enough to go round, and so they prevented the deer from becoming extinct by making them sacred to the kings. It's much more interesting to write about that than about sex, which most of your audience knows about.

INTERVIEWER: Have you ever worked closely with a publisher who has suggested ideas to you?

WEST: No. I write books to find out about things. I wrote *Saint Augustine* because, believe it or not, there was no complete life in English at the time.

INTERVIEWER: Have you never had a close relationship with an editor, who has helped you after the books were written?

WEST: No. I never met anybody with whom I could have discussed books before or after. One doesn't have people on one's wavelength as completely as that. And I very rarely found the *New Yorker* editors any good.

INTERVIEWER: They have a tremendous reputation.

WEST: I don't know why.

INTERVIEWER: When you read, do you just follow your imagination completely?

WEST: Well, I've had eighty-five years to read in.

INTERVIEWER: I wondered whether you made book lists?

WEST: Yes, I do, but I'm often disappointed. I do think modern novels are boring on the whole. Somebody told me I ought to read a wonderful thing about how a family of children buried Mum in a cellar under concrete and she began to smell. But that's the sole point of the story. Mum just smells. That's all that happens. It is not enough.

INTERVIEWER: This is a new Ian McEwan, isn't it? I thought you, in your book on Augustine, made a marvelous comment which applies to him and to some of the other fashionable novelists now. You say that Augustinianism is "the ring-fence, in which the modern mind is still prisoner." I think that Ian McEwan is very Augustinian in his sense of unmovable evil in human life.

WEST: Yes, but he doesn't really do very much with it, does he? This thing just presents you with the hairs along people's groins and the smell, and very little else.

INTERVIEWER: Do you feel this relates to your feeling about the will to die in people, that this kind of very black outlook on the human body and human emotions is part of the suicidal streak that you've written about in both individuals and in society?

WEST: Oh, I suppose it is. It's very farfetched, isn't it? One rarely recognizes the smell of Mum under the concrete, does one? I don't know. I cannot see the abysmal silliness of a lot of novels. Did you read a book called *The Honey Tree*? By Janice Elliott. If you didn't read it, it's no use talking about it. It's all about people who take a house and fornicate all over it, and they all have children, and their swollen bodies are a great source of satisfaction to Mrs. Elliott, and paternity does all sorts of things to men which I doubt, don't you?

INTERVIEWER: Perhaps. I believe you admire A. L. Barker.

WEST: Enormously, but I'm the only person who does, so far as I can make out. I think she's the best novelist now writing, not always, but I think *The Middling* is a magnificent novel. And *A Source of Embarrassment*, about the woman who knew she was going to die. This last book, *The Heavy Feather*, is so good I can't believe it, and nobody likes it. And they are wrong. I am exaggerating, of course. Lots of people do admire her, but not enough.

INTERVIEWER: What are the particular qualities that you think she has that others at the moment haven't?

WEST: She really tells you what people do, the extraordinary things that people think, how extraordinary circumstances are, and how unexpected the effect of various incidents. There's a terribly good thing in *The Heavy Feather*, where a woman goes home and there's a railway accident. The train is just jarred and the poor woman is sitting with a suitcase over her head. The suitcase falls on top of the woman sitting opposite her and kills her. This woman has been saying how happy she is and how all her children love her and how ideal her life is. Then the other, when she gets home, finds she's taken the woman's suitcase instead of her own, and it's got the address and she goes to take back the suitcase and try and get her own from the husband, who turns out to be Hindustani. The woman was white, and he's living there with a Hindustani girl and they're both terrified because they have been waiting for this white woman, who had no children and wasn't adored and was utterly miserable. The people come off the page to tell you what this would be like. You feel: Now I understand this better. And she also has in the book very good heterosexuals and very good homosexuals . . . with the different quality quite marked.

INTERVIEWER: Yes. Would you place her as high as the women writers that you have said overcome the problem of being female in their writing? I am thinking of Madame de Sévigné, Madame de La Fayette, Jane Austen, Willa Cather, Virginia Woolf, Colette.

WEST: Oh, she's almost better than anybody, I think. She's much better than Iris Murdoch, I think. But then Iris Murdoch I like enormously except when she begins to clown and be funny, because I don't think she ever is very funny. She writes curious books on goodness. Have you read her philosophic works? I can't make head or tail of them. They're better written than anything else she writes. They are so strange. She says that one has to study what goodness is by looking at good people. She says that the trouble with good people is that, if they're men, usually very little is known about them because they're so obscure, and, as for women, goodness is rarely found in women except in the inarticulate mothers of large families, which is just such an idiotic remark, you can't believe it. Is she pulling one's leg? One hopes so. But even so, why?

INTERVIEWER: Do you have a high opinion of Ivy Compton-Burnett?

WEST: She had her own stereotype, and wrote too many books exactly like each other in form. But it was a damn good form. At the time of a rising in South Africa, when it seemed that the colored races were going to burst forth and one was afraid that the white suburbs were being set on fire, I managed to get in happy nights reading the novels of Ivy Compton-Burnett. But it was very funny that people believed in her story of herself. She was a nanny, and you had only to meet her to see it; all her stories are nanny stories, about how awful the family is. She was very, very clever. You'd have to be very tasteless not to see she had something unique to give her age . . .

INTERVIEWER: How do you feel about Doris Lessing?

WEST: I wish I knew her. I think she's a marvelous writer. There's a peculiar book about European refugees in Africa, but it fascinates. It's beautifully done, the play side of philosophy. They were talking about all their ideas and it was as if the children were trying to go into a shop and buy things not with coins but with butterscotch or toffee apples. It's very curious. Yes, she's the only person who absolutely gets the mood of today right, I think. An absolutely wonderful writer. She wrote a picaresque novel, *The Children of Violence*, I thought was very fine. Who got the Booker Prize? Does anybody know? [Iris Murdoch won it for *The Sea, The Sea*, after this meeting.]

INTERVIEWER: Do you follow prizes?

WEST: Not very much. I was on the Booker Prize Committee twice. It almost drove me mad. I think they give people prizes too late. This is a sad thought. They've been heard of as failures and they have become conditioned to failure, so it is rather wide of the point. It's nice for them, though.

INTERVIEWER: Do you feel that public taste has declined as expressed in things like prizes?

WEST: People in England read books. I have read Mr. McEwan, and I read new books all the time, whether I review them or not, but you see, most people in America are reading the same books over and over again. They read Scott Fitzgerald and Hemingway and James Joyce and Nabokov, and they haven't moved on anywhere for years.

INTERVIEWER: John Gross says in his book on the English man of letters that we are now as far from Joyce as Joyce was from George Eliot, but in terms of the progress of literature, we haven't moved at all.

WEST: Yes. It's curious. People have no desire to read anything new. It is bad that English is taught in universities. It's bad over here, where it's sometimes not badly taught, but over there, where it's horribly badly taught, it simply stops the thing in its traces.

INTERVIEWER: Because people always look back on the past?

WEST: They don't even look onto the past. They look onto the certified past. There really were beautiful writers in America like G. W. Cable, who wrote about the South in the middle of last century. It's very rich, rather Balzacian sort of stuff about the South, New Orleans and so on. But nobody reads him now.

INTERVIEWER: Why do you think English is so badly taught in America?

WEST: It's an absurd error to put modern English literature in the curriculum. You should read contemporary literature for pleasure or not read it at all. You shouldn't be taught to monkey with it. It's ghastly to think of all the little girls who are taught to read *To the Lighthouse*. It's not really substantial food for the young because there's such a strong feeling that Virginia Woolf was doing a set piece and it didn't really matter very much. She was putting on an act. Shakespeare didn't put on an act. But *Orlando* is a lovely original splash, a beautiful piece of fancy. Leonard Woolf had a tiresome mind. When you read his books about

Malaya, and then the books of the cadets who went out there, he's so petty, and they have such an enthusiasm and such tolerance for the murderous habits of the natives. But he was certainly good to Virginia. I couldn't forgive Vanessa Bell for her awful muddy decorations and those awful pictures of Charlotte Brontë. And I hated Duncan Grant's pictures too. The best thing that was ever said about Bloomsbury was said by a lovely butler of mine. At dinner one evening, they began to talk of Faulkner's book in which someone uses a corncob for the purposes of rape. They were being terribly subtle, and doing this and that gesture over the table. The butler came in to my son Anthony's room and asked, "Do you know where they keep the Faulkners? It seems they're very saucy.". . . Virginia Woolf's criticism was much better than criticism others were writing then.

INTERVIEWER: Amongst critics, do you admire Cyril Connolly? Or Malcolm Muggeridge?

WEST: Connolly? What an extraordinary thing to ask! He was a very good editor of *Horizon*, but he wasn't an interesting person. As for writing, he was fond of it, as you might say. But he didn't know much about it, did he? I've got no opinion of Muggeridge. He's very nice and friendly. What ever have I read of his in the past? I can never think Christ is grateful for being alluded to as if He were a lost cause.

INTERVIEWER: Did you want to write about trials?

WEST: Not at all. I had done it once or twice, when I was very hard up, when I was young, just to get some money, and so I learnt how to do them, and then I used to sit and listen to William Joyce [Lord Haw-Haw, hanged 1945] when he was broadcasting. Then I arranged to go to his trial because I was interested in him. A man called Theo Matthew, who was director of public prosecutions, though not a prosecuting sort of person, said, "I wish you'd report a lot of these trials because otherwise they will go unnoticed because there is so little newsprint." He said, "Really, if you will consider it as war work, it would be extremely valuable." So I did that for one book [*The New Meaning of Treason*, 1947] and then I did it for another [*A Train of Powder*, 1955]. Most of the people in Intelligence didn't agree with my views. I don't know whether it had any effect on them at all. Someone asked me recently how did I think Intelligence had found out John Vassal? [British spy, jailed in 1963]. It seemed to me such a silly question. He had it tattooed on his forehead. I never know how people don't find out spies.

INTERVIEWER: Are you interested in espionage still?

WEST: I won't say I'm interested in spies, but they do turn up in my life in quite funny ways. There was a man called Sidney Reilly, who was a famous spy, a double agent. My mother-in-law was very upset because my husband married me instead of the daughter of a civil servant. My husband's mother thought she was a nice Catholic girl, who'd be so nice for my husband, and it always tickled me because it gradually emerged that this girl was the mistress of this *very* famous and very disreputable spy. It was a wonderful thing to have in your pocket against your mother-in-law. My mother-in-law was an enormous, huge woman, and extremely pathetic. She had had her life broken up so often. By the First World War, and then the Second. Between the wars she was perfectly happy going to tea at those old-fashioned tea places they had—Rumpelmayer's. But her other son was very ill and he went out to Australia and he had a weak lung, and she went to see him and she got caught by the war there. If you like Rumpelmayer's, you wouldn't want to be in Australia for six years.

INTERVIEWER: Do you enjoy reviewing for the *Sunday Telegraph*?

WEST: Yes, I do. I do. I would feel awfully cut off if I didn't review; I think it's such a good discipline. It makes you really open your mind to the book. Probably you wouldn't, if you just read it.

INTERVIEWER: Oh, yes. It concentrates one, yes. I thought your review of Christopher Isherwood's *Christopher and His Kind* was dazzling. You demolished him.

WEST: I was so horrified by the way he treated the little German pansy. Also I thought it must have been so disgusting for the people in the village on the Greek island. I know Greeks love money, but I think a lot of money would have to pass before you'd be reconciled to Isherwood making such a noise.

INTERVIEWER: When I read your review, I was completely convinced by your argument, that it was an extraordinary sort of obliviousness that comes from class privilege.

WEST: Well, I didn't want to make a butt of him. Do you know, a bookseller's assistant said to him, "What do you think of Rebecca West's review of your book?" and he is alleged to have said such a lovely thing: "I shall think of some way of turning it to my advantage." You can't think how bad reviewing was when I first started to review, so dull and so dreadful. Nobody good but Lady Robert Cecil, one of the Salisbury family.

INTERVIEWER: But your reviews were absolutely sparkling. I love the essay you wrote about *The Uncles*.

WEST: Oh, Bennett was horrible about it. He was a horrible mean-spirited hateful man. I hated Arnold Bennett.

INTERVIEWER: But you were very nice about him.

WEST: Well, I thought so, and I think he was sometimes a very good writer. I do think *The Old Wives' Tale* is very good, don't you? He was a horrible man.

INTERVIEWER: Was he in a position to make things difficult for you then?

WEST: Yes. He was not nice. He lived with these two women, the French woman to whom he was married and also the woman who was with him when he died. He was always telling other people how tiresome these women were. It was all very, as people say, unchivalrous.

INTERVIEWER: English writing hasn't really produced the kind of giants it produced in the twenties. The stagnation of English writing since then is extraordinary. Joyce, Virginia Woolf, Wells, Shaw: all these people were writing, and who have we got to compare now?

WEST: I find Tom Stoppard just as amusing as I ever found Shaw. Very amusing, both as a playwright and as himself. But I'm not now an admirer of Shaw. It was a poor mind, I think. I liked his wife so much better. He *was* conceited, but in an odd way. Usually, you know, it's people shouting to keep their spirits up, but he really did think he was better than most people. I thought that book on Yeats's postbag was so good, letters that people wrote to Yeats. Did you read that? It's absolutely delightful. It's got delightful things like a very nicely phrased letter from a farmer, saying that he understands Yeats writes about supernatural matters and can he recommend a reliable witch? You know, charming things like that.

INTERVIEWER: Did you meet Yeats?

WEST: Yes. He wasn't a bit impressive and he wasn't my sort of person at all. He boomed at you like a foghorn. He was there one time when Philip Guedalla and two or three of us were all very young, and were talking nonsense about murderers in Shakespeare and whether a third murderer ever became a first murderer by working hard or were they, sort of, hereditary slots? Were they like Japanese specialists and one did one kind of murder, another did another? It was really awfully funny. Philip was very funny to be with. Then we started talking about something on the Western Isles but Yeats wouldn't join in, until we fussed round and were nice to him. But we were all wrong; what he liked was solemnity and, if you were big enough, heavy enough, and strong enough, he loved you. He loved great big women. He would have been mad about Vanessa Redgrave.

INTERVIEWER: Is your Irish birth important to you?

WEST: Frightfully, yes. I loved my family. I have a great affiliation to relations of mine called Denny. The present man is an architect, Sir Anthony Denny. He's exactly like Holbein's drawing of his ancestor, Anthony Denny, which I think is a great testimonial. Anthony Denny lives up in the Cotswolds and he and his wife are most glamorous people in a very quiet way. They have two charming sons, one of them paints very well, and they adopted a child, a Vietnamese child. Tony went out to see his brother, who had fever there, and he was walking along a quay and one of the refugee babies, who was sitting about, suddenly ran up to him and clasped him round the knees and looked up in his face. So he just said, "I'll have this one"—and took him home. It was a most lovely reason. The Dennys did nice things like that. And then my father used to speak about this cousin in Ireland, in the west of Ireland, called Dickie Shoot. Dickie Shoot beggared himself by helping people.

INTERVIEWER: I always think it's astonishing how much literature Protestant Ireland has produced.

WEST: I don't think they're very poetical people or sensitive people really, but what a lot of literature they've produced compared with the Scotch, who I think have really deeper emotions. It's most peculiar.

INTERVIEWER: Shaw. Wilde. Whatever one thinks of their quality, there they are. Samuel Beckett. All from Protestant Irish stock.

WEST: You know, an Irish priest said a most beautiful thing to me the other day, and I absolutely loved it. He looked at those books and said—a very old man he is, he's older than I am, he must be over ninety—and he said to me, "What are you doing with all your books, when you're dead? You must have planned for them." I said, "I'm giving those Oxford dictionaries to the grandson of Oscar Wilde, Merlin Holland." And he said, "Oh, how beautiful that makes it all. It's rather as if it hadn't happened." I said, "What do you mean?" He said, "Well, your family lives in Fitzwilliam Square and Wilde's people lived in Merrion Square and it's such a natural thing to do for a family in Fitzwilliam Square to give their Oxford dictionary to the son of a family living in Merrion Square." Almost as if it hadn't happened. He couldn't have added a word to it. I love Merlin. I went to see him out in Beirut with his mother, which was rather a trial. She's Australian in a big way but you know, it was so extraordinary, the glimpse I had of her. He was very fond of a ballet dancer, and we went out to lunch. We went up to her house, and after dinner Mrs. Holland, who is plump and sixty-something, got up and she turned on one of the records, *Swan Lake*, and danced to it, as she'd learnt to, and she was quite beautiful. Obviously she should have been a dancer.

INTERVIEWER: Do you think it has become easier for women to follow their vocations?

WEST: I don't know. It's very hard. I've always found I've had too many family duties to enable me to write enough. I would have written much better and I would have written much more. Oh, men, whatever they may say, don't really have any barrier between them and their craft, and certainly I had.

INTERVIEWER: What inspired you later to write your great book on Yugoslavia? Was it the contact with the people?

WEST: What I was interested in really was wandering about with Henry. I wanted to write a book on Finland, which is a wonderful case of a small nation with empires here and there, so I learnt Finnish and I read a Finnish novel. It was all about people riding bicycles. But then, when I went to Yugoslavia, I saw it was much more exciting with Austria and Russia and Turkey, and so I wrote that. I really did enjoy it terribly, loved it. I loved writing about St. Augustine, too. I like writing about heretics, anyway.

INTERVIEWER: You consider Augustine a heretic, do you?

WEST: Oh, no, he wasn't a heretic. Most of his life he wasn't at all a nice man, but that's quite a different thing. I like to think about people like the Donatists, who were really suffering agonies of one kind and another because the Roman Empire was splitting up and it was especially uncomfortable to be in Roman Africa. But they didn't know anything about economics, and did know about theology. Theology had taught them that if you suffered, it was usually because you'd offended God: so they invented an offense against God, which was that unworthy priests were celebrating the Sacraments. So that satisfied them and then they went round the country, looting and getting the food and the property they wanted because they said that they were punishing heretics. I think it's wonderful that in the past people overlooked things that now seem to us quite obvious, and thought they were doing things for the reasons they weren't, and tried to remedy them by actions. Perhaps there's some quite simple thing we'll think of some day, which will make us much happier.

—MARINA WARNER
1981

5. Dorothy Parker

Dorothy Parker was born Dorothy Rothschild in West End, New Jersey, in 1893, and was educated partly in a convent school. In 1916 she worked for *Vogue* at ten dollars a week; then she became drama critic for *Vanity Fair*. Her first collection of verse, *Enough Rope*, appeared in 1927. That same year she accepted a book-reviewing stint for *The New Yorker*, her columns appearing over the signature "Constant Reader." She became famous as a wit among the group that met at the Round Table in the Hotel Algonquin, and there was a time when everything bright or malicious said in New York was ascribed to Dorothy Parker.

In 1929 Parker won the O. Henry Prize for "Big Blonde," a story which was included in her first collection, *Laments for the Living* (1930). A second collection of stories was *After Such Pleasures* (1933). *Here Lies* (1939) included all her fiction published to that time. She wrote three plays: *Close Harmony* (with Elmer Rice, 1924), *The Coast of Illyria* (1949), and *The Ladies of the Corridor* (with Arnaud d'Usseau, 1953). Although she preferred the dramatic form, her plays never achieved the popularity of her verse and her short stories. Her collections of verse were all best-sellers, a rare occurrence in American publishing. They include *Sunset Gun* (1928), *Death and Taxes* (1931), and her collected poems *Not So Deep as a Well* (1936).

The Portable Dorothy Parker (1944), which includes both verse and fiction complete, was one of the most popular volumes in a famous series. Alexander Woollcott once said of her work that it was "so potent a distillation of nectar and wormwood, of ambrosia and deadly night-shade, as might suggest to the rest of us that we write far too much." Parker died in 1967.

and, on consoles and desk and table, photographs of himself at two
and a half and five and seven and nine, framed in broad mirror
bands.   Whenever his mother settled in a new domicile, and she
removed often, those photographs were the first things out of the
luggage.   The boy hated them.   He had had to pass his fifteenth
birthday before his body had caught up with his head; there was that head -
presentments of his former selves, that pale, enormous blob.
Once he had asked his mother to put the pictures somewhere else -
preferably some small, dark place that could be locked.   But he
had had the bad fortune to make his request on one of the occasions
when she was given to weeping suddenly and long.   So the photographs stood out on parade, with their frames twinkling away.

There were twinkings, too, to the silver top of the
fat crystal cocktail shaker, but the liquid low within the crystal
was pale and dull.   There was no shine, either, to the glass his
mother held.   It was cloudy from the clutch of her
hand, and on the inside there were oily dribbles of what it had
contained.

His mother shut the door by which she had admitted him
and followed him into the room.   She looked at him with her head
tilted to the side.

"Well, aren't you going to kiss me?" she said in a
charming, wheedling voice, the voice of a little, little girl.
"Aren't you, you beautiful big ox, you?"

"Sure," he said.   He bent down toward her, but she
stepped suddenly away.   A sharp change came over her.   She drew
herself tall, with her shoulders back and her head flung high.
Her upper lip lifted over her teeth, and her gaze came cold beneath

Oliver Harrington

Dorothy Parker

At the time of this interview, Dorothy Parker was living in a midtown New York hotel. She shared her small apartment with a youthful poodle which had run of the place and had caused it to look, as Mrs. Parker said apologetically, somewhat "Hogarthian": newspapers spread about the floor, picked lamb chops here and there, and a rubber doll—its throat torn from ear to ear—which Mrs. Parker lobbed left-handed from her chair into corners of the room for the poodle to retrieve—as it did, never tiring of the opportunity. The room was sparsely decorated, its one overpowering fixture being a large dog portrait, not of the poodle, but of a sheepdog owned by the author Philip Wylie and painted by his wife. The portrait indicated a dog of such size that if it were real, would have dwarfed Mrs. Parker. She was a small woman, her voice gentle, her tone often apologetic, but occasionally, given the opportunity to comment on matters she felt strongly about, her voice rose almost harshly, and her sentences were punctuated with

observations phrased with lethal force. Hers was still the wit which
made her a legend as a member of the Round Table of the Al-
gonquin—a humor whose particular quality seemed a coupling of
brilliant social commentary with a mind of devastating inven-
tiveness. She seemed able to produce the well-turned phrase for
any occasion. A friend remembered sitting next to her at the theater
when the news was announced of the death of the stolid Calvin
Coolidge. "How do they know?" whispered Mrs. Parker.

Readers of this interview, however, will find that Mrs. Parker
had only contempt for the eager reception accorded her wit. "Why
it got so bad," she had said bitterly, "that they began to laugh
before I opened my mouth." And she had a similar attitude toward
her value as a serious writer.

But Mrs. Parker was her own worst critic. Her three books of
poetry may have established her reputation as a master of light
verse, but her short stories were essentially serious in tone—serious
in that they reflected her own life, which was in many ways an
unhappy one—and also serious in their intention. Franklin P.
Adams described them in an introduction to her work: "Nobody
can write such ironic things unless he has a deep sense of injustice—
injustice to those members of the race who are the victims of the
stupid, the pretentious and the hypocritical."

INTERVIEWER: Your first job was on Vogue, wasn't it? How did
you go about getting hired, and why Vogue?

PARKER: After my father died there wasn't any money. I had
to work, you see, and Mr. Crowninshield, God rest his soul, paid
twelve dollars for a small verse of mine and gave me a job at ten
dollars a week. Well, I thought I was Edith Sitwell. I lived in a
boarding house at 103rd and Broadway, paying eight dollars a
week for my room and two meals, breakfast and dinner. Thorne
Smith was there, and another man. We used to sit around in the
evening and talk. There was no money, but Jesus we had fun.

INTERVIEWER: What kind of work did you do at Vogue?

PARKER: I wrote captions. "This little pink dress will win you
a beau," that sort of thing. Funny, they were plain women work-

ing at *Vogue*, not chic. They were decent, nice women—the nicest women I ever met—but they had no business on such a magazine. They wore funny little bonnets and in the pages of their magazine they virginized the models from tough babes into exquisite little loves. Now the editors are what they should be: all chic and worldly; most of the models are out of the mind of a Bram Stoker, and as for the caption writers—*my* old job— they're recommending mink covers at seventy-five dollars apiece for the wooden ends of golf clubs "—for the friend who has everything." Civilization is coming to an end, you understand.

INTERVIEWER: Why did you change to *Vanity Fair*?

PARKER: Mr. Crowninshield wanted me to. Mr. Sherwood and Mr. Benchley—we always called each other by our last names— were there. Our office was across from the Hippodrome. The midgets would come out and frighten Mr. Sherwood. He was about seven feet tall and they were always sneaking up behind him and asking him how the weather was up there. "Walk down the street with me," he'd ask, and Mr. Benchley and I would leave our jobs and guide him down the street. I can't tell you, we had more fun. Both Mr. Benchley and I subscribed to two undertaking magazines: *The Casket* and *Sunnyside*. Steel yourself: *Sunnyside* had a joke column called "From Grave to Gay." I cut a picture out of one of them, in color, of how and where to inject embalming fluid, and had it hung over my desk until Mr. Crown-inshield asked me if I could possibly take it down. Mr. Crown-inshield was a lovely man, but puzzled. I must say we behaved extremely badly. Albert Lee, one of the editors, had a map over *his* desk with little flags on it to show where our troops were fighting during the First World War. Every day he would get the news and move the flags around. I was married, my husband was overseas, and since I didn't have anything better to do I'd get up half an hour early and go down and change his flags. Later on, Lee would come in, look at his map, and he'd get very serious about spies—shout, and spend his morning moving his little pins back into position.

INTERVIEWER: How long did you stay at *Vanity Fair*?

PARKER: Four years. I'd taken over the drama criticism from P.G. Wodehouse. Then I fixed three plays—one of them *Caesar's Wife*, with Billie Burke in it—and as a result I was fired.

INTERVIEWER: You *fixed* three plays?

PARKER: Well, *panned*. The plays closed and the producers, who were the big boys—Dillingham, Ziegfeld, and Belasco—didn't like it, you know. *Vanity Fair* was a magazine of no opinion, but *I* had opinions. So I was fired. And Mr. Sherwood and Mr. Benchley resigned their jobs. It was all right for Mr. Sherwood, but Mr. Benchley had a family—two children. It was the greatest act of friendship I'd known. Mr. Benchley did a sign, "Contributions for Miss Billie Burke," and on our way out we left it in the hall of *Vanity Fair*. We behaved very badly. We made ourselves discharge chevrons and wore them.

INTERVIEWER: Where did you all go after *Vanity Fair*?

PARKER: Mr. Sherwood became the motion-picture critic for the old *Life*. Mr. Benchley did the drama reviews. He and I had an office so tiny that an inch smaller and it would have been adultery. We had *Parkbench* for a cable address, but no one ever sent us one. It was so long ago—before you were a gleam in someone's eyes—that I doubt there *was* a cable.

INTERVIEWER: It's a popular supposition that there was much more communication between writers in the twenties. The Round Table discussions in the Algonquin, for example.

PARKER: I wasn't there very often—it cost too much. Others went. Kaufman was there. I guess he was sort of funny. Mr. Benchley and Mr. Sherwood went when they had a nickel. Franklin P. Adams, whose column was widely read by people who wanted to write, would sit in occasionally. And Harold Ross, the *New Yorker* editor. He was a professional lunatic, but I don't know if he was a great man. He had a profound ignorance. On one of Mr. Benchley's manuscripts he wrote in the margin opposite "Andromache," "Who he?" Mr. Benchley wrote back, "You keep out of this." The only one with stature who came to the Round Table was Heywood Broun.

INTERVIEWER: What was it about the twenties that inspired people like yourself and Broun?

PARKER: Gertrude Stein did us the most harm when she said, "You're all a lost generation." That got around to certain people and we all said, "Whee! We're lost." Perhaps it suddenly brought to us the sense of change. Or irresponsibility. But don't forget that, though the people in the twenties seemed like flops, they weren't. Fitzgerald, the rest of them, reckless as they were, drinkers as they were, they worked damn hard and all the time.

INTERVIEWER: Did the "lost generation" attitude you speak of have a detrimental effect on your own work?

PARKER: Silly of me to blame it on dates, but so it happened to be. Dammit, it *was* the twenties and we had to be smarty. I *wanted* to be cute. That's the terrible thing. I should have had more sense.

INTERVIEWER: And during this time you were writing poems?

PARKER: My verses. I cannot say poems. Like everybody was then, I was following in the exquisite footsteps of Miss Millay, unhappily in my own horrible sneakers. My verses are no damn good. Let's face it, honey, my verse is terribly dated—as anything once fashionable is dreadful now. I gave it up, knowing it wasn't getting any better, but nobody seemed to notice my magnificent gesture.

INTERVIEWER: Do you think your verse writing has been of any benefit to your prose?

PARKER: Franklin P. Adams once gave me a book of French verse forms and told me to copy their design, that by copying them I would get precision in prose. The men you imitate in verse influence your prose, and what I got out of it was precision, all I realize I've ever had in prose writing.

INTERVIEWER: How did you get started in writing?

PARKER: I fell into writing, I suppose, being one of those awful children who wrote verses. I went to a convent in New York—The Blessed Sacrament. Convents do the same things progressive schools do, only they don't know it. They don't teach you how to read; you have to find out for yourself. At my convent we *did* have a textbook, one that devoted a page and a half to Adelaide Ann Proctor; but we couldn't read Dickens; he was vulgar, you know. But *I* read him and Thackeray, and I'm the one woman you'll ever know who's read every word of Charles Reade, the author of *The Cloister and the Hearth*. But as for helping me in the outside world, the convent taught me only that if you spit on a pencil eraser it will erase ink. And I remember the smell of oilcloth, the smell of nuns' garb. I was fired from there, finally, for a lot of things, among them my insistence that the Immaculate Conception was spontaneous combustion.

INTERVIEWER: Have you ever drawn from those years for story material?

PARKER: All those writers who write about their childhood! Gentle God, if I wrote about mine you wouldn't sit in the same room with me.

INTERVIEWER: What, then, would you say is the source of most of your work?

PARKER: Need of money, dear.

INTERVIEWER: And besides that?

PARKER: It's easier to write about those you hate—just as it's easier to criticize a bad play or a bad book.

INTERVIEWER: What about "Big Blonde"? Where did the idea for that come from?

PARKER: I knew a lady—a friend of mine who went through holy hell. Just say I knew a woman once. The purpose of the writer is to say what he feels and sees. To those who write fantasies—the Misses Baldwin, Ferber, Norris—I am not at home.

INTERVIEWER: That's not showing much respect for your fellow women, at least not the writers.

PARKER: As artists they're not, but as providers they're oil wells; they gush. Norris said she never wrote a story unless it was fun to do. I understand Ferber whistles at her typewriter. And there was that poor sucker Flaubert rolling around on his floor for three days looking for the right word. I'm a feminist, and God knows I'm loyal to my sex, and you must remember that from my very early days, when this city was scarcely safe from buffaloes, I was in the struggle for equal rights for women. But when we paraded through the catcalls of men and when we chained ourselves to lamp posts to try to get our equality—dear child, we didn't foresee *those* female writers. Or Clare Boothe Luce, or Perle Mesta, or Oveta Culp Hobby.

INTERVIEWER: You have an extensive reputation as a wit. Has this interfered, do you think, with your acceptance as a serious writer?

PARKER: I don't want to be classed as a humorist. It makes me feel guilty. I've never read a good tough quotable female humorist, and I never was one myself. I couldn't do it. A "smartcracker" they called me, and that makes me sick and unhappy. There's a hell of a distance between wisecracking and wit. Wit has truth in it; wisecracking is simply calisthenics with words. I didn't mind so much when they were good, but for a long time anything that was called a crack was attributed to me—and then they got the shaggy dogs.

INTERVIEWER: How about satire?

PARKER: Ah, satire. That's another matter. They're the big boys. If I'd been called a satirist there'd be no living with me. But by satirist I mean those boys in the other centuries. The people we call satirists now are those who make cracks at topical topics and consider themselves satirists—creatures like George S. Kaufman and such who don't even know what satire is. Lord knows, a writer should show his times, but not show them in wisecracks. Their stuff is not satire; it's as dull as yesterday's newspaper. Successful satire has got to be pretty good the day after tomorrow.

INTERVIEWER: And how about contemporary humorists? Do you feel about them as you do about satirists?

PARKER: You get to a certain age and only the tried writers are funny. I read my verses now and I ain't funny. I haven't been funny for twenty years. But anyway there aren't any humorists any more, except for Perelman. There's no need for them. Perelman must be very lonely.

INTERVIEWER: Why is there no need for the humorist?

PARKER: It's a question of supply and demand. If we needed them, we'd have them. The new crop of would-be humorists doesn't count. They're like the would-be satirists. They write about topical topics. Not like Thurber and Mr. Benchley. Those two were damn well read and, though I hate the word, they were cultured. What sets them apart is that they both had a point of view to express. That is important to all good writing. It's the difference between Paddy Chayefsky, who just puts down lines, and Clifford Odets, who in his early plays not only sees but has a point of view. The writer must be aware of life around him. Carson McCullers is good, or she used to be, but now she's withdrawn from life and writes about freaks. Her characters are grotesques.

INTERVIEWER: Speaking of Chayefsky and McCullers, do you read much of your own, or the present generation of writers?

PARKER: I will say of the writers of today that some of them, thank God, have the sense to adapt to their times. Mailer's *The Naked and the Dead* is a great book. And I thought William Styron's *Lie Down in Darkness* an extraordinary thing. The start of it took your heart and flung it over there. He writes like a god. But for most of my reading I go back to the old ones—for comfort. As you get older you go much farther back. I read *Vanity Fair* about a dozen times a year. I was a woman of eleven when I first read it—the thrill of that line "George Osborne lay dead with a bullet through his head." Sometimes I read, as an elegant friend of mine calls them, "who-did-its." I love Sherlock Holmes. My life is so untidy and he's so neat. But as for living novelists, I suppose E. M. Forster is the best, not knowing what that is, but at least he's a semi-finalist, wouldn't you think? Somerset Maugham once said to me, "We have a novelist over here, E. M. Forster, though I don't suppose he's familiar to you." Well, I could have kicked him. Did he think I carried a papoose on my back? Why, I'd go on my hands and knees to get to Forster. He once wrote something I've always remembered: "It has never happened to me that I've had to choose between betraying a friend and betraying my country, but if it ever does so happen I hope I have the guts to betray my country." Now doesn't that make the Fifth Amendment look like a bum?

INTERVIEWER: Could I ask you some technical questions? How do you actually write out a story? Do you write out a draft and then go over it or what?

PARKER: It takes me six months to do a story. I think it out and then write it sentence by sentence—no first draft. I can't write five words but that I change seven.

INTERVIEWER: How do you name your characters?

PARKER: The telephone book and from the obituary columns.

INTERVIEWER: Do you keep a notebook?

PARKER: I tried to keep one, but I never could remember where I put the damn thing. I always say I'm going to keep one tomorrow.

INTERVIEWER: How do you get the story down on paper?

PARKER: I wrote in longhand at first, but I've lost it. I use two fingers on the typewriter. I think it's unkind of you to ask. I know so little about the typewriter that once I bought a new one because I couldn't change the ribbon on the one I had.

INTERVIEWER: You're working on a play now, aren't you?

PARKER: Yes, collaborating with Arnaud d'Usseau. I'd like to do a play more than anything. First night is the most exciting thing in the world. It's wonderful to hear your words spoken. Unhappily, our first play, *The Ladies of the Corridor*, was not a success, but writing that play was the best time I ever had, both for the privilege and the stimulation of working with Mr. d'Usseau and because that play was the only thing I have ever done in which I had great pride.

INTERVIEWER: How about the novel? Have you ever tried that form?

PARKER: I wish to God I could do one, but I haven't got the nerve.

INTERVIEWER: And short stories? Are you still doing them?

PARKER: I'm trying now to do a story that's purely narrative. I think narrative stories are the best, though my past stories make themselves stories by telling themselves through what people say. I haven't got a visual mind. I hear things. But I'm not going to do those *he-said she-said* things any more, they're over, honey, they're over. I want to do the story that can only be told in the narrative form, and though they're going to scream about the rent, I'm going to do it.

INTERVIEWER: Do you think economic security an advantage to the writer?

PARKER: Yes. Being in a garret doesn't do you any good unless you're some sort of a Keats. The people who lived and wrote well in the twenties were comfortable and easy-living. They were able to find stories and novels, and good ones, in conflicts that came out of two million dollars a year, not a garret. As for me, I'd like to have money. And I'd like to be a good writer. These two can come together, and I hope they will, but if that's too adorable, I'd rather have money. I hate almost all rich people, but I think I'd be darling at it. At the moment, however, I like to think of Maurice Baring's remark: "If you would know what the Lord God thinks of money, you have only to look at those to whom he gives it." I realize that's not much help when the wolf comes scratching at the door, but it's a comfort.

INTERVIEWER: What do you think about the artist being supported by the state?

PARKER: Naturally, when penniless, I think it's superb. I think that the art of the country so immeasurably adds to its prestige that if you want the country to have writers and artists—persons who live precariously in our country—the state must help. I do not think that any kind of artist thrives under charity, by which I mean one person or organization giving him money. Here and there, this and that—that's no good. The difference between the state giving and the individual patron is that one is charity and the other isn't. Charity is murder and you know it. But I do think that if the government supports its artists, they need have no feeling of gratitude—the meanest and most sniveling attribute in the world—or baskets being brought to them, or apple-polishing. Working for the state—for Christ's sake, are you grateful to your employers? Let the state see what its artists are trying to do—like France with the Academie Française. The artists are a part of their country and their country should recognize this, so both it and the artists can take pride in their efforts. Now I mean that, my dear.

INTERVIEWER: How about Hollywood as provider for the artist?

PARKER: Hollywood money isn't money. It's congealed snow, melts in your hand, and there you are. I can't talk about Hollywood. It was a horror to me when I was there and it's a horror to look back on. I can't imagine how I did it. When I got away from it I couldn't even refer to the place by name. "Out there," I called it. You want to know what "out there" means to me? Once I was coming down a street in Beverly Hills and I saw a Cadillac about a block long, and out of the side window was a wonderfully slinky mink, and an arm, and at the end of the arm a hand in a white suede glove wrinkled around the wrist, and in the hand was a bagel with a bite out of it.

INTERVIEWER: Do you think Hollywood destroys the artist's talent?

PARKER: No, no, no. I think nobody on earth writes down. Garbage though they turn out, Hollywood writers aren't writing down. That is their best. If you're going to write, don't pretend to write down. It's going to be the best you can do, and it's the fact that it's the best you can do that kills you. I want so much to write well, though I know I don't, and that I didn't make it. But during and at the end of my life, I will adore those who have.

INTERVIEWER: Then what is it that's the evil in Hollywood?

PARKER: It's the people. Like the director who put his finger in Scott Fitzgerald's face and complained, "Pay *you*. Why, you ought to pay us." It was terrible about Scott; if you'd seen him you'd have been sick. When he died no one went to the funeral, not a single soul came, or even sent a flower. I said, "Poor son of a bitch," a quote right out of *The Great Gatsby*, and everyone thought it was another wisecrack. But it was said in dead seriousness. Sickening about Scott. And it wasn't only the people, but also the indignity to which your ability was put. There was a picture in which Mr. Benchley had a part. In it Monty Woolley had a scene in which he had to enter a room through a door on which was balanced a bucket of water. He came into the room covered with water and muttered to Mr. Benchley, who had a part in the scene, "Benchley? Benchley of *Harvard*?" "Yes," mumbled Mr. Benchley and he asked, "Woolley? Woolley of *Yale*?"

INTERVIEWER: How about your political views? Have they made any difference to you professionally?

PARKER: Oh, certainly. Though I don't think this "blacklist" business extends to the theater or certain of the magazines, in Hollywood it exists because several gentlemen felt it best to drop names like marbles which bounced back like rubber balls about people they'd seen in the company of what they charmingly called "commies." You can't go back thirty years to Sacco and Vanzetti. I won't do it. Well, well, well, that's the way it is. If all this means something to the good of the movies, I don't know what it is. Sam Goldwyn said, "How'm I gonna do decent pictures when all my good writers are in jail?" Then he added, the infallible Goldwyn, "Don't misunderstand me, they all ought to be hung." Mr. Goldwyn didn't know about "hanged." That's all there is to say. It's not the tragedies that kill us, it's the messes. I can't stand messes. I'm not being a smartcracker. You know I'm not when you meet me—don't you, honey?

—MARION CAPRON
1956

6. Lillian Hellman

Lillian Hellman was born on June 20, 1905, in New Orleans. Except for occasional visits to her Southern relatives, she spent her childhood in New York, where she had moved at the age of five. In 1923 she entered New York University. She did not graduate, however, and after transferring to Columbia for one semester left college for good in 1924 to work as a publisher's assistant for Horace Liveright. In 1925 she married playwright-author Arthur Kober. During their seven years of marriage she worked as a reviewer for the *New York Herald-Tribune* and as a play reader (one of her discoveries was Vicki Baum's *Grand Hotel*). A year after her divorce from Kober in 1932, she began work on what was to be her first produced play. With the guidance of Dashiell Hammett, who remained her lifelong friend, she finished the play in 1934: *The Children's Hour* opened that year on Broadway and ran for six hundred ninety-one performances.

Her plays continue to be produced regularly: *Days to Come* (1936); *The Little Foxes* (1939); *Watch on the Rhine*, which won the New York Drama Critics' Circle Award in 1941; *The Searching Wind* (1944); *Another Part of the Forest* (1946); *The Autumn Garden* (1951); and *Toys in the Attic* (1960). She also wrote a number of adaptations: *Montserrat* (1949), based on Emmanuel Robles's novel; *The Lark* (1955), based on Jean Anouilh's play; and *My Mother, My Father and Me* (1963), based on Burt Blechman's novel *How Much*. She wrote the libretto for the musical *Candide* (1956) and the film script *The Chase* (1966). Among her other screenplays are *Dark Angel* (1935), *These Three* (the first film version of *The Children's Hour*—1935–1936), *Dead End* (1937), *The Little Foxes* (1940), *North Star* (1943), and *The Searching Wind* (1945). She edited *Selected Letters of Anton Chekhov* in 1955. In 1970, three of her autobiographical works, *An Unfinished Woman*, *Pentimento*, and *Scoundrel Time*, a personal account of the House Un-American Activities Committee trials in the 1950s, were published in one volume, entitled *Three*. Hellman died in 1984.

CAL

Miss Zan she had two helpings frozen fruit cream and she tell
that honored guest, she tell him that you make the best frozen
fruit cream in all the south.

ADDIE
(Smiles, pleased)

Did she? Well, save her a little. She like it right before
she go to bed.

(Cal nods, exits. After a second the
dining room doors are opened and quickly
closed again by BIRDIE HUBBARD. Birdie
is a woman of about forty, with a pretty,
well-bred, faded face. Her movements are
usually nervous and timid, but now, as she
comes running into the room, she is gay
and excited) *don't understand p.4.*

BIRDIE
(Running to the bell-cord)

My, Addie. What a good dinner. Just as good as good can be.

ADDIE

You look pretty this evening, Miss Birdie, and young. *more casual*

BIRDIE
(Laughing, pleased)

Me, young!
(ADDIE looks at her as she rings the
bell again)

I want one of the kitchen boys to run home for me. He's to
look in my desk drawer, the left drawer, and bring my music
album right away. Mr. Marshall is very anxious to see it
because of his father and the opera in Chicago. Mr. Marshall *— too much for*
is such a polite man with his manners, and very educated and *college!*
cultured —
(CAL appears at the door)

Oh, Cal. Tell Simon or one of the boys to run down to our
house and look in my desk, the left drawer, and —

(The dining room doors are opened and quickly
closed by OSCAR HUBBARD. He is a tall, thin-
faced man in his late forties)

OSCAR
(Sharply)

Birdie.

BIRDIE
(Turning, nervously)

Oh. Oscar. I was just sending Simon for my music album.

OSCAR
(To Cal) *album*

Never mind about Simon. Miss Birdie has changed her mind.

Manuscript page from The Little Foxes

ANNE HOLLANDER

Lillian Hellman

Miss Hellman spent her summers in a comfortable white house at the bottom of a sandbank in the town of Vineyard Haven, Massachusetts, on the island of Martha's Vineyard. There was nothing of old Cape Cod about it; a modern house, with lots of big windows and a wooden deck facing on the harbor. Miss Hellman observed the ferries of the Woods Hole–Martha's Vineyard–Nantucket Steamship Authority, weighted down with passengers and automobiles, as they pushed through the harbor on their midsummer schedule and disgorge ever more visitors upon this teeming, heterogeneous resort. It was a measure of Miss Hellman's dedication to her work that she achieved so much in her exposed situation, not half a mile from the ferry dock. Here she stayed with her maid, and a big barking poodle that discouraged few of the peak-of-the-season visitors who trooped through her parlor.

Behind this new house and out of view as it sits on top of the sandbank, is the old house, which Miss Hellman sold after Dashiell

Hammett died. A frame house with yellow painted shingles and climbing roses, plainer and more regional in its architecture, like a Yankee farmhouse of the last century, it had a complex of boxlike rooms where Miss Hellman's guests thronged. Removed from these, on the far east wing of the house, stood a tower formed by the shell of an old Cape Cod windmill. Up in this windmill tower was the room where Dashiell Hammett lived; he always escaped there when company came. He had been an invalid since the war; he became a recluse and at the end of his life talked to almost no one. Hammett was a thin, finely built man and very tall—when he was seen walking in delicate silence, in the cruel wasting of his illness, down a crowded sidewalk on his way to the library, unrecognized, unknown, forgotten, the proudness of his bearing set him off from the summer people.

Occasionally a stranger would come in the house uninvited and catch Dashiell Hammett off guard. He might be reading in an easy chair. Miss Hellman would introduce him, and he would elegantly rise and shake hands. Like many a famous writer who detests being disturbed in his private self, a million miles from any social confrontation, he had learned to scare off the intruder with his smile. Here he was luckier than most, for rather than looking pained and fraudulent, rather than a predictable Sam Spade/Humphrey Bogart hard-guy leer, the smile Dashiell Hammett produced on his clear-eyed, lean, aristocratic face was so nearly beatific that it disarmed the intruder long enough for Dashiell Hammett, with no more than a how-do-you-do, to vanish from the room. The armchair or the book gave his only evidence. Even the invited dinner guest coming punctually into the room would know the same ectoplasmic presence, when Miss Hellman, the laughter mingled in her greeting, immediately explained what Dash had said—what his joking exit line had been on, it seemed, the instant of your entrance. He was elusive but never aloof. Through the medium of Miss Hellman it was possible to carry on a running extrasensory conversation. A question to him, put through to her, on one evening (as how to clean a meerschaum pipe) or a request for an opinion (on somebody's writing, on something President Eisenhower did) was sure to be answered on another *evening. And five years before the meeting with Miss Hellman, a request had been put in writing for a* Paris Review *interview. He was by then at the end of his tether, often too weak to take his meals at the table. An answer came: "Sorry. Don't think it would work. Lilly will explain." Which she did, though neither by design nor by coincidence, in this interview. On a table in the parlor where she talked was a framed snapshot of Dashiell Hammett as he looked in World War II as a corporal in the Army Service Forces. He is lighting his cigarette with a PX-Zippo lighter and looking every inch a soldier in his impeccably creased suntans and overseas cap tilted toward the right of his head of white hair.*

Miss Hellman's voice had a quality, not to be captured on the page, of being at once angry, funny, slyly feminine, sad, affectionate, and harsh. While talking here she often allowed her laughter, like an antidote to bitterness, to break into her thoughts and give a more generous dimension to her comments, which, in print, may seem at first glance merely captious. These pages were compiled from three afternoon conversations in the more than usually harrying conditions of the Labor Day weekend on Martha's Vineyard, while Miss Hellman drove herself to finish a movie script for Sam Spiegel. There were many interruptions—telephone calls and people coming and going in the room. Such circumstances cannot excuse but may in part explain some of the interviewers' unrehearsed and too eagerly "literary" questions.

INTERVIEWER: Before you wrote plays, did you write anything else?

HELLMAN: Yes, short stories, a few poems. A couple of the stories were printed in a long-dead magazine called *The Paris Comet* for which Arthur Kober worked. Arthur and I were married and living in Paris. Let's see, about 1928, 1929, somewhere in there. They were very lady-writer stories. I reread them a few years ago. The kind of stories where the man puts his fork down and the woman knows it's all over. You know.

INTERVIEWER: Was it Dashiell Hammett who encouraged you to write plays?

HELLMAN: No. He disliked the theater. He always wanted me

to write a novel. I wrote a play before *The Children's Hour* with Louis Kronenberger called *The Dear Queen*. It was about a royal family. A royal family who wanted to be bourgeois. They kept running away to be middle class, and Dash used to say the play was no good because Louis would laugh only at his lines and I would laugh only at mine.

INTERVIEWER: Which of your plays do you like best?

HELLMAN: I don't like that question. You always like best the last thing you did. You like to think that you got better with time. But you know it isn't always true. I very seldom reread the plays. The few times I have, I have been pleasantly surprised by things that were better than I had remembered and horrified by other things I had thought were good. But I suppose *Autumn Garden*. I suppose I think it is the best play, if that is what you mean by "like."

INTERVIEWER: Somebody who saw you watch the opening night in Paris of Simone Signoret's adaptation of *The Little Foxes* said that through the performance you kept leaving your seat and pacing the vestibule.

HELLMAN: I jump up and down through most performances. But that particular night I was shaken by what I was seeing. I like *Little Foxes*, but I'm tired of it. I don't think many writers like best their best-known piece of work, particularly when it was written a long time ago.

INTERVIEWER: What prompted you to go back to the theme and the characters of *The Little Foxes*? Only seven years later you wrote *Another Part of the Forest*.

HELLMAN: I always intended to do *The Little Foxes* as a trilogy. Regina in *The Little Foxes* is about thirty-eight years old, and the year is 1900. I had meant to take up with her again in about 1920 or 1925, in Europe. And her daughter, Alexandra, was to have become maybe a spinsterish social worker, disappointed, a rather angry woman.

INTERVIEWER: In the third act of *The Little Foxes* is a speech which carries the burden of the play. It says there are people who eat the earth and all the people on it, like the locusts in the Bible. And there are the people who let them do it. "Sometimes I think it ain't right to stand by and watch them do it." At the end of this play Alexandra decides that she is not going to be one of those passive people. She is going to leave her mother.

HELLMAN: Yes, I meant her to leave. But to my great surprise, the ending of the play was taken to be a statement of faith in Alexandra, in her denial of her family. I never meant it that way. She did have courage enough to leave, but she would never have the force or vigor of her mother's family. That's what I meant. Or maybe I made it up afterward.

INTERVIEWER: These wheelers and dealers in your plays—the gouging, avaricious Hubbards. Had you known many people like that?

HELLMAN: Lots of people thought it was my mother's family.

INTERVIEWER: Might you ever write that third play?

HELLMAN: I'm tired of the people in *The Little Foxes*.

INTERVIEWER: In *Regina*, the opera Marc Blitzstein based on *The Little Foxes*, the badness of Regina is most emphatic.

HELLMAN: Marc and I were close friends but we never collaborated. I had nothing to do with the opera. I never saw Regina that way. You have no right to see your characters as good or bad. Such words have nothing to do with people you write about. Other people see them that way.

INTERVIEWER: You say in your introduction that *The Children's Hour* is about goodness and badness.

HELLMAN: Goodness and badness is different from good and bad people, isn't it? *The Children's Hour*—I was pleased with the results—was a kind of exercise. I didn't know how to write a play and I was teaching myself. I chose, or Dashiell Hammett chose for me, an actual law case, on the theory that I would do better with something that was there, had a foundation in fact. I didn't want to write about myself at the age of twenty-six. The play was based on a law case in a book by William Roughead. I changed it, of course, completely, by the time I finished. The case took place in Edinburgh in the nineteenth century, and was about two old-maid schoolteachers who ran a sort of second-rate private school. A little Indian girl—an India Indian—had been enrolled by her grandmother in the school. She brought charges of Lesbianism against the two teachers. The two poor middle-aged ladies spent the rest of their lives suing, sometimes losing, sometimes winning, until they no longer had any money and no school.

INTERVIEWER: As a rule does the germ of a play come to you abstractly? Do you work from a general conception?

HELLMAN: No, I've never done that. I used to say that I saw a play only in terms of the people in it. I used to say that because I believed that is the way you do the best work. I have come now to think that it is people *and* ideas.

INTERVIEWER: Have characters invented themselves before you write them?

HELLMAN: I don't think characters turn out the way you think they are going to turn out. They don't always go your way. At least they don't go my way. If I wanted to start writing about you, by page ten I probably wouldn't be. I don't think you start with a person. I think you start with the parts of many people. Drama has to do with conflict in people, with denials. But I don't really know much about the process of creation and I don't like talking about it.

INTERVIEWER: Is there something mysterious in what a play evokes as art and the craft of writing it?

HELLMAN: Sure. That is really the only mystery because theories may work for one person and not for another. It's very hard, at least for me, to have theories about writing.

INTERVIEWER: But you had to begin with a clear idea of what the action of the play would be?

HELLMAN: Not always. Not as I got older. It was bright of Hammett to see that somebody starting to write should have a solid foundation to build on. It made the wheels go easier. When I first started to write I used to do two or three page outlines. Afterward, I didn't.

INTERVIEWER: Do you think the kind of play you do—the well-made play, one which runs the honest risk of melodrama for a purpose—is going to survive?

HELLMAN: I don't know what survives and what doesn't. Like everybody else, I hope I will survive. But survival won't have anything to do with well-made or not well-made, or words like "melodrama." I don't like labels and -isms. They are for people who raise or lower skirts because that's the thing you do for this year. You write as you write, in your time, as you see your world. One form is as good as another. There are a thousand ways to write, and each is as good as the other if it fits you, if you are any good. If you can break into a new pattern along the way, and it opens things up, and allows you more freedom, that's something. But not everything, maybe even not much. Take any form, and if you're good—

INTERVIEWER: Do you have to do with the casting of your plays?

HELLMAN: Yes.

INTERVIEWER: Do you feel you were well served always?

HELLMAN: Sometimes, sometimes not. *Candide* and *My Mother, My Father and Me* were botched, and I helped to do the botching. You never know with failures who has done the harm. *Days to Come* was botched. The whole production was botched, including my botching. It was an absolute horror of a failure. I mean the curtain wasn't up ten minutes and catastrophe set in. It was just an awful failure. Mr. William Randolph Hearst caused a little excitement by getting up in the middle of the first act and leaving with his party of ten. I vomited in the back aisle. I did. I had to go home and change my clothes. I was drunk.

INTERVIEWER: Have you enjoyed the adaptations you have done of European plays?

HELLMAN: Sometimes, not always. I didn't like Anouilh's *The Lark* very much. But I didn't discover I didn't like it until I was halfway through. I liked *Montserrat*. I don't seem to have good luck with adaptations. I got nothing but pain out of *Candide*. That's a long story. No, I had a good time on *Candide* when I was working alone. I am not a collaborator. It was a stormy collaboration. But I had a good time alone.

INTERVIEWER: *Candide* was a box-office failure, but obviously it was a success. The record is very popular.

HELLMAN: It has become a cult show. It happens. I'm glad.

INTERVIEWER: Do you think *My Mother, My Father and Me* was a cult show?

HELLMAN: It opened during the newspaper strike, and that was fatal. Yes, I guess we were a cult show. Oddly enough, mostly with jazz musicians. The last week the audience was filled with jazz musicians. Stan Getz had come to see it and liked it, and he must have told his friends about it. I hope it will be revived because I like it. Off Broadway. I had wanted it done off Broadway in the beginning.

INTERVIEWER: Can you comment on your contemporaries— Arthur Miller?

HELLMAN: I like *Death of a Salesman*. I have reservations about it, but I thought it was an effective play. I like best *View from the Bridge*.

INTERVIEWER: *After the Fall*?

HELLMAN: So you put on a stage your ex-wife who is dead from suicide and you dress her up so nobody can mistake her. Her name is Marilyn Monroe, good at any box office, so you cash in on her, and cash in on yourself, which is maybe even worse.

INTERVIEWER: In an important subplot of this play a man who was once briefly a communist names a close friend before a congressional committee.

HELLMAN: I couldn't understand all that. Miller felt differently once upon a time, although I never much liked his House Un-American Committee testimony: a little breast-beating and a little apology. And recently I went back to reread it and liked it even less. I suppose, in the play, he was being tolerant: those who betrayed their friends had a point, those who didn't also had a point. Two sides to every question and all that rot.

INTERVIEWER: And Tennessee Williams?

HELLMAN: I think he is a natural playwright. He writes by sanded fingertips. I don't always like his plays—the last three or four seem to me to have gone off, kind of way out in a conventional way. He is throwing his talent around.

INTERVIEWER: Mary McCarthy wrote in a review that you get the feeling that no matter what happens Mr. Williams will be rich and famous.

HELLMAN: I have the same feeling about Miss McCarthy.

INTERVIEWER: She has accused you of, among other things, a

certain "lubricity," of an overfacility in answering complex questions. Being too facile, relying on contrivance.

HELLMAN: I don't like to defend myself against Miss McCarthy's opinions, or anybody else's. I think Miss McCarthy is often brilliant and sometimes even sound. But, in fiction, she is a lady writer, a lady magazine writer. Of course, that doesn't mean that she isn't right about me. But if I thought she was, I'd quit. I would like critics to like my plays because that is what makes plays successful. But a few people I respect are the only ones whose opinions I've worried about in the end.

INTERVIEWER: There is a special element in your plays—of tension rising into violence. In *Days to Come* and *Watch on the Rhine* there are killings directly on stage. Was there possibly, from your association with Dashiell Hammett and his work, some sort of influence, probably indirect, on you?

HELLMAN: I don't think so, I don't think so. Dash and I thought differently and were totally different writers. He frequently objected to my use of violence. He often felt that I was far too held up by how to do things, by the technique. I guess he was right. But he wasn't writing for the theater and I was.

INTERVIEWER: You have written a lot of movies?

HELLMAN: Let's see. I wrote a picture called *The Dark Angel* when I first started. I did the adaptation of *Dead End*. I did the adaptation of *The Little Foxes*. Right now I'm doing a picture called *The Chase*.

INTERVIEWER: Did you ever worry about Hollywood being a dead end for a serious writer?

HELLMAN: Never. I wouldn't have written movies if I'd thought that. When I first went out to Hollywood one heard talk from writers about whoring. But you are not tempted to whore unless you want to be a whore.

INTERVIEWER: The other night when we listened to Pete Seeger sing his folk songs you seemed nostalgic.

HELLMAN: I was moved by seeing a man of conviction again.

INTERVIEWER: We aren't making them like that any more?

HELLMAN: Not too many. Seeger's naïveté and the sweetness,

the hard work, the depth of belief I found touching. He reminded me of very different times and people. There were always X number of clowns, X number of simple-minded fools, X number of fashionables who just went along with what was being said and done, but there were also remarkable people, people of belief, people willing to live by their beliefs. Roosevelt gave you a feeling that you had something to do with your government, something to do with better conditions for yourself and for other people. With all its foolishness, the thirties were a good time and I often have regrets for it. Many people of my age make fun of that period, and are bitter about it. A few do so out of a genuine regret for foolish things said or foolish things done—but many do so because belief is unfashionable now and fear comes with middle age.

INTERVIEWER: Do people still mention your statement before the House Un-American Activities Committee: "I can't cut my conscience to fit this year's fashions"?

HELLMAN: Yes.

INTERVIEWER: Did that put you in contempt of Congress?

HELLMAN: No, I never was in contempt. They brought no contempt charges at the end of that day. My lawyer, Joseph Rauh, was so proud and pleased. He was afraid I would be harmed because I might have waived my rights under the Fifth Amendment.

INTERVIEWER: You took the stand that you would tell the committee all they wanted to know about you, but you weren't going to bring bad trouble upon innocent people no matter if they had been fooled?

HELLMAN: We sent a letter* saying that I would come and testify about myself as long as I wasn't asked questions about other people. But the committee wasn't interested in that. I think they knew I was innocent, but they were interested in other people. It was very common in those days, not only to talk about other people, but to make the talk as interesting as possible. Friendly

---

* Following the interview is the text of this letter. The Committee rejected the proposal contained in the letter.

witnesses, so-called, would often make their past more colorful than ever was the case. Otherwise you might turn out to be dull. I thought mine was a good position to take—I still think so.

INTERVIEWER: Was it something of a custom among theater people in those days, when they were going to name some old acquaintance to a committee, to call him beforehand and let him know? Just to be fair and square, as it were?

HELLMAN: Yes. They would telephone around among their friends. In several cases the to-be-injured people actually gave their permission. They understood the motive of their friends' betrayal—money, injury to a career. Oh, yes, there was a great deal of telephoning around. Kind of worse than testifying, isn't it?—the fraternity of the betrayers and the betrayed. There was a man in California who had been barred from pictures because he had been a communist. After a while he was broke, this Mr. Smith, and his mother-in-law, who was getting bored with him—anybody would have been bored with him—said that he could have a little piece of land. So he started to build a two-room house, and he borrowed the tools from his closest friend, his old college roommate, Mr. Jones. He had been working on his house for about seven or eight months and almost had it finished when Mr. Jones arrived to say that he had to have the tools back because, he, Mr. Jones, was being called before the committee the next day and was going to name Mr. Smith and thought it was rather unethical for Mr. Smith to have his tools while he was naming him. I don't know whether the house ever got finished. Clowns, they were.

INTERVIEWER: A little-known aspect of Lillian Hellman is that she was the inspiration for Dashiell Hammett's Nora Charles, the loyal wife of Nick Charles, the detective-hero of *The Thin Man*. That marriage is beautifully evoked in the book and was played by William Powell and Myrna Loy in the movies.

HELLMAN: Yes.

INTERVIEWER: Didn't it give you some gratification?

HELLMAN: It did, indeed.

INTERVIEWER: When Myrna Loy turned into her, then she became the perfect wife.

HELLMAN: Yes. I liked that. But Nora is often a foolish lady. She goes around trying to get Nick into trouble.

INTERVIEWER: And that was about you both?

HELLMAN: Well, Hammett and I had a good time together. Most of it, not all of it. We were amused by each other.

INTERVIEWER: Was it because of that book that Gertrude Stein invited you to dinner?

HELLMAN: Miss Stein arrived in America and said that there were two people that she wanted to meet. They were both in California at that minute—Chaplin and Dash. And we were invited to dinner at the house of a friend of Miss Stein; Charlie Chaplin, Dash and myself, Paulette Goddard, Miss Toklas, our host and hostess, and another man. There was this magnificent china and lace tablecloth. Chaplin turned over his coffee cup, nowhere near Stein, just all over this beautiful cloth, and the first thing Miss Stein said was, "Don't worry, it didn't get on me." She was miles away from him. She said it perfectly seriously. Then she told Dash he was the only American writer who wrote well about women. He was very pleased.

INTERVIEWER: Did he give you any credit for that?

HELLMAN: He pointed to me, but she didn't pay any attention. She wasn't having any part of me. I was just a girl around the table. I talked to Miss Toklas. We talked about food. It was very pleasant.

INTERVIEWER: Did you know Nathanael West?

HELLMAN: He managed a hotel, the Sutton Hotel. We all lived there half free, sometimes all free. Dash wrote *The Thin Man* at the Sutton Hotel. Pep West's uncle or cousin owned it, I think. He gave Pep a job out of kindness. There couldn't have been any other reason. Pep liked opening letters addressed to the guests. He was writing, you know, and he was curious about everything and everybody. He would steam open envelopes, and I would help him. He wanted to know about everybody.

Dash had the Royal Suite—three very small rooms. And we had to eat there most of the time because we didn't have enough money to eat any place else. It was awful food, almost spoiled.

I think Pep bought it extra cheap. But it was the depression and I couldn't get a job. I remember reading the manuscript of *Balso Snell* in the hotel. And I think he was also writing *Lonelyhearts* at that time. Dash was writing *The Thin Man*. The hotel had started out very fancy—it had a swimming pool. I spent a good deal of time in the swimming pool . . . I had nothing else to do with myself.

Then the Perelmans* bought a house in Bucks County. We all went down to see it. There was a dead fish in a closet. I don't know why I remember that fish. Later we would all go down for weekends, to hunt. I have a snapshot of the Perelmans and Dash and me and Pep and Bob Coates.

Even in a fuzzy snapshot you can see that we are all drunk. We used to go hunting. My memory of those hunting trips is of trying to be the last to climb the fence, with the other guns in front of me, just in case. Pep was a good shot. He used to hunt with Faulkner. So was Dash.

INTERVIEWER: Did Faulkner come around a lot in those days?

HELLMAN: Faulkner and Dash liked each other. Dash's short stories were selling, the movies were selling. So we had a lot of money, and he gave it away and we lived fine. Always, he gave it away—to the end of his life when there wasn't much, any more. We met every night at some point for months on end, during one of Faulkner's New York visits. We had literary discussions. A constant argument about Thomas Mann. This must have taken up weeks of time.

INTERVIEWER: Was Faulkner quiet?

HELLMAN: He was a gallant man, very Southern. He used to call me Miss Lillian. I never was to see him much after that period, until a few years ago when I saw him a couple of times. We remembered the days with Dash, and he said what a good time in his life that was and what a good time we had had together.

INTERVIEWER: Was any play easy to write?

HELLMAN: *Autumn Garden* was easier than any other.

* S. J. Perelman was West's brother-in-law.

INTERVIEWER: At the very end of the play, the retired general, Griggs, makes one of the rare speeches in your plays that is of a remotely "philosophic" nature.

HELLMAN: Dash wrote that speech. I worked on it over and over again but it never came right. One night he said, "Go to bed and let me try." Dash comes into this interview very often, doesn't he?

INTERVIEWER: "That big hour of decision, the turning point in your life, the someday you've counted on when you'd suddenly wipe out your past mistakes, do the work you'd never done, think the way you'd never thought, have what you'd never had, it just doesn't come suddenly. You trained yourself for it while you waited—or you've let it all run past you and frittered yourself away."

HELLMAN: Yes, the basic idea was his. Dash was hipped on the subject. I think I believe that speech . . . I know I do. . . . Dash worked at it far harder than I ever have, as his death proved. He wasn't prepared for death, but he was prepared for the trouble and the sickness he had, and was able to bear it—I think, because of this belief—with enormous courage, and quietness.

INTERVIEWER: What is the sensation the writer has when he hears his own words from the mouth of somebody else? Of even the most gifted actor?

HELLMAN: Sometimes you're pleased and the words take on meanings they didn't have before, larger meanings. But sometimes it is the opposite. There is no rule. I don't have to tell you that speech on the stage is not the speech of life, not even the written speech.

INTERVIEWER: But do you hear dialogue spoken when you are writing it?

HELLMAN: I guess I do. Anyway, I read it to myself. I usually know in the first few days of rehearsals what I have made actors stumble over, and what can or cannot be cured.

INTERVIEWER: Do you have disputes with actors who want their lines changed?

HELLMAN: Not too many. I took a stubborn stand on the first play and now I have a reputation for stubbornness.

INTERVIEWER: Is that because you have written always to be read, even more than to be acted?

HELLMAN: Partly. But I had learned early that in the theater, good or bad, you'd better stand on what you did. In *Candide* I was persuaded to do what I didn't believe in, and I am no good at all at that game. It wasn't that the other people were necessarily wrong, I just couldn't do what they wanted. With age, I guess, I began to want to be agreeable.

INTERVIEWER: Would you mind if your plays were never produced again but only read?

HELLMAN: I wouldn't like it. Plays are there to be acted. I want both.

INTERVIEWER: The famous Hemingway dialogue, the best of it, turns to parody when actors speak it verbatim in adaptations of his work.

HELLMAN: That's right. It shows up, it shows up. That's just what I meant by listening to the actor. Writing for the theater is a totally different form. But then, if you want to be good and hope people will also read the plays, then it becomes a question of making sure the two forms come together. Very often in the printed form, you must recast a sentence. I do it—when I'm not too lazy—for the published version. But in minor ways, like changing the place of a verb, or punctuation. I overpunctuate for theater scripts.

INTERVIEWER: Do you think the political message in some of your plays is more important than the characters and the development?

HELLMAN: I've never been interested in political messages, so it is hard for me to believe I wrote them. Like every other writer, I use myself and the time I live in. The nearest thing to a political play was *The Searching Wind*, which is probably why I don't like it much any more. But even there I meant only to write about nice, well-born people who, with good intentions, helped to sell out a world.

INTERVIEWER: Maybe this was one play in which you were more concerned with a situation of crisis than with your characters?

HELLMAN: Yes. But I didn't know that when I was writing it. I felt very strongly that people had gotten us into a bad situation—gotten us into a war that could have been avoided if fascism had been recognized early enough.

INTERVIEWER: What were you doing in those war years?

HELLMAN: In 1944 I was invited by the Russians to come on a kind of cultural mission. Maybe because they were producing *Watch on the Rhine* and *The Little Foxes* in Moscow.

INTERVIEWER: What were those productions like?

HELLMAN: *The Little Foxes* was an excellent production. *Watch on the Rhine* was very bad. I had thought it would be the other way around. I would go to rehearsals of *Watch on the Rhine* with Serge Eisenstein, and when I made faces or noises, he would say, "Never mind, never mind. It's a good play. Don't pay any attention to what they are doing. They can't ruin it." I saw a great deal of Eisenstein. I was very fond of him.

INTERVIEWER: When did you discover that you could no longer earn money by writing for the movies?

HELLMAN: I learned about the black-listing by accident in 1948. Wyler and I were going to do *Sister Carrie*. Somebody, I think Mr. Balaban, told Wyler that I couldn't be hired. That unwritten, unofficial, powerful black list stayed in effect until two or three years ago.

INTERVIEWER: Weren't you offered clearance if you would sign something? If you made an appropriate act of contrition?

HELLMAN: Later. Shortly after the first black-listing I was offered a contract by Columbia Pictures—a contract that I had always wanted—to direct, produce, and write, all three or any. And a great, great deal of money. But it came at the time of the famous movie conference of top Hollywood producers. They met to face the attacks of the Red-baiters and to appease them down. A new clause went into movie contracts. I no longer remember the legal phrases, but it was a lulu. I didn't sign the contract.

INTERVIEWER: What did you think about what was happening?

HELLMAN: I was so unprepared for it all, so surprised McCarthy was happening in America. So few people fought, so few people spoke out. I think I was more surprised by that than I was by McCarthy.

INTERVIEWER: People in the theater or pictures?

HELLMAN: Yes, and literary people and liberals. Still painful to me, still puzzling. Recently I was asked to sign a protest about Polish writers. I signed it—it was a good protest, I thought—and went out to mail it. But I tore it up when I realized not one of the people protesting had ever protested about any of us.

INTERVIEWER: What did you think was going to happen?

HELLMAN: I thought McCarthy would last longer than he did. I thought the whole period would be worse and longer than it was. You know, I was very worried about Dash. He was a sick man and I was scared that he might go back to prison and get sicker—I lived for a long time in fear that he would go back and not get good medical treatment and be alone and— But jail hadn't worried him much or he pretended it hadn't. It amused him to act as if jail was like college. He talked about going to jail the way people talk about going to college. He used to make me angry. . . .

INTERVIEWER: *The Maltese Falcon* was taken off the shelves of the U.S.I.S. libraries when Roy Cohn and David Schine were riding high. Dashiell Hammett was called before Senator McCarthy's committee.

HELLMAN: Yes. It was on television and I watched it. They called Dash, and Dash was a handsome man, a remarkably handsome man, and he looked nice. One of the senators, I think McCarthy, said to him, "Mr. Hammett, if you were in our position, would you allow your books in U.S.I.S. libraries?" And he said, "If I were you, Senator, I would not allow any libraries." A good remark. McCarthy laughed. Nobody else did, but McCarthy did. Dash had an extremely irritating habit of shrugging his shoulders. For years I would say, "Please don't shrug your shoulders." I don't know why it worried me, but it did. He was shrugging his shoulders like mad at the committee. He'd give an answer, and he'd shrug his shoulders with it. And when he was finished and got to the airport he rang me up and said, "Hey, how did you like it? I was shrugging my shoulders just for you."

INTERVIEWER: Did that period—and its effect on people—appeal to you as a subject?

HELLMAN: I've never known how to do it. It was really a clownish period. It was full of clowns talking their heads off, apologizing, inventing sins to apologize for. And other clowns, liberals, who just took to the hills. Ugly clowning is a hard thing to write about. Few people acted large enough for drama and not pleasant enough for comedy.

INTERVIEWER: Then you went to England to do a movie?

HELLMAN: I used to try to explain that it wasn't as bad as they thought it was. And it wasn't. They were exaggerating it because they don't always like us very much. So much talk about fascism here and how many people were in jail. The only time I ever met Richard Crossman, he didn't know I knew Hammett. Hammett was in jail, and Crossman said what a disgrace that was. "What's the matter with all of you, you don't lift a finger for this man? It couldn't happen here, we'd have raised a row." I told him I had lifted a finger.

INTERVIEWER: Did you ever think of living abroad as other Americans were doing?

HELLMAN: I was tempted to stay in England, but I couldn't. I like this country. This is where I belong. Anyway, I don't much like exiles. But I used to try to persuade Dash to go away, just to save his life. He had emphysema. He caught tuberculosis in the First World War and emphysema in the Second. He had never been to Europe. He used to laugh when I suggested his leaving here. He had a provincial dislike of foreigners, and an amused contempt for Russian bureaucracy. He didn't understand all of our trotting around Europe. Thought it was a waste of time.

INTERVIEWER: Did he laugh at the idea that they admired him over there?

HELLMAN: No. He liked it but it didn't interest him much. When I told him that André Gide admired him, he made a joke which you can't print.

INTERVIEWER: Let's be bold.

HELLMAN: All right. He said, "I wish that fag would take me out of his mouth."

INTERVIEWER: Whom did he want to admire his work?

HELLMAN: Like most writers he wanted to be admired by good writers. He had started off as a pulp writer, you know, and had a wide audience—he wrote a lot for a pulp mystery magazine, *The Black Mask*. But I believe Dash took himself very seriously as a writer from the beginning.

INTERVIEWER: He helped you with your work. Did you help him with his?

HELLMAN: No, no.

INTERVIEWER: Did he show you his novels while he was writing them?

HELLMAN: *The Thin Man* and some stories, and a novel unfinished at his death. The other novels were written before I met him.

INTERVIEWER: But he worked very painstakingly with you, on your work.

HELLMAN: Oh, yes, and was very critical of me. The rules didn't apply the other way. I had many problems writing *The Little Foxes*. When I thought I had got it right, I wanted Dash to read it. It was five o'clock in the morning. I was pleased with this sixth version, and I put the manuscript near his door with a note, "I hope *this* satisfies you." When I got up, the manuscript was outside my door with a note saying, "Things are going pretty well if you will just cut out the liberal blackamoor chitchat."

INTERVIEWER: He meant the Negro servants talking?

HELLMAN: Yes. No other praise, just that.

INTERVIEWER: So you knew you were all right?

HELLMAN: No, I wrote it all over again. He was generous with anybody who asked for help. He felt that you didn't lie about writing and anybody who couldn't take hard words was about to be shrugged off, anyway. He was a dedicated man about writing. Tough and generous.

INTERVIEWER: Was he always reasonably successful?

HELLMAN: Oh, no. He earned a kind of living at first, but pulp magazines didn't pay much. He was not really discovered until shortly before I met him, in 1930. He had been writing for a long time.

INTERVIEWER: He read constantly?

HELLMAN: Enormously. He had little formal education. He quit school at thirteen to work. He was the most widely read person I ever knew. He read anything, just anything. All kinds of science books, farm books, books on making turtle traps, tying knots, novels—he spent almost a year on the retina of the eye. I got very tired of retinas. And there was a period of poisonous plants and Icelandic sagas and how to take the muddy taste from lake bass. I finally made a rule that I would not listen to any more retina-of-the-eye talk or knot talk or baseball talk or football talk.

INTERVIEWER: Do you consider yourself to be closely tied to the theater and to "theater people"?

HELLMAN: In the early days I didn't think it out, but I stayed away from them. I was frightened of competing. I felt that the further I stayed away, the better chance I had. No, I don't know too many theater people.

INTERVIEWER: A man who has known both breeds said that on the whole writers are even more narcissistic and nastier and more competitive than people in show biz.

HELLMAN: Hard to know the more or less. But people in the theater are usually generous with money and often with good will. Maybe the old-troupers world—having to live together and sharing. Writers are interesting people, but often mean and petty. Competing with each other and ungenerous about each other. Hemingway was ungenerous about other writers. Most writers are. Writers can be the stinkers of all time, can't they?

INTERVIEWER: The playwright knows dangers that are different from those the novelists know?

HELLMAN: Yes, because failure is faster in the theater. It is necessary that you not become frightened of failure. Failure in the theater is more dramatic and uglier than in any other form of writing. It costs so much, you feel so guilty. In the production of *Candide*, for the first time in my life, I guess, I was worried by all this. It was bad for me.

INTERVIEWER: Writing about the Lincoln Center Repertory in the *New York Review of Books,* Elizabeth Hardwick said that the trouble with the present theater is that it is all professionalism and is divorced from literature.

HELLMAN: Yes, of course she was right. There shouldn't be any difference between writing for the theater and writing for anything else. Only that one has to know the theater. Know it. To publish a novel or a poem one doesn't have to know print types or the publishing world. But to do a play, no matter how much one wishes to stay away from it, one has to *know* the theater. Playwrights have tried to stay away, including Shaw and Chekhov, but in the end, they were involved. Chekhov used to send letters of instructions and angry notes. A play is not only on paper. It is there to share with actors, directors, scene designers, electricians.

INTERVIEWER: Do you believe there are many talented writers working at present?

HELLMAN: Yes, but nothing like the period when I was very young, in the twenties. That was a wonderfully talented generation, the one before mine. But, you know, I think there's talent around now. Maybe not great talent, but how often does that occur anyway? It is good that we have this much. And there are signs now of cutting up. They are not always to my taste, but that doesn't matter. Cutting up is a form of belief, a negative expression of it, but belief.

INTERVIEWER: The hard professionalism in writers of that generation, like Ring Lardner, Dashiell Hammett, or Dorothy Parker, seems very unfashionable now. Young writers take themselves very seriously as highbrows and artists.

HELLMAN: The writer's intention hasn't anything to do with what he achieves. The intent to earn money or the intent to be famous or the intent to be great doesn't matter in the end. Just what comes out. It is a present fashion to believe that the best writing comes out of a hophead's dream. You pitch it around and paste it up. So sentimental.

INTERVIEWER: Sentimental or romantic?

HELLMAN: Romantic and sentimental. I am surprised, for example, at the sentimentality in much of Genet, and surprised that people are romantic enough not to see its sentimentality. I mean a sentimental way of looking at life, at sex, at love, at the way you live or the way you think. It is interesting that the "way-out" is not the sharpness of a point of view or the toughness, but just tough words and tough actions, masking the romantic. Violence, in space, is a romantic notion. Antibourgeois in an old-fashioned sense.

INTERVIEWER: Philip Rahv said the old idea of *épatisme* is dead. You can no longer scandalize the bourgeois. He may be vicious about defending his property; but as to morality, he is wide open to any and all nihilistic ideas.

HELLMAN: Yes, indeed. He has caught up. That is what words like "the sexual revolution" mean, I guess—the bourgeois sexual revolution. I agree with Philip. "Epataying" is just a sticking out of the tongue now, isn't it? The tongue or other organs.

INTERVIEWER: You have seen a lot of the contemporary theater in Europe. How does it compare with ours?

HELLMAN: The British have more talented young men and women than we have here, but I doubt if they are major talents. Genet and Ionesco are interesting men, but they are not to my taste in the theater. Beckett is the only possibly first-rate talent in the world theater. But he must grow larger, the scale's too small. We don't know much about the Russian theater. Obviously, it hasn't produced good playwrights. Certainly not when I was there. But Russian production, directing, and acting are often wonderful. But that's a dead end. When the major talents are directors, actors, and scene designers—that's dead-end theater. Fine to see, but it ain't going nowhere. You have to turn out good new writers.

INTERVIEWER: What about the revival of Brecht?

HELLMAN: Brecht was the truest talent of the last forty or fifty years. But a great deal of nonsense has been written about Brecht. Brecht himself talked a great deal of nonsense. Deliberately, I think. He was a showman and it is showman-like in the theater to have theories. But that doesn't matter. What a wonderful play *Galileo* is. Writers talk too much.

INTERVIEWER: What do you want to do next?

HELLMAN: I am going to edit that anthology. I had a struggle with myself because Dash would not have wanted it. He didn't want the short stories printed again. But I decided that I was going to have to forget what he wanted. Someday even the second copyrights will expire and the stories will be in public domain. I don't really know why he didn't want them reprinted—maybe because he was too sick to care. It will be a hard job. I have already started the introduction and I find it very difficult to write about so complex a man, and even I knew so little of what he was. I am not sure I can do it in the end, but I am going to have a try. But I don't know his reasons. Probably when you're sick enough you don't care much. He went through a bad time.

—JOHN PHILLIPS
—ANNE HOLLANDER
1965

May 19, 1952

Honorable John S. Wood
Chairman
House Committee on Un-American Activities

Dear Mr. Wood:

As you know, I am under subpoena to appear before your Committee on May 21, 1952.

I am most willing to answer all questions about myself. I have nothing to hide from your Committee and there is nothing in my life of which I am ashamed. I have been advised by counsel that under the Fifth Amendment I have a constitutional privilege to decline to answer any questions about my political opinions, activities and associations, on the grounds of self-incrimination. I do not wish to claim this privilege. I am ready and willing to testify before representatives of our Government as to my own opinions and my own actions, regardless of any risks or consequences to myself.

But I am advised by counsel that if I answer the Committee's questions about myself, I must also answer questions about other people and that if I refuse to do so, I can be cited for contempt. My counsel tells me that if I answer questions about myself, I will have waived my rights under the Fifth Amendment and could be forced legally to answer questions about others. This is very difficult for a layman to understand. But there is one principle that I do understand: I am not willing, now or in the future, to bring bad trouble to people who, in my past association with them, were completely innocent of any talk or any action that was disloyal or subversive. . . .

But to hurt innocent people whom I know many years ago in order to save myself is, to me, inhuman and indecent and dishonorable. I cannot and will not cut my conscience to fit this year's fashions, even though I long ago came to the conclusion that I was not a political person and could have no comfortable place in any political group. . . .

I am prepared to waive the privilege against self-incrimination and to tell you anything you wish to know about my views or actions if your Committee will agree to refrain from asking me to name other people. If the Committee is unwilling to give me this assurance, I will be forced to plead the privilege of the Fifth Amendment at the hearing.

A reply to this letter would be appreciated.

Sincerely yours,
LILLIAN HELLMAN

7. Eudora Welty

Eudora Welty has lived almost all of her life in Jackson, Mississippi, where she was born in 1909. She attended Mississippi State College for Women for two years and received her A.B. from the University of Wisconsin in 1929. After a year at the Columbia School of Advertising, she returned to Jackson in 1932 to pursue her writing. Since then she has departed only for a rare visit to Europe, an annual trip to New York, and an occasional reading at a college.

The short story has always been her forte, although she has written a number of novels: *The Robber Bridegroom* (1942), *Delta Wedding* (1946), *The Ponder Heart* (1954), *Losing Battles* (1970), and *The Optimist's Daughter* (1972), which won the Pulitzer Prize.

Her first published story, "Death of a Traveling Salesman," appeared in 1936 in *Manuscript*, an obscure quarterly. During the next five years she was published in many distinguished periodicals, most frequently in *The Southern Review*. Her first collection of stories, *A Curtain of Green*, did not appear until 1941. It was followed by three more collections: *The Wide Net* (1943), *The Golden Apples* (1949), and *The Bride of Innisfallen* (1955). She has also written a children's book, *The Shoe Bird* (1964), and published a collection of photographs, *One Time, One Place* (1971). Her first work of nonfiction, *The Eye of the Story: Selected Essays and Reviews*, appeared in 1978, and *One Writer's Beginnings*, her autobiography, was published in 1984. In all her work, her scene has been the South.

Miss Welty was recipient of the Creative Arts Medal for Fiction at Brandeis University, 1966. She is a member of the National Institute of Arts and Letters and has since 1958 been an honorary consultant in American letters of the Library of Congress. She has been awarded the National Medal for Literature, the National Institute of Arts and Letters' Gold Medal, and the Modern Language Association's Commonwealth Award.

"Bywy River, my father killed his last bear. Blessed old

Dragged her home,
sow / Laid her adross ~~the~~ doorstep."

"Granny! Did you ever have a _father_? And _mother_?" cried.

Elvie.

"Mama said, 'Take that back where you found it, Mr. Blaikie.

You're nothing but bragging now,'" said Granny.

~~"What when, Granny about Elvie pleaded~~

~~"Was you ~~~~ Elvie pleaded to know~~

"Was you _born_?" Elvie pleaded to know. "Granny!

Like Lady May?"

"Granny'd like _her_ picture taken!" Aunt Beck divined. "Ninety

today!"

"With all of us!" cried Aunt Birdie. "A picture with Granny

in the middle. Haul her out here in the broil, see what you can

get, Sister Cleo!"

Miss Beulah was summoned, and stood at center back, the ~~Beecham~~

Beechum   (The men squatted or reclined on the ground.
~~and~~ wives lined up at her sides. ⟩Granny sat composed in the cen-

ter, and for the only time that day drew the pipe from her pocket,

in order to pose with it cocked in her mouth. ~~Then~~ The aunts as

one dropped their hands before them, as if called to the door in

their aprons. ~~But~~ ~~as Aunt Nannie, her heart began was like~~

~~sleeved arms~~ ~~were folded across it~~ ~~front.~~

Has Cleo a
world? or are
they only
picking?

© Jill Krementz

Eudora Welty

During Eudora Welty's brief stay in New York, we met in her room at the Algonquin Hotel an hour or so after her train had arrived in Penn Station. She had given me the wrong room number, so I first saw her peering out of her door as the elevator opened. A tall, large-boned, gray-haired woman greeted me apologetically. She was admittedly nervous about being interviewed, particularly on a tape recorder. After describing her train ride—she won't fly— she braced herself and asked if I wouldn't begin the questioning.

Once the interview (which appeared in the 1972 Fall issue of The Paris Review) got under way, she grew more at ease. As she herself might say, she was not "unforthcoming." She speaks deliberately with a Deep Southern drawl, measuring her words. She is extremely private and won't answer anything personal about herself or about friends.

INTERVIEWER: You wrote somewhere that we should still tolerate Jane Austen's kind of family novel. Is Austen a kindred spirit?

WELTY: *Tolerate*? I should just think so! I love and admire all she does, and profoundly, but I don't read her or anyone else for "kindredness." The piece you're referring to was written on assignment for *Brief Lives*, an anthology Louis Kronenberger was editing. He did offer me either Jane Austen or Chekhov, and Chekhov I do dare to think is more "kindred." I feel closer to him in spirit, but I couldn't read Russian, which I felt whoever wrote about him should be able to do. Chekhov is one of us—so close to today's world, to my mind, and very close to the South—which Stark Young pointed out a long time ago.

INTERVIEWER: Why is Chekhov close to today's South?

WELTY: He loved the singularity in people, the individuality. He took for granted the sense of family. He had the sense of fate overtaking a way of life, and his Russian humor seems to me kin to the humor of a Southerner. It's the kind that lies mostly in character. You know, in *Uncle Vanya* and *The Cherry Orchard*, how people are always gathered together and talking and talking, no one's really listening. Yet there's a great love and understanding that prevails through it, and a knowledge and acceptance of each other's idiosyncracies, a tolerance of them, and also an acute enjoyment of the dramatic. Like in *The Three Sisters*, when the fire is going on, how they talk right on through their exhaustion, and Vershinin says, "I feel a strange excitement in the air," and laughs and sings and talks about the future. That kind of responsiveness to the world, to whatever happens, out of their own deeps of character seems very Southern to me. Anyway, I took a temperamental delight in Chekhov, and gradually the connection was borne in upon me.

INTERVIEWER: Do you ever return to Virginia Woolf?

WELTY: Yes. She was the one who opened the door. When I read *To the Lighthouse*, I felt, Heavens, *what is this*? I was so excited by the experience I couldn't sleep or eat. I've read it many times since, though more often these days I go back to her diary. Any day you open it to will be tragic, and yet all the marvelous things she says about her work, about working, leave you filled with joy that's stronger than your misery for her. Remember— "I'm not very far along, but I think I have my statues against the sky"? Isn't that beautiful?

INTERVIEWER: About your own work, are you surprised that *Losing Battles* was on the best-seller list—a first for you, I believe?

WELTY: It occurred to me right at first it must be a fluke—that whoever had that place on the best-seller list had just got up and given me his seat—let the lady sit down, she's tottering. Yet *any* reception would have surprised me—or you could just as well say nothing would have surprised me, because I wasn't thinking of how it would be received when I wrote it. I thought about the opinion of a handful of friends I would love to have love that book, but not about the public.

INTERVIEWER: Do you write for your friends?

WELTY: At the time of writing, I don't write for my friends or myself, either; I write for *it*, for the pleasure of *it*. I believe if I stopped to wonder what So-and-so would think, or what I'd feel like if this were read by a stranger, I would be paralyzed. I care what my friends think, very deeply—and it's only after they've read the finished thing that I really can rest, deep down. But in the writing, I have to just keep going straight through with only the *thing* in mind and what it dictates.

It's so much an inward thing that reading the proofs later can be a real shock. When I received them for my first book—no, I guess it was for *Delta Wedding*—I thought, *I* didn't write this. It was a page of dialogue—I might as well have never seen it before. I wrote to my editor, John Woodburn, and told him something had happened to that page in the typesetting. He was kind, not even surprised—maybe this happens to all writers. He called me up and read me from the manuscript—word for word what the proofs said. Proofs don't shock me any longer, yet there's still a strange moment with every book when I move from the position of writer to the position of reader, and I suddenly see my words with the eyes of the cold public. It gives me a terrible sense of exposure, as if I'd gotten sunburned.

INTERVIEWER: Do you make changes in galleys?

WELTY: I correct or change words, but I can't rewrite a scene or make a major change because there's a sense then of someone looking over my shoulder. It's necessary, anyway, to trust that moment when you were sure at last you had done all you could, done your best for that time. When it's finally in print, you're delivered—you don't ever have to look at it again. It's too late to worry about its failings. I'll have to apply any lessons this book has taught me toward writing the next one.

INTERVIEWER: Is *Losing Battles* a departure from your previous fiction?

WELTY: I wanted to see if I could do something that was new for me: translating every thought and feeling into action and speech, speech being another form of action—to bring the whole life of it off through the completed gesture, so to speak. I felt that I'd been writing too much by way of description, of introspection on the part of my characters. I tried to see if I could make everything shown, brought forth, without benefit of the author's telling any more about what was going on inside the characters' minds and hearts. For me, this makes almost certainly for comedy—which I love to write best of all. Now I see it might be a transition toward writing a play.

INTERVIEWER: Did you know what you were going to write before you put it on paper?

WELTY: Yes, it was there in my head, but events proliferated as I went along. For instance, I thought all the action in the novel would be contained in one day and night, but a folder started to fill up with things marked "Next A.M." I didn't foresee the stories that grew out of the stories—that was one of the joys of working the novel out. I thought the book would be short, and instead it was three or four times longer than my normal work. There's no way of estimating its original length because I had great chunks of things in paper clips which weren't numbered until they went to the printer. And I must have thrown away at least as much as I kept in the book.

INTERVIEWER: Did you learn anything new about writing dialogue?

WELTY: I believe so. In its beginning, dialogue's the easiest thing in the world to write when you have a good ear, which I think I have. But as it goes on, it's the most difficult, because it has so many ways to function. Sometimes I needed to make a speech do three or four or five things at once—reveal what the character said but also what he thought he said, what he hid, what others were going to think he meant, and what they mis-understood, and so forth—all in his single speech. And the speech would have to keep the essence of this one character, his whole particular outlook in concentrated form. This isn't to say I suc-ceeded. But I guess it explains why dialogue gives me my greatest pleasure in writing. I used to laugh out loud sometimes when I wrote it—the way P. G. Wodehouse is said to do. I'd think of some things my characters would say, and even if I couldn't use it, I would write the scene out just to let them loose on some-thing—my private show.

INTERVIEWER: Where does the dialogue come from?

WELTY: Familiarity. Memory of the way things get said. Once you have heard certain expressions, sentences, you almost never forget them. It's like sending a bucket down the well and it always comes up full. You don't know you've remembered, but you have. And you listen for the right word, in the present, and you hear it. Once you're into a story everything seems to apply—what you overhear on a city bus is exactly what your character would say on the page you're writing. Wherever you go, you meet part of your story. I guess you're tuned in for it, and the right things are sort of magnetized—if you can think of your ears as magnets. I could hear someone saying—and I had to cut this out—"What, you never ate goat?" And someone answering, "Goat! Please don't say you serve *goat* at this reunion. I wasn't told it was *goat* I was served. I thought—" and so on, and then the recipe, and then it ended up with—I can't remember exactly now—it ended with, "You can do a whole lot of things with vinegar." Well, all these things I would just laugh about and think about for so long and put them in. And then I'd think, that's just plain indulgence. Take it out! And I'd take it out.

INTERVIEWER: Are you an eavesdropper?

WELTY: I'm not as much as I used to be, or would like to be, because I don't hear as well as I used to, or there's too much other noise everywhere. But I've heard some wonderful remarks. Well, in the South, everybody stays busy talking all the time—they're not sorry for you to overhear their tales. I don't feel in helping myself I ever did anything underhanded. I was *helping out*.

INTERVIEWER: Do you think this oral tradition, so to speak, accounts for your vigorous use of dialogue?

WELTY: I think it accounts for the pleasure people take in a story told. It's a treasure I helped myself to. I took it for my ways and means, and that's proper and justified: Our people talk that way. They learn and teach and think and enjoy that way. Southerners do have, they've inherited, a narrative sense of human destiny. This may or may not come out in *Losing Battles*. A reunion is everybody remembering together—remembering and relating when their people were born and what happened in their lives, what that made happen to their children, and how it was that they died. There's someone to remember a man's whole life, every bit of the way along. I think that's a marvelous thing, and I'm glad I got to know something of it. In New York you may have the greatest and most congenial friends, but it's extraordinary if you ever know anything about them except that little wedge of their life that you meet with the little wedge of your life. You don't get that sense of a continuous narrative line. You never see the full circle. But in the South, where people don't move about as much, even now, and where they once hardly ever moved away at all, the pattern of life was always right there.

INTERVIEWER: Would you say that Southerners—Deep Southerners—are more open than Northerners?

WELTY: I think we have a sort of language we all understand and speak—a shorthand of some kind, based on familiarity—but I'm not sure we're more open. We may not tell as much as we think we do, and we may not hide as much as we think we do. We're just more used to talking—as you can see—and the subject doesn't especially cut us down.

INTERVIEWER: And that profoundly affects your fiction?

WELTY: I think that's what gives a pattern to it, and a sense of its shape to me. I do want to say that I'm only speaking for myself when I speak of Southern qualities, because I don't know how other people work. It may be entirely different, especially with a genius like William Faulkner, who had such a comprehensive sense of the whole deep, deep past and more far-reaching, bred-in country knowledge than I have, which is so valuable, besides all the rest of his equipment that I don't need to tell you about.

INTERVIEWER: Did you know Faulkner?

WELTY: Slightly and over a long period of time, but not well. I liked him ever so much. We met at a dinner party in Oxford, just old friends of his and old friends of mine, which was the right way for it to happen, and it was just grand. We sang hymns, and we sang some old ballads—and the next day he invited me to go sailing. If we ever met in New York, we just talked about being in Oxford. *He* didn't bring up writing, and if he didn't, you know *I* wasn't going to bring it up! But when he was working in Hollywood, he once wrote me a two-line letter—this was long before we met—and told me he liked a little book of mine called *The Robber Bridegroom* and said would I let him know if he could ever do anything for me. It was on a little piece of notebook paper, written in that fine, neat, sort of unreadable hand, in pencil—and I've lost it.

INTERVIEWER: Did you feel at all influenced by his presence?

WELTY: I don't honestly think so. It is hard to be sure about such things. I was naturally in the deepest awe and reverence of him. But that's no help in your own writing. Nobody can help you but yourself. So often I'm asked how I could have written a word with William Faulkner living in Mississippi, and this question amazes me. It was like living near a big mountain, something majestic—it made me happy to know it was there, all that work of his life. But it wasn't a helping or hindering presence. Its magnitude, all by itself, made it something remote in my own working life. When I thought of Faulkner it was when I *read*.

On the other hand, he didn't seem remote to everybody in being our great writer. I know a story about him, though he never knew anybody knew of it, I'd bet. Mississippi is full of writers, and I heard this from the person it was told to. A lady had decided she'd write a novel and got along fine till she came to the love scene. "So," she told my friend, "I thought, there's William Faulkner, sitting right up there in Oxford. Why not send it to William Faulkner and ask him?" So she sent it to him, and time went by, and she didn't ever hear from him, and so she called him up. Because there he was. She said, "Mr. Faulkner, did you ever get that love scene I sent you?" He said yes, he had got it. And she said, "Well, what did you think of it?" And he said, "Well, honey, it's not the way I'd do it—but you go *right ahead*." Now, wasn't that gentle of him?

INTERVIEWER: Do people give you unpublished manuscripts to read? I mean, women especially tend to write voluminous historical novels, and I wonder if any of them are in Jackson.

WELTY: I wouldn't be surprised. I don't think there's any neck of the woods they're not in. Yes, I get sent manuscripts, but those historical and Gothic novels are really a subject on which I know nothing, and I say so. There is, in point of fact, a good deal of writing talent in general around our state now—a lot of good young ones, serious ones.

INTERVIEWER: Did you ever feel part of a literary community, along with people like Flannery O'Connor, Carson McCullers, Katherine Anne Porter, or Caroline Gordon?

WELTY: I'm not sure there's any dotted line connecting us up, though all of us knew about each other, and all of us, I think, respected and read each other's work and understood it. And some of us are friends of long standing. I don't think there was any passing about of influences, but there's a lot of pleasure in thinking in whose lifetimes your own lifetime has happened to come along. Of course, Katherine Anne Porter was wonderfully generous to me from the beginning. At the time I began sending my first stories to *The Southern Review*, she read them and wrote to me from Baton Rouge inviting me to come down to see her. It took me, I suppose, six months or a year to fully get up my nerve. Twice I got as far as Natchez and turned around and came back. But I finally did get there, and Katherine Anne couldn't have been more welcoming. Later on, she wrote the introduction to my first book of stories, and I owe her very much for that. We've been friends all these years.

INTERVIEWER: How would you feel about a biography about yourself?

WELTY: Shy, and discouraged at the very thought, because to me a writer's work should be everything. A writer's whole feeling, the force of his whole life, can go into a story—but what he's worked for is to get an objective piece down on paper. That should be read instead of some account of his life, with that understanding—here is something which now exists and was made by the hands of this person. Read it for what it is. It doesn't even matter too much whose hands they were. Well, of course, it does—I was just exaggerating to prove my point. But your private life should be kept private. My own I don't think would particularly interest anybody, for that matter. But I'd guard it; I feel strongly about that. They'd have a hard time trying to find something about me. I think I'd better burn everything up. It's best to burn letters, but at least I've never kept diaries or journals. All my manuscripts I've given to the Department of Archives and History in Jackson as they came out because that's my hometown and the director is a lifelong friend. But I don't give them everything. I must have a trunk full of stuff that I didn't give because I didn't think it was anybody's else's concern, or that anybody would even care to see my mistakes and false turns. Like about eating goat and all the million things that I left out.

INTERVIEWER: Why do *Losing Battles* and *Delta Wedding* take place back in the 1920s and 1930s?

WELTY: It was a matter of setting the stage and confining the story. These are both family stories, and I didn't want them inhibited by outward events I couldn't control. In the case of *Delta Wedding*, I remember I made a careful investigation to find the year in which nothing very terrible had happened in the Delta by way of floods or fires or wars which would have taken the men away. I settled it by the almanac. It was a little inconvenient for me because I myself was only a little girl during the era I was writing about—that's why I let a little girl be the observer of part of it. In the case of *Losing Battles*, I wanted to write about a family who had *nothing*. A bare stage. I chose the time that was the very hardest, when people had the least and the stage could be the barest—and that was the Depression, of course.

INTERVIEWER: Do you prefer working with a bare stage?

WELTY: In this case, it was in order to overcrowd it with people. I start with ideas about character and situation, and the technique grows out of these as I grow into the work. It's different, of course, for every story. In *Losing Battles* I wanted to write about people who had nothing at all and yet had all the resources of their own character and situation to do what they could about their lives.

INTERVIEWER: Were you familiar with plantation life when you wrote *Delta Wedding*?

WELTY: No, but I had some friends who came from there, and I used to hear their stories, and I'd be taken on picnics and visits there. Family visits. The Delta is very rich and visually striking, but completely flat. I would find it maddening after days with nothing but the horizon. Just before you reach it, there are high bluffs, and to get in you plunge down a deep hill, and from then on there's nothing but flatness. Some of the things I saw and heard began to stick. Some family tales and sayings are right in the book, though by now I can't remember which are true and which are made up.

INTERVIEWER: John Crowe Ransom wrote in a review that *Delta Wedding* might well be "one of the last novels in the tradition of the Old South."

WELTY: I revere Mr. Ransom, but his meaning here is not quite clear to me. I wasn't trying to write a novel of the Old South. I don't think of myself as writing out of any special tradition, and I'd hesitate to accept that sanction for *Delta Wedding*. I'd hesitate still more today because the term itself, "Old South," has a connotation of something unreal and not quite straightforward.

INTERVIEWER: Your parents weren't from the Deep South originally. Do you think that contributed to your ironic perspective?

WELTY: It may have given me balance. But other factors mattered more. My father's father owned a farm in Southern Ohio, and my mother's father was a country lawyer and farmer in West Virginia, and both my mother's parents came from Virginia families made up mostly of teachers and preachers. Some of these wrote for newspapers or kept journals, though none wrote fiction. But the family influence I felt came from the important fact that they all loved to read and that I was brought up with books. Yet my parents would have been the people they were, people of character, no matter where they were from, and I would have been their child wherever I was born. I'm a native Southerner, but as a writer I think background matters most in how well it teaches you to look around and see clearly what's there and in how deeply it nourishes your imagination.

INTERVIEWER: "Where is the Voice Coming From?" is about the Medgar Evers assassination and must be your only topical story.

WELTY: I'm certain it is. It pushed up through something else I was working on. I had been having a feeling of uneasiness over the things being written about the South at that time because most of them were done in other parts of the country, and I thought most were synthetic. They were perfectly well-intentioned stories but generalities written from a distance to illustrate generalities. When that murder was committed, it suddenly crossed my consciousness that I knew what was in that man's mind because I'd lived all my life where it happened. It was the strangest feeling of horror and compulsion all in one. I tried to write from the interior of my own South, and that's why I dared to put it in the first person. The title isn't very good; I'd like to get a better one. At the time I wrote it—it was overnight—no one knew who the murderer was, and I just meant by the title that whoever was speaking, I—the writer—knew, was in a position to know, what the murderer must be saying and why.

INTERVIEWER: Do real events hinder you in writing?

WELTY: Well, if you write about an actual event, you can't shape it the way you can an imaginary one. In "The Voice" I was writing about the real thing, and at the point of its happening. I was like a real-life detective trying to discover who did it. I don't mean the name of the murderer but his *nature*. That's not really a short-story writer's prerogative, or is it? Anyway, as events went to prove, I think I came close to pinpointing the mind, but I went a bit wide of the mark in placing the social background of the person arrested for it. As a friend of mine said, "You thought it was a Snopes, and it was a Compson." However, in some ways, that isn't a very lasting distinction any more.

INTERVIEWER: Do you see a difference between your early stories in *A Curtain of Green* and *The Wide Net* where you deal more with the grotesque and grim than you do in *The Bride of the Innisfallen*?

WELTY: It's a difference not really in subject matter so much as in the ways I approached it. In those early stories I'm sure I needed the device of what you call the "grotesque." That is, I hoped to differentiate characters by their physical qualities as a way of showing what they were like inside—it seemed to me then the most direct way to do it. This is an afterthought, though. I don't suppose I did it as consciously as all that, and I didn't know it was the easiest way. But it is easier to show somebody as lonely if you make him deaf and dumb than if you go feeling your way into his mind. And there was another reason for making the boy in "First Love" a deaf character: one of the other characters— Aaron Burr—was a real person. I couldn't invent conversation for him as I could for an imaginary character, so I had him speak in front of a deaf boy who could report and interpret him in his own way—that is, to suit the story. It's instinctive for a writer to show acute feeling or intense states of emotion by translating it into something visible—red hair, if nothing else. But it's not necessary. I believe I'm writing about the same inward things now without resorting to such obvious devices. But all devices— and the use of symbols is another—must come about organically, out of the story. I feel emphatic about that.

INTERVIEWER: Are you also talking here about other early stories like "Lily Daw and the Three Ladies" and "Petrified Man"?

WELTY: Well, when I wrote my first stories, I wrote much faster, and it failed to occur to me that I could write them any other way, and perhaps better the second time. They show all the weaknesses of the headlong. I never rewrote, I just wrote. The plots in these stories are weak because I didn't know enough to worry about plots. In the dialogue stories, they came into being exactly as the dialogue led them along. I didn't realize their real weakness until I began reading stories in public—and my ear told me. They could have been made stronger so easily. Sometimes I fixed them up a little for my readings—cut, transposed—small things, just to see the difference.

INTERVIEWER: What inspired "Powerhouse"?

WELTY: I wrote it in one night after I'd been to a concert and dance in Jackson where Fats Waller played. I tried to write my idea of the life of the traveling artist and performer—not Fats Waller himself, but any artist—in the alien world and tried to put it in the words and plot suggested by the music I'd been listening to. It was a daring attempt for a writer like me—as daring as it was to write about the murderer of Medgar Evers on *that* night—and I'm not qualified to write about music or performers. But trying it pleased me then, and it still does please me.

INTERVIEWER: Are there problems with ending a story?

WELTY: Not so far, but I could have made mistakes without knowing it yet. It's really part of plotting to know the exact moment you're through. I go by my ear, and this may trick me. When I read, I hear what's on the page. I don't know whose voice it is, but some voice is reading to me, and when I write my own stories, I hear it, too. I have a visual mind, and I *see* everything I write, but I have to hear the words when they're put down. Oh, that sounds absurd. This is not the same as working with dialogue, which of course is another, specialized, kind of hearing.

INTERVIEWER: Your first stories were about Paris.

WELTY: It's not worth remembering. That was when I was a college freshman, sixteen years old. Oh, you know, I was writing about the great world, of which I only knew Jackson, Mississippi. But part of it stemmed from my sense of mystery in people and places, and that's legitimate and lifelong. As for Paris, I remember a sentence I opened one story with, to show you how bad I was: "Monsieur Boule inserted a delicate dagger in Mademoiselle's left side and departed with a poised immediacy." I like to think I didn't take myself seriously then, but I did.

INTERVIEWER: When you sent out "Death of a Traveling Salesman," how did you know you had ended your apprenticeship?

WELTY: I was just beginning it! I was thrilled to find that out.

I hadn't conceived of a story's actually being taken. A boy up the street, an old friend, Hubert Creekmore, who's dead now, knew all about sending stories out. He was a writer who started before I did and published many good novels and poems. I wouldn't let him read anything I wrote but just asked him, "Hubert, do you know where I can send this?"—and he said to John Rood of *Manuscript*. So I sent it off, and John Rood took it, and of course I was flabbergasted. So was Hubert! I believe I've always been lucky—my work has always landed safely and among friends.

INTERVIEWER: You were lucky to escape the novel-first requirement that publishers seem to impose upon young writers. They're wary of short story collections.

WELTY: I owe that to John Woodburn, my first editor, who was then at Doubleday, and to Diarmuid Russell, my agent and friend of many years now. I owe it to my nature, too, because I never wrote anything that didn't spring naturally to mind and engage my imagination.

INTERVIEWER: Compared to your stories, I see your novels as looser, freer, happier works which enjoy reconciliations and a final sense of communion.

WELTY: My natural temperament is one of positive feelings, and I really do work for resolution in a story. I don't think we often see life resolving itself, not in any sort of perfect way, but I like the fiction writer's feeling of being able to confront an experience and resolve it as art, however imperfectly and briefly— to give it a form and try to embody it—to hold it and express it in a story's terms. You have more chance to try it in a novel. A short story is confined to one mood, to which everything in the story pertains. Characters, setting, time, events, are all subject to the mood. And you can try more ephemeral, more fleeting things in a story—you can work more by suggestion—than in a novel. Less is resolved, more is suggested, perhaps.

INTERVIEWER: You reserve the short story for the ephemeral and the novel for the resolution?

WELTY: I can only say such things after the fact. If I'd known I was going to finish *Losing Battles* as a long novel, I don't know that I'd have begun it. I'm a short-story writer who writes novels the hard way, and by accident. You see, all my work grows out of the work itself. It seems to set its form from the idea, which is complete from the start, and a sense of the form is like a vase into which you pour something and fill it up. I have that completely in mind from the beginning, and I don't realize how far I can wander and yet come back. The flexibility and freedom are exciting to me, not being used to them, and they are hard to come by. But no one could have enjoyed more learning those lessons than I did. There's no end to what can be tried, is there? So better luck next time.

INTERVIEWER: Do you think critics have made too much of you as a regional writer, taking off from your own essays on the subject?

WELTY: I don't mind being called a regional writer. It's the critic's job to place and judge. But the critic can't really have a say in what a writer chooses to write about—that's the writer's lone responsibility. I just think of myself as writing about human beings, and I happen to live in a region, as do we all, so I write about what I know—it's the same case for any writer living anywhere. I also happen to love my particular region. If this shows, I don't mind.

INTERVIEWER: Is place your source of inspiration?

WELTY: Not only that, it's my source of knowledge. It tells me the important things. It steers me and keeps me going straight, because place is a definer and a confiner of what I'm doing. It helps me to identify, to recognize and explain. It does so much for you of itself. It saves me. Why, you couldn't write a story that happened nowhere. I couldn't, anyway. I couldn't write anything that abstract. I wouldn't be interested in anything that abstract.

INTERVIEWER: How about the function of place in "No Place for You, My Love"?

WELTY: That story is the one that place did the most for. It really wrote the story. I saw that setting only one time—the Delta of the Mississippi River itself, down below New Orleans where it winds toward the Gulf—one time only. Which smote me. It started the story and made it for me—and *was* the story, really. At its very least, place is essential, though. Time and place make the framework that any story's built on. To my mind, a fiction writer's honesty begins right there, in being true to those two facts of time and place. From there, imagination can take him anywhere at all.

You can equally well be true, I feel, to an *impression* of place. A new place seen in a flash may have an impact almost as strong as the place you've grown up in, one you're familiar with down to the bone and know what it's like without having to think. I've written about place from either one extreme or the other but not from partial familiarity or guessing—there's no solidity there.

INTERVIEWER: "Music from Spain" takes place in San Francisco.

WELTY: That's using impression of place. I was in San Francisco for only three or four months—that's seeing it in a flash. That story was all a response to a place, an act of love at first sight. It's written from the point of view of the stranger, of course—the only way to write about a strange place. On the other hand, I couldn't write a story laid in New York, where I've come so many times—because it's both familiar and unfamiliar, a no man's land.

INTERVIEWER: Where is Morgana, in *The Golden Apples*?

WELTY: It's a made-up Delta town. I was drawn to the name because I always loved the conception of *Fata Morgana*—the illusory shape, the mirage that comes over the sea. All Delta places have names after people, so it was suitable to call it Morgana after some Morgans. My population might not have known there was such a thing as *Fata Morgana*, but illusions weren't unknown to them, all the same—coming in over the cottonfields.

INTERVIEWER: Do you see a similarity between Miss Eckhart in *The Golden Apples* and Julia Mortimer in *Losing Battles*, both being schoolteachers who were civilizing agents and therefore outsiders?

WELTY: It doesn't have to be "therefore"—though mine were indeed outsiders. I suppose they are kin, but teachers like those are all over the South and maybe everywhere else, too—dedicated, and losing their battles, but not losing them every time. I went all through grammar school in Jackson under a principal all of us who went there still remember and talk about—Miss

Lorena Duling. This isn't to say I based my character on her, but she gave me insight into what it meant to be a great teacher. And so was my mother one. All her teaching was done by the time I came along, but she told me stories about it. She taught in the little mountain schools in West Virginia, riding to her school on horseback and crossing the river in a boat, teaching children older than she was—she started at fifteen. I think it was my mother who made seventeen silver dollars the first month she taught, and after that they never could quite come up to that high a standard—which also happened to Miss Julia Mortimer. The shaping influence of teachers like that stays real for a lifetime.

INTERVIEWER: I see another group of characters forming a pattern in your work. Virgie Rainey, in *The Golden Apples*, is an individualist and outsider and similar in that respect to Robbie Reid of *Delta Wedding* and Gloria Short of *Losing Battles*.

WELTY: In looking back I can see the pattern. It's funny—when I'm writing, I never see a repeat I make in large or small degree. I learn about it later. In Jackson they were recently doing a play of *The Ponder Heart* when I had just finished writing *Losing Battles*. The new novel was so fresh in my mind, whereas I hadn't thought of *The Ponder Heart* for years. But when I sat in at rehearsals, I kept seeing bits and pieces come up that I thought I had invented for *Losing Battles*, and there they were in another version in *Ponder Heart*. So I thought, it's sort of dismaying, but there it is. Your mind works that way. Yet they occur to me as new every time.

INTERVIEWER: Do you write when you're away from home?

WELTY: I've found it possible to write almost anywhere I've happened to try. I like it at home better because it's much more convenient for an early riser, which I am. And it's the only place where you can really promise yourself time and keep out interruptions. My ideal way to write a short story is to write the whole first draft through in one sitting, then work as long as it takes on revisions, and then write the final version all in one, so that in the end the whole thing amounts to one long sustained effort. That's not possible anywhere, but it comes nearest to being possible in your own home.

INTERVIEWER: Do you typewrite?

WELTY: Yes, and that's useful—it helps give me the feeling of making my work objective. I can correct better if I see it in typescript. After that, I revise with scissors and pins. Pasting is too slow, and you can't undo it, but with pins you can move things from anywhere to anywhere, and that's what I really love doing—putting things in their best and proper place, revealing things at the time when they matter most. Often I shift things from the very beginning to the very end. Small things—one fact, one word—but things important to me. It's possible I have a reverse mind and do things backwards, being a broken left-hander. Just so I've caught on to my weakness.

INTERVIEWER: You rewrite considerably?

WELTY: Yes, I do. Some things I let alone from first to last—the kernel of the story. You know enough not to touch something if it's right. The hardest thing for me is getting people in and out of rooms—the mechanics of a story. A simple act of putting on clothes is almost impossible for me to describe without many false starts. You have to be quick and specific in conveying that sort of action or fact, and also as neat and quiet about it as possible so that it doesn't obtrude. And I find that very challenging, especially to describe an action that I don't do very well myself, like sewing. I made Aunt Lexie in *Losing Battles* a poor sewer so that I wouldn't have to describe it too well. The easiest things to write about are emotions.

INTERVIEWER: And yet the most difficult thing would seem to be the hidden reaches of the human heart, the mystery, those impalpable emotions.

WELTY: For a writer those things are what you start with. You wouldn't have started a story without that awareness—that's what made you begin. That's what makes a character, projects the plot. Because you write from the inside. You can't start with how people look and speak and behave and come to know how they feel. You must know exactly what's in their hearts and minds before they ever set visible foot on the stage. You must know all, then not tell it all, or not tell too much at once: simply the right thing at the right moment. And the same character would be written about entirely differently in a novel as opposed to a short story. In a story you don't go into a character in order to develop him. He was born full grown, and he's present there to perform his part in the story. He's subservient to his function, and he doesn't exist outside it. But in a novel, he may. So you may have to allow for his growth and maybe hold him down and not tell everything you know, or else let him have his full sway—make room for a hero, even, in more spacious premises.

INTERVIEWER: Can you talk objectively about your language, perhaps about your use of metaphor?

WELTY: I don't know how to because I think of the actual writing as having existence only in the story. When I think of something, I put it into a narrative form, not in analytical form, and so anything I say would be artificial. Which reminds me of an Armenian friend of mine, an artist, who told me that his dreams all happened in the same place. When he went to bed, he'd imagine himself on a sled going down a steep hill; at the foot of the hill was a little town, and by the time he reached it, he was asleep, and his dreams happened right there. He didn't know why or how. And to go to the ridiculous and yet the sublime, there's W. C. Fields, who read an analysis of how he juggled. He couldn't juggle for six years afterwards. He'd never known that was how it was done. He'd just thrown up the balls and juggled.

—LINDA KUEHL
1972

8. Mary McCarthy

Mary McCarthy was born in Seattle, Washington, on June 21, 1912, and was raised by grandparents, uncles, and aunts after her parents died of influenza in 1918. At the age of eight she won a state prize for an article entitled "The Irish in American History." She was educated at the Forest Ridge Convent in Seattle, Annie Wright Seminary in Tacoma, and Vassar College, where she was graduated in 1933. At Vassar she was elected to Phi Beta Kappa in her senior year.

After her graduation from college she began to write book reviews for the *Nation* and the *New Republic*. In 1936 and 1937 she was an editor for Covici Friede, and from 1937 to 1948 she was an editor and theater critic for the *Partisan Review*. During this period she wrote articles, stories, and finally novels.

Her son was born in 1938. After her divorce from Edmund Wilson, she taught for a short time at Bard College and at Sarah Lawrence. She was a Guggenheim Fellow during 1949 and 1950, and again in 1959 and 1960. In 1949 she received the *Horizon* prize, and in 1957 a National Institute grant.

The author of numerous works of fiction and criticism, her books include *The Company She Keeps* (1942), *The Groves of Academe* (1952), *A Charmed Life* (1955), *Memories of a Catholic Girlhood* (1957), *The Stones of Florence* (1959), *The Group* (1963), *The Writing on the Wall and Other Literary Essays* (1970), and *Ideas and the Novel* (1980). In 1984 McCarthy won both the Edward McDowell Award and the National Award for Literature. She is a member of the National Institute of Arts and Letters. Her autobiography, *How I Grew*, was published in 1987.

who would advise me about budgeting and not letting friends make long-distance calls on my wire. But all that was normal; it was happening to everybody and nobody could feel it as a profound or permanent change, for it was like the life of a college student prolonged; middle-class college students always overspent their allowances and ran up bills that scared them because they couldn't pay. ~~########~~ The thirties proper, which I was inducted into in about 1936, were something harsher. They were Armageddon. This panel itself, in a way is rather thirtyish. The idea behind it is that we (or you) are sitting in judgment on a period of history. The thirties are being presented as a choice. Are you for them or against them, and as you answer, so will you be defined. The rhetorical form that best expresses the thirties is the debate. Today, perhaps, it is the panel, which recognizes the possibility of shades of opinion; in the thirties, the meetings of this sort that I remember ~~########~~ featured only a pair of antagonists. People used to tell about a debate, so called, at the University of Chicago, when President Hutchins represented Aristotle, Mortimer Adler represented Aquinas, and a student wearing a dunce-cap (yes, literally) represented Hume. Thus the debate shaded into the trial, and in the thirties the weaker member of a pair of debaters found himself, always, on trial. This state of war, of incessant belligerency, was not confined to politics. It infected literature, education, psychiatry, art. The word, reconciliation, which was often used at that time, testifies to the state of belligerency. Certain mediators were always trying to "reconcile" Freud with Marx, as or, they tried to reconcile a little later, Freud with religion. A common form of speech was "How do you reconcile what you say with---?" In practice, there were were some very strange reconciliations. The tiara at the Waldorf strike; the gold evening dress to go to Madrid in the Spanish Civil War. Those women were trying to reconcile the twenties (fun) with the thirties. There was a strong affinity (unconscious) in the thirties for the absurd. Looking back, people remember grotesque and unbelievable events, events that flew, as they say, in the face of Nature. But I will come back to that in a minute.

The thirties are presented now, nostalgically, as a time of freedom. Not so.

Manuscript page from an article by Mary McCarthy.

Mary McCarthy

The interview took place in the living room of the apartment in Paris where Miss McCarthy was staying during the winter of 1961. It was a sunny, pleasant room, not too large, with long windows facing south toward the new buildings going up along the Avenue Montaigne. A dining-cum-writing table stood in an alcove at one end; on it were a lamp, some books and papers, and a rather well-worn portable typewriter. At the other end of the room were several armchairs and a low sofa where Miss McCarthy sat while the interview was recorded. On this early spring afternoon (it was March 16), the windows were open wide, letting in a warm breeze and the noise of construction work nearby. An enormous pink azalea bloomed on the balcony, and roses graced a small desk in one corner.

Miss McCarthy settled down on the sofa and served coffee. She was wearing a simple beige dress with little jewelry—a large and rather ornate ring was her one elaborate ornament. She is a woman of medium height, dark, with straight hair combed back from a center part into a knot at the nape of her neck; this simple coiffure sets off a profile of beautiful, almost classic regularity. Her smile is a generous one, flashing suddenly across her face, crinkling up her wide-set eyes. She speaks not quickly, but with great animation and energy, gesturing seldom, and then only with a slight casual motion of her wrists and hands. Her sentences are vigorously punctuated with emphatic verbal stresses and short though equally emphatic pauses. In general, she impresses one as a woman who combines a certain gracefulness and charm with positively robust and somewhat tense assurance; it is typical of her that she matches the tremendously elegant carriage of her arms and neck and handsomely poised head with a deliberate, almost jerky motion in taking a step.

While Miss McCarthy's conversation was remarkably fluent and articulate, she would nevertheless often interrupt herself, with a kind of nervous carefulness, in order to reword or qualify a phrase, sometimes even impatiently destroying it and starting again in the effort to express herself as exactly as possible. Several times during the interview she seized upon a question in such a way that one felt she had decided upon certain things she wanted to say about herself and would willy-nilly create the opportunity to do so. At other moments, some of them hilarious—her gifts for pitiless witticism are justifiably celebrated—she would indulge in unpremeditated extravagances of description or speculation that she would then laughingly censor as soon as the words were out of her mouth. She was extremely generous in the matter of silly or badly worded questions, turning them into manageable ones by the nature of her response. In all, her conversation was marked by a scrupulous effort to be absolutely fair and honest, and by a kind of natural and exuberant enjoyment of her own intellectual powers.

INTERVIEWER: Do you like writing in Europe?

MCCARTHY: I don't really find much difference. I think if you stayed here very long, you'd begin to notice a little difficulty about language.

INTERVIEWER: Did you write about Europe when you first came here after the war?

MCCARTHY: Only in that short story, "The Cicerone." That was in the summer of 1946. We were just about the only tourists because you weren't allowed to travel unless you had an official reason for it. I got a magazine to give me some sort of *carnet*.

INTERVIEWER: Did the old problem, the American in Europe, interest you as a novelist?

MCCARTHY: I suppose at that time, at least in that story somewhat, it did. But no, not further. For one thing, I don't know whether I cease to feel so much like an American or what; New York is, after all, so Europeanized, and so many of one's friends are European, that the distinction between you as an American and the European blurs. Also Europe has become so much more Americanized. No, I no longer see that Jamesian distinction. I mean, I see it in James, and I could see it even in 1946, but I don't see it any more. I don't feel any more this antithesis of Young America, Old Europe. I think that's really gone. For better or worse, I'm not sure. Maybe for worse.

INTERVIEWER: What about the novel you're writing while you're here—have you been working on it a long time?

MCCARTHY: Oh, years! Let me think, I began it around the time of the first Stevenson campaign. Then I abandoned it and wrote the books on Italy, and *A Charmed Life*, and *Memories of a Catholic Girlhood*. When did I begin this thing again? A year ago last spring, I guess. Part of it came out in *Partisan Review*. The one called "Dotty Makes an Honest Woman of Herself."

INTERVIEWER: Is it unfair to ask you what it will be about?

MCCARTHY: No, it's very easy. It's called *The Group*, and it's about eight Vassar girls. It starts with the inauguration of Roosevelt, and—well, at first it was going to carry them up to the present time, but then I decided to stop at the inauguration of Eisenhower. It was conceived as a kind of mock-chronicle novel. It's a novel about the idea of progress, really. The idea of progress seen in the female sphere, the feminine sphere. You know, home economics, architecture, domestic technology, contraception, childbearing; the study of technology in the home, in the playpen, in the bed. It's supposed to be the history of the loss of faith in progress, in the idea of progress, during that twenty-year period.

INTERVIEWER: Are these eight Vassar girls patterned more or less after ones you knew when you were there in college?

MCCARTHY: Some of them are drawn pretty much from life, and some of them are rather composite. I've tried to keep myself out of this book. Oh, and all their mothers are in it. That's the part I almost like the best.

INTERVIEWER: Just the mothers, not the fathers?

MCCARTHY: Not the fathers. The fathers vaguely figure, offstage and so on, but the mothers are really monumentally present!

INTERVIEWER: Does it matter to you at all where you write?

MCCARTHY: Oh, a nice peaceful place with some good light.

INTERVIEWER: Do you work regularly, every morning, say?

MCCARTHY: Normally; right now I haven't been. Normally I work from about nine to two, and sometimes much longer—if it's going well, sometimes from nine to seven.

INTERVIEWER: Typewriter?

MCCARTHY: Typewriter, yes. This always has to get into a *Paris Review* interview! I very rarely go out to lunch. That's a rule. I've been accepting lunch dates recently—*why* didn't I remember that? My excuse—the excuse I've been forgetting—is simply that I don't go out to lunch! And in general, I don't. That was the best rule I ever made.

INTERVIEWER: Once you've published part of a novel separately, in a magazine or short-story collection, do you do much work on it afterwards, before it is published in the novel itself?

MCCARTHY: It depends. With this novel, I have.

INTERVIEWER: Speaking not of a novel, but of your autobiography, I remember that you published parts of *Memories of a Catholic Girlhood* as one section in *Cast a Cold Eye*. You changed the story about your nickname a great deal, reducing it to just a small incident in *Catholic Girlhood*.

MCCARTHY: I couldn't *bear* that one! It had appeared years ago in *Mademoiselle*, and when I put it in *Cast a Cold Eye*, I didn't realize how much I disliked it. When I came to put *Catholic Girlhood* together, I simply couldn't stand it, and when I was reading the book in proof, I decided to tear it out, to reduce it to a tiny tiny incident. As it stood, it was just impossible, much too rhetorical.

INTERVIEWER: When you publish chapters of a book separately on their own, do you think of them as chapters, or as independent short stories?

McCARTHY: As chapters, but if somebody, a magazine editor, thought they were what *Partisan Review* calls a "self-contained chapter," all right, but I've never tried to make them into separate units. If one happens to be, all right—if they want to publish it as such. The *New Yorker* has given me surprises: they've printed things that I would never have thought could stand by themselves. But *they* thought so.

INTERVIEWER: Did you, when you saw them in print?

McCARTHY: Surprisingly, yes.

INTERVIEWER: What about in your first novel, *The Company She Keeps*?

McCARTHY: Those chapters were written originally as short stories. About halfway through, I began to think of them as a kind of unified story. The same character kept reappearing, and so on. I decided finally to call it a novel, in that it does in a sense tell *a* story, one story. But the first chapters were written without any idea of there being a novel. It was when I was doing the one about the Yale man that I decided to put the heroine of the earlier stories in that story too. The story of the Yale man is not a bit autobiographical, but the heroine appears anyway, in order to make a unity for the book.

INTERVIEWER: Were you also interested simply in the problem of writing one story from various different points of view, in experimenting with the different voices?

McCARTHY: There were no voices in that. I don't think I was really very much interested in the technical side of it. It was the first piece of fiction I had ever written, I mean I'd never made any experiments before. I was too inexperienced to worry about technical problems.

INTERVIEWER: You hadn't written any fiction before then?

McCARTHY: No. Well, in college I had written the tiniest

amount of fiction: very bad short stories, very unrealized short
stories, for courses, and that was all. I once started a detective
story to make money—but I couldn't get the murder to take place!
At the end of three chapters I was still describing the characters
and the milieu, so I thought, this is not going to work. No corpse!
And that was all. Then I simply did *The Company She Keeps*,
and was only interested in the technical side from the point of
view of establishing the truth, of trying to re-create what happened. For instance, the art-gallery story was written in the first
person because that's the way you write that kind of story—a study
of a curious individual.

INTERVIEWER: You imply that most of the stories were distinctly
autobiographical.

MCCARTHY: They all are more or less, except the one about the
Yale man.

INTERVIEWER: Is this distinction between autobiography and
fiction clear in your mind before you begin writing a story, or
does it become so as you write? Or is there no such distinction?

MCCARTHY: Well, I think it depends on what you're doing. Let's
be frank. Take "The Man in the Brooks Brothers Shirt"; in that
case it was an attempt to describe something that really happened—though naturally you have to do a bit of name-changing
and city-changing. And the first story, the one about the divorce:
that was a stylization—there were no proper names in it or anything—but still, it was an attempt to be as exact as possible about
something that had happened. The Yale man was based on a real
person, John Chamberlain, actually, whom I didn't know very
well. But there it was an attempt to make this real man a broad
type. You know, to use John Chamberlain's boyish looks and a
few of the features of his career, and then draw all sorts of other
Yale men into it. Then the heroine was put in, in an imaginary
love affair, which *had* to be because she had to be in the story.
I always thought that was all very hard on John Chamberlain,
who was married. But of course he knew it wasn't true, and he
knew that I didn't know him very well, and that therefore in the
story he was just a kind of good-looking clotheshanger. Anything
else that I've written later—I may make a mistake—has been on

the whole a fiction. Though it may have autobiographical elements in it that I'm conscious of, it has been conceived as a fiction, even a thing like *The Oasis*, that's supposed to have all these real people in it. The whole story is a complete fiction. Nothing of the kind ever happened; after all, it happens in the future. But in general, with characters, I do try at least to be as exact as possible about the essence of a person, to find the key that works the person both in real life and in the fiction.

INTERVIEWER: Do you object to people playing the *roman à clef* game with your novels?

MCCARTHY: I suppose I really ask for it, in a way. I *do* rather object to it at the same time, insofar as it deflects attention from what I'm trying to do in the novel. What I really do is take real plums and put them in an imaginary cake. If you're interested in the cake, you get rather annoyed with people saying what species the real plum was. In *The Groves of Academe*, for instance. I had taught at Bard College and at Sarah Lawrence, but I didn't want to make a composite of those two places: I really wanted to make a weird imaginary college of my own. I even took a trip to the Mennonite country in Pennsylvania to try to find a perfect location for it, which I found—now where was it? Somewhere near Ephrata—yes, it was Lititz, Pennsylvania, the home of the pretzel. There's a very charming old-fashioned sort of academy, a girls' college there—I'd never heard of it before and can't remember the name. It had the perfect setting, I thought, for this imaginary college of mine. Anyway, I would get terribly annoyed if people said it had to do with Sarah Lawrence, which it had almost no resemblance to. It was quite a bit like Bard. Sarah Lawrence is a much more *borné* and dull place than Bard, or than my college. And of course I was even more annoyed if they said it was Bennington. There was not supposed to be anything there of Bennington at all!

INTERVIEWER: When were you at Bard?

MCCARTHY: '45 to '46.

INTERVIEWER: And at Sarah Lawrence?

MCCARTHY: I was there just for one term, the winter of '48.

INTERVIEWER: Did you enjoy teaching?

MCCARTHY: I adored teaching at Bard, yes. But the students were so poor at Sarah Lawrence that I didn't much enjoy it there. I don't think anyone I knew who was teaching there then did. But at Bard it was very exciting. It was all quite mad, crazy. I had never taught before, and I was staying up till two in the morning every night trying to keep a little bit behind my class. Joke.

INTERVIEWER: Did they ask you to teach "Creative Writing"?

MCCARTHY: I've always refused to teach creative writing. Oh, I had in addition to two courses, about seven or eight tutorials, and some of those tutees wanted to study creative writing. I think I finally weakened and let one boy who was utterly ungifted for it study creative writing because he was so incapable of studying anything else.

INTERVIEWER: But mostly it was these two courses.

MCCARTHY: Yes, and then you had to keep up with all these students. I had one boy doing all the works of James T. Farrell and a girl who was studying Marcus Aurelius and Dante. That was fun. That one I did the work for. And one girl was doing a thesis on Richardson; that was just hopeless. I mean, I couldn't even try to keep up with teaching Russian novels, and, say, Jane Austen—who in my course came under the head of "Modern Novel"—*and* all the works of Richardson. So I could never tell, you know, whether she had read what she was supposed to have read, because I couldn't remember it! Everything was reversed! The student was in a position to see whether the professor was cheating, or had done her homework. Anyway, everybody ended up ill after this year—you know, various physical ailments. But it was exciting, it was fun. The students were fun. The bright ones were bright, and there wasn't much of a middle layer. They were either bright or they were just cretins. I must say, there are times when you welcome a B student.

I liked teaching because I loved this business of studying. I found it quite impossible to give a course unless I'd read the material the night before. I absolutely couldn't handle the material unless it was fresh in my mind. Unless you give canned lectures, it really has to be—though that leads, I think, to all sorts of very whimsical, perhaps, and capricious interpretations; that is, you see the whole book, say *Anna Karenina*, in terms that are perhaps dictated by the moment. One wonders afterwards whether one's interpretation of *Anna Karenina* that one had rammed down the throats of those poor students was really as true as it seemed to one at the time.

INTERVIEWER: Which books did you teach in the "Modern Novel"?

MCCARTHY: Well, you had to call everything at Bard either modern or contemporary, or the students wouldn't register for it. Everyone thinks this a joke, but it was true. I originally was going to teach a whole course on critical theory, from Aristotle to T. S. Eliot or something, and only three students registered for it, but if it had been called "Contemporary Criticism," then I think we would have had a regular class. So we called this course "The Modern Novel," and it began with Jane Austen, I think, and went up, well, certainly to Henry James. That was when I taught novels in pairs. I taught *Emma* and *Madame Bovary* together. Then *The Princess Casamassima*, with the anarchist plot in it and everything, with *The Possessed*. *The Red and the Black* with *Great Expectations*. And *Fontamara* with something. I only taught novels I liked.

INTERVIEWER: Would it be roughly the same list, were you teaching the course now? Or do you have new favorites?

MCCARTHY: Oh I don't know, I might even add something like *Dr. Zhivago* at the end. I would probably do some different Dickens. I've read an awful lot of Dickens over again since then. Now I think I'd teach *Our Mutual Friend* or *Little Dorritt*.

INTERVIEWER: Why did you start reading Dickens over again?

MCCARTHY: I don't know, I got interested in Dickens at Bard, and then at Sarah Lawrence. Another stimulus was a book done by a man called Edgar Johnson, a biographer of Dickens. Anthony West had attacked it in the *New Yorker*, and this made me so angry that I reviewed the book, and that set off another kind of chain reaction. I really *passionately* admire Dickens.

INTERVIEWER: Could I go back for a moment to what you said about your early writing at college? I think you said that *The*

Company She Keeps was the first fiction you ever wrote, but that was some years after you left Vassar, wasn't it?

MCCARTHY: Oh, yes. You know, I had been terribly discouraged when I was at Vassar, and later, by being told that I was really a critical mind, and that I had no creative talent. Who knows? they may have been right. This was done in a generous spirit, I don't mean that it was harsh. Anyway, I hadn't found any way at all, when I was in college, of expressing anything in the form of short stories. We had a rebel literary magazine that Elizabeth Bishop and Eleanor Clark were on, and Muriel Rukeyser and I. I wrote, not fiction, but sort of strange things for this publication.

INTERVIEWER: A rebel magazine?

MCCARTHY: There was an official literary magazine, which we were all against. Our magazine was anonymous. It was called *Con Spirito*. It caused a great sort of scandal. I don't know why— it was one of these perfectly innocent undertakings. But people said, "How awful, it's anonymous." The idea of anonymity was of course to keep the judgment clear, especially the editorial board's judgment—to make people read these things absolutely on their merits. Well anyway, *Con Spirito* lasted for only a few numbers. Elizabeth Bishop wrote a wonderful story for it which I still remember, called "Then Came the Poor." It was about a revolution, a fantasy that took place in modern bourgeois society, when the poor invade, and take over a house.

INTERVIEWER: When you left Vassar, what then?

MCCARTHY: Well, I went to New York, and I began reviewing for the *New Republic* and the *Nation*—right away. I wrote these little book reviews. Then there was a series about the critics. The *Nation* wanted a large-scale attack on critics and book-reviewers, chiefly those in the *Herald Tribune*, the *Times*, and the *Saturday Review*, and so on. I had been doing some rather harsh reviews, so they chose me as the person to do this. But I was so young, I think I was twenty-two, that they didn't *trust* me. So they got Margaret Marshall, who was the assistant literary editor then, to do it with me: actually we divided the work up and did separate pieces. But she was older and was supposed to be—I don't know— a restraining influence on me; anyway, someone more respon-

sible. That series was a great sensation at the time, and it made
people very mad. I continued just to do book reviews, maybe one
other piece about the theater, something like the one on the
literary critics. And then nothing more until *Partisan Review*
started. That was when I tried to write the detective story—before
Partisan Review. To be exact, *Partisan Review* had existed as a
Stalinist magazine, and then it had died, gone to limbo. But after
the Moscow trials, the PR boys, Rahv and Phillips, revived it,
got a backer, merged with some other people—Dwight Macdonald and others—and started it again. As an anti-Stalinist magazine. I had been married to an actor, and was supposed to know
something about the theater, so I began writing a theater column
for them. I didn't have any other ambitions at all. Then I married
Edmund Wilson, and after we'd been married about a week, he
said, "I think you have a talent for writing fiction." And he put
me in a little room. He didn't literally lock the door, but he said,
"Stay in there!" And I did. I just sat down, and it just came. It
was the first story I had ever written, really: the first story in *The
Company She Keeps*. Robert Penn Warren published it in the
Southern Review. And I found myself writing fiction to my great
surprise.

INTERVIEWER: This was when you became involved in politics,
wasn't it?

MCCARTHY: No. Earlier. In 1936, at the time of the Moscow
trials. That changed absolutely everything. I got swept into the
whole Trotskyite movement. But by accident. I was at a party. I
knew Jim Farrell—I'd reviewed one of his books, I think it was
Studs Lonigan—in any case, I knew Jim Farrell, and I was asked
to a party given by his publisher for Art Young, the old *Masses*
cartoonist. There were a lot of Communists at this party. Anyway,
Farrell went around asking people whether they thought Trotsky
was entitled to a hearing and to the right of asylum. I said yes,
and that was all. The next thing I discovered I was on the let-
terhead of something calling itself the American Committee for
the Defense of Leon Trotsky. I was furious, of course, at this use
of my name. Not that my name had any consequence, but still,
it was mine. Just as I was about to make some sort of protest, I

began to get all sorts of calls from Stalinists, telling me to get off the committee. I began to see that other people were falling off the committee, like Freda Kirchwey—she was the first to go, I think—and this cowardice impressed me so unfavorably that naturally I didn't say anything about my name having got on there by accident, or at least without my realizing. So I stayed.

I began to know all the people on the committee. We'd attend meetings. It was a completely different world. Serious, you know. Anyway, that's how I got to know the PR boys. They hadn't yet revived the *Partisan Review*, but they were both on the Trotsky committee, at least Philip was. We—the committee, that is—used to meet in Farrell's apartment. I remember once when we met on St. Valentine's Day and I thought, Oh, this is so strange, because I'm the only person in this room who realizes that it's Valentine's Day. It was true! I had a lot of rather rich Stalinist friends, and I was always on the defensive with them, about the Moscow Trial question, Trotsky, and so on. So I had to inform myself, really, in order to conduct the argument. I found that I was reading more and more, getting more and more involved in this business. At the same time I got a job at Covici Friede, a rather left-wing publishing house now out of business, also full of Stalinists. I began to see Philip Rahv again because Covici Friede needed some readers' opinions on Russian books, and I remembered that he read Russian, so he came around to the office, and we began to see each other. When *Partisan Review* was revived I appeared as a sort of fifth wheel—there may have been more than that—but in any case as a kind of appendage of *Partisan Review*.

INTERVIEWER: Then you hadn't really been interested in politics before the Moscow trials?

MCCARTHY: No, not really. My first husband had worked at the Theater Union, which was a radical group downtown that put on proletarian plays, and there were lots of Communists in that. Very few Socialists. And so I knew all these people; I knew that kind of person. But I wasn't very sympathetic to them. We used to see each other, and there were a lot of jokes. I even marched in May Day parades. Things like that. But it was all . . . fun. It was all done in that spirit. And I remained, as the *Partisan Review* boys said, absolutely bourgeois throughout. They always said to me very sternly, "You're really a throwback. You're really a twenties figure."

INTERVIEWER: How did you react to that?

MCCARTHY: Well, I suppose I was wounded. I was a sort of gay, good-time girl, from their point of view. And they were men of the thirties. Very serious. That's why my position was so insecure on *Partisan Review*; it wasn't exactly insecure, but . . . lowly. I mean, in *fact*. And that was why they let me write about the theater, because they thought the theater was of absolutely no consequence.

INTERVIEWER: How did the outbreak of the war affect your political opinion? The *Partisan Review* group split apart, didn't it?

MCCARTHY: At the beginning of the war we were all isolationists, the whole group. Then I think the summer after the fall of France—certainly before Pearl Harbor—Philip Rahv wrote an article in which he said in a measured sentence, "In a certain sense, this is our war." The rest of us were deeply shocked by this, because we regarded it as a useless imperialist war. You couldn't beat Fascism that way: "Fight the enemy at home," and so on. In other words, we reacted to the war rather in the manner as if it had been World War I. This was after Munich, after the so-called "phony war." There was some reason for having certain doubts about the war, at least about the efficacy of the war. So when Philip wrote this article, a long controversy began on *Partisan Review*. It split between those who supported the war, and those who didn't. I was among those who didn't—Edmund Wilson also, though for slightly different reasons. Dwight Macdonald and Clement Greenberg split off, and Dwight founded his own magazine, *Politics*, which started out as a Trotskyite magazine, and then became a libertarian, semi-anarchist one. Meyer Schapiro was in this group, and I forget who else. Edmund was really an unreconstructed isolationist. The others were either Marxist or libertarian. Of course there was a split in the Trotskyite movement at that period.

Toward the end of the war, I began to realize that there was something hypocritical about my position—that I was really supporting the war. I'd go to a movie—there was a marvelous documentary called *Desert Victory* about the British victory over Rommel's Africa Corps—and I'd find myself weeping madly when Montgomery's bagpipers went through to El Alamein. In other words, cheering the war, and on the other hand, being absolutely against Bundles for Britain, against Lend Lease—this was after Lend Lease, of course—against every practical thing. And suddenly, I remember—it must have been the summer of '45 that I first said this aloud—I remember it was on the Cape, at Truro. There were a lot of friends, Chiaromonte, Lionel Abel, Dwight, et cetera, at my house—by this time I was divorced from Edmund, or separated, anyway. And I said, "You know, I think I, and all of us, are really *for* the war." This was the first time this had been said aloud by me. Dwight indignantly denied it. "I'm *not* for the war!" he said. But he was. Then I decided I wanted to give a blood transfusion. And I practically had to get cleared! Now no one was making me do this, but I felt I had to go and get cleared by my friends first. Was it wrong of me to support the war effort by giving a blood transfusion? It was agreed that it was all right. All this *fuss!* So I gave a blood transfusion, just one. Some other people were doing it too, I believe, independently, at the same time, people of more or less this tendency. That is the end of that story.

Years later, I realized I really thought that Philip had been right, and that the rest of us had been wrong. Of course we didn't know about the concentration camps: the death camps hadn't started at the beginning. All that news came in fairly late. But once this news was in, it became clear—at least to me, and I still believe it—that the only way to have stopped it was in a military way. That only the military defeat of Hitler could stop this, and it had to be stopped. But it took a long, long time to come to this view. You're always afraid of making the same mistake over again. But the trouble is you can always correct an earlier mistake like our taking the attitude to World War II as if it were World War I, but if you ever try to project the correction of a mistake into the future, you may make a different one. That is, many people now are talking about World War III as if it were World War II.

INTERVIEWER: What I don't see, though, is how all this left you once the war was over.

MCCARTHY: Actually, as I remember, after the war was the very best period, politically, that I've been through. At that time, it seemed to me there was a lot of hope around. The war was over! Certain—perhaps—mistakes had been recognized. The bomb had been dropped on Hiroshima, and there was a kind of general repentance of this fact. This was before the hydrogen bomb; and we never even dreamed that the Russians were going to get the atomic bomb. The political scene looked free. This was not only true for us—it seemed a good moment. At least there was still the hope of small libertarian movements. People like Dwight and Chiaromonte and I used to talk about it a great deal, and even Koestler was writing at that period about the possibility of founding oases—that's where I took the title of that book from. It seemed possible still, utopian but possible, to change the world on a small scale. Everyone was trying to live in a very principled way, but with quite a lot of energy, the energy that peace had brought, really. This was the period of the Marshall Plan, too. It was a good period. Then of course the Russians got the atom bomb, and the hydrogen bomb came. That was the end of *any* hope, or at least any hope that I can see of anything being done except in a massive way.

INTERVIEWER: How do you characterize your political opinion now?

MCCARTHY: Dissident!

INTERVIEWER: All the way round?

MCCARTHY: Yes! No, I still believe in what I believed in then— I still believe in a kind of libertarian socialism, a decentralized socialism. But I don't see any possibility of achieving it. That is, within the span that I can see, which would be, say, to the end of my son's generation, your generation. It really seems to me sometimes that the only hope is space. That is to say, perhaps the most energetic—in a bad sense—elements will move on to a new world in space. The problems of mass society will be transported into space, leaving behind this world as a kind of Europe, which then eventually tourists will visit. The Old World. I'm only half joking. I don't think that the problem of social equality has ever been solved. As soon as it looks as if it were going to be solved, or even as if it were going to be confronted,—say, as at the end of the eighteenth century—there's a mass move to a new continent which defers this solution. After '48, after the failure of the '48 revolutions in Europe, hope for an egalitarian Europe really died, and the '48-ers, many of them, went to California in the Gold Rush as '49-ers. My great-grandfather, from central Europe, was one of them. The Gold Rush, the Frontier was a substitute sort of equality. Think of Chaplin's film. And yet once the concept of equality had entered the world, life becomes intolerable without it; yet life continues without its being realized. So it may be that there will be another displacement, another migration. The problem, the solution, or the confrontation, will again be postponed.

INTERVIEWER: Do you find that your critical work, whether it's political or literary, creates any problems in relation to your work as a novelist?

MCCARTHY: No, except that you have the perpetual problem, if somebody asks you to do a review, whether to interrupt what you're writing—if you're writing a novel—to do the review. You have to weigh whether the subject interests you enough, or whether you're tired at that moment, emotionally played out by the fiction you're writing. Whether it would be a good thing to stop and concentrate on something else. I just agreed to and did a review of Camus' collected fiction and journalism. That *was* in some way connected with my own work, with the question of the novel in general. I thought, yes, I will do this because I want to read all of Camus and decide what I think about him finally. (Actually, I ended up almost as baffled as when I started.) But in general, I don't take a review unless it's something like that. Or unless Anthony West attacks Dickens. You know. Either it has to be some sort of thing that I want very much to take sides on, or something I'd like to study a bit, that I want to find out about anyway. Or where there may, in the case of study, be some reference—very indirect—back to my own work.

INTERVIEWER: This is quite a change from the time when you wrote criticism and never even thought of writing fiction. But now you consider yourself a novelist? Or don't you bother with these distinctions?

MCCARTHY: Well, I suppose I consider myself a novelist. Yes. Still, whatever way I write was really, I suppose, formed critically. That is, I learned to write reviews and criticism and then write novels so that however I wrote, it was formed that way. George Eliot, you know, began by translating Strauss, began by writing about German philosophy—though her philosophic passages are not at all good in *Middlemarch*. Nevertheless, I *think* that this kind of training really makes one more interested in the subject than in the style. Her work certainly doesn't suffer from any kind of stylistic frippery. There's certainly no voluminous drapery around. There is a kind of concision in it, at her best—that passage where she's describing the character of Lydgate—which shows, I think, the critical and philosophic training. I've never liked the conventional conception of "style." What's confusing is that style usually means some form of fancy writing—when people say, oh yes, so and so's such a "wonderful stylist." But if one means by style the voice, the irreducible and always recognizable and alive thing, then of course style is really everything. It's what you find in Stendhal, it's what you find in Pasternak. The same thing you find in a poet—the sound of, say, Donne's voice. In a sense, you can't go further in an analysis of Donne than to be able to place this voice, in the sense that you recognize Don Giovanni by the voice of Don Giovanni.

INTERVIEWER: In speaking of your own writing, anyway, you attribute its "style" to your earlier critical work—then you don't feel the influence of other writers of fiction?

MCCARTHY: I don't think I have any influences. I think my first story, the first one in *The Company She Keeps*, definitely shows the Jamesian influence—James is so terribly catching. But beyond that, I can't find any influence. That is, I can't as a detached person—as detached as I can be—look at my work and see where it came from the point of view of literary sources.

INTERVIEWER: There must be certain writers, though, that you are *drawn* to more than others.

MCCARTHY: Oh, yes! But I don't think I write like them. The writer I really like best is Tolstoi, and I *know* I don't write like Tolstoi. I wish I did! Perhaps the best English prose is Thomas Nash. I don't write at all like Thomas Nash.

INTERVIEWER: It would seem also, from hints you give us in your books, that you like Roman writers as well.

MCCARTHY: I did when I was young, very much. At least, I adored Catullus, and Juvenal; those were the two I really passionately loved. And Caesar, when I was a girl. But you couldn't say that I had been influenced by *Catullus*! No! And Stendhal I like very, very much. Again, I would be happy to write like Stendhal, but I don't. There are certain sentences in Stendhal that come to mind as how to do it if one could. I can't. A certain kind of clarity and brevity—the author's attitude summed up in a sentence, and done so simply, done without patronizing. Some sort of joy.

INTERVIEWER: It's a dangerous game to play, the influence one.

MCCARTHY: Well in some cases it's easy to see, and people themselves acknowledge it, and are interested in it, as people are interested in their genealogy. I simply can't find my ancestors. I was talking to somebody about John Updike, and he's another one I would say I can't find any sources for.

INTERVIEWER: Do you like his writing?

MCCARTHY: Yes. I've not quite finished *Rabbit, Run*—I must get it back from the person I lent it to and finish it. I thought it was very good, and so stupidly reviewed. I'd read *Poorhouse Fair*, which I thought was really remarkable. Perhaps it suffered from the point-of-view problem, the whole virtuosity of doing it through the eyes of this old man sitting on the veranda of the poorhouse, through his eyes with their refraction, very old eyes, and so on. I think, in a way, this trick prevents him saying a good deal in the book. Nevertheless, it's quite a remarkable book. But anyway, I nearly didn't read *Rabbit, Run* because I thought, Oh my God! from reading those reviews. The reviewers seemed to be under the impression that the hero was a terrible character. It's incredible! No, I think it's the most interesting American novel I've read in quite a long time.

INTERVIEWER: What about others? Did you like *Henderson the Rain King*?

MCCARTHY: Well, yes, the first part of *Henderson* I think is marvelous. The vitality! I still think it's an amusing novel right through the lions, almost like a French eighteenth-century novel, or *conte*, very charming. But it doesn't have this tremendous blast of vitality that the first part has, and it doesn't have the density.

INTERVIEWER: What other recent American novels have you been interested by?

MCCARTHY: Well, name one. There really aren't any! I mean, are there? I can't think of any. I don't like Salinger, not at all. That last thing isn't a novel anyway, whatever it is. I don't like it. Not at all. It suffers from this terrible sort of metropolitan sentimentality and it's so narcissistic. And to me, also, it seemed so false, so calculated. Combining the plain man with an absolutely megalomaniac egoism. I simply can't stand it.

INTERVIEWER: What do you think of women writers, or do you think the category "woman writer" should not be made?

MCCARTHY: Some women writers make it. I mean, there's a certain kind of woman writer who's a capital W, capital W. Virginia Woolf certainly was one, and Katherine Mansfield was one, and Elizabeth Bowen is one. Katherine Anne Porter? Don't think she really is—I mean, her writing is certainly very feminine, but I would say that there wasn't this "WW" business in Katherine Anne Porter. Who else? There's Eudora Welty, who's certainly not a "Woman Writer." Though she's become one lately.

INTERVIEWER: What is it that happens to make this change?

MCCARTHY: I think they become interested in décor. You notice the change in Elizabeth Bowen. Her early work is much more masculine. Her later work has much more drapery in it. Who else? Jane Austen was never a "Woman Writer," I don't think. The cult of Jane Austen pretends that she was, but I don't think she was. George Eliot *certainly* wasn't, and George Eliot is the kind of woman writer I admire. I was going to write a piece at some point about this called "Sense and Sensibility," dividing women writers into these two. I *am* for the ones who represent sense, and so was Jane Austen.

INTERVIEWER: Getting away from novels for a moment, I'd like to ask you about *Memories of a Catholic Girlhood* if I might. Will you write any more autobiography?

MCCARTHY: I was just reading—oh God, actually I *was* just starting to read Simone de Beauvoir's second volume, *La Force de l'Age*, and she announces in the preface that she can't write about her later self with the same candor that she wrote about her girlhood.

INTERVIEWER: You feel that too?

MCCARTHY: On this one point I agree with her. One has to be really old, I think, really quite an old person—and by that time I don't know what sort of shape one's memory would be in.

INTERVIEWER: You don't agree with her on other points?

MCCARTHY: I had an interview with *L'Express* the other day, and I gave Simone de Beauvoir the works. Let's not do it twice. I think she's pathetic, that's all. This book is supposed to be better, more interesting anyway, than the first one because it's about the thirties, and everyone wants to read about the thirties. And her love affair with Sartre, which is just about the whole substance of this book, is supposed to be very touching. The book *is* more interesting than the first one. But I think she's odious. A mind totally bourgeois turned inside out.

INTERVIEWER: I have something else to ask, apropos of *Memories of a Catholic Girlhood*. There are certain points, important points and moments in your novels, where you deepen or enlarge the description of the predicament in which a character may be by reference to a liturgical or ecclesiastical or theological parallel or equivalence. What I want to know is, is this simply a strict use of analogy, a technical literary device, or does it indicate any conviction that these are valid and important ways of judging a human being?

MCCARTHY: I suppose it's a reference to a way of thinking about a human being. But I think at their worst they're rather just literary references. That is, slightly show-off literary references. I have a terrible compulsion to make them—really a dreadful compulsion. The first sentence of *The Stones of Florence* begins, "How can you stand it? This is the first thing, and the last thing, the eschatological question that the visitor leaves echoing in the air behind him." Something of that sort. Well, everybody was after me to take out that word. I left it out when I published that chapter in the *New Yorker*, but I put it back in the book. No, I do have this great compulsion to make those references. I think I do it as a sort of secret signal, a sort of looking over the heads of the readers who don't recognize them to the readers who do understand them.

INTERVIEWER: If these references *are* only literary ones, secret signals, then they are blasphemous.

MCCARTHY: Yes, I see what you mean. I suppose they are. Yes, they are secret jokes, they are blasphemies. But—I think I said something of this in the introduction of *Catholic Girlhood*—I think that religion offers to Americans (I mean the Roman Catholic religion) very often the only history and philosophy they ever get. A reference to it somehow opens up that historical vista. In that sense it is a device for deepening the passage.

INTERVIEWER: Could we go back to your novels for a moment? I'd like to ask you about how you begin on them. Do you start with the characters, the situation, the plot? What comes first? Perhaps that's too hard a question, too general.

MCCARTHY: Very hard, and I'm awfully specific. I can really only think in specific terms, at least about myself. *The Groves of Academe* started with the plot. The plot and this figure: there can't be the plot without this figure of the impossible individual, the unemployable professor and his campaign for justice. Justice, both in quotes, you know, and serious in a way. What *is* justice for the unemployable person? That was conceived from the beginning as a plot: the whole idea of the reversal at the end, when Mulcahy is triumphant and the President is about to lose his job or quit, when the worm turns and is triumphant. I didn't see exactly what would happen in between; the more minute details weren't worked out. But I did see that there would be his campaign for reinstatement and then his secret would be discovered. In this case that he had *not* been a Communist. A *Charmed Life* began with a short story; the first chapter was written as a short story. When I conceived the idea of its being a novel, I think about all I knew was that the heroine would have to die in the end. Everybody objected to that ending, and said that it was terrible to have her killed in an automobile accident in the last paragraph—utterly unprepared for, and so on. But the one thing I knew absolutely certainly was that the heroine had to die in the end. At first I was going to have her have an abortion, and have her die in the abortion. But that seemed to me so trite. Then I conceived the idea of having her drive on the correct side of the road and get killed, because in this weird place everyone is always on the wrong side of the road. But all that is really implicit in the first chapter.

INTERVIEWER: So the charge that readers are unprepared for the last paragraph you feel is unfair?

MCCARTHY: There may be something wrong with the novel, I don't know. But it was always supposed to have a fairy tale element in it. New Leeds is *haunted!* Therefore nobody should be surprised if something unexpected happens, or something catastrophic, for the place is also pregnant with catastrophe. But it may be that the treatment in between was too realistic, so that the reader was led to expect a realistic continuation of everything going on in a rather moderate way. It was, to some extent, a symbolic story. The novel is supposed to be about doubt. All the characters in different ways represent doubt, whether it is philosophical or ontological doubt as in the case of the strange painter who questions everything—"Why don't I murder my grandmother?" and so on. Or the girl's rather nineteenth-century self-doubt, doubt of the truth, of what she perceives. In any case, everyone is supposed to represent one or another form of doubt. When the girl finally admits to herself that she's pregnant, and also recognizes that she must do something about it, in other words, that she has to put up a real stake—and she does put up a real stake—at that moment she becomes mortal. All the other characters are immortal. They have dozens of terrible accidents, and they're all crippled in one way or another, and yet they have this marvelous power of survival. All those drunks and human odds and ends. Anyway, the girl makes the decision—which from the point of view of conventional morality is a wicked decision—to have an abortion, to kill life. Once she makes this decision, she becomes mortal, and doesn't belong to the charmed circle any more. As soon as she makes it, she gets killed—to get killed is simply a symbol of the fact that she's mortal.

INTERVIEWER: You say that her decision makes her mortal. But her decision has also included someone else, the painter.

MCCARTHY: Yes, yes. I see what you mean. I hadn't thought of that, that when she asks somebody to help her it implies some sort of social bond, some sort of mutual bond between people in society, while the rest of these people are still a community of isolates.

INTERVIEWER: His joining her in this mortal, social bond, that doesn't make him mortal as well? He is still a part of the charmed circle?

MCCARTHY: He's too sweet to be mortal! Well, he's a comic figure, and I have this belief that all comic characters are immortal. They're eternal. I believe this is Bergson's theory too. He has something, I'm told, about comic characters being *figé*. Like Mr. and Mrs. Micawber: they all have to go on forever and be invulnerable. Almost all Dickens' characters have this peculiar existence of eternity, except the heroes, except Pip, or Nicholas Nickleby, or David Copperfield.

INTERVIEWER: What other characters in your novels do you consider—

MCCARTHY: The comic ones? Who knows whether they're immortal! As far as I'm concerned, they're immortal!

INTERVIEWER: Then you haven't thought of this distinction between "mortal" and "immortal" in relation to characters in other of your novels besides *A Charmed Life*?

MCCARTHY: I didn't think of this distinction until just recently, and not in connection with myself. It's just at this very moment—*now* talking with you—that I'm thinking of it in connection with myself. I would say that it is a law that applies to *all* novels: that the comic characters are *figé*, are immortal, and that the hero or heroine exists in time, because the hero or heroine is always in some sense equipped with purpose.

The man in *The Groves of Academe*. Well, he's immortal, yes. He is a comic villain, and villains too always—I think—partake in this comic immortality. I *think* so. I'm not sure that you couldn't find an example, though, of a villain it wasn't true of. In Dickens again. In the late novels, somebody like Bradley Headstone, the schoolmaster, he's a mixed case. He's certainly not a villain in the sense of, say, the villain in *Little Dorritt*, who belongs to the old-fashioned melodramatic immortal type of villain. Headstone is really half a hero, Steerforth is half a hero, and therefore they don't conform to this.

This all came to me last year, this distinction, when I was thinking about the novel. Not my novel: The Novel.

But maybe that's really part of the trouble I'm having with *my* novel! These girls are all essentially comic figures, and it's awfully hard to make anything happen to them. Maybe this is really the trouble! Maybe I'm going to find out something in this interview! That the whole problem is *time!* I mean for me, in this novel. The passage of time, to show development. I think maybe my trouble is that these girls are comic figures, and that therefore they really can't develop! You see what I mean? They're not all so terribly comic, but most of them are.

How're they ever going to progress through the twenty years between the inauguration of Roosevelt and the inauguration of Eisenhower? This has been the great problem, and here I haven't had a form for it. I mean, all I know is that they're supposed to be middle-aged at the end.

Yes, I think maybe that *is* the trouble. One possibility would be . . . I've been introducing them one by one, chapter by chapter. They all appear at the beginning, you know, like the beginning of an opera, or a musical comedy. And then I take them one by one, chapter by chapter. I have been bringing each one on a little later on in time. But perhaps I can make bigger and bigger jumps so that you could meet, say, the last one when she is already middle-aged. You see what I mean. Maybe this would solve the problem. One five years later, another eight years later, and so on. I could manage the time problem that way. This has been very fruitful! Thank you!

INTERVIEWER: I want to ask you about the problem of time in the novel. You have written that a novel's action cannot take place in the future. But you have said that the action described in *The Oasis* all takes place in the future.

MCCARTHY: *The Oasis* is not a novel. I don't classify it as such. It was terribly criticized, you know, on that ground; people objected, said it wasn't a novel. But I never meant it to be. It's a *conte*, a *conte philosophique*.

INTERVIEWER: And *A Charmed Life* you say has fairy-tale elements.

MCCARTHY: I'm not sure any of my books are novels. Maybe none of them are. Something happens in my writing—I don't mean it to—a sort of distortion, a sort of writing on the bias, seeing things with a sort of swerve and swoop. *A Charmed Life*, for instance. You know, at the beginning I make a sort of inventory of all the town characters, just telling who they are. Now I did this with the intention of describing, well, this nice, ordinary, old-fashioned New England town. But it ended up differently. Something is distorted, the description takes on a sort of extravagance—I don't know exactly how it happens. I know I don't mean it to happen.

INTERVIEWER: You say in one of your articles that perhaps the fault lies simply in the material which the modern world affords, that it itself lacks—

MCCARTHY: Credibility? Yes. It's a difficulty I think all modern writers have.

INTERVIEWER: Other than the problem of arrangement of time, are there other specific technical difficulties about the novel you find yourself particularly concerned with?

MCCARTHY: Well, the whole question of the point of view, which tortures everybody. It's the problem that everybody's been up against since Joyce, if not before. Of course James really began it, and Flaubert even. You find it as early as *Madame Bovary*. The problem of the point of view, and the voice: *style indirect libre*—the author's voice, by a kind of ventriloquism, disappearing in and completely limited by the voices of his characters. What it has meant is the complete banishment of the author. I would like to restore the author! I haven't tried yet, but I'd like to try after this book, which is as far as I can go in ventriloquism. I would like to try to restore the author. Because you find that if you obey this Jamesian injunction of "Dramatize, dramatize," and especially if you deal with comic characters, as in my case, there is so much you can't say because you're limited by these mentalities. It's just that a certain kind of intelligence—I'm not only speaking of myself, but of anybody, Saul Bellow, for example—is more or less absent from the novel, and has to be, in accordance with these laws which the novel has made for itself. I think one reason that everyone—at least I—welcomed *Dr. Zhivago* was that you had the author in the form of the hero. And this beautiful tenor voice, the hero's voice and the author's—this marvelous voice, and this clear sound of intelligence. The Russians have never gone through the whole development of the novel you find in Joyce, Faulkner, et cetera, so that Pasternak was slightly unaware of the problem! But I think this technical development has become absolutely killing to the novel.

INTERVIEWER: You say that after this novel about the Vassar girls, you—

MCCARTHY: I don't know what I'm going to do, but I want to try something that will introduce, at least back into my work, my own voice. And not in the disguise of a heroine. I'm awfully sick of my heroine. I don't mean in this novel: my heroine of the past. Because the sensibility in each novel got more and more localized with this heroine, who became an agent of perception, et cetera.

Let me make a jump now. The reason that I enjoyed doing those books on Italy, the Venice and Florence books, was that I was writing *in my own voice*. One book was in the first person, and one was completely objective, but it doesn't make any difference. I felt, you know, now I can talk freely! The books were written very fast, the Venice one faster. Even the Florence book, with masses of research in it, was written very fast, with a great deal of energy, with a kind of liberated energy. And without the peculiar kind of painstakingness that's involved in the dramatization that one does in a novel, that is, when nothing can come in that hasn't been perceived through a character. The technical difficulties are so great, in projecting yourself, in feigning an alien consciousness, that too much energy gets lost, I think, in the masquerade. And I think this is not only true of me.

INTERVIEWER: How did you come to write those books about Florence and Venice?

MCCARTHY: By chance. I was in Paris, just about to go home to America, and somebody called up and asked if I would come and have a drink at the Ritz before lunch, that he wanted to ask me something. It was an intermediary from the Berniers, who edit *L'Oeil*. They were in Lausanne, and this man wanted to know whether I would write a book on Venice for them. I had been in Venice once for ten days, years ago, but it seemed somehow adventurous. And there were other reasons too. So I said yes. I went out to meet the Berniers in Lausanne. I had absolutely no money left, about twenty dollars, and I thought, what if all this is a terrible practical joke? You know. I'll get to Lausanne and there won't be any of these people! There'll be nobody! I ran into Jay Laughlin that night, and he said that his aunt was in Lausanne at the moment, so that if anything happened to me, I could call on her! But in any case, I went to Lausanne, and they were real, they were there. And we drove to Venice together.

I knew nothing about the subject—maybe I exaggerate my ignorance now—but I was *appalled*. I was afraid to ask any questions—whenever I'd ask a question Georges Bernier would shudder because it revealed such absolutely terrifying depths of ignorance. So I tried to be silent. I'd never heard before that there was more than one Tiepolo, or more than one Tintoretto, that there was a son. I vaguely knew Bellini, but didn't have any idea there were three Bellinis. Things like that. I couldn't have been expected to know Venetian history, but actually Venetian history is very easy to bone up on, and there isn't much. But the art history! And I considered myself a reasonably cultivated person! My art history was of the most fragmentary nature!

But it was fun, and then that led me into doing the Florence book. I didn't want to, at first. But everything in Venice, in Italy for that matter, really points to Florence, everything in the Renaissance anyway, like signposts on a road. Whenever you're near discovery, you're near Florence. So I felt that this was all incomplete; I thought I had to go to Florence. It was far from my mind to write a book. Then various events happened, and slowly I decided, All right, I would do the book on Florence. After that I went back to Venice and studied the Florentines in Venice, just for a few days. It was *so* strange to come back to Venice after being immersed in Florence. It looked so terrible! From an architectural point of view, *so* scrappy and nondescript, if you'd been living with the Florentine substance and monumentality, and intellectuality of architecture. At first coming back was a real shock. Oh, and I discovered I liked history! And I thought, my God, maybe I've made a mistake. Maybe I should have been an historian.

INTERVIEWER: It would also appear that you discovered you loved Brunelleschi.

MCCARTHY: Oh, yes! Yes! Also, I felt a great, great congeniality—I don't mean with Brunelleschi personally, I would flatter myself if I said that—but with the history of Florence, the Florentine temperament. I felt that through the medium of writing about this city I could set forth what I believed in, what I was for; that through this city, its history, its architects and painters— more its sculptors than its painters—it was possible for me to say what I believed in. And say it very affirmatively, even though this all ended in 1529, you know, long before the birth of Shakespeare.

INTERVIEWER: In reading the Florence book, I remember being very moved by the passage where you talk of Brunelleschi, about his "absolute integrity and essence," that solidity of his, both real and ideal. When you write about Brunelleschi, you write about this sureness, this "being-itself," and yet as a novelist—in *The Company She Keeps* for instance—you speak of something so very different, and you take almost as a theme this fragmented unplaceability of the human personality.

MCCARTHY: But I was very young then. I think I'm really not interested in the quest for the self any more. Oh, I suppose everyone continues to be interested in the quest for the self, but what you feel when you're older, I think, is that—how to express this—that you really must *make* the self. It's absolutely useless to look for it, you won't find it, but it's possible in some sense to make it. I don't mean in the sense of making a mask, a Yeatsian mask. But you finally begin in some sense to make and to choose the self you want.

INTERVIEWER: Can you write novels about that?

MCCARTHY: I never have. I never have, I've never even thought of it. That is, I've never thought of writing a developmental novel in which a self of some kind is discovered or is made, is forged, as they say. No. I suppose in a sense I don't know any more today than I did in 1941 about what my identity is. But I've stopped looking for it. I must say, I believe much more in truth now than I did. I do believe in the solidity of truth much more. Yes. I believe there is a truth, and that it's knowable.

—ELISABETH SIFTON
1961

9. Elizabeth Hardwick

Elizabeth Hardwick was born in Lexington, Kentucky, in 1916. She came to New York to attend graduate school at Columbia University in the 1940s, and has for the most part lived in the city ever since. For many years she was married to the American poet Robert Lowell. In addition to her long association with *Partisan Review*, she is a founder and advisory editor of *The New York Review of Books*, the editor of *The Selected Letters of William James* (1961), and the author of three novels—*The Ghostly Lover* (1945), *The Simple Truth* (1955), and *Sleepless Nights* (1979)— and three collections of essays—*Seduction and Betrayal: Women and Literature* (1974), *A View of My Own: Essays in Literature and Society* (1980), and *Bartleby in Manhattan and Other Essays* (1983).

Winner of a Guggenheim Fellowship and many other prizes, Hardwick was the first woman recipient of the George Jean Nathan Award for dramatic criticism in 1967. She is a member of the American Academy of Arts & Letters.

&.

The beginning of June was hot. I took a journey and, of course,
everything was ~~different and strange~~ [new]. When you travel your first discovery is that ~~somehow~~ you [do not] ~~no longer~~ exist. The phlox bloomed in its
faded purples; on the hillside, phallic pines. Foreigners in the arcades,
in the ~~little~~ [basket] shops. A steamy haze blurred the lines of the hills. A
dirty, exhausting sky. Already, ~~it seemed,~~ the summer was passing
away. Soon the boats would be gathered in, ferries roped to the dock.

I ~~was~~ [am] looking for the fosselized, for something-- persons and
places thick and encrusted with final shape; instead there are many,
many minnows, wildly swimming, trembling, vigilant to escape the net.

Kentucky-- that ~~was~~ [is] certainly ~~always~~ part of it. My mother
lived as a girl in so many North Carolina towns they are confused
in my [mind]. Raleigh and Charlotte. ~~Those two I remember.~~ She hardly knew
her own parents; they died quickly as people did then of whatever was
in the air-- pneumonia, diphtheria, tuberculosis. I never knew a
person so indifferent to the past. It was as if she didn't know who
she was. ~~in some sense.~~ She had brothers and sisters and was raised
by them, passing their names down to us. I met one of her sisters when I was a
Child. She ran a hotel in asheville, north Carolina,
Her face, my mother's, is not quite clear to me. A boneless, soft
prettiness, with small brown eyes and the scarcest of eyebrows, darkened
with a lead pencil. ~~Not a face easy to describe.~~

1962

Dearest M: Here I am back in New York, on 67th Street in a high
steep place with long, dirty windows. ~~It is quite nice, but,~~ In the late

Elizabeth Hardwick

Elizabeth Hardwick lives on the West Side of Manhattan, on a quiet street near enough to Central Park to have heard the crowds and speakers at the great political demonstrations in Sheep's Meadow. Her apartment is light and spacious. "Like modern architecture," she says, "it looks much better in photographs." The building was designed for artists, and the living room is dominated by a large window. Behind the enormous plants and the freestanding tiles, one can see a comforting fixture of urban life: a fire escape.

Her home is clearly that of a writer constantly at work, and strewn throughout is a lifetime's accumulation of furniture, objects, paintings, posters, photographs, records, heirlooms, and countless books. On either side of the living room are more books: ceiling-high shelves of histories, fiction, and poetry. It is a working library, collected with her late husband, the poet Robert Lowell. The daily effort to keep a large library in order has made Hardwick favor paperbacks, preferably those lightweight and storable ones that can be whipped out on a bus or an airplane—nonsmoking section—without too much fuss.

Just as there are books everywhere that indicate the life of the mind, so one frequently comes upon notebooks and notepads on the coffee table, on the dining room table, things in which she has jotted down lines, questions, ideas. The typewriter goes from room to room, one day upstairs in her study, the next morning downstairs. And then there are the manuscripts of former as well as current students from her various writing classes, which she will read and comment on extensively.

This interview took place in her home, where she occasionally puttered, setting stray books in their places as we talked.

INTERVIEWER: I have the feeling you don't like to talk about yourself, at least not in a formal way.

HARDWICK: Well, I do a lot of talking and the "I" is not often absent. In general I'd rather talk about other people. Gossip, or as we gossips like to say, character analysis.

INTERVIEWER: *Sleepless Nights* is reticent, perhaps, but it certainly has the tone of lived experience, of a kind of autobiography.

HARDWICK: I guess so. After all, I wrote it in the first person and used my own name, Elizabeth. Not very confessional, however. And not entirely taken from life, rather less than the reader might think.

INTERVIEWER: Many of the essays in *Seduction and Betrayal* have an oddly personal tone. The stress on certain parts of the texts shows that you have dug things out in an unusual, somehow urgent manner, as if you had lived them. I'm thinking of the Jane Carlyle essay and your way of looking at Ibsen's *Rosmersholm*.

HARDWICK: Jane Carlyle was real, but of course I didn't *really* know her, as the saying goes. The people in *Rosmersholm* are figures of Ibsen's imagination.

INTERVIEWER: What is the reason for your deep attraction to Ibsen?

HARDWICK: I don't know that I have a deep attraction for Ibsen. Sometimes I think he's an awful dolt . . . wooden, and in certain plays stolidly grandiose like the mountains that are such an unfortunate apotheosis in *Little Eyolf* and *When We Dead Awaken*. I don't like the poetic Ibsen, but I have found myself deeply engaged by the beauty, you might call it, of the old Ibsen domestic misery.

INTERVIEWER: Someone once said to me that he was fascinated by your essay on *Rosmersholm*, about the triangle between the man and the two women. But when he went to the play he couldn't always find your ideas there on the page. What do you make of that?

HARDWICK: I certainly hope what I said is on Ibsen's pages and of course I think it is. Still, you're not writing an essay to give a résumé of the plots. You choose to write because you think you have something fresh to say on a topic. That is, if you're writing from choice and not just as a journeyman doing a job. Perhaps it's true that in reading certain works, not all works, I do sometimes enter a sort of hallucinatory state and I think I see undercurrents and light in dark places about the imagined emotions and actions. This often stimulates me to write, particularly about novels. Of course the text is the object, the given, and the period is not often one's own and if there is anything detestable it is the looking at fictional characters as if they were your friends. I have found that horrible inclination among students, more and more so. They don't know the difference between calling a character "silly" and realizing that they are reading a masterpiece of created, located, visionary "silliness." I think every reader and critic falls into a hallucinatory state and that is as true of the technocrats, the deconstructionists, as of any others.

INTERVIEWER: When you say "hallucinatory state," are you trying to describe how the creative process works for you?

HARDWICK: Perhaps "hallucinatory" is too strong or too mysterious a word. What I meant was that in reading books and planning to write about them, or maybe just in reading certain books, you begin to see all sorts of not quite expressed things, to make connections, sometimes to feel you have discovered or felt certain things the author may not have been entirely conscious of. It's a sort of creative or "possessed" reading and that is why I think even the most technical of critics do the same thing, by their means making quite mysterious discoveries. But as I said, the text is always the first thing. It has the real claim on you, of course.

INTERVIEWER: Do you fall into this state when you write fiction?

HARDWICK: I don't fall into a state at all. I just meant to describe something happening in the brain when it is stimulated by reading imaginative works. As for writing fiction, well, you don't have any primary text, of course. You have to create that, and yet the struggle seems to be to uncover things by language, to find out what you mean and feel by the sheer effort of writing it down. By expression you discover what you wish to express or what can be expressed, by you. Things that are vague in the beginning have to be made concrete. Often, what you thought was the creative idea ahead of you vanishes or becomes something else.

INTERVIEWER: What comes first in sitting down to write—I guess we're talking about fiction. Is it a concept? Is it a character? Is it a scene?

HARDWICK: It takes many things to make a work of fiction, but I suppose it is true that there is a kind of starting point in the mind, a point that may be different for each piece of work. Sometimes I have had the impulse to begin fiction from a single line I had in my head.

INTERVIEWER: Can you give an example?

HARDWICK: I remember that I started writing *Sleepless Nights* because of a single line. The line was: "Now I will start my novel, but I don't know whether to call myself I or she."

INTERVIEWER: Was this a first line, a beginning line?

HARDWICK: No, it was to be the last line of the opening scene. I published the first chapter in *The New York Review of Books* and the line was the ending of the scene. But as I went on to write the book, I did call the narrator "I" and so I deleted the line from the final text. Some readers noticed the omission and asked me about it. I think now that I could have retained the line and just gone on with the narrative "I," as if to say I had made the decision.

INTERVIEWER: What did the line mean to you? That you knew it was going to be an autobiographical novel?

HARDWICK: Of course that line is not a theme. It is a wondering aloud about structure and also meant to indicate that sometimes in novels the use of the third person is really a disguise for the first person. I mean certain fictions have the strong feeling of autobiography even if they are written in the third person. It's something a sensitive reader can feel.

INTERVIEWER: When you started *Sleepless Nights* did you know anything more than that it would be an autobiographical novel?

HARDWICK: I wrote the first scene, starting with a description of a place and then going on to the writing of an imaginary letter to "Dearest M." The opening scene dominated the book, set the tone, and then, of course, as I worked on it I had to write the book—that is, create scenes, encounters, and so on.

INTERVIEWER: Has the impulse for writing ever started from a last line?

HARDWICK: Maybe not a last line, but a notion of the ending can be a useful stimulus.

INTERVIEWER: Does the opening paragraph mostly concern mood? Or plot? Or character?

HARDWICK: I don't have many plots and perhaps as a justification I sometimes think: if I want a plot I'll watch *Dallas*. I think it's mood. No, I mean tone. Tone arrived at by language. I can't write a story or an essay until I can, by revision after revision, get the opening tone right. Sometimes it seems to take forever, but when I have it I can usually go on. It's a matter of the voice, how you are going to approach the task at hand. It's all language and rhythm and the establishment of the relation to the material, of who's speaking, not speaking as a person exactly, but as a mind, a sensibility.

INTERVIEWER: Can you always arrive at the tone you want?

HARDWICK: No, I can't, and when that happens I put the work aside. But I've noticed that the effort is always useful. I mostly use the things, sometime, somewhere, that I've abandoned. They've been worked on, exist, if only in a few pages—and the old yellow pages flaking away in a drawer turn out to be useful. I don't know what I'm thinking about a particular thing until I have some kind of draft. It's the actual execution that tells me what I want to say, what I always wanted to say when I started.

INTERVIEWER: What do you mean when you say that you don't know what is in your mind until you've written it?

HARDWICK: I'm not sure I understand the process of writing. There is, I'm sure, something strange about imaginative concentration. The brain slowly begins to function in a different way, to make mysterious connections. Say, it is Monday, and you write a very bad draft, but if you keep trying, on Friday, words, phrases, appear almost unexpectedly. I don't know why you can't do it on Monday, or why I can't. I'm the same person, no smarter, I have nothing more at hand.

INTERVIEWER: Do you find that unique with yourself?

HARDWICK: I think it's true of a lot of writers. It's one of the things writing students don't understand. They write a first draft and are quite disappointed, or often *should* be disappointed. They don't understand that they have merely begun, and that they may be merely beginning even in the second or third draft. For the great expansive prose writers, obviously this isn't the case. Somehow everything is available to them all the time. That's the real prose gift.

INTERVIEWER: What writers have had this gift?

HARDWICK: Tolstoy, Dickens, Henry James. All the greatly productive geniuses. I am very struck by the revisions of Henry James. They seem to me always interesting, but in the end quite minor—changes in a few words, shiftings. The powers of concentration the great writers show are extraordinarily moving.

INTERVIEWER: Are there any tricks or devices that seem to help?

HARDWICK: For me, writing has not become easier after all these years. It is harder—perhaps because of the standards you set for your work. I suppose you have, by effort, a greater command than you imagine. The fact that writing remains so difficult is what puzzles.

INTERVIEWER: What is it about the writing process that gives you the most pleasure?

HARDWICK: The revision. That's what I like, working on a page or a scene.

INTERVIEWER: What about help with revision? Did Cal [Robert Lowell] ever help you with the books or essays?

HARDWICK: Not really. His suggestions were always wonderful, but so general I couldn't make much use of them. And he was always revising his own work and showing it to me and to his friends. He was revising something from the moment he got up until the moment he went to sleep, if only in his head, and so much of the time with him when you were alone was spent reading and talking to him about what he had done during the day. And that was very pleasant to me, it was always very interesting reading it, and it wasn't just to me that he read his work in progress. I have noticed the same method with other poets. I can remember having dear old I. A. Richards to dinner, and we weren't sitting there very long before the sheaf came out of the pocket of his coat, and he read his new poems, and that was wonderful.

INTERVIEWER: You didn't offer your own work in progress in that way?

HARDWICK: Well, it was a little bit different, you know, prose being longer, and it's not quite the same as seeing a quatrain at the end of the day. Cal did read my work, of course, and he was very encouraging and nice about it, and all of that, but it wasn't the same as going over each little part.

INTERVIEWER: How about the intellectual content of the essays?

HARDWICK: I must say he often looked discomfited on that score. Sometimes he thought I was too snippy.

INTERVIEWER: Really? He'd ask you to de-snip?

HARDWICK: I remember in one of the first issues of *The New York Review* I wrote a piece about a biographical book on Robert Frost. It was more or less mild, but Cal was quite annoyed— annoyed for a short time. I noticed in Randall Jarrell's letters that he gave a bit of approval to my Frost essay and so I said to myself, "O.K., Cal?" On the whole, Cal was encouraging. He liked women writers and I don't think he ever had a true interest in a woman who wasn't a writer—an odd turn-on indeed and one I've noticed not greatly shared. Women writers don't tend to be passive vessels or wives, saying, "Oh, that's good, dear."

INTERVIEWER: Was it stimulating to your own work to be involved in that sort of tremendously volatile writers' atmosphere?

HARDWICK: What do you mean "involved"? That would have been my atmosphere no matter what. Literature was always my passion. I do remember however that I was once asked if I had felt overpowered by Lowell's work, meaning, I guess, if it overpowered my own. I said, "Well, I should hope so." I had great regard and admiration for it. Learned from him and from it, got pleasure from it.

INTERVIEWER: If you could say what was particularly enriching about your life with Lowell, what would it be? The spirit of it, or technical literary matters?

HARDWICK: The quality of his mind—quite the most thrilling I've known. Once at dinner something came up about what people you have known whom you considered to be geniuses. Mary McCarthy was there. We all thought for a while and Mary and I came up with the same two names. Cal and Hannah Arendt.

INTERVIEWER: What do you think is the essential piece of equipment a writer must have?

HARDWICK: Well, you know, there is such a thing as talent, a bit of talent. I'll leave it at that.

INTERVIEWER: Given the talent, should writers be concerned with the issues of the times . . . things like that?

HARDWICK: Not necessarily. Of course they usually *are* concerned with the issues of the times in some way. The variety and strangeness of literary works is amazing. You wake up one morning and someone's done something a little bit new, something fresh and genuine, a new accent, quality of experience, way of composing and structuring. That's very beautiful to me. I am very happy when I see an interesting, gifted struggle with fictional form. I know as well as the next person that many fine things use traditional methods of narration and there will be, naturally, much that is traditional in those who experiment. Here I am not talking about a great innovator like Joyce, but about lesser struggles. When I open a new work of fiction I like to notice the way it is constructed, to learn something from it. Like Milan Kundera's latest novel, *The Unbearable Lightness of Being*. The narrator comes in and out and yet the form shifts to stories, to feelings, actions the narrator could not have known. I think it is done successfully there. There is always the problem of who is seeing, who is thinking. I am excited when I feel the author is trying to cope with this dilemma—and it is often a compositional dilemma.

INTERVIEWER: Can talent be taught?

HARDWICK: Perhaps not. I try to uncover what talent may be hiding by teaching creative reading. That turns out to be rather difficult—to read as a writer reads. I guess that is what I meant by reading in a "hallucinatory state." Not the perfect phrase.

INTERVIEWER: What state of mind are you in when the writing seems to be moving along?

HARDWICK: I don't know. I don't know why I am so helplessly led to condensation in both my fiction and my essays. Some people find it hard to follow my meaning because I don't spell it out, not entirely. My writing is simple but I like to be sort of emphatic and then let it go. I remember when I was writing exams in school I'd be the first one finished. All these people writing away. As I look back on it I think I didn't want to tell the teacher what he already knew, but to try to get at things from an angle—nothing very grand, just a little twist. That little twist always got me an A *minus*.

INTERVIEWER: In your first novel, *The Ghostly Lover*, and in your early short stories that appeared in various magazines, you seemed to be a Southern writer. And then you became much more identified with New York. Why is that?

HARDWICK: I don't like to quote myself, but since one doesn't have many ideas—or perhaps just *I* don't have many ideas—I will have to quote what I said in a Southern literature discussion. That is, that being a Southern writer is a decision, not a fate. Naturally, I love the best Southern writing and spent my youth, up through the university, in Lexington, Kentucky, a very beautiful and interesting place. But I think a critical, defining moment came into my life one summer. I had received a fellowship to LSU, a magical place then, with the *Southern Review* and all sorts of brilliant writers around. And then in August I suddenly didn't want to go and instead I went to Columbia . . . and without a fellowship. I'm amazed I was accepted.

INTERVIEWER: And then what happened?

HARDWICK: Well, ever trendy, I decided I had to specialize in the seventeenth century because that was the time of the Metaphysical poets, John Donne and so on. That was the hot period. After the first seminar I woke up and thought, I don't even know when the seventeenth century was! Of course I rushed out and read some books fast, filling in my literary knowledge, which began in 1920. It was all rather fun. It was New York and even back home I had been reading *Partisan Review* and had already been a Communist and an ex-Communist, Left variety, before I got here.

INTERVIEWER: Is that true?

HARDWICK: Yes, I wouldn't say it otherwise.

INTERVIEWER: I remember you once said that your dream when you were young was to be a Jewish intellectual.

HARDWICK: I said that as a joke, but it was more or less true. What I meant was the enlightenment, a certain deracination which I value, an angular vision, love of learning, cosmopolitanism, a word that practically means Jewish in Soviet lexicography. Right now, I'd say my remark depended upon which Jewish intellectual. I am not sympathetic with the political attitudes of certain members of the New Right who happen to be Jewish intellectuals, and less sympathetic to the Christian Right, most of whom are scarcely to be called intellectuals at all. I don't like the chauvinism, the militarism, the smugness, and the Social Darwinism, that jargon term, the support of Ronald Reagan . . . and all the rest.

INTERVIEWER: How do you feel about the religiosity of the New Right, the fundamentalists, and Reagan's courting of them?

HARDWICK: I think the fundamentalists' and Reagan's use of religion is an appalling blasphemy. The idea that God wants a strong America. Many Americans will naturally want a strong America, but I don't know that God is in agreement. I hadn't thought of Him as being a patriot . . . I hadn't thought of Him as in a state of desire except against idolaters, and as we know from the Old Testament it is very easy to sink into idolatry, which a good deal of the flag-waving is just now. As for evangelizing Christians, their vulgarization of the Scriptures surpasses belief, their incredible assumption of Jesus as a pal in the cheering stand.

INTERVIEWER: Are you interested in religion?

HARDWICK: Of course, even though I'm a nonbeliever. I was brought up a Presbyterian. I still feel an attachment to the Presbyterian Church, where I know all the hymns and where I first felt the beauty and resonance of the Scriptures. Actually, when I lived in New England I was surprised to find that the denomination hardly existed there—not that if it had I was ready to put on my pumps and trot off every Sunday. The Scotch and the Scotch-Irish, which my mother's family were, mostly migrated to the upper South, especially to North Carolina, where she grew up. In New England you're supposed to think that the Presbyterians and the Congregationalists are more or less the same, but my seventeenth-century studies told me otherwise.

INTERVIEWER: What are you trying to say about religion . . . as a nonbeliever?

HARDWICK: I don't know. It may sound glib but I suppose for me religion is a vast, valuable museum . . . and, yes, I know the treasures of it are not the same as going to the Louvre . . . although now that I think of it, there's a good deal of overlapping, isn't there?

INTERVIEWER: Do you see any literary influence of the New Right, of the neo-conservatives?

HARDWICK: I don't know about influence, but I do see that, as always, cultural and political attitudes swim along in the same bloodstream. Defense of American values, as these notions are called, can have a wide swing, picking up all sorts of things like homosexuals or fast women who are not doing their bit for the preservation of the American family. . . . For myself, I like many homosexuals and many self-absorbed, childless women, and I can't see them as a menace to the republic, or even to Republicans. Some of my best friends . . . and so on.

INTERVIEWER: Do you find any conservative attitudes specifically literary?

HARDWICK: I notice the creeping development of what I would call the Conservative Realism, because it brings to mind the intellectual follies of Socialist Realism. You get the idea that disaffected, even laid-back, attitudes in fiction, certain choices of despairing subject matter, are contemptible in a writer residing in the fullness of the United States. Certain tones of reflection are seen as a snide assault on the Free World.

INTERVIEWER: For instance?

HARDWICK: It's a rich field but I happen to remember a particular review of Ann Beattie's stories which said, "They seem treacherous to the energy and heroic idealism that are her country's saving grace." Now, I ask you! That appeared in *Partisan Review*, which is not a neo-con magazine, but "bore from within," as we used to say. Also, there is Norman Podhoretz's consignment of Henry Adams and all his works to the ash heap of history.

INTERVIEWER: You have taught a great deal. Why do you think many writers resent teaching? Do you agree with them that it interferes in subtle ways with their own writing?

HARDWICK: Nothing interferes with my own writing except my often irresolute character and of course the limitations of my talent.

INTERVIEWER: You seem rather accommodating and modest and yet you can be aggressive in your writing.

HARDWICK: And not only in my writing, alas. I don't like aggressiveness and I detest anger, a quality some feminists and many psychiatrists think one should cultivate in order to express the self. I was astonished by the number of obituaries of Lillian Hellman that spoke with reverence of her anger. I don't see anger as an emotion to be cultivated and, in any case, it is not in short supply.

INTERVIEWER: Can you talk a bit about your background—school, childhood?

HARDWICK: Childhood? I came from a large family and many of my brothers and sisters were older than I, and I learned from them since they were, most of them, going to college when I was growing up. It was not an intellectual atmosphere, but a stimulating one. Like all writers I know of, the early days were dominated by a love of reading, just reading, like eating, anything around. It was not until I got to the University of Kentucky that the range of books was quite suddenly and very excitingly extended. I had some extraordinary teachers, some of the refugees from Europe, and very smart friends, some clever and "know-it-all" from New York, which appealed to me, and some very bright and lovable from just down home. I was not aware of any intellectual deprivation and there was none in the general sense. But aren't we all self-educated, and of course our self-education never includes all of the things we would like to know or need to know.

INTERVIEWER: And your career?

HARDWICK: Is it a career? I mean is that the right word for being a writer? It's a strange life. . . . The most peculiar thing about it is that when you write you are required to think and having once noticed that, you observe how little the rest of life makes such a demand. It demands something else, many things of course, but not sitting and thinking the way you must when you write, when you revise, when you abandon, start over, refine, all of that. About my own efforts, I sometimes feel I can say, well, I'm doing my best, or have done my best. That is not the supreme thrill for one who has spent her life reading superb writings of all kinds. But I am happy to do what I can.

INTERVIEWER: Some young women I know think of you as very fortunate to have your place in things, your work and so forth.

HARDWICK: As I have grown older I see myself as fortunate in many ways. It is fortunate to have had all my life this passion for studying and enjoying literature and for trying to add a bit to it as interestingly as I can. This passion has given me much joy, it has given me friends who care for the same things, it has given me employment, escape from boredom, everything. The greatest gift is the passion for reading. It is cheap, it consoles, it distracts, it excites, it gives you knowledge of the world and experience of a wide kind. It is a moral illumination.

INTERVIEWER: Do you think there are special difficulties in being a woman writer?

HARDWICK: Woman writer? A bit of a crunch trying to get those two words together . . . I guess I would say no special difficulty, just the usual difficulties of the arts.

INTERVIEWER: So you feel it's the same for men and women?

HARDWICK: Nothing is the same for men and women.

INTERVIEWER: Not the same and . . . what else?

HARDWICK: Actually I have noticed lately a good deal of bitchiness with regard to certain women writers. Susan Sontag, for instance. The public scourging she was subjected to from all sides seemed to me disgusting and unworthy.

INTERVIEWER: What "public scourging" are you referring to?

HARDWICK: A sort of extended flap about a speech she made at a public gathering in which she spoke of communism as "fascism with a human face" and other matters. This was followed by attacks from the Left and the Right that seemed to go on for months. She was also scorned for writing so much about Europeans, the French particularly. I think her being a woman, a learned one, a *femme savante*, had something to do with it. As an intellectual with very special gifts and attitudes, it was somehow felt that this made her a proper object for ridicule of a coarse kind. I believe the tone was different because she was seen as a very smart, intellectually ambitious woman.

INTERVIEWER: Intellectual woman? Aren't you yourself one of them?

HARDWICK: Let me quote from *The Land of Ulro*, the latest book by the poet Czeslaw Milosz. "The history of my stupidity would fill many volumes."

INTERVIEWER: But, these days, women writers fare about as well as men, don't they?

HARDWICK: In general, of course. Just as many atrocious women writers are laughing all the way to the bank as men. But I do feel there is an inclination to punish women of what you might call presumption of one kind or another.

INTERVIEWER: Which women?

HARDWICK: For instance, Joan Didion and Renata Adler. I haven't found two books recently that have seemed to me more imaginative, intelligent, and original than *Democracy* and *Pitch Dark*. In the reviews, at least in many of them, I felt a note of contempt and superiority, often expressed in a lame, inept effort to parody. . . . And when you think of what the big guys have been turning out! And the ponderous, quaking reviews they receive!

INTERVIEWER: You mean they're getting away with something? What big guys?

HARDWICK: Never mind, never mind.

INTERVIEWER: What about reviewers today?

HARDWICK: I notice that many of them in very important places haven't written anything except their reviews, their quick, short reviews, composed with an air of easy authority. For the most part, I think the authority should be in some way earned. Well, they pass the night perhaps. . . . When a real writer discusses literature and culture you will notice a difference in style, in carefulness, and you will actually find ideas, illuminations, oddities and not merely yes-or-no opinions.

INTERVIEWER: Are you saying it's not entirely fair for a critic to do nothing but practice criticism?

HARDWICK: No. Let me say that criticism, analysis, reflection is a natural response to the existence in the world of works of art. It is an honorable and even an exalted endeavor. Without it, works of art would appear in a vacuum, as if they had no relation to the minds experiencing them. It would be a dismal, unthinkable world with these shooting stars arousing no comment, leaving no trace. But it is the mind of the critic, somehow, the establishment of his own thought and values, that counts; and that establishment is the authority of the voice, whether it comes from creative work in the arts or creative work in criticism. When I read a review, a mere short review, I am more interested at first in who is doing the reviewing than in the work under discussion. The name, what is attached to it by previous work, by serious thought, tells me whether it is likely to have any meaning or value for me. It is not a question of right or wrong specific opinions, but of the quality of the mind.

INTERVIEWER: You have been criticized for your review of Simone de Beauvoir's *The Second Sex* in *A View of My Own*. Would you still stand on that?

HARDWICK: No, I wouldn't. It's a wonderful, remarkable book. Nothing that has come since on the matter of women compares to it. When I wrote my comments I was thinking of existentialism and the idea that one can choose and not be dominated by the given . . . something like that. And of course thinking back on my remarks I see how much has changed since the 1950s, especially in the manner of life for women. You are still weaker than men in muscular force, but can sleep in the streets if you like, even, alas, if that is the only place you have to sleep, and go to Arabia in your jeans and knapsack . . . and much, much more.

INTERVIEWER: I was present a few years ago at a panel discussion where you were asked who was the greatest American female novelist, and you said Henry James. I had the feeling you meant something serious about that.

HARDWICK: Such remarks don't bear scrutiny. Did I actually say that? I do remember saying once that maybe the greatest female novelist in English was Constance Garnett. Sometimes I try to lighten the gloom of discussions but I notice that no one laughs. Instead you see a few people writing down the name.

INTERVIEWER: I have the impression that in your most recent stories about New York—"The Bookseller," "Back Issues," and "On the Eve"—you are using the city almost as a text and the characters you have chosen are instruments of decoding. Or is that too mechanistic for the way you place these people, catch the start and stop of their lives?

HARDWICK: I don't know about decoding New York. It's a large place, oh yes. And it's a place, isn't it? Still very much a place, or so I think. There's not much good feeling about New York, in spite of the T-shirts and the "Big Apple" and so on.

INTERVIEWER: You seem to be faithful to it.

HARDWICK: I like cities, big cities and even medium-sized cities. If I were traveling about America, I'd always want to spend the night downtown. If I could still find downtown. Yes, I'm faithful to New York, one might say. It's ours, our country's, our great metropolis. Many people no longer like the melting pot notion and seem to feel there are too many poor trying to be melted in the great vat. Of course everybody hates poor people. They're a damned nuisance. Always wanting something. Perhaps they used to be a part of the scheme of things, a part of nature, always with us and so on. But you might say they don't fit in anymore, or so I think many people see it.

INTERVIEWER: In a talk at the Columbia School of Architecture, you spoke of the increasing "Bombayism" of New York. What did you mean?

HARDWICK: Well, Bombay is called the New York of India, and I guess New York is becoming the Bombay of the U.S. What I had in mind was the increasing separation of the classes, the gap, as of another species. The streets filled with Untouchables. Just look the other way and move on. The intractable, milling others for whom you have no solution. Roll up the window of the limo. Step aside and into a cab. . . . New York is a city of the rich and the poor. It's a terrible place for the middle classes, and for what you would call the workers who run the elevators, build the buildings, clerk in the stores, cook in the restaurants. Manhattan is not for them. They get on the subway and go to the other boroughs at night. So the culture of the city, the vitality, the promise is more and more restricted. There's not a foot of living space and what there is is so overpriced as to raise the dead. That is a violation of the contract of the city as we knew it. When you think of old New York, I, at least, don't think of the patricians, but of the Lower East Side and Harlem—both are gone, wiped out as images of promise, change, relief from the old country or from the South or whatever, as places that created styles like the jazziness of Harlem that captivated Europe and the experience of generations of immigrants.

INTERVIEWER: Are you trying to express this in the fiction you're working on?

HARDWICK: I know that I can't. I realize how narrow my knowledge of the city is. I can't take it in as a whole. I feel I know less about it than when I first came here, but I very much like to think about it and care about it. I am using it as the landscape of my fiction just now, but whether I can make an image of the city itself I don't know. Everything in the stories I have done recently is imaginary. I even had to go to the Public Library and look around.

INTERVIEWER: You mean in "Back Issues" where you met the Greek?

HARDWICK: I've never met a Greek in my life.

INTERVIEWER: The shop in "The Bookseller" reminded me of every secondhand shop I've seen in Manhattan.

HARDWICK: I hardly ever go into a bookstore because, instead of buying, I would like to give away about five thousand of my seven thousand books, which are weighing on me like some suffocating plague.

INTERVIEWER: I'll take them.

HARDWICK: They're yours. Bring your van. I can't find those I want, thousands have not been dusted in years. I miss the time when I used to go into the old secondhand shops, looking for the modern classics. What a pleasure that was, not having them and finding them. And then to get volumes of history, all the odd tomes.

INTERVIEWER: What do you think of the state of publishing just now?

HARDWICK: Insofar as making money is concerned it is better now not to be an *author* when you write a book. Being a writer just mucks it up. I see that when I look at the best-seller list of books by movie stars and doctors, although some *literateurs* make money, fortunately. But of course the best-seller list, poor old thrashed dog, is not what things are about. Otherwise I don't think publishing changes much. It's still sort of a running faucet and words and pages pour out. I doubt that many worthwhile books don't make it to the printing presses. I like sometimes to think otherwise.

INTERVIEWER: Why do you like to think otherwise?

HARDWICK: Just the idea that something brilliant and unacceptable, something too quirky and original is being created. In general I guess I feel that what we have is what is there.

INTERVIEWER: Do you feel that the European novel, the Latin American novel, the African novel, the dissident writings are superior to what is being done here?

HARDWICK: Superior, who knows? In some ways, I suppose we are left behind in the great themes that arrive from the feeling of displacement and loss. V. S. Naipaul said something about English fiction—it's all tea parties or something like that. We seem to have divorce and adultery and being young with your parents and being a bit gay here and there, or quite gay—can I still say queer?—and drinking beer at the truck stop instead of getting ahead. But we live in a world of displaced, agonized talents who have lost country and language and family and whose condition represents so much of this century. The survival of those talents, the imaginative rendering of their experience is extraordinarily moving and large. Of course it's all in the telling. We are a protected country even though so many of us are whipped to a frenzy about the dangers around us and feel the best thing we can do for our citizens is to push them into a siege mentality. But meanwhile . . . meanwhile, you can be quite happy and make quite a good living crying havoc and getting out the siege vote. Let me say that I would not want our country overrun in order to create fiction and poetry. All I'm saying is that the introversion of our literature just now makes it narrower than the exile writing. But everyone knows that.

INTERVIEWER: Who are the readers?

HARDWICK: I don't know. It is thought that the present young generation doesn't know much about literature, hasn't read much . . . and yet a lot of the writing of the last decades is full of parodies, mimicry, learned references of a sort and readers seem to get it. I always wonder who buys the books. "100,000 in print," the ads say. Fifty thousand may have come from knowing that the first fifty thousand bought the book. That's okay. Especially if it's something of value. I don't think it's a good idea for writers to think too much about the publishing world. I sense in a good many books, even in books by the best writers, an anxiety about how it will do in the marketplace. You can feel it on the page, a sort of sweat of calculation. As if to say, well, it will be a few years before the next one and I had better be sure I don't let this chance to make some money pass by. But no more about publishing.

INTERVIEWER: Okay, no more about publishing. May I ask you how you feel about growing older?

HARDWICK: You can always ask. Or perhaps no one need ask. Just another piece of rotten luck. No, I haven't found anything good to say about it. Not a condition that can be recommended. Its only value is that it spares you the opposite, not growing older. People do cling to consciousness, and under the most dreadful circumstances. It shows you that it is all we have, doesn't it? Waking up, the first and the last privilege, waking up once more.

INTERVIEWER: Do you think it is more painful for women than for men?

HARDWICK: More about women and men? About something so burdensome it doesn't seem valuable to make distinctions. Oh, the dear grave. I like what Gottfried Benn wrote, something like, "May I die in the spring when the ground is soft and easy to plough."

INTERVIEWER: I notice that you quote poets a lot.

HARDWICK: Well, you don't exactly quote prose I guess, although I often remember prose lines and sayings.

INTERVIEWER: Has the reading of poetry and the knowing of poets influenced your own style? Some have thought so.

HARDWICK: I don't know. Certainly Cal had a great influence on every aspect of my life. In literary matters, his immense learning and love of literature were a constant magic for me. As an influence on my own writing, that is more difficult to figure out. . . . Let me shift the subject a little. Maybe I was led to this by Cal's library, led to the prose written by poets. The poet's prose is one of my passions. I like the offhand flashes, the absence of the lumber in the usual prose . . . the quickness, the deftness, confidence, and even the relief from spelling everything out, plank by plank.

INTERVIEWER: Can you give an example?

HARDWICK: Well, here is a beautiful sentence, just right, inspired, a bit of prose I've memorized. It is by Pasternak. It goes:

"The beginning of April surprised Moscow in the white stupor of returning winter. On the seventh, it began to thaw for the second time, and on the fourteenth when Mayakovsky shot himself, not everyone had yet become accustomed to the novelty of spring." I love the rhythm of "the beginning of April . . . on the seventh . . . on the fourteenth" and the way the subject, Mayakovsky's suicide, is honored by the beauty of this introduction to the account. It's in *Safe Conduct*, Pasternak's autobiographical writing.

INTERVIEWER: Perhaps this leads to the subject of biography. You had a review in *The New York Times* of a biography of Katherine Anne Porter. There you had some rough things to say about the present practice.

HARDWICK: Last summer I had a striking experience. On the same day I received two letters, written by different people, each saying she was writing a biography of an author recently dead, an author not at all a household word. Two letters on the same day. I didn't know the author, but perhaps I'll merit a footnote in the book saying I did not know her. Or be thanked in the preface. Biography is a scrofulous cottage industry, done mostly by academics who get grants and have a good time going all over the place interviewing. How seldom it is that one has ever heard of the person writing the biography. What are the models, what are the qualifications? And it is not only the full-scale computer printout that these things are, but the books brought forth by lovers, friends from youth, cousins, whatever. I remember how horrified Dickens was when he met, in later life, the model for Dora in *David Copperfield*. Now Dora would hire a hack and write about Dickens. I have just read *Auden in Love* by Dorothy Farnan, the stepmother of Chester Kallman. I quite disapprove of the impertinence and the celestial glow around herself and her intimacy. Both Auden and Chester would be *mute, motionless, aghast*. Such books diminish the celebrated object and aggrandize the biographer or memoirist. I understand from the reviews of a new book about Agee that the swarm and smarm of little "facts" degrade the memory most of us have of Agee. Think how sweet Trelawny now appears; and De Quincey's beautiful memories of the Lake Poets, candid indeed, are almost a valentine because there is some equity between the subject and the author. And serious, incomparable reflection.

INTERVIEWER: How do you feel about Ian Hamilton's biography of Lowell?

HARDWICK: Hamilton is very intelligent and a very fine writer. Still the book is composed along contemporary lines and there is too little of Hamilton in it since most of the stage is given to raw documentation. When I finished it, I was reminded of Sir Walter Raleigh's executioner, who said, "There is not another such head to be chopped off!"

INTERVIEWER: Are you working on any fiction now? A future novel?

HARDWICK: Oh, yes. What are you working on? When one writer asks another that, he immediately apologizes, as if for a *gaffe*. . . . I might say I'm working on working on a novel. . . . I do hope I'll be writing a novel. I have some of it, but it is slow, of course, the writing. I hope not the work. Yes, I am writing fiction.

—DARRYL PINCKNEY
1984

10. Nadine Gordimer

Nadine Gordimer was born in 1923, in Springs, the Transvaal, a small town near Johannesburg, South Africa. Her father was a Jewish watchmaker who had immigrated from Lithuania at the age of thirteen; her mother was an Englishwoman. Raised "on the soft side" of South Africa's color bar, her concern with South Africa's apartheid system plays a large role in her novels.

Gordimer began writing at the age of nine; six years later she published her first story in *Forum*, a Johannesburg weekly. Though her formal education was interrupted by illness and she was taught primarily by a private tutor, Gordimer did study for one year at the University of Witwatersrand in 1945. Her first collection of short stories, *Face to Face*, was published in 1949. Gordimer is the author of nine novels, including *The Conservationist* (1976), which was awarded the Booker Prize, *Burger's Daughter* (1980), *July's People* (1981), and most recently, *A Sport of Nature* (1987). Her eight short story collections include *A Soldier's Embrace* (1980) and *Something Out There* (1984), and a collection of her essays, *The Essential Gesture: Writing, Politics and Places* was published in 1988. Her first novel, *The Lying Days*, appeared in 1953.

Honored internationally for her work, she has received, among other awards, the W. H. Smith Literary Award, and the James Tait Black Memorial Prize. France honored her with its Grand Aigle d'Or in 1975, and the University of Leuven in Belgium awarded her a doctorate of literature in 1980. She is an honorary member of the American Academy of Arts & Letters and serves as vice-president of PEN International.

you0ve escaped altogether. Because without the Kafka will-

power you can(t reach out or be caught (the same thing, here)

in nothing and nowhere. I was going to call it a desert,

from old habit, but where's the sand, where's the camels,

where's the air?— I'm still _mensch_ enough to crack a joke—

you see? Oh but I forgot—you didn't like my jokes, my

                                   unfortunately you had no life in you,
fooling around with kids. My poor boy, in all those books

and diaries and letters (the ones you posted, to strangers,
                        it   before you put the words
to women) you said a hundred times you were unfit for xkifet

xthaughxyxxxputxthexwxrxx in my mouth, in your literary way,
                                    youxhadxnexiifexinxyxxy
in xhxxxxxxtxxjx (maginary letter: you were 'unfit for life',

and so death was natural, how would you say, naturally to you.
                                          of vigour
It doesn't come so easily to a man like me I was, I can tell

you, and so here I am writing, talking— I don't know if there

is a word for this Anyway, it's Hermann Kafka; I outlived

youxxandxinxxxxxxyxxenexxfxthexwxrxx you, there, the same as

here.

    That is what you really accuse me of, you know, in

sixty or so pages the length of that letter varies a bit bit

xxxxxx from language to language, of course it's been translated

into everything but— I don't know what, Hottentot and Iceland-

ic to Chinese, though you wrote it 'for me' in German.)

I outlived you, not for seven years, as an old sick man, after

you died, but while you were young and alive. It's clear

as daylight, from the examples you give of being afraid of

me, from the time you were a little boy. You were not

afraid, you were envious. At first, when I took you swimming

and you say you felt yourself a nothing, puny and weak,

beside my big, strong naked body in the change-house, all

right, you say you were proud of such a father, a father

with a fine physique... And may I remind you that father

A page from a Nadine Gordimer short story.

Hugo Cassirer

Nadine Gordimer

This interview with Nadine Gordimer was conducted in two parts—in the fall of 1979, when she was in America on a publicity tour for her most recent novel, Burger's Daughter, *and in the spring of 1980, when she was here to see her son graduate from college.*

Our first meeting was in a room set aside for us by her publisher, The Viking Press—one of those conference rooms made cozy by lots of books, and claustrophobic by its lack of windows. The hotel room where our second meeting took place was slightly more conducive to amiable conversation. But Gordimer does not waste words in conversation any more than she does in her prose. On both occasions she was ready to begin our interview the moment I walked in the door and ready to end it the moment the hour she had suggested for our meeting was up. Her clarity and mental focus allow her to express a great deal in a short amount of time.

A petite, birdlike, soft-spoken woman, Gordimer manages to combine a fluidity and gentleness with the seemingly restrained and highly structured workings of her mind. It was as if the forty-odd years that she had devoted to writing had trained her to distill passion—and as a South African writer she is necessarily aware of being surrounded by passion on all sides—into form, whether of the written or spoken word. At the same time, she conveyed a sense of profound caring about the subject matter of her writing; those subjects natural to any writer concerned with the human condition, but set, in her case, in the heightened context of South African life. Her manner seemed to say, "Yes, these are important subjects we're discussing. Now let's get through talking about them so I can get back to the business of writing about them."

INTERVIEWER: Do you have seasons in South Africa, or is it hot all year round?

GORDIMER: Oh no, we have seasons. Near the equator, there's very little difference in the seasons. But right down where we are, at the end of the continent, and also high up where I live in Johannesburg—6,000 feet up—you have very different seasons. We have a sharp, cold winter. No snow—it's rather like your late fall or early spring—sunny, fresh, cold at night. We have a very definite rainy season. But you don't see rain for about half the year. You forget that rain exists. So it's a wonderful feeling when you wake up one day, and you smell the rain in the air. Many of the old houses, like ours, have galvanized iron or tin roofs. It's very noisy when there's a heavy rain—it just gallops down on the roof. The house that I was brought up in had a tin roof, so it's one of my earliest memories, lying in bed and listening to the rain . . . and hail, which, of course, on a tin roof is deafening.

INTERVIEWER: When was your first trip out of South Africa?

GORDIMER: My first trip out was to what was then called Rhodesia—Zimbabwe. That might seem very much the same thing as South Africa to you, but it isn't. Zimbabwe is Central Africa, subtropical, shading into tropical. But my first real trip out was much later. I had already published two books—I was thirty years old. I went to Egypt, on my way to England, and America.

Perhaps it was a good transition. In London I felt at home, but in an unreal way—I realized when I got there that my picture of London came entirely from books. Particularly Dickens and Virginia Woolf. The writers who, I'd thought, had impressed me with the features of English life, like Orwell, did not have this evocation when I was actually in the place; they were not writers with a strong sense of place. Woolf and Dickens obviously were. So that when I walked around in Chelsea I felt that this was definitively Mrs. Dalloway's country. I remember I stayed in a hotel near Victoria Station. And at night, these dark, sooty buildings, the dampness when one leant against a wall—absolutely decayed buildings . . .

INTERVIEWER: Were you as unprepared for this first trip off the African continent, and as awed by it, as Rebecca in your novel, *Guest of Honour*?

GORDIMER: No, my mother, who hadn't been back to England for about twenty years, prepared me. She provided me with woolly underwear and whatnot, which I threw away after I arrived. But Rebecca's trip to Switzerland . . . I think descriptions of impressions from the air are something that writers nowadays have to be careful of. Like train journeys in mid-nineteenth century literature . . . they made such a change in people's lives. They produced a . . . leap in consciousness, especially so far as time was concerned. I can imagine what it must have been, the thought of taking a train that was to go rushing through the countryside. There were so many descriptions of trains in the literature of the day. But I think writers must be careful now not to overdo the use of travel as a metaphor for tremendous internal changes. "The journey" now is by air, and think of how many writers use this—in my own books it appears in *The Conservationist* and in *Guest of Honour*. And indeed, in *Burger's Daughter*, Rosa Burger takes her first trip out of South Africa; I had to resist the temptation to talk about the journey—I describe only the landing, because that particular piece of the landscape could be useful later on.

INTERVIEWER: Was this trip to England a sort of "back to the roots" expedition?

GORDIMER: No. But it brought an understanding of what I was, and helped me to shed the last vestiges of colonialism. I didn't know I was a colonial, but then I had to realize that I was. Even though my mother was only six when she came to South Africa from England, she still would talk about people "going home." But after my first trip out, I realized that "home" was certainly and exclusively—Africa. It could never be anywhere else.

INTERVIEWER: What brought your parents to South Africa?

GORDIMER: The same thing brought them both. They were part of the whole colonial expansion. My maternal grandfather came out in the 1890s with a couple of brothers. South Africa was regarded as a land of opportunity for Europeans. And indeed, he went prospecting for diamonds in Kimberley. I don't think he found very much—maybe some small stones. After that, his entire life was the stock exchange. He was what we call a "tickey-snatcher." A tickey was a tiny coin like a dime—alas, we don't have it anymore. It was equal to three English pence. "Tickey" is a lovely word, don't you think? Well, my grandfather was a tickey-snatcher on the stock exchange, which meant that he sat there all day, and that he bought and sold stocks—making a quick buck.

My father's story is really not such a happy one. He was born in Lithuania, and he went through the whole Jewish pogrom syndrome, you know. He had hardly any schooling. There wasn't any high school for Jewish kids in his village. His father was a shipping clerk and there were twelve children. I'm sure they must have been very poor. Their mother was a seamstress. As soon as my father was twelve or thirteen the idea was that he would just go—*somewhere*, either to America or wherever—it was the time of the great expansion, you know, the early 1900s. So his was the classic Ellis Island story—thirteen years old, not speaking a word of English, traveling in the hold of a ship, but all the way to Africa instead of America—it must have been extraordinary. He was a very unadventurous man; he didn't have a strong personality—he was timid. He still is a mystery to me. I wonder if he didn't burn himself out in this tremendous initial adventure, whether it wasn't really too much for him, and once having found a niche for himself somewhere, he just didn't have the guts to become much of a personality. There was something *arrested* about my father.

INTERVIEWER: What did he do once he got to Africa?

GORDIMER: Like many poor Jews—one either became a shoe-maker, a tailor, or a watchmaker. He had learned watchmaking. All he had was a little bag with his watchmaking tools. He went to the Transvaal, to the goldfields. He took his little suitcase and went around the mines and asked the miners if anybody wanted a watch fixed. And he would take the watches away to a little room he had somewhere: he would just sit there and mend watches. Then he bought a bicycle and he'd go back round the mines. But by the time I came on the scene he had a little jeweler's shop and he was no longer a watchmaker—he employed one. Indeed, he imported his brother-in-law from Russia to do it. By now my father was the tycoon of the family. He brought *nine* sisters out of Lithuania—the poor man—saving up to bring one after the other. I found out later that he hated them all—we didn't ever have family gatherings. I don't know why he hated them so much.

INTERVIEWER: Where exactly was this jeweler's shop?

GORDIMER: In a little town called Springs, which was thirty miles from Johannesburg. I grew up in a small, gold-mining town of about 20,000 people.

INTERVIEWER: What were the schools like there?

GORDIMER: Well, I've had little formal education, really. I had a very curious childhood. There were two of us—I have an elder sister—and I was the baby, the spoiled one, the darling. I was awful—brash, a show-off, a dreadful child. But maybe that had something to do with having a lot of energy that didn't find any outlet. I wanted to be a dancer—this was my passion, from the age of about four to ten. I absolutely adored dancing. And I can still remember the pleasure, the release, of using the body in this way. There was no question but that I was to be a dancer, and I suppose maybe I would have been. But at the age of ten, I suddenly went into a dead faint one day, having been a very skinny but very healthy child. Nobody took much notice. But then it happened again. So I was taken to the family doctor, and it was discovered that I had an incredibly rapid heartbeat. Nobody had noticed this; it was, I suppose, part of my excitability and liveliness. It was discovered that I had an enlarged thyroid gland, which causes a fast heartbeat and makes one hyperactive. Well, I've since discovered that this isn't a serious malady at all. It happens to hundreds of people—usually at puberty. But my mother got very alarmed. This rapid pulse should have been ignored. But my mother was quite sure that it meant that I had a "bad heart." So she went immediately to the convent where I attended school and told the nuns, "This child mustn't have any physical training, she mustn't play tennis, she mustn't even swim." At ten, you know, you don't argue with your mother— she tells you you're sick, you believe her. When I would be about to climb stairs, she would say, "Now, take it slowly, *remember your heart*." And then of course the tragedy was that I was told I mustn't dance anymore. So the dancing stopped like that, which was a terrible deprivation for me.

It's really only in the last decade of my life that I've been able to face all this. When I realized what my mother had done to me, I went through, at the age of twenty, such resentment—this happens to many of us, but I *really* had reason. When I was thirty, I began to understand why she did it, and thus to pity her. By the time she died in '76 we were reconciled. But it was an extraordinary story.

In brief, my mother was unhappily married. It was a dreadful marriage. I suspect she was sometimes in love with other men; but my mother would never have dreamt of having an affair. Because her marriage was unhappy, she concentrated on her children. The chief person she was attracted to was our family doctor. There's no question. I'm sure it was *quite* unconscious, but the fact that she had this "delicate" daughter, about whom she could be constantly calling the doctor—in those days doctors made house calls, and there would be tea and cookies and long chats—made her keep my "illness" going in this way. Probably I was being wrongly treated anyway, so that what medication should have cleared up, it didn't, and symptoms persisted. Of course, I began to feel terribly important. By that time I was reading all sorts of books that led me to believe my affliction made me very interesting. I was growing up with this legend that I was very delicate, that I had something wrong with my heart.

When I was eleven—I don't know how my mother did this—she took me out of school completely. For a year I had no education at all. But I read tremendously. And I retreated into myself, I became very introspective. She changed my whole character. Then she arranged for me to go to a tutor for three hours a day. She took me there at ten in the morning and picked me up at one. It was such incredible loneliness—it's a terrible thing to do to a child. There I was, all on my own, doing my work; a glass of milk was brought to me by this woman—she was very nice, but I had no contact with other children. I spent my whole life, from eleven to sixteen, with older people, with people of my mother's generation. She carted me around to tea parties—I simply lived her life. When she and my father went out at night to dinner she took me along . . . I got to the stage where I could really hardly talk to other children. I was a little old woman.

INTERVIEWER: What about your sister's relationship to you during this time?

GORDIMER: My sister is four years older than I am. She went away to university; she wasn't really a companion to me. I stopped going to the tutor when I was fifteen or sixteen. So that was the extent of my formal education.

When I was twenty-one or twenty-two, already a published writer, I wanted to go to university to get a little more formal education. But since I hadn't matriculated, I could only do occasional courses at the University of the Witwatersrand—that's Afrikaans for "ridge of white waters." There was something called "general studies"—this was just after the war, and there were lots of veterans who had interrupted their education, and so it was very nice for me—there were people my own age mixed up with the others. A few years ago I gave a graduation address at that same university.

INTERVIEWER: Are you one of these writers to whom they're always trying to give honorary degrees?

GORDIMER: I don't accept them in South Africa. I've taken

one—in Belgium in 1981, from the University of Leuven. It turned out to be quite extraordinary, because the man who got an honorary degree with me, Monsignor Oscar Romero, was assassinated two weeks later in El Salvador. In Belgium he had given the most marvelous address. He was such a striking man. He received a standing ovation for about eight minutes from the students. And two weeks later he was lying on the floor of a church, dead.

INTERVIEWER: How long did you go to university?

GORDIMER: One year. This was the first time in my life I'd mixed with blacks, and was more or less the beginning of my political consciousness. Perhaps the good thing about being carted around with my parents was that they would sit playing gin rummy or something while I wandered around the host's house seeing what I could find to read. I discovered everybody from Henry Miller to Upton Sinclair. It was Sinclair's *The Jungle* that really started me thinking about politics: I thought, good God, these people who are exploited in a meat-packing factory—they're just like blacks here. And the whole idea that people came to America, not knowing the language, having to struggle in sweat shops . . . I didn't relate this to my own father, because my father was bourgeois by then . . . but I related it to the blacks. Again, what a paradox that South Africa was the blacks' *own country*, but they were recruited just as if they had been migrant workers for the mines. So I saw the analogy. And that was the beginning of my thinking about my position vis-à-vis blacks. But though I didn't know anything—I was twelve or thirteen, and leading the odd kind of life I did, living in books—I began to think about these things before, perhaps, I was ready for them. When I got to university, it was through mixing with other people who were writing or painting that I got to know black people as equals. In a general and inclusive, nonracial way, I met people who lived in the world of ideas, in the world that interested me passionately.

In the town where I lived, there was no mental food of this kind at all. I'm often amazed to think how they live, those people, and what an oppressed life it must be, because human beings *must* live in the world of ideas. This dimension in the human psyche is very important. It was there, but they didn't know how to express it. Conversation consisted of trivialities. For women, household matters, problems with children. The men would talk about golf or business or horseracing or whatever their practical interests were. Nobody ever talked about, or even around, the big things—life and death. The whole existential aspect of life was never discussed. I, of course, approached it through books. Thought about it on my own. It was as secret as it would have been to discuss my parents' sex life. It was something so private, because I felt that there was nobody with whom I could talk about these things, just *nobody*. But then, of course, when I was moving around at university, my life changed. From Europe—it was just after the war—came Existentialism, and at home in South Africa there was great interest in movements of the Left, and black national movements. At that time, the Communist party and various other leftist movements were not banned. So there were all sorts of Marxist discussion groups. This was an area of thought and conviction I simply never had heard mentioned before. I'd only read about it. And there, of course, were people who were mixing with blacks. So it was through people who were writing, painting, or acting that I started mixing with blacks.

INTERVIEWER: What did you do after that year at university? Did you begin any political activity?

GORDIMER: No, you see I was writing then—a lot. I was concentrating tremendously on writing. I wasn't really interested in politics. My approach to living as a white supremacist, perforce, among blacks, was, I see now, the humanist approach, the individualistic approach. I felt that all I needed, in my own behavior, was to ignore and defy the color bar. In other words, my own attitude toward blacks seemed to be sufficient action. I didn't see that it was pretty meaningless until much later.

INTERVIEWER: Were you living on your own then?

GORDIMER: No, I wasn't. In that way I was extremely backward. But you have to look at the kind of dependency that had been induced in me at the crucial age of ten. When other kids were going off to the equivalent of what's known as "summer camp"— "Nadine can't go camping, she's got a *bad heart*! If people go on a hike, she can't go. She's got to stay with mama." A child like that becomes very corrupt, a kind of jester, an entertainer for grown-ups. Especially at the age of fifteen and sixteen. Adults find you charming. You flirt with other people's husbands instead of with boys your own age. It's a very corrupting thing. I was rather a good mimic. Perhaps it was the beginning of having an ear for dialogue? So I would take off people. Grown-ups would sit around at drink parties, getting a little tight, and there was Nadine prancing around, rather cruelly imitating people whom they knew. It didn't occur to them that the moment their backs were turned I was doing it to them as well.

At any rate, I was still living at home when I went to university, and I used to commute by train into Johannesburg. Then my sister got married and lived in Johannesburg, so that when I didn't want to go home I would go to her, which was very nice for me, to have a base there. But I still didn't have the guts, I don't know why, to move out of home, the mining town of Springs. And you see, I wasn't earning enough by my writing, heaven knows, to live on. I was doing something that no kid does nowadays—I was living off my father. On the other hand, my needs were so modest. It never occurred to me that one would want a car— now every kid has a jalopy—this was just not the kind of thing that I would have dreamt of. All I wanted was to buy books. I earned enough with my writing here and there to do this, and of course I also used the library tremendously, which, again, people don't seem to do so much anymore. When I talk to young writers, and I say, "Have you read this or that?"—"Well, no, but books are so expensive . . ."—I say, "Well for God's sake! The central library is a wonderful library. For heaven's sake, use it! You're never going to be able to write if you don't read!"

INTERVIEWER: Perhaps the isolation of your childhood helped you to become a writer—because of all the time it left you for reading—lonely though it must have been.

GORDIMER: Yes . . . perhaps I would have become a writer anyway. I was doing a bit of writing before I got "ill." I wanted to be a journalist as well as a dancer. You know what made me want to become a journalist? Reading Evelyn Waugh's *Scoop* when I was about eleven. Enough to make anybody want to be a journalist! I absolutely adored it. I was already reading a lot, obviously, but of course I was reading without any discrimination. I would go to the library and wander around, and one book led to another. But I think that's the best way. An Oxford student who is doing a thesis on my writing came to visit me in Johannesburg the other day. I did something I've not done before. I told him, "Right, here are boxes of my papers, just do what you like." I liked him so much—he was so very intelligent and lively. I would meet him at lunch. He would emerge, and so would I, from our separate labors. Suddenly he brought out a kid's exercise book—a list, that I'd kept for about six months when I was twelve, of books that I'd read, and I'd written little book reviews. There was a review of *Gone With the Wind*. Do you know what was underneath it? My "review" of Pepys's *Diary*. And I was still reading kids' books at the time, devouring those, and I didn't see that there was any difference between these and *Gone With the Wind* or Pepys's *Diary*.

INTERVIEWER: Were you publishing stories in the *New Yorker* before you published your first book?

GORDIMER: No. I published a book of stories in South Africa, in 1949. I must have started publishing stories in the *New Yorker* when I was twenty-six. I had one story in the *New Yorker*, and several in journals like *Virginia Quarterly Review*, the *Yale Review*—the traditional places where young writers in the fifties submitted their work. Then my first book was published abroad—a book of short stories.

INTERVIEWER: You sent your manuscripts around to these magazines?

GORDIMER: No, no, by that time I had an agent. It came about that I had an agent in New York. I never sent anything on impulse to those magazines, because I wasn't familiar at all with American publications. The publications I was familiar with were the English ones. Of course, publishers in those days usually watched magazines. And my first publisher, Simon and Schuster, became interested in me through reading that first story of mine in the *New Yorker*. Katharine White became my editor and friend at the *New Yorker*. She told me, years after, that all those other stories which were in my first book had already been submitted to the *New Yorker* via my agent. But they had been read by the slush-pile people. She had never seen them, and she regretted very much that she hadn't. But of course these things happen. And I don't quite know how that *one* story surfaced.

INTERVIEWER: Who was your agent?

GORDIMER: My agent was an extraordinary man called Sidney Satenstein. He was an extremely rich man who loved writers. He had no children, and I think writers were his children. He had very few writers really, because he wasn't principally an agent. I came to him through somebody who knew him and knew my work and said, "It's ridiculous—you should have an agent abroad." He was such an incredible man—a sort of John O'Hara character, or even coarser, really. He spent half his time flying to Las Vegas to gamble, or to Florida to play golf. He was a kind of caricature rich American. He always had a cigar in his mouth. He was big, and wore the most ghastly clothes—checked trousers and things like that. He was an absolute darling. Of course he gave me a completely false idea of what an agent was. When I met him I was exactly thirty—though he had taken me on in my mid-twenties—and he was in his mid-sixties. He established a sort of fatherly relationship with me, very fond. Strangely enough, he really liked my writing, which surprised me. One wouldn't have thought that my writing—especially my stories—would have interested *him*. But they did. He was incredible. He knew the circumstances of my life. I was newly divorced, I had a small child—a baby, indeed, eighteen months old—and I had no money. And he really fought for me. If somebody bought something of mine—and after all, I was totally unknown—he insisted that I was a hot property. He got sufficient money for me to live on. When Simon and Schuster bought my first book of stories, they wanted to know if I was writing a novel, and indeed I was. And again he pushed them to give me what would now be considered a *teeny* advance, the amount someone would get to write a line today, but then publishers were not so generous, nor writers so demanding. But at least they gave me a modest sum that I could live on. And once the book was well along, and they saw part of it, Satenstein said to them, you've just *got* to give her more, she's got nothing. So they gave me another advance—all due to him. He used to send me enormous bottles of French perfume. The times I came here—twice—while he was alive, he threw parties for me at the 21 Club, with caviar and sturgeon . . . he had a big heart, and style.

Unfortunately, he died—of a heart attack—just when I began to get known and make a success. He deserved better, because it would have been terribly exciting for him. At least he was able to be thrilled with the response to my first novel. Though not a best seller—I've never been that—it was a big critical success here . . . a completely unknown writer with a front page review in *The New York Times*.

INTERVIEWER: What role do you feel politics and the constant conflict it evokes in South Africa have played in your development as a writer?

GORDIMER: Well, it has turned out to have played a very important role. I would have been a writer anyway; I was writing before politics impinged itself upon my consciousness. In my writing, politics comes through in a didactic fashion very rarely. The kind of conversations and polemical arguments you get in *Burger's Daughter*, and in some of my other books—these really play a very minor part. For various reasons to do with the story, they had to be there. But the real influence of politics on my writing is the influence of politics on people. Their lives, and I believe their very personalities, are changed by the extreme political circumstances one lives under in South Africa. I am dealing with people; here are people who are shaped and changed by politics. In that way my material is profoundly influenced by politics.

INTERVIEWER: Do you see that as an advantage for a writer?

GORDIMER: Not really. Life is so apparently amorphous. But as soon as you burrow down this way or that . . . you know Goethe's maxim? "Thrust your hand deep into life, and whatever you bring up in it, that is you, that is your subject." I think that's what writers do.

INTERVIEWER: If you had grown up in a country that was not politically oppressed, might you have become a more abstract writer?

GORDIMER: Maybe. Take a writer whom I admire tremendously, the greatest American short-story writer ever, Eudora Welty. In a strange way, if she had lived where I've lived, she might have turned these incredible gifts of hers more outward—she might have written more, she might have tackled wider subjects. I hesitate to say this, because what she's done she's done wonderfully. But the fact is that she hasn't written very much; I don't think she ever developed fully her gifts as a novelist. She was not forced by circumstance to come to grips with something different. And I don't believe it's just a matter of temperament, because my early writing had qualities similar to hers. I got to hate that word about my work—"sensitive." I was constantly being compared to Katherine Mansfield. I am *not* by nature a political creature, and even now there is so much I don't like in politics, and in political people—though I admire tremendously people who are politically active—there's so much lying to oneself, self-deception, there has to be—you don't make a good political fighter unless you can pretend the warts aren't there.

INTERVIEWER: Do you have the same complaint about Virginia Woolf's novels as you do with Eudora Welty's?

GORDIMER: No, because Virginia Woolf extended herself the other way. I mean she really concentrated totally on that transparent envelope that she'd find for herself. There are two ways to knit experience, which is what writing is about. Writing is making sense of life. You work your whole life and perhaps you've made sense of one small area. Virginia Woolf did this incomparably. And the complexity of her human relationships, the economy with which she managed to portray them . . . staggering. But you can't write a novel like *Burger's Daughter* with the sensibility of a Virginia Woolf. You have to find some other way. You're always trying to find some other way. I'm interested in both ways of writing. I started off by being interested in that transparent envelope.

INTERVIEWER: Was Woolf a big influence when you began writing?

GORDIMER: Midway, I think—after I'd been writing for about five years. She can be a very dangerous influence on a young writer. It's easy to fall into the cadence. But the content isn't there. The same could be said for a completely different kind of writer like Dos Passos, or Hemingway. You've got to be very careful, or you do if you are a writer like me, starting out with an acute sensibility and a poor narrative gift. My narrative gift was weak in my early novels—they tend to fall into beautiful set pieces. It was only with *The Late Bourgeois World*, which was published in 1966, that I began to develop narrative muscle. From then on, my struggle has been not to lose the acute sensitivity— I mean the acuteness of catching nuance in behavior (not in description, because as you get more mature that falls into place) and to marry it successfully to a narrative gift. Because the kind of subjects that are around me, that draw me, that I see motivating me, require a strong narrative ability.

INTERVIEWER: Do you feel that your political situation—the political situation in South Africa—gave you a particular incentive as a writer?

GORDIMER: No. For instance, in *Burger's Daughter*, you could say on the face of it that it's a book about white Communists in South Africa. But to me, it's something else. It's a book about commitment. Commitment is not merely a political thing. It's part of the whole ontological problem in life. It's part of my feeling that what a writer does is to try to make sense of life. I think that's what writing is, I think that's what painting is. It's seeking that thread of order and logic in the disorder, and the incredible waste and marvelous profligate character of life. What all artists are trying to do is to make sense of life. So you see, I would have found my themes had I been an American or an English writer. They are there if one knows where to look . . . if one is pushed from within.

INTERVIEWER: How do you feel that fiction from relatively non-oppressed countries compares with that produced in countries where the political situation necessitates a certain amount of political consciousness?

GORDIMER: To me, it's all a matter of the quality of the writing. To me, that is everything. I can appreciate a tremendously subjective and apolitical piece of writing. If you're a writer, you can make the death of a canary stand for the whole mystery of death. That's the challenge. But, of course, in a sense you are "lucky" if you have great themes. One could say that about the Russians in the nineteenth century. Would they have been the wonderful writers they are if they hadn't had that challenge? They also had the restrictions that we chafe against in South Africa—censorship, and so on. And yet it seems on the face of it to have had only a good effect on writing. Then I think it depends. It can have a deleterious effect. In South Africa, among young blacks who are writing—it's difficult for them to admit it, but they know this— they have to submit to an absolute orthodoxy within black consciousness. The poem or the story or the novel must follow a certain line—it's a kind of party line even though what is in question is not a political party, but it *is*, in the true sense of the word, a party line. For example, nobleness of character in blacks must be shown. It's pretty much frowned upon if there's a white character who is human. It's easy enough to understand this and it's important as a form of consciousness-raising for young blacks to *feel* their own identity, to recite poems which simply exalt blackness and decry everything else, and often to exalt it in crude terms, in crude images, clichés. That's fine as a weapon of propaganda in the struggle, which is what such writing is, primarily. But the *real* writers are victims of this, because as soon as they stray from one or two clearly defined story lines, they're regarded as . . .

INTERVIEWER: Traitors. Are there many blacks writing and publishing in South Africa?

GORDIMER: There are a lot, and there's a fairly good relationship between black and white writers. Literature is one of the few areas left where black and white feel some identity of purpose; we all struggle under censorship, and most white writers feel a strong sense of responsibility to promote, defend, and help black writers where possible.

INTERVIEWER: *Burger's Daughter* was banned three weeks after it was published, wasn't it?

GORDIMER: Yes, and it remained banned for several months. Then it was unbanned. I was pleased, as you can imagine. Not only for myself, but because it established something of a precedent for other writers, since there are in that book blatant contraventions of certain Acts. In that book I published a document that was a real document, distributed by the students in the 1976 riots in Soweto, and banned by the government. It's in the book with all the misspellings and grammatical mistakes . . . everything exactly as it was; and indeed that's important because, as Rosa points out, these kids rioted because they felt their education wasn't good enough. And when you read the text of that pathetic little pamphlet you can see what the young blacks meant, because that's as well as they could write at the age of sixteen or seventeen, when they were ready to matriculate. So here is one example where, indeed, I flagrantly crossed the line to illegality. Now that the book has been unbanned, it's going to be a difficult thing for the censors to ban other books on evidence of such transgressions.

INTERVIEWER: Why was the book unbanned?

GORDIMER: If I hadn't been a writer who's known abroad and if this hadn't been a book that happened to receive serious attention at a high level abroad—it obviously made the censors feel rather foolish—the book would not have been released. So there we are.

INTERVIEWER: Is it common for a book to be unbanned?

GORDIMER: Well, not so quickly. Of my two previous books, one, *A World of Strangers*, was banned for twelve years, and the other, entitled *The Late Bourgeois World*, for ten; after that length of time most books are pretty well dead.

INTERVIEWER: How does a book get banned?

GORDIMER: First of all, if the book is imported, the authorities embargo it. In other words, it's just like any other cargo arriving at the docks. It is embargoed at Customs and the customs officer sends the book off to the Censorship Board. He's got a list of suspects. For instance, a South African writer like myself would be on it, you see, because they know the kind of subjects I've chosen, and, in any case, I've had three books banned previously. So would somebody like James Baldwin; several of his books were banned. Then there's another way that books get embargoed with the possible outcome of a ban. After normal distribution, somebody, some Mother Grundy, old busybody, reads a book that's already in the bookshops, objects to it, and sends it off to the Censorship Board with a complaint. On the recommendation of just one person, a committee will read the book to see if it's "objectionable." But while it's being read by the censors, it's under embargo, which means that although there are copies in the bookshops the bookseller can't sell them; he's got to put them away, take them off the shelves. Sometimes the book is then released. It happened to my novel, *A Guest of Honour*; it happened to *The Conservationist*. *The Conservationist*, I think, was held by the censors for ten weeks, which is iniquitous because the first ten weeks in a book's life are crucial from the point of view of sales. Then it was released by the director of the board. The members of the censor's committee—there are a number of those, usually with three people comprising a committee—read the book, each writes an independent report, and if these concur that the book should be banned or released, right, it's done. If they don't concur, then a fourth person has to be brought in. If they concur that the book is undesirable, then it is banned. The author isn't told. The decision is published in the government gazette, which is published once a week. And that's the end of the book.

INTERVIEWER: What happens then? Is it like what happened with *Ulysses*? Do people scrounge around frantically trying to get hold of it and hide it when policemen walk by?

GORDIMER: People do, people do. Books are usually banned only for sale and distribution but not for *possession*, so that if you've already bought the book you may keep it; but you may not lend it to me or the person across the road, and you may not sell it.

INTERVIEWER: You can't lend it?

GORDIMER: No. This, of course, is perfectly ridiculous. Everybody lends banned books all the time. But people are very nervous, for instance, about buying them abroad or having them sent. They're rather too timid about that. They don't like to have to smuggle them in.

INTERVIEWER: So there isn't much smuggling going on?

GORDIMER: Some people don't, some do. But with some of us, it's a point of honor always to do this.

INTERVIEWER: To smuggle?

GORDIMER: Yes, of course. It's a legitimate form of protest. But unfortunately, when a book is banned, very few copies get around.

INTERVIEWER: Getting back to the idea that oppressed societies produce better writers . . .

GORDIMER: Well, I don't know. I think in the case of Latin American countries, they seem to have experienced so many forms of oppression and for so long that it's become a normal state. But notice that they all write about the same thing . . . the themes are as obsessive as the African ones. *The* theme among the remarkable Latin American writers is the corrupt dictator. Nevertheless, despite the sameness of theme, I regard this as the most exciting fiction in the world being written today.

INTERVIEWER: Which Latin American novelists?

GORDIMER: García Márquez, of course. Hardly necessary even to name Borges. Borges is the only living successor to Franz Kafka. Alejo Carpentier was absolutely wonderful. *The Kingdom of the Earth* is an exquisite little novel—it's brilliant. Then there's Carlos Fuentes, a magnificent writer. Mario Vargas Llosa. And Manuel Puig. These just roll off my tongue quickly; there are others. But always there's this obsessive theme—the corrupt dictator. They all write about it; they're obsessed by it.

INTERVIEWER: I suppose that an oppressed culture such as South Africa's creates the possibility for heroes to exist, and that this is why some of your novels, such as *A Guest of Honour* and *Burger's Daughter,* have heroes as their motivating force.

GORDIMER: Well, you know, it amazes me . . . I come to America, I go to England, I go to France . . . nobody's at risk.

They're afraid of getting cancer, losing a lover, losing their jobs, being insecure. It's either something that you have no control over, like death—the atom bomb—or it's something with which you'd be able to cope anyway, and that is not the end of the world; you'll get another job or you'll go on state relief or something of this nature. It's only in my own country that I find people who voluntarily choose to put everything at risk—in their personal life. I mean to most of us, the whole business of falling in love is so totally absorbing, nothing else matters. It's happened to me. There have been times in my life when I have put the person I was in love with far ahead of my work. I would lose interest, I wouldn't even care if the book was coming out. I'd forget when it was being published and I wouldn't worry about the reception it got because I was in such a state of anguish over some man. And yet the people I know who are committed to a *political* cause never allow themselves to be deflected by this sort of personal consideration or ambition.

INTERVIEWER: How do you think romantic love manifests itself in families such as Rosa's, where people's passions lie in politics?

GORDIMER: This is what interested me so much, and this is what I partly tried to explore in the relationship between that girl and her family, who loved her, exploited her, but at the same time felt that they were doing this not for each other or to each other, but because the *cause* demanded it.

INTERVIEWER: We get only very brief glimpses of the love affair between Burger and his wife. In fact, the reader hardly gets any picture either of their relationship or of Rosa's mother at all.

GORDIMER: That was one of the points that's fascinated me about such people: you could know them very well, and yet even in their intimate relations with one another they remained intensely secretive; it's part of the discipline that you have to have. I have a very, very close friend—no character in the book is modeled on her, I might add—but much that I know or have discovered intuitively about such people started with my fascination with her. She has been my closest friend for many years—she's a political exile now—and we've talked nights and days. She's one of the few people for whom I suppose I'd put myself physically at risk if there were to be cause. There are so many things I don't know about her that normally would come out in confidences between people who are as close as we are, and it's because of her political commitment that I can't ask her and she won't tell me. I think that this could extend even to family relationships. It's part of the discipline that the more you know, the more dangerous you are to the people around you. If you and I are working together in an underground movement, the less I know about you the better.

INTERVIEWER: We've talked about the South American writers you admire. What about other writers?

GORDIMER: Lots of novelists say they don't read other novelists, contemporary ones. If this is true, it's a great pity. Imagine, if you had lived in the nineteenth century and not read the writers that we now turn back to so lovingly, or even if you had lived in the twentieth century and hadn't read Lawrence or Hemingway, Virginia Woolf and so on. At different times in my life I've— liked is not the word—I've been psychologically *dependent* upon different writers. Some have remained influential in my life and some haven't, and some I suppose I've forgotten and do them an injustice by not mentioning. When I first began to write, I wrote short stories, and of course I still do; I've written a great many. It's a form that I love to write and to read. I was very influenced by American, Southern, short-story writers. Eudora Welty was a great influence on me. Years later, when I met Eudora, visited her in Jackson, there were such parallels between the way she was living, even then, and my life: a black man was mowing the lawn! There was a kind of understanding. Of course, this really had nothing to do with the fact that I thought she was a superb short-story writer. Katherine Anne Porter was an influence on me. Faulkner. Yes. But, again, you see, one lies, because I'm sure that when we were doing the five-finger exercises of short-story writing, Hemingway must have influenced *everybody* who began to write in the late forties, as I did. Proust has been an influence on me, all my life—an influence so deep it frightens me . . . not only in my writing, but in my attitudes to life. Then later came Camus, who was quite a strong influence, and Thomas

Mann, whom I've come to admire more and more. E. M. Forster, when I was a young girl; when I was in my twenties—he was very important to me. And I still think *Passage to India* is an absolutely wonderful book that cannot be killed by being taught in the universities.

INTERVIEWER: In what way did Hemingway influence you?

GORDIMER: Oh, through his short stories. The reduction, you know, and also the use of dialogue. Now I think a great failure in Hemingway's short stories is the omnipresence of Hemingway's voice. People do not speak for themselves, in their own thought patterns; they speak as Hemingway does. The "he said," "she said" of Hemingway's work. I've cut these attributions out of my novels, long ago. Some people complain that this makes my novels difficult to read. But I don't care. I simply cannot stand he-said/she-said any more. And if I can't make readers *know* who's speaking from the tone of voice, the turns of phrase, well, then I've failed. And there's nothing anyone can do about it.

INTERVIEWER: It certainly enforces concentration when one is reading your novels.

GORDIMER: Yes.

INTERVIEWER: The dashes are very effective.

GORDIMER: Oh, that's very old. It started with Sterne's *Tristram Shandy*.

INTERVIEWER: What technique did you use that was the same?

GORDIMER: A kind of interior monologue that jumps about from different points of view. In *The Conservationist*, sometimes it's Mehring speaking from inside himself, observing, and sometimes it's a totally dispassionate view from outside.

INTERVIEWER: It's a much more standard narrative technique than that of *Burger's Daughter*.

GORDIMER: Well, no, it isn't you know. In *The Conservationist* you've got interior monologue and you have a real narrator. It's not always Mehring speaking. But the line between when he is and when he isn't is very vague, my theory being that the central personality is there, whether it's being observed from outside or whether from inside—it's the same entity.

INTERVIEWER: You mentioned that the way in which you came

up with the structure of *Burger's Daughter*, in which Rosa is always speaking to somebody, was from the idea that when one is writing one always has a listener in mind.

GORDIMER: Oh, no, not in your writing, in your *life*. I believe that in your life, in your thoughts when you are alone, you are always addressing yourself to somebody.

INTERVIEWER: And you are not doing this when you write?

GORDIMER: No, because you're no longer yourself when you're writing; you're projecting into other people. But I think in your life, and sometimes even in the conduct of your life, you're imagining that some particular person is seeing your actions. And you're turning away, sometimes, from others.

INTERVIEWER: How has Faulkner influenced you? Do you see any similarities in the structure of *Burger's Daughter* and, say, *As I Lay Dying*?

GORDIMER: No, none at all, and I don't think there could be any influence there. I think the big time when people influence you is when you're very young and you start to write; after that you slough off what you don't need and you painfully hammer out your own style.

INTERVIEWER: There's a similarity between the way your method of narration in *Burger's Daughter* and some of Faulkner's books address themselves to the relative nature of "truth."

GORDIMER: Yes. Well, of course it is a method that points out the relativity of truth. The point I'm trying to make is about the relationship between style and point of view; in a sense, style is the point of view, or the point of view is the style.

INTERVIEWER: Right, and that's why you choose to structure your narratives in the way that you do.

GORDIMER: And then it was Proust who said that style is the moment of identification between the writer and his situation. Ideally that is what it should be—one allows the situation to dictate the style.

INTERVIEWER: So that you are expressing a point of view, with the style that you choose, about the way life is in South Africa.

GORDIMER: Yes. I'm expressing a point of view of the way life is for that particular person and the people around her (in the case of *Burger's Daughter*), and, by extension, a view of life itself.

INTERVIEWER: In Conor Cruise O'Brien's review of *Burger's Daughter*, which appeared in *The New York Review of Books*, he says that your novel is constructed with a "properly deceptive art." He talks about how the construction makes the book seem as if it were a book in which nothing happens, and then several cataclysmic things do, in fact, happen. I was wondering if you have any response.

GORDIMER: For me again, so little of the construction is objectively conceived. It's organic and instinctive and subconscious. I can't tell you how I arrive at it. Though, with each book, I go through a long time when I know what I want to do and I'm held back and puzzled and appalled because I don't know before I begin to write how I'm going to do it, and I always fear that I can't do it. You see, in *Guest of Honour*, I wrote a political book, a book that needed certain objective entities relating to and acting upon the character's life in particular. And I wrote that book as a conventional narrative so that at the point where there was indeed a big party congress there was no difficulty then in presenting it almost like a play. Then I wrote *The Conservationist*, where I chose to ignore that one had to explain anything at all. I decided that if the reader didn't make the leap in his mind, if the allusions were puzzling to him—too bad. But the narrative would have to carry the book in the sense of what is going on in the characters' minds and going on in their bodies; the way they believed things that they did *really were*. Either the reader would make the leap or not, and if the reader was puzzled now and then—too bad. In other words, the novel was full of private references between the characters. Of course, you take a tremendous risk with such a narrative style, and when you do succeed, I think it's the ideal. When you don't, of course, you irritate the reader or you leave him puzzled. Personally, as a reader, I don't mind being puzzled. Perhaps the writer doesn't know the consequences implied in his/her books, because there's a choice of explanations; and, as a reader, I enjoy that. To me, it's an important part of the exciting business of reading a book, of being stirred, and of having a mind of your own. And so, as a writer, I take the liberty of doing this.

INTERVIEWER: You don't consciously create a complete structure before you begin writing a novel?

GORDIMER: No. For *Burger's Daughter*, perhaps four or five pages of very scrappy notes for the whole book. But, for me, those half sentences or little snatches of dialogue are tremendously important; they are the core of something. And I've only got to look at them, and know that that's the next stage in the book that I'm coming to.

INTERVIEWER: Is this the way you usually write your novels?

GORDIMER: Yes. With me it's really a very natural process once I get started. An organic process.

INTERVIEWER: How long do you prepare before you get started?

GORDIMER: It's so difficult for me to say because, looking back at *Burger's Daughter*, for example, I know that I've been fascinated by the kind of person Rosa is for many years. It's as if the secret of a life is there, and slowly I'm circling, coming closer and closer to it. Perhaps there are other themes that present themselves but finally spin off instead of drawing me to them. I suppose one's ready for different things at different times in one's life. And also, in a country where so much is changing, the quality of life around one is changing; so that perhaps I wouldn't be attracted now to write the book that I wrote ten years ago, and vice versa.

INTERVIEWER: So you feel that the way your books are written is more an inevitable phenomenon than a conscious choice.

GORDIMER: I don't think any writer can say why he chooses this or that or how a theme impinges itself. It may have been around for a long time and then a stage comes in your life when your imagination is ready for it and you can deal with it.

INTERVIEWER: I wanted to ask you about *The Conservationist*, in which death is almost an obsessive theme. There are certain sections where it is continually brought up in ritualized ways: the man hopping up from his grave in different people's minds throughout the book, and the ritual of killing the goat to get back at Solomon's injury . . .

GORDIMER: In *The Conservationist* there's a resurrection theme, and that is also a political theme. At the end of the book there's a disguised message. The slogan of the biggest banned liberation movement, a kind of battle cry widely adopted, is the African word, "mayibuye." This means, "Africa, come back." You can see the whole idea of resurrection is there. And if you look at the end of *The Conservationist* you'll see that this thought is reworded, but it is actually what is said when the unknown man is reburied: that although he is nameless and childless, he has all the children of other people around him; in other words, the future. He has people around him who are not his blood brothers and sisters but who stand for them. And that he has now been put with proper ceremony into his own earth. He has taken possession of it. There's a suggestion of something that has been planted, that is going to grow again.

INTERVIEWER: This theme is repeated in one of your short stories—"Six Feet of the Country."

GORDIMER: Yes. But the repetition is in reverse: "Six Feet" was written years before *The Conservationist*. Oddly enough, that early story is based on a true incident.

INTERVIEWER: Do you have a fascination with death?

GORDIMER: Not consciously, but then . . . how can any thinking person not have? Death is really the mystery of life, isn't it? If you ask, "What happens when we die? Why do we die?" you are asking, "Why do we live?" Unless one has a religion . . . Without a religious explanation, one has only the Mount Everest argument: "I climb it because it's there. I live because there is the gift of life." It's not an answer, really, it's an evasion. Or, "I think my purpose on this earth is to make life better." Progress is the business of making life more safe and more enjoyable . . . fuller, generally. But that justification, it stops short of death, doesn't it? The only transcendent principle is that you are then seeking to improve the human lot for future generations. But we still don't get past the fact that it's a turnabout business; it's your turn and then it's mine, and life is taken up by somebody else. Human beings are never reconciled to this. In my own life I am made puzzled and uneasy by my attitude and that of others to death.

If somebody dies young it's so terrible, it's such a tragedy, and the sense of waste is so strong; you think of all the promise that was there. And then if people live into old age, there's the horror of decay, especially—it's awful to say—but especially with exceptional people; when you see their minds going and their bodies falling to pieces, and they want to die and you want them to die, then that's equally terrible. So it's the mere fact of death that we can't accept? We say it's terrible if people die young, and we say it's terrible if they go on living too long.

INTERVIEWER: Are you a religious or mystical person?

GORDIMER: I'm an atheist. I wouldn't even call myself an agnostic. I am an atheist. But I think I have a basically religious temperament, perhaps even a profoundly religious one. I went through a stage in my life when I was about thirty-two or thirty-three years old—when I was very fascinated by the writings of Simone Weil. In the end, her religious philosophy left me where I was. But I felt that there was something there that answered to a need that I felt, *my* "need for roots" that she wrote about so marvelously. I couldn't find the same solution.

INTERVIEWER: How do you feel about Conor Cruise O'Brien's idea about there being Christian overtones in *Burger's Daughter*?

GORDIMER: Well, I'm thinking of that. I'm sure that many of my friends, people who know me well, laughed because they know that, as I say, I'm an atheist. But he hit on something that is there in me, a certain inclination—more than that—a pull. Perhaps, brought up differently in a different milieu, in a different way, I might have been a religious person.

INTERVIEWER: Then there is the resurrection of the black man in *The Conservationist*.

GORDIMER: But of course the idea of resurrection comes from the Greeks, from the Egyptians. You can begin to believe in a collective unconscious without having religious beliefs.

INTERVIEWER: I've noticed that sensual elements play a key role in your writing: smells, textures, sexuality, bodily functions. You don't write about the so-called "beautiful people," the leisured class of South Africa, and the beautiful environment in which they must live. In fact, I noticed that almost all of the white women in your *Selected Stories* are physically and mentally both highly unattractive and middle-class. Does this reflect the way in which you view white colonialists in your country?

GORDIMER: I don't make such judgments about people. After all, I'm a white colonial woman myself, of colonial descent. Perhaps I know us too well through myself. But if somebody is partly frivolous or superficial, has moments of cruelty or self-doubt, I don't write them off, because I think that absolutely everybody has what are known as human failings. My black characters are not angels either. All this role-playing that is done in a society like ours—it's done in many societies, but it's more noticeable in ours—sometimes the role is forced upon you. You fall into it. It's a kind of song-and-dance routine, and you find yourself, and my characters find themselves, acting out these preconceived, ready-made roles. But, of course, there are a large number of white women of a certain kind in the kind of society that I come from who . . . well, the best one can say of them is that one can excuse them because of their ignorance of what they have allowed themselves to become. I see the same kind of women here in the U.S. You go into one of the big stores here and you can see these extremely well-dressed, often rather dissatisfied-looking, even sad-looking middle-aged women, rich, sitting trying on a dozen pairs of shoes; and you can see they're sitting there for the morning. And it's a terribly agonizing decision, but maybe the heel should be a little higher or maybe . . . should I get two pairs? And a few blocks away it's appalling to see in what poverty and misery other people are living in this city, New York. Why is it that one doesn't criticize that American woman the same way one does her counterpart in South Africa? For me, the difference is that the rich American represents class difference and injustice, while in South Africa the injustice is based on both class *and* race prejudice.

INTERVIEWER: What about the "beautiful people" of South Africa?

GORDIMER: They're featured very prominently in an early book of mine called *A World of Strangers* but very rarely since then, until the character of Mehring in *The Conservationist*. They are not the most interesting people in South Africa, believe me . . . although they may regard themselves as such.

INTERVIEWER: Is it intentional that so often the physical details of characters are not brought home strongly in your work? One gets a very strong sense of the mind's workings in major characters, but often a very limited sense of what they actually look like.

GORDIMER: I think that physical descriptions of people should be minimal. There are exceptions—take Isaac Bashevis Singer. He very often starts off a story by giving you a full physical description. If you look very closely at the description, of course it's extremely good. He stamps character on a twist of the nose or a tuft of red beard. My own preference is for physical description to come piecemeal at times when it furthers other elements in the text. For instance, you might describe a character's eyes when another character is looking straight into them so it would be natural . . . a feature of that particular moment in the narrative. There might be another scene later, where the character whose eyes you've described is under tension, and is showing it by tapping her foot or picking at a hangnail—so if there was something particular about her hands, that would be the time to talk about them. I'm telling you this as if it were something to be planned. It isn't. It comes at the appropriate moment.

INTERVIEWER: In the introduction to your *Selected Stories*, you say that: "My femininity has never constituted any special kind of solitude, for me. In fact, my only genuine connection with the social life of the town (when I was growing up) was through my femaleness. As an adolescent, at least, I felt and followed sexual attraction in common with others; that was a form of communion I could share. Rapunzel's hair is the right metaphor for this femininity: by means of it I was able to let myself out and live in the body, with others, as well as—alone—in the mind." You go on to say you "question the existence of the specific solitude of woman-as-intellectual when that woman is a writer, because when it comes to their essential faculty as writers, all writers are androgynous beings."

What about the process of becoming a writer, of becoming an androgynous being? Isn't that a struggle for women?

GORDIMER: I hesitate to generalize from my own experience. I would consider it an arrogance to state my own experience as true for all women. I really haven't suffered at all from being a woman. It's inconceivable, for example, that I could ever have become interested in a man who regarded women as nonbeings. It's never happened. There would be a kind of war between us. I just take it for granted, and it has always happened, that the men in my life have been people who treated me as an equal. There was never any question of fighting for this. I'm somebody who has lived a life as a woman. In other words, I've been twice married, I've brought up children, I've done all the things that women do. I haven't avoided or escaped this, supposing that I should have wished to, and I don't wish to and never wished to. But, as I say, I don't generalize, because I see all around me women who are gifted and intelligent who *do* have these struggles and who indeed *infuriate* me easier. But I did manage to maintain it when my children were young, I suppose, by being rather ruthless. I think writers, artists, are very ruthless, and they have to be. It's unpleasant for other people, but I don't know how else we can manage. Because the world will never make a place for you. My own family came to understand and respect this. Really, when my children were quite small they knew that in my working hours they must leave me alone; if they came home from school and my door was closed, they left and they didn't turn on the radio full blast. I was criticized for this by other people. But my own children don't hold it against me. I still had time that I spent with them. What I have also sacrificed, and it hasn't been a sacrifice for me, is a social life; and as I've got older, I'm less and less interested in that. When I was young I did go through some years when I enjoyed party-going very much and stayed out all night. But in the end, the loss next day, the fact that I had a hangover and that I couldn't work, quickly outweighed the pleasure; and, as time has gone by, I've kept more and more to myself. Because a writer doesn't only need the time when he's actually writing—he or she has got to have time to think and time just to let things work out. Nothing is worse for this than society. Nothing is worse for this than the abrasive, if enjoyable, effect of other people.

INTERVIEWER: What conditions do you find to be most conducive to writing?

GORDIMER: Well, nowhere very special, no great, splendid desk and cork-lined room. There have been times in my life, my God, when I was a young divorced woman with a small child living in a small apartment with thin walls when other people's radios would drive me absolutely mad. And that's still the thing that bothers me tremendously—*that* kind of noise. I don't mind people's voices. But Muzak or the constant clack-clack of a radio or television coming through the door . . . well, I live in a suburban house where I have a small room where I work. I have a door with direct access to the garden—a great luxury for me—so that I can get in and out without anybody bothering me or knowing where I am. Before I begin to work I pull out the phone and it stays out until I'm ready to plug it in again. If people really want you, they'll find you some other time. And it's as simple as that, really.

INTERVIEWER: How long do you usually work every day? Or do you work every day?

GORDIMER: When I'm working on a book I work every day. I work about four hours nonstop, and then I'll be very tired and nothing comes anymore, and then I will do other things. I can't understand writers who feel they shouldn't have to do any of the ordinary things of life, because I think that this is necessary; one has got to keep in touch with that. The solitude of writing is also quite frightening. It's quite close sometimes to madness, one just disappears for a day and loses touch. The ordinary action of taking a dress down to the dry cleaner's or spraying some plants infected with greenfly is a very sane and good thing to do. It brings one back, so to speak. It also brings the world back. I have formed the habit, over the last two books I've written, of spending half an hour or so reading over what I'd written during the day just before I go to bed at night. Then, of course, you get tempted to fix it up, fuss with it, at night. But I find that's good. But if I've been with friends or gone out somewhere, then I won't do that. The fact is that I lead a rather solitary life when I'm writing.

INTERVIEWER: Is there a time of day that's best?

GORDIMER: I work in the morning. That's best for me.

INTERVIEWER: How long does it usually take you to write a book?

GORDIMER: It depends. The shortest has been about eighteen months. *Burger's Daughter* took me four years.

INTERVIEWER: Four years of steady writing?

GORDIMER: I wrote one or two other things, small things. Sometimes when I'm writing I get a block, and so I stop and write a short story, and that seems to set me going. Sometimes when I'm writing a book I get ideas for stories, and they're just tucked away. But alas, as I get older, I get fewer ideas for short stories. I used to be teeming with them. And I'm sorry about that because I like short stories.

INTERVIEWER: What about writer's block? Is that a problem for you?

GORDIMER: No. And I say so, as you see, with hesitation and fear and trembling because you always feel that that demon is waiting behind the back of your brain.

INTERVIEWER: You have the short story to loosen you up?

GORDIMER: Yes, and occasionally I do some nonfiction piece, usually something involving travel. For me, this is a kind of relaxation. During the time I was writing *Burger's Daughter* I did two such pieces.

INTERVIEWER: You don't even have minor fits of procrastination, endless cups of tea or things like that?

GORDIMER: No, no. Though I do have, not blocks but . . . problems moving on from one stage to the next; particularly when I've got something done with and it's worked well. For instance, I finished that chapter with Brandt Vermeulen, you know, the nationalist in *Burger's Daughter*, which went unexpectedly well. I simply wrote it just like that and it all came right. I had been dreading it. I had been dreading getting the tone of voice and everything right. And then, knowing where I was going on from there, there was suddenly an inability to get out of that mood and into another; and so there were perhaps a few awful days; because when that happens, I don't stop and do something else. I sit in front of that paper for the normal time that I would be writing. And then, well, I break through.

INTERVIEWER: There's no specific routine that gets you from the bedroom or the living room into the writing room, bridging that terrifying gap between not writing and writing?

GORDIMER: No—that's the advantage if you're free to choose the time you're going to write. That's the advantage of writing in the morning. Because then one gets up and in one's subconscious mind one knows: I am going to write. Whatever small thing you have to do, such as talking to other people at breakfast, it's only done with one part of you, so to speak; just done on the surface. The person with whom I live, my husband, understands this and has for a very long time. And he knows that to say to me at breakfast, "What shall we do about so-and-so?" or, "Would you read this letter?"—he knows that isn't the time to ask. I get irritable, and irritated, I don't want to be asked to do things then. And I don't want to phone an order to the grocer at that time. I just want to be left alone to eat my breakfast. Ideally, I like to walk around a bit outside, which you can do, of course, with a garden. But I often think that even that becomes a kind of procrastination because it's so easy then to see a weed that one has to stop and pull up and then one sees some ants and wonders, where are they going? So the best thing to do is to go into the room and close the door and sit down.

INTERVIEWER: Do you go through much revision of your work?

GORDIMER: As time goes by, less and less. I used to. When I was young, I used to write three times as much as the work one finally reads. If I wrote a story, it would be three times the final length of that story. But that was in the very early times of my writing. Short stories are a wonderful discipline against overwriting. You get so used to cutting out what is extraneous.

INTERVIEWER: Do you ever find critics useful?

GORDIMER: Yes, but you must remember they're always after the event, aren't they? Because then the work's already done. And the time you find you agree with them is when they come to the same conclusions you do. In other words, if a critic objects to something that I know by my lights is right, that I did the best I could and that it's well done, I'm not affected by the fact that somebody didn't like it. But if I have doubts about a character or something that I've done, and these doubts are confirmed by a critic, then I feel my doubts confirmed and I'm glad to respect that critic's objections.

INTERVIEWER: Frequently writers say they don't read reviews because even one bad review among ten shining ones can be devastating.

GORDIMER: Of course, it depends very much on the reviewer. There are people who are not reviewers, one or two, to whom I give my books to read, perhaps even in manuscript. I am sick with apprehension while they are reading them. And certainly there are certain reviewers I would be very wounded by if they were to say, "Well, this one's rotten."

INTERVIEWER: But this hasn't happened yet.

GORDIMER: Not yet. With *Burger's Daughter* I've had, out of perhaps fifty or sixty reviews, two bad ones.

INTERVIEWER: You say that writers are androgynous. Do you recognize any difference between masculine and feminine writing, such as say, Woolf's versus Hemingway's writing?

GORDIMER: Hemingway is such an extreme example, and his writing is really an instance of machismo, isn't it? Henry James could have been a woman. E. M. Forster could have been. George Eliot could have been a man. I used to be too insistent on this point that there's no sex in the brain; I'm less insistent now—perhaps I'm being influenced by the changing attitude of women toward themselves in general? I don't think there's anything that women writers don't know. But it may be that there are certain aspects of life that they can deal with a shade better, just as I wonder whether any woman writer, however great, could have written the marvelous war scenes in *War and Peace*. By and large, I don't think it matters a damn what sex a writer is, so long as the work is that of a real *writer*. I think there *is* such a thing as "ladies' writing," for instance, feminine writing; there are "authoresses" and "poetesses." And there are men, like Hemingway, whose excessive "manliness" is a concomitant part of their writing. But with so many of the male writers whom I admire, it doesn't matter too much. There doesn't seem to be anything *they* don't know, either. After all, look at Molly Bloom's soliloquy. To me, that's the ultimate proof of the ability of either sex to understand and convey the inner workings of the other. No woman was ever "written" better by a woman writer. How did Joyce know? God knows how, and it doesn't matter. When I was a young woman, a young girl, I wrote a story about a man who had lost his leg. He couldn't accept this, the reality of it, until he was sitting recuperating in the garden and saw a locust that had its leg off; he saw the locust struggling because it felt its leg was still there. I don't know how I wrote that story, somehow I just imagined myself into it. A psychiatrist once told me it was a perfect example of penis envy.

INTERVIEWER: Is there anything, new or otherwise, that you hope to do with your writing in the future?

GORDIMER: I would always hope to find the one right way to tackle whatever subject I'm dealing with. To me, that's the real problem, and the challenge of writing. There's no such feeling as a general achievement. You cannot say that because I have managed to say what I wanted to say in one book, that it is now inside me for the next, because the next one is going to have a different demand. And until I find out how to write it, I can't tackle it.

INTERVIEWER: In other words, you don't know the question until you have the answer?

GORDIMER: Yes. I would like to say something about how I feel in general about what a novel, or any story, ought to be. It's a quotation from Kafka. He said, "A book ought to be an ax to break up the frozen sea within us."

—JANNIKA HURWITT
1980

11. Anne Sexton

Born on November 9, 1928, Anne Sexton was brought up in Wellesley, Massachusetts, attended Garland Junior College, and at twenty married a salesman. She became a fashion model in Boston and had two daughters. When her second child was born, she suffered a mental breakdown and twice tried to commit suicide. For a number of years she was in and out of mental hospitals.

At the age of thirty, as a means of recovery, Anne Sexton started writing. With the publication of each book, grants and awards followed. *To Bedlam and Part Way Back* (1960) led to admittance to Radcliffe's Institute for Independent Study. *All My Pretty Ones* (1962) brought her the first traveling fellowship offered by the American Academy of Arts and Letters (1963–64), a Ford Foundation grant in playwriting (1964–65), and the first literary-magazine travel grant from the Congress for Cultural Freedom (1965). In 1965 her *Selected Poems* appeared in England, and she was elected a Fellow of the Royal Society of Literature in London. Her third book, *Live or Die* (1966), won the Pulitzer Prize and the Shelley Award from the Poetry Society of America. Five more books followed: *Love Poems* (1969), *Transformations* (1971), *The Book of Folly* (1972), *The Death Notebooks* (1974), and *An Awful Rowing Towards God* (1975).

In 1972 she served as Cranshaw Professor of Literature at Colgate University and was a Professor of Creative Writing at Boston University from 1970 to 1974. She took her own life on October 4, 1974.

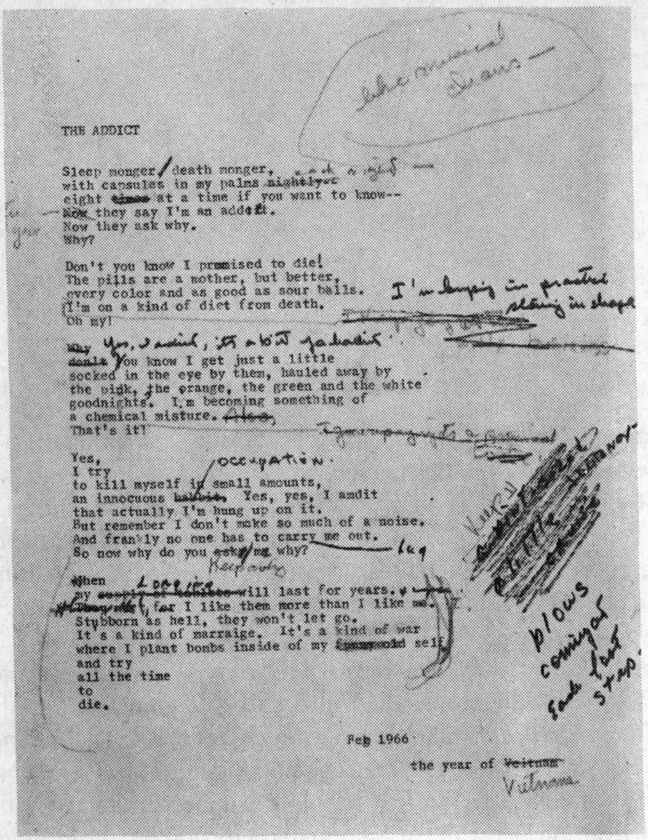

THE ADDICT

Sleep monger / death monger, ~~and night~~
with capsules in my palms ~~nightly~~
eight ~~times~~ at a time if you want to know--
~~Now~~ they say I'm an add~~i~~ct.
Now they ask why.
Why?

Don't you know I promised to die!
The pills are a mother, but better,
every color and as good as sour balls.
(I'm on a kind of diet from death.
Oh my!

~~Why~~ Yes, I ~~said,~~ ~~it about~~ paradise
~~don't~~ You know I get just a little
socked in the eye by them, hauled away by
the pink, the orange, the green and the white
goodnights. I'm becoming something of
a chemical mixture. ~~Also~~
That's it?

Yes,
                        occupation
I try
to kill myself in small amounts,
an innocuous ~~hobbie~~. Yes, yes, I admit
that actually I'm hung up on it.
But remember I don't make so much of a noise.
And frankly no one has to carry me out.
So now why do you ~~asking~~ why?   say

~~When~~ ~~I am living~~
my ~~something of habits~~ will last for years. ~~y~~
~~something~~ ~~for~~ I like them more than I like me.
Stubborn as hell, they won't let go.
It's a kind of marraige. It's a kind of war
where I plant bombs inside of my ~~funny cold~~ self
and try
all the time
to
die.

                              Feb 1966

                    the year of ~~Veitnam~~
                              Vitnum

Handwritten annotations: like musical scans — / I'm dying in practise / relaxing in sleep / blows coming of good luck stops

Rollie McKenna

Anne Sexton

*The interview took place over three days in the middle of August
1968. When asked about dates of publications or other events,
Anne Sexton kept saying, "Let me think, I want this to be ac-
curate," and she'd use the births of her children as reference dates
to chronicle the event in question. Sometimes her distinctions between real and imagined life blurred, as in scenes from Pirandello.
Often, her answers sounded like incantations, repetitious chants
that, if pared down, would lose something of their implications,
and so, for the most part, they are preserved in their entirety. Even
when replying from written notes, she read with all the inflections
and intonations of—as she described her readings—"an actress in
her own autobiographical play."*

INTERVIEWER: You were almost thirty before you began writing
poetry. Why?

SEXTON: Until I was twenty-eight I had a kind of buried self who didn't know she could do anything but make white sauce and diaper babies. I didn't know I had any creative depths. I was a victim of the American Dream, the bourgeois, middle-class dream. All I wanted was a little piece of life, to be married, to have children. I thought the nightmares, the visions, the demons would go away if there was enough love to put them down. I was trying my damndest to lead a conventional life, for that was how I was brought up, and it was what my husband wanted of me. But one can't build little white picket fences to keep nightmares out. The surface cracked when I was about twenty-eight. I had a psychotic break and tried to kill myself.

INTERVIEWER: And you began to write after the nervous breakdown?

SEXTON: It isn't quite as simple as all that. I said to my doctor at the beginning, "I'm no good; I can't do anything; I'm dumb." He suggested I try educating myself by listening to Boston's educational TV station. He said I had a perfectly good mind. As a matter of fact, after he gave me a Rorschach test, he said I had creative talent that I wasn't using. I protested, but I followed his suggestion. One night I saw I. A. Richards on educational television reading a sonnet and explaining its form. I thought to myself, "I could do that, maybe; I could try." So I sat down and wrote a sonnet. The next day I wrote another one, and so forth. My doctor encouraged me to write more. "Don't kill yourself," he said. "Your poems might mean something to someone else someday." That gave me a feeling of purpose, a little cause, something to *do* with my life, no matter how rotten I was.

INTERVIEWER: Hadn't you written limericks before that?

SEXTON: I did write some light verse—for birthdays, for anniversaries, sometimes thank-you notes for weekends. Long before, I wrote some serious stuff in high school; however, I hadn't been exposed to any of the major poets, not even the minor ones. No one taught poetry at that school. I read nothing but Sara Teasdale. I might have read other poets, but my mother said as I graduated from high school that I had plagiarized Sara Teasdale. Something about that statement of hers . . . I had been writing a poem a day for three months, but when she said that, I stopped.

INTERVIEWER: Didn't anyone encourage you?

SEXTON: It wouldn't have mattered. My mother was top billing in our house.

INTERVIEWER: In the beginning, what was the relationship between your poetry and your therapy?

SEXTON: Sometimes, my doctors tell me that I understand something in a poem that I haven't integrated into my life. In fact, I may be concealing it from myself, while I was revealing it to the readers. The poetry is often more advanced, in terms of my unconscious, than I am. Poetry, after all, milks the unconscious. The unconscious is there to feed it little images, little symbols, the answers, the insights I know not of. In therapy, one seeks to hide sometimes. I'll give you a rather intimate example of this. About three or four years ago my analyst asked me what I thought of my parents having intercourse when I was young. I couldn't talk. I knew there was suddenly a poem there, and I selfishly guarded it from him. Two days later, I had a poem, entitled, "In the Beach House," which describes overhearing the primal scene. In it I say, "Inside my prison of pine and bedspring,/over my window sill, under my knob,/it is plain they are at/the royal strapping." The point of this little story is the image, "the royal strapping." My analyst was quite impressed with that image, and so was I, although I don't remember going any further with it then. About three weeks ago, he said to me, "Were you ever beaten as a child?" I told him that I had been when I was about nine. I had torn up a five-dollar bill that my father gave to my sister; my father took me into his bedroom, laid me down on his bed, pulled off my pants, and beat me with a riding crop. As I related this to my doctor, he said, "See, that was quite a royal strapping," thus revealing to me, by way of my own image, the intensity of that moment, the sexuality of that beating, the little masochistic seizure—it's so classic, it's almost corny. Perhaps it's too intimate an example, but then both poetry and therapy are intimate.

INTERVIEWER: Are your poems still closely connected to your therapy as in the past?

SEXTON: No. The subject of therapy was an early theme—the

process itself as in "Said the Poet to the Analyst," the people of my past, admitting what my parents were really like, the whole Gothic New England story. I've had about eight doctors, but only two that count. I've written a poem for each of the two—"You, Doctor Martin" and "Cripples and Other Stories." And that will do. Those poems are about the two men as well as the strange process. One can say that my new poems, the love poems, come about as a result of new attitudes, an awareness of the possibly good as well as the possibly rotten. Inherent in the process is a rebirth of a sense of self, each time stripping away a dead self.

INTERVIEWER: Some critics admire your ability to write about the terror of childhood guilts, parental deaths, breakdowns, suicides. Do you feel that writing about the dark parts of the human psyche takes a special act of courage?

SEXTON: Of course, but I'm tired of explaining it. It seems to be self-evident. There are warnings all along the way. "Go— children—slow." "It's dangerous in there." The appalling horror that awaits you in the answer.

INTERVIEWER: People speak of you as a primitive. Was it so natural for you to dig so deeply into the painful experiences of your life?

SEXTON: There was a part of me that was horrified, but the gutsy part of me drove on. Still, part of me was appalled by what I was doing. On the one hand I was digging up shit, with the other hand, I was covering it with sand. Nevertheless, I went on ahead. I didn't know any better. Sometimes, I felt like a reporter researching himself. Yes, it took a certain courage, but as a writer one has to take the chance on being a fool . . . yes, to be a fool, that perhaps requires the greatest courage.

INTERVIEWER: Once you began writing, did you attend any formal classes to bone up on technique?

SEXTON: After I'd been writing about three months, I dared to go into the poetry class at the Boston Center for Adult Education taught by John Holmes. I started in the middle of the term, very shy, writing very bad poems, solemnly handing them in for the eighteen others in the class to hear. The most important aspect of that class was that I felt I belonged somewhere. When I first got sick and became a displaced person, I thought I was quite alone, but when I went into the mental hospital, I found I wasn't, that there were other people like me. It made me feel better—more real, sane. I felt, "These are my people." Well, at the John Holmes class that I attended for two years, I found I belonged to the poets, that I was *real* there, and I had another, "These are my people." I met Maxine Kumin, the poet and novelist, at that class. She is my closest friend. She is part superego, part sister, as well as pal of my desk. It's strange because we're quite different. She is reserved, while I tend to be flamboyant. She is an intellectual, and I seem to be a primitive. That is true about our poetry as well.

INTERVIEWER: You once told me, "I call Maxine Kumin every other line." Is that a slight exaggeration?

SEXTON: Yes. But often, I call her draft by draft. However, a lot of poems I did without her. The year I was writing my first book, I didn't know her well enough to call that often. Later, when she didn't approve of such poems as "Flee on Your Donkey"—that one took four years to complete—I was on my own. Yet once, she totally saved a poem, "Cripples and Other Stories."

INTERVIEWER: In the early days, how did your relatives react to the jangling of family skeletons?

SEXTON: I tried not to show my relatives any of the poems. I do know that my mother snuck into my desk one time and read "The Double Image" before it was printed. She told me just before she died that she liked the poem, and that saved me from some added guilt. My husband liked that poem, too. Ordinarily, if I show him a poem, something I try not to do, he says, "I don't think that's too hotsy-totsy," which puts me off. I try not to do it too often. My in-laws don't approve of the poems at all. My children do—with a little pain, they do.

INTERVIEWER: In your poems, several family skeletons come out of the camphor balls—your father's alcoholic tendencies, your mother's inability to deal with your suicide attempt, your great-aunt in a straitjacket. Is there any rule you follow as to which skeletons you reveal and which you don't?

SEXTON: I don't reveal skeletons that would hurt anyone. They may hurt the dead, but the dead belong to me. Only once in a while do they talk back. For instance, I don't write about my husband or his family, although there are some amazing stories there.

INTERVIEWER: How about Holmes or the poets in your class, what did they say?

SEXTON: During the years of that class, John Holmes saw me as something evil and warned Maxine to stay away from me. He told me I shouldn't write such personal poems about the madhouse. He said, "That isn't a fit subject for poetry." I knew no one who thought it was; even my doctor clammed up at that time. I was on my own. I tried to mind them. I tried to write the way the others, especially Maxine, wrote, but it didn't work. I always ended up sounding like myself.

INTERVIEWER: You have said, "If anything influenced me, it was W. D. Snodgrass's 'Heart's Needle.' " Would you comment on that?

SEXTON: If he had the courage, then I had the courage. That poem about losing his daughter brought me to face some of the facts about my own life. I had lost a daughter, lost her because I was too sick to keep her. After I read the poem, "Heart's Needle," I ran up to my mother-in-law's house and brought my daughter home. That's what a poem should do—move people to action. True, I didn't keep my daughter at the time—I wasn't ready. But I was beginning to be ready. I wrote a disguised poem about it, "Unknown Girl in the Maternity Ward." The pain of the loss . . .

INTERVIEWER: Did you ever meet Snodgrass?

SEXTON: Yes. I'd read "Heart's Needle" in *The New Poets of England and America.* I'd written about three quarters of *To Bedlam and Part Way Back* at the time, and I made a pilgrimage to Antioch Writer's Conference to meet and to learn from Snodgrass. He was a surprising person, surprisingly humble. He encouraged me, he liked what I was doing. He was the first established poet to like my work, and so I was driven to write harder and to allow myself, to dare myself to tell the whole story. He also suggested that I study with Robert Lowell. So I sent Mr. Lowell some of my poems and asked if he would take me into the class. By then I'd had poems published in *The New Yorker* and around a bit. At any rate, the poems seemed good enough for Lowell, and I joined the class.

INTERVIEWER: Which poems did you submit to Lowell?

SEXTON: As far as I can remember, the poems about madness— "You, Doctor Martin," "Music Swims Back to Me" . . . about ten or fifteen poems from the book.

INTERVIEWER: Was this before or after Lowell published *Life Studies*?

SEXTON: Before. I sent him the poems in the summer; the following spring *Life Studies* came out. Everyone says I was influenced by Robert Lowell's revelation of madness in that book, but I was writing *To Bedlam and Part Way Back*, the story of my madness, before *Life Studies* was published. I showed my poems to Mr. Lowell as he was working on his book. Perhaps I even influenced him. I have never asked him. But stranger things have happened.

INTERVIEWER: And when was your first book, *To Bedlam and Part Way Back*, published?

SEXTON: It was accepted that January; it wasn't published for a year and a half after that, I think.

INTERVIEWER: Where was Lowell teaching then?

SEXTON: The class met at Boston University on Tuesdays from two to four in a dismal room. It consisted of some twenty students. Seventeen graduates, two other housewives who were graduates or something, and a boy who had snuck over from M.I.T. I was the only one in that room who hadn't read *Lord Weary's Castle*.

INTERVIEWER: And Lowell, how did he strike you?

SEXTON: He was formal in a rather awkward New England sense. His voice was soft and slow as he read the students' poems. At first I felt the impatient desire to interrupt his slow, line by line readings. He would read the first line, stop, and then discuss it at length. I wanted to go through the whole poem quickly and then go back. I couldn't see any merit in dragging through it until you almost hated the damned thing, even your own poems, especially your own. At that point, I wrote to Snodgrass about my impatience, and his reply went this way, "Frankly, I used to nod my head at his every statement, and he taught me more than a whole gang of scholars could." So I kept my mouth shut, and Snodgrass was right. Robert Lowell's method of teaching is intuitive and open. After he had read a student's poem, he would read another evoked by it. Comparison was often painful. He worked with a cold chisel, with no more mercy than a dentist. He got out the decay, but if he was never kind to the poem, he was kind to the poet.

INTERVIEWER: Did you consult Robert Lowell on your manuscript of *To Bedlam and Part Way Back* before you submitted it to a publisher?

SEXTON: Yes. I gave him a manuscript to see if he thought it was a book. He was enthusiastic on the whole, but suggested that I throw out about half of it and write another fifteen or so poems that were better. He pointed out the weak ones, and I nodded and took them out. It sounds simple to say that I merely, as he once said, "jumped the hurdles that he had put up," but it makes a difference who puts up the hurdles. He defined the course, and acted as though, good race horse that I was, I would just naturally run it.

INTERVIEWER: Ultimately, what can a teacher give a writer in a creative-writing class?

SEXTON: Courage, of course. That's the most important ingredient. Then, in a rather plain way, Lowell helped me to distrust the easy musical phrase and to look for the frankness of ordinary speech. Lowell is never impressed with a display of images or sounds—those things that a poet is born with anyhow. If you have enough natural imagery, he can show you how to chain it in. He didn't teach me what to put into a poem, but what to leave out. What he taught me was taste—perhaps that's the only thing a poet can be taught.

INTERVIEWER: Sylvia Plath was a member of Lowell's class also, wasn't she?

SEXTON: Yes. She and George Starbuck heard that I was auditing Lowell's class. They kind of joined me there for the second term. After the class, we would pile in the front seat of my old Ford, and I would drive quickly through the traffic to the Ritz.

I would always park illegally in a "Loading Only Zone," telling them gaily, "It's O.K., we're only going to get loaded." Off we'd go, each on George's arm, into the Ritz to drink three or four martinis. George even has a line about this in his first book of poems, *Bone Thoughts*. After the Ritz, we would spend our last pennies at the Waldorf Cafeteria—a dinner for seventy cents— George was in no hurry. He was separated from his wife; Sylvia's Ted [Hughes] was busy with his own work, and I had to stay in the city for a seven P.M. appointment with my psychiatrist . . . a funny three.

INTERVIEWER: In Sylvia Plath's last book, written just before her suicide, she was submerged by the theme of death, as you are in your book, *Live or Die*. Did you ever get around to talking about death or your suicides at the Ritz?

SEXTON: Often, very often. Sylvia and I would talk at length about our first suicide, in detail and in depth—between the free potato chips. Suicide is, after all, the opposite of the poem. Sylvia and I often talked opposites. We talked death with burned-up intensity, both of us drawn to it like moths to an electric light bulb, sucking on it. She told the story of her first suicide in sweet and loving detail, and her description in *The Bell Jar* is just that same story. It is a wonder we didn't depress George with our egocentricity; instead, I think, we three were stimulated by it— even George—as if death made each of us a little more real at the moment.

INTERVIEWER: In a BBC interview, Sylvia Plath said, "I've been very excited by what I feel is the new breakthrough that came with, say, Robert Lowell's *Life Studies* . . . this intense break- through into very serious, very personal emotional experience, which I feel has been partly taboo. . . . I think particularly of the poetess Anne Sexton, who writes also about her experiences as a mother; as a mother who's had a nervous breakdown, as an extremely emotional and feeling young woman. And her poems are wonderfully craftsmanlike poems, and yet they have a kind of emotional psychological depth, which I think is something perhaps quite new and exciting." Do you agree that you influ- enced her?

SEXTON: Maybe. I did give her a sort of daring, but that's all she should have said. I remember writing to Sylvia in England after her first book, *The Colossus*, came out and saying something like, "If you're not careful, Sylvia, you will out-Roethke Roethke." She replied that I had guessed accurately. But maybe she buried her so-called influences deeper than that, deeper than any one of us would think to look, and if she did, I say, "Good luck to her!" Her poems do their own work. I don't need to sniff them for distant relatives: I'm against it.

INTERVIEWER: Did Sylvia Plath influence your writing?

SEXTON: Her first book didn't interest me at all. I was doing my own thing. But after her death, with the appearance of *Ariel*, I think I was influenced, and I don't mind saying it. In a special sort of way, it was daring again. She had dared to do something quite different. She had dared to write hate poems, the one thing I had never dared to write. I'd always been afraid, even in my life, to express anger. I think the poem, "Cripples and Other Stories," is evidence of a hate poem somehow, though no one could ever write a poem to compare to her "Daddy." There was a kind of insolence in them, saying, "Daddy, you bastard, I'm through." I think the poem, "The Addict," has some of her speech rhythms in it. She had very open speech rhythms, something that I didn't always have.

INTERVIEWER: You have said, "I think the second book lacks some of the impact and honesty of the first, which I wrote when I was so raw that I didn't know any better." Would you describe your development from the second book to the third and from your third to the fourth?

SEXTON: Well, in the first book, I was giving the experience of madness; in the second book, the causes of madness; and in the third book, finally, I find that I was deciding whether to live or to die. In the third I was daring to be a fool again—raw, "uncooked," as Lowell calls it, with a little camouflage. In the fourth book, I not only have lived, come on to the scene, but loved, that sometime miracle.

INTERVIEWER: What would you say about the technical development from book to book?

SEXTON: In *Bedlam*, I used very tight form in most cases, feeling that I could express myself better. I take a kind of pleasure, even now, but more especially in *Bedlam*, in forming a stanza, a verse, making it an entity, and then coming to a little conclusion at the end of it, of a little shock, a little double rhyme shock. In my second book, *All My Pretty Ones*, I loosened up and in the last section didn't use any form at all. I found myself to be surprisingly free without the form which had worked as a kind of superego for me. The third book I used less form. In *Love Poems*, I had one long poem, eighteen sections, that is in form, and I enjoyed doing it in that way. With the exception of that and a few other poems, all of the book is in free verse, and I feel at this point comfortable to use either, depending on what the poem requires.

INTERVIEWER: Is there any particular subject which you'd rather deal with in form than in free verse?

SEXTON: Probably madness. I've noticed that Robert Lowell felt freer to write about madness in free verse, whereas it was the opposite for me. Only after I had set up large structures that were almost impossible to deal with did I think I was free to allow myself to express what had really happened. However in *Live or Die*, I wrote "Flee on Your Donkey" without that form and found that I could do it just as easily in free verse. That's perhaps something to do with my development as a human being and understanding of myself, besides as a poet.

INTERVIEWER: In *Live or Die*, the whole book has a marvelous structured tension—simply by the sequence of the poems which pits the wish to live against the death instinct. Did you plan the book this way? Lois Ames speaks of you as wishing to write more "live" poems because the "die" poems outnumbered them.

SEXTON: I didn't plan the book any way. In January of 1962, I started collecting new poems the way you do when a book is over. I didn't know where they would go or that they would go anywhere, even into a book. Then at some point, as I was collecting these poems, I was rereading *Henderson the Rain King* by Saul Bellow. I had met Saul Bellow at a cocktail party about a year before, and I had been carrying *Henderson the Rain King* around in my suitcase everywhere I traveled. Suddenly there I was meeting Saul Bellow, and I was overenthusiastic. I said, "Oh, oh, you're Saul Bellow, I've wanted to meet you," and he ran from the room. Very afraid. I was quite ashamed of my exuberance, and then sometime, a year later, reading *Henderson the Rain King* over again, at three in the morning, I wrote Saul Bellow a fan letter about Henderson, saying that he was a monster of despair, that I understood his position because Henderson was the one who had ruined life, who had blown up the frogs, made a mess out of everything. I drove to the mail box then and there! The next morning I wrote him a letter of apology.

Saul Bellow wrote me back on the back of a manuscript. He said to me, "Luckily, I have a message to you from the book I am writing [which was *Herzog*]. I have both your letters—the good one which was written that night at three A.M. and then the contrite one, the next day. One's best things are always followed by apoplectic, apologetic seizure. Monster of despair could be *Henderson*'s subtitle." The message that he had encircled went this way, "With one long breath caught and held in his chest, he fought his sadness over his solitary life. Don't cry you idiot, live or die, but don't poison everything." And in circling that and in sending it to me, Saul Bellow had given me a message about my whole life. That I didn't want to poison the world, that I didn't want to be the killer; I wanted to be the one who gave birth, who encouraged things to grow and to flower, not the poisoner. So I stuck that message up over my desk and it was a kind of hidden message. You don't know what these messages mean to you, yet you stick them up over your desk or remember them or write them down and put them in your wallet. One day I was reading a quote from Rimbaud that said, "Anne, Anne, flee on your donkey," and I typed it out because it had my name in it and because I wanted to flee. I put it in my wallet, went to see my doctor, and at that point was committed to a hospital for about the seventh or eighth time. In the hospital, I started to write the poem, "Flee on Your Donkey," as though the message had come to me at just the right moment. Well, this was true with Bellow's quote from his book. I kept it over my desk, and when I went to Europe, I pasted it in the front of my manuscript. I kept it there as a quotation with which to preface my book. It must have just hit me one day that *Live or Die* was a damn good title for the book I was working on. And that's what it was all about, what all those poems were about. You say there's a tension there and a structure, but it was an unconscious tension and an unconscious structure that I didn't know was going on when I was doing it.

INTERVIEWER: Once you knew the title of the book, did you count up the "live" poems and count up the "die" poems and then write any more poems because of an imbalance?

SEXTON: No, no, that's far too rigid. You can't write a poem because of an imbalance. After that I wrote "Little Girl, My Stringbean, My Lovely Woman." Then I wrote a play, then "A Little Uncomplicated Hymn" and other poems. Some were negative, and some were positive. At this time I knew that I was trying to get a book together. I had more than enough for a book, but I knew I hadn't written out the live or die question. I hadn't written the poem "Live." This was bothering me because it wasn't coming to me. Instead of that, "Cripples and Other Stories" and "The Addict" were appearing, and I knew that I wasn't finishing the book, that I hadn't come to the cycle, I hadn't given a reason. There's nothing I could do about this and then suddenly, our dog was pregnant. I was supposed to kill all the puppies when they came; instead, I let them live, and I realized that if I let *them* live, that I could let *me* live, too, that after all I wasn't a killer, that the poison just didn't take.

INTERVIEWER: Although you received a European traveling fellowship from the American Academy of Arts and Letters, there are, to date, very few poems published about your European experience. Why?

SEXTON: First of all poems aren't post cards to send home. Secondly I went to Europe with a purpose as well as with a grant. My great-aunt, who was really my best childhood friend, had sent letters home from Europe the three years that she lived there. I had written about this in a poem called "Some Foreign Letters."

I had her letters with me as I left for Europe, and I was going to walk her walks and go to her places, live her life over again, and write letters back to her. The two poems that I did write about Europe mention the letters. In "Crossing the Atlantic," I mention that I have read my grandmother's letters and my mother's letters. I had swallowed their words like Dickens, thinking of Dickens' journals in America. The second poem, "Walking in Paris," was written about my great-aunt, how she used to walk fourteen or fifteen miles a day in Paris, and I call her Nana. Some critics have thought I meant Zola's Nana, but I didn't any more than I meant the Nana in Peter Pan. However the letters were stolen from my car in Belgium. When I lost the letters in Brussels, that was the end of that kind of poem that I had gone over there to write.

INTERVIEWER: You were to go abroad for a year, but you only stayed two months. Do you want to comment on that?

SEXTON: Two and a half months. I got sick over there; I lost my sense of self. I had, as my psychiatrist said, "a leaky ego" and I had to come home. I was in the hospital for a while, and then I returned to my normal life. I had to come home because I need my husband and my therapist and my children to tell me who I am. I remember, I was talking with Elizabeth Hardwick on the phone and saying, "Oh, I feel so guilty. I couldn't get along without my husband. It's a terrible thing, really, a modern woman should be able to do it." Although I may be misquoting her, I may have remembered it the way I needed to hear it, she said to me, "If I were in Paris without my husband, I'd hide in a hotel room all day." And I said, "Well, think of Mary McCarthy." And Elizabeth Hardwick said, "Mary McCarthy, she's never been without a man for a day in her life."

INTERVIEWER: From 1964 to 1965, you held a Ford Foundation Grant in playwriting and worked at Boston's Charles Street Playhouse. How did you feel writing something that had to be staged?

SEXTON: I felt great! I used to pace up and down the living room shouting out the lines, and what do they call it . . . for walking around the stage . . . *blocking* out the play as I would go along.

INTERVIEWER: Was the play [*Mercy Street*] ever performed?*

SEXTON: There were little working performances at the Charles Playhouse when we had time. It was pretty busy there. Now and then they would play out a scene for me, and then I would rewrite it and send it in to the director special delivery. He would call me up the next morning and say, "It's not right," and then I would work on it again, send it to him that evening, and then the next morning, he'd call, and so on it went. I found that I had one whole character in the play who was unnecessary because, as they acted it, the director had that person be quiet and say nothing. I realized that that dialogue was totally unnecessary, so I cut out that character.

INTERVIEWER: Did you find that the themes in your poetry overlapped into your play? Was your play an extension of your poetry?

SEXTON: Yes. Completely. The play was about a girl shuffling between her psychiatrist and a priest. It was the priest I cut out, realizing that she really wasn't having a dialogue with him at all. The play was about all the subjects that my poems are about— my mother, my great-aunt, my father, and the girl who wants to kill herself. A little bit about her husband, but not much. The play is really a morality play. The second act takes place after death.

INTERVIEWER: Many of your poems are dramatic narratives. Because you're accustomed to handling a plot, was it easy for you to switch from verse to scene writing?

SEXTON: I don't see the difference. In both cases, the character is confronting himself and his destiny. I didn't know I was writing scenes; I thought I was writing about people. In another context— helping Maxine Kumin with her novel—I gave her a bit of advice. I told her, "Fuck structure and grab your characters by the time balls." Each one of us sits in our time; we're born, live and die. She was thinking this and that, and I was telling her to get inside her characters' lives—which she finally did.

* Editor's Note: *Mercy Street* was eventually produced at New York's American Place Theater in 1969.

INTERVIEWER: What were your feelings when you received the Pulitzer Prize for Poetry for *Live or Die* in 1967?

SEXTON: Of course, I was delighted. It had been a bad time for me. I had a broken hip, and I was just starting to get well, still crippled, but functioning a little bit. After I received the prize, it gave me added incentive to write more. In the months following, I managed to write a poem, "Eighteen Days Without You," in fourteen days—an eighteen-section poem. I was inspired by the recognition that the Pulitzer gave me, even though I was aware that it didn't mean all that much. After all, they have to give a Pulitzer Prize every year, and I was just one in a long line.

INTERVIEWER: Do you write a spate of poems at one time, or are you disciplined by a writing schedule?

SEXTON: Well, I'm very dissatisfied with the amount I write. My first book—although it took three years to complete—was really written in one year. Sometimes ten poems were written in two weeks. When I was going at that rate, I found that I could really work well. Now I tend to become dissatisfied with the fact that I write poems so slowly, that they come to me so slowly. When they come, I write them; when they don't come, I don't. There's certainly no disciplined writing schedule except for the fact that when a poem comes a person must be disciplined and ready, flexing his muscles. That is, they burst forth, and you must put everything else aside. Ideally it doesn't matter what it is unless your husband has double pneumonia, or the child breaks his leg. Otherwise, you don't tear yourself away from the typewriter until you must sleep.

INTERVIEWER: Do the responsibilities of wife and mother interfere with your writing?

SEXTON: Well, when my children were younger, they interfered all the time. It was just my stubbornness that let me get through with it at all, because here were these young children saying, "Momma, Momma," and there I was getting the images, structuring the poem. Now my children are older and creep around the house saying, "Shh, Mother is writing a poem." But then again, as I was writing the poem, "Eighteen Days Without You"—the last poem in *Love Poems*—my husband said to me,

"I can't stand it any longer, you haven't been with me for days."
That poem originally was "Twenty-one Days Without You" and
it became "Eighteen Days" because he had cut into the inspiration; he demanded my presence back again, into his life, and
I couldn't take that much from him.

INTERVIEWER: When writing, what part of the poem is the
prickliest part?

SEXTON: Punctuation, sometimes. The punctuating can change
the whole meaning, and my life is full of little dots and dashes.
Therefore, I have to let the editors help me punctuate. And,
probably the rhythm. It's the thing I have to work hardest to get
in the beginning—the feeling, the voice of the poem, and how
it will come across, how it will feel to the reader, how it feels to
me as it comes out. Images are probably the most important part
of the poem. First of all, you want to tell a story, but images are
what are going to shore it up and get to the heart of the matter—
but I don't have to work too hard for the images—they have to
come—if they're not coming, I'm not even writing a poem, it's
pointless. So I work hardest to get the rhythm, because each
poem should have its own rhythm, its own structure. Each poem
has its own life, each one is different.

INTERVIEWER: How do you decide a length of line? Does it
have something to do with the way it looks on a page as well as
how many beats there are to a line?

SEXTON: How it looks on a page. I don't give a damn about the
beats in a line, unless I want them and need them. These are
just tricks that you use when you need them. It's a very simple
thing to write with rhyme and with rhythmic beat—those things
anyone can do nowadays; everyone is quite accomplished at that.
The point, the hard thing, is to get the true voice of the poem,
to make each poem an individual thing, give it the stamp of your
own voice, and at the same time to make it singular.

INTERVIEWER: Do you ever find yourself saying, "Oh, yes, I've
explored that in another poem," and discarding a poem?

SEXTON: No, because I might want to explore it in a new way
. . . I might have a new realization, a new truth about it. Recently
I noticed in "Flee on Your Donkey" that I had used some of the

same facts in *To Bedlam and Part Way Back*, but I hadn't realized them in their total ugliness. I'd hidden from them. This time was really raw and really ugly and it was all involved with my own madness. It was all like a great involuted web, and I presented it the way it really was.

INTERVIEWER: Do you revise a great deal?

SEXTON: Constantly.

INTERVIEWER: Do you have any ritual which gets you set for writing?

SEXTON: I might, if I felt the poem come on, put on a certain record, sometimes the "Bachianas Brasileiras" by Villa-Lobos. I wrote to that for about three or four years. It's my magic tune.

INTERVIEWER: Is there any time of day, any particular mood that is better for writing?

SEXTON: No. Those moments before a poem comes, when the heightened awareness comes over you, and you realize a poem is buried there somewhere, you prepare yourself. I run around, you know, kind of skipping around the house, marvelous elation. It's as though I could fly, almost, and I get very tense before I've told the truth—hard. Then I sit down at the desk and get going with it.

INTERVIEWER: What is the quality of feeling when you're writing?

SEXTON: Well, it's a beautiful feeling, even if it's hard work. When I'm writing, I know I'm doing the thing I was born to do.

INTERVIEWER: Do you have any standard by which you judge whether to let an image remain in a poem, or be cut?

SEXTON: It's done with my unconscious. May it do me no ill.

INTERVIEWER: You've said, "When I'm working away on a poem, I hunt for the truth . . . It might be a poetic truth, and not just a factual one." Can you comment on that?

SEXTON: Many of my poems are true, line by line, altering a few facts to get the story at its heart. In "The Double Image," the poem about my mother's death from cancer and the loss of my daughter, I don't mention that I had another child. Each poem has its own truth. Furthermore, in that poem, I only say that I was hospitalized twice, when in fact, I was hospitalized five times in that span of time. But then, poetic truth is not necessarily autobiographical. It is truth that goes beyond the immediate self, another life. I don't adhere to literal facts all the time; I make them up whenever needed. Concrete examples give a verisimilitude. I want the reader to feel, "Yes, yes, that's the way it is." I want them to feel as if they were touching me. I would alter any word, attitude, image, or persona for the sake of a poem. As Yeats said, "I have lived many lives, I have been a slave and a prince. Many a beloved has sat upon my knee, and I have sat upon the knee of many a beloved. Everything that has been shall be again."

INTERVIEWER: There Yeats is talking about reincarnation.

SEXTON: So am I. It's a little mad, but I believe I am many people. When I am writing a poem, I feel I am the person who should have written it. Many times I assume these guises; I attack it the way a novelist might. Sometimes I become someone else, and when I do, I believe, even in moments when I'm not writing the poem, that I am that person. When I wrote about the farmer's wife, I lived in my mind in Illinois; when I had the illegitimate child, I nursed it—in my mind—and gave it back and traded life. When I gave my lover back to his wife, in my mind, I grieved and saw how ethereal and unnecessary I had been. When I was Christ, I felt like Christ. My arms hurt, I desperately wanted to pull them in off the Cross. When I was taken down off the Cross and buried alive, I sought solutions; I hoped they were Christian solutions.

INTERVIEWER: What prompted you to write "In the Deep Museum," which recounts what Christ could have felt if he were still alive in the tomb? What led you to even deal with such a subject?

SEXTON: I'm not sure. I think it was an unconscious thing. I think I had a kind of feeling Christ was speaking to me and telling me to write that story . . . the story he hadn't written. I thought to myself, this would be the most awful death. The Cross, the Crucifixion, which I so deeply believe in, has almost become trite, and that there was a more humble death that he might have had to seek for love's sake, because his love was the greatest thing about him—not his death.

INTERVIEWER: Are you a believing nonbeliever? Your poems, such as "The Division of Parts" and "With Mercy for the Greedy," suggest you would like to believe, indeed struggle to believe, but can't.

SEXTON: Yes. I fight my own impulse. There is a hard-core part of me that believes, and there's this little critic in me that believes nothing. Some people think I'm a lapsed Catholic.

INTERVIEWER: What was your early religious training?

SEXTON: Half-assed Protestant. My Nana came from a Protestant background with a very stern patriarchal father who had twelve children. He often traveled in Europe, and when he came back and brought nude statues into his house, the minister came to call and said, "You can't come to church if you keep these nude statues." So he said, "All right, I'll never come again." Every Sunday morning he read the Bible to his twelve children for two hours, and they had to sit up straight and perfect. He never went to church again.

INTERVIEWER: Where do you get the "juice" for your religious poetry?

SEXTON: I found, when I was bringing up my children, that I could answer questions about sex easily. But I had a very hard time with the questions about God and death. It isn't resolved in my mind to this day.

INTERVIEWER: Are you saying then that questions from your children are what prompted you to think about these poems— that doesn't sound quite right.

SEXTON: It isn't. I have visions—sometimes ritualized visions— that come to me of God, or of Christ, or of the Saints, and I feel that I can touch them almost . . . that they are part of me. It's the same "Everything that has been shall be again." It's reincarnation, speaking with another voice . . . or else with the Devil. If you want to know the truth, the leaves talk to me every June.

INTERVIEWER: How long do your visions last? What are they like?

SEXTON: That's impossible to describe. They could last for six months, six minutes, or six hours. I feel very much in touch with things after I've had a vision. It's somewhat like the beginning of writing a poem; the whole world is very sharp and well defined, and I'm intensely alive, like I've been shot full of electric volts.

INTERVIEWER: Do you try to communicate this to other people when you feel it?

SEXTON: Only through the poems, no other way. I refuse to talk about it, which is why I'm having a hard time now.

INTERVIEWER: Is there any real difference between a religious vision and a vision when you're mad?

SEXTON: Sometimes, when you're mad, the vision—I don't call them visions, really—when you're mad, they're silly and out of place, whereas if it's a so-called mystical experience, you've put everything in its proper place. I've never talked about my religious experiences with anyone, not a psychiatrist, not a friend, not a priest, not anyone. I've kept it very much to myself—and I find this very difficult, and I'd just as soon leave it, if you please.

INTERVIEWER: A poem like "The Division of Parts" has direct reference to your mother's dying. Did those excruciating experiences of watching someone close to you disintegrate from cancer force you to confront your own belief in God or religion?

SEXTON: Yes, I think so. The dying are slowly being rocked away from us and wrapped up into death, that eternal place. And one looks for answers and is faced with demons and visions. Then one comes up with God. I don't mean the ritualized Protestant God, who is such a goody-goody . . . but the martyred saints, the crucified man . . .

INTERVIEWER: Are you saying that when confronted with the ultimate question, death, that your comfort comes, even though watered down, from the myths and fables of religion?

SEXTON: No myth or fable ever gave me any solace, but my own inner contact with the heroes of the fables, as you put it, my very closeness to Christ. In one poem about the Virgin Mary, "For the Year of the Insane," I believed that I was talking to Mary, that her lips were upon my lips; it's almost physical . . . as in many of my poems. I become that person.

INTERVIEWER: But is it the fact in your life of someone you know dying that forces you into a vision?

SEXTON: No, I think it's my own madness.

INTERVIEWER: Are you more lucid, in the sense of understanding life, when you are mad?

SEXTON: Yes.

INTERVIEWER: Why do you think that's so?

SEXTON: Pure gift.

INTERVIEWER: I asked you, are you a believing disbeliever. When something happens like a death, are you pushed over the brink of disbelieving into believing?

SEXTON: For a while, but it can happen without a death. There are little deaths in life, too—in your own life—and at that point, sometimes you are in touch with strange things, otherworldly things.

INTERVIEWER: You have received a great deal of fan mail from Jesuits and other clergy. Do any of them interpret what you write as blasphemy?

SEXTON: No. They find my work very religious, and take my books on retreats, and teach my poems in classes.

INTERVIEWER: Why do you feel that most of your critics ignore this strain of religious experience in your poetry?

SEXTON: I think they tackle the obvious things without delving deeper. They are more shocked by the other, whereas I think in time to come people will be more shocked by my mystical poetry than by my so-called confessional poetry.

INTERVIEWER: Perhaps your critics, in time to come, will associate the suffering in your confessional poetry with the kind of sufferers you take on in your religious poetry.

SEXTON: You've summed it up perfectly. Thank you for saying that. That ragged Christ, that sufferer, performed the greatest act of confession, and I mean with his body. And I try to do that with words.

INTERVIEWER: Many of your poems deal with memories of suffering. Very few of them deal with memories that are happy ones. Why do you feel driven to write more about pain?

SEXTON: That's not true about my last book, which deals with joy. I think I've dealt with unhappy themes because I've lived them. If I haven't lived them, I've invented them.

INTERVIEWER: But surely there were also happy moments, joyous, euphoric moments in those times as well.

SEXTON: Pain engraves a deeper memory.

INTERVIEWER: Are there any poems you wouldn't read in public?

SEXTON: No. As a matter of fact, I sing "Cripples and Other Stories" with my combo to a Nashville rhythm.

INTERVIEWER: What is your combo?

SEXTON: It's called "Her Kind"—after one of my poems. One of my students started putting my poems to music—he's a guitarist, and then we got an organist, a flutist, and a drummer. We call our music "Chamber Rock." We've been working on it and giving performances for about a year. It opens up my poems in a new way by involving them in the sound of rock music, letting my words open up to sound that can be actually heard, giving a new dimension. And it's quite exciting for me to hear them that way.

INTERVIEWER: Do you enjoy giving a reading?

SEXTON: It takes three weeks out of your life. A week before it happens, the nervousness begins, and it builds up to the night of the reading when the poet in you changes into a performer. Readings take so much out of you because they are a reliving of the experience, that is, they are happening all over again. I am an actress in my own autobiographical play. Then there is the love . . . When there is a coupling of the audience and myself, when they are really with me, and the Muse is with me, I'm not coming alone.

INTERVIEWER: Can you ever imagine America as a place where thousands of fans flock to a stadium to hear a poet, as they do in Russia?

SEXTON: Someday, perhaps. But our poets seem to be losing touch. People flock to Bob Dylan, Janis Joplin, the Beatles—these are the popular poets of the English-speaking world. But I don't worry about popularity; I'm too busy.

INTERVIEWER: At first your poetry was a therapeutic device. Why do you write now?

SEXTON: I write because I'm driven to—it's my bag. Though after every book, I think there'll never be another one. That's the end of that. Good-by, good-by.

INTERVIEWER: And what advice would you give to a young poet?

SEXTON: Be careful who your critics are. Be specific. Tell almost the whole story. Put your ear close down to your soul and listen hard.

INTERVIEWER: Louis Simpson criticized your poetry, saying, "A poem titled 'Menstruation at Forty' was the straw that broke this camel's back." Is it only male critics who balk at your use of the biological facts of womanhood?

SEXTON: I haven't added up all the critics and put them on different teams. I haven't noticed the gender of the critic especially. I talk of the life-death cycle of the body. Well, women tell time by the body. They are like clocks. They are always fastened to the earth, listening for its small animal noises. Sexuality is one of the most normal parts of life. True, I get a little uptight when Norman Mailer writes that he screws a woman anally. I like Allen Ginsberg very much, and when he writes about the ugly vagina, I feel awful. That kind of thing doesn't appeal to me. So I have my limitations, too. Homosexuality is all right with me. Sappho was beautiful. But when someone hates another person's body and somehow violates it—that's the kind of thing I mind.

INTERVIEWER: What do you feel is the purpose of poetry?

SEXTON: As Kafka said about prose, "A book should serve as the axe for the frozen sea within us." And that's what I want from a poem. A poem should serve as the axe for the frozen sea within us.

INTERVIEWER: How would you apply the Kafka quote to your new book, *Love Poems*?

SEXTON: Well, have you ever seen a sixteen-year-old fall in love? The axe for the frozen sea becomes imbedded in her. Or have you ever seen a woman get to be forty and never have any love in her life? What happens to her when she falls in love? The axe for the frozen sea.

INTERVIEWER: Some people wonder how you can write about yourself, completely ignoring the great issues of the times, like the Vietnam war or the civil-rights crisis.

SEXTON: People have to find out who they are before they can confront national issues. The fact that I seldom write about public issues in no way reflects my personal opinion. I am a pacifist. I sign petitions, etc. However, I am not a polemicist. "The Fire Bombers"—that's a new poem—is about wanton destruction, not about Vietnam, specifically; when Robert Kennedy was killed, I wrote about an assassin. I write about human emotions; I write about interior events, not historical ones. In one of my love poems, I say that my lover is unloading bodies from Vietnam. If that poem is read in a hundred years, people will have to look up the war in Vietnam. They will have mixed it up with the Korean or God knows what else. One hopes it will be history very soon. Of course, I may change. I could use the specifics of the war for a backdrop against which to reveal experience, and it would be just as valid as the details I am known by. As for the civil-rights issue, I mentioned that casually in a poem, but I don't go into it. I think it's a major issue. I think many of my poems about the individual who is dispossessed, who must play slave, who cries "Freedom Now," "Power Now," are about the human experience of being black in this world. A black emotion can be a white emotion. It is a crisis for the individual as well as the nation. I think I've been writing black poems all along, wearing my white mask. I'm always the victim . . . but no longer!

—BARBARA KEVLES
1968

12. Cynthia Ozick

Born in New York City's Yorkville on April 17, 1928 and raised in the Pelham Bay section of the Bronx, Cynthia Ozick attended P.S. 71 and Hunter College High School. She received her B.A. from New York University, where she was inducted into Phi Beta Kappa, and her M.A. from Ohio State University, where her master's thesis was "Parable in the Later Novels of Henry James."

Ozick is the author of three novels, *Trust* (1966), *The Cannibal Galaxy* (1983), and, most recently, *The Messiah of Stockholm* (1987); three collections of short stories, *The Pagan Rabbi and Other Stories* (1971), *Bloodshed and Three Novellas* (1976), and *Levitation: Five Fictions* (1982); and a collection of essays, *Art & Ardor* (1983). In 1986, she was named the first recipient of the Rea Award for the short story, given annually to a living American writer whose short stories have made a significant contribution to the form. Her other awards include the American Academy of Arts and Letters Award for Literature, three O. Henry First Prizes for the short story, a Guggenheim fellowship, and, in 1983, the National Institute of Arts and Letters Mildred and Harold Strauss Living Award.

Ozick lives in New Rochelle, New York.

A manuscript page from Cynthia Ozick's essay "Good Novelists, Bad Citizens," published in The New York Times Book Review.

© Ricki Rosen

Cynthia Ozick

A few words about the collaborative process that yielded the text that follows: initially, Ozick was concerned that her spoken words would later betray her in print. "Conversation is air," she said, and asked whether I might submit questions to be answered in writing. I made an acceptable counterproposal: I would ask questions, Ozick would type out her answers.

I sent no questions beforehand. Instead, we sat down at the dining room table of her New Rochelle home on a June day in 1985. I turned on my tape recorder, she turned on her electric typewriter. I asked a question, she typed out her answer and then read it to me. Ozick is a rapid typist and the exchange flowed quickly. It was a conversation, with the typing giving pause for thought. We drank tea and I munched on cookies. Occasionally we would drift into conversation lost to the typescript but captured on tape. The end product was a manuscript which when amended by her oral comments doubled in length. At a later date, Ozick reviewed and revised her spoken comments. Her changes, true to our intent, were more of a copyedit than a rewrite. "Whoever thinks the taped voice is 'true to life' is in error," she wrote me later. "It is false to life. But I am satisfied with the interview."

I had feared that the rigorous intellect evidenced in Cynthia Ozick's essays and stories would be matched in person by a severe manner. But what is most disarming about Ozick in person is her gentleness, sensitivity, and directness, which put the visitor at ease. At as great a length as I interviewed Ozick, or more, she later interviewed me, with interest, sympathy and encouragement.

INTERVIEWER: You write all night. Have you always done so?

OZICK: [*Speaking, not yet typing*] Always. I've written in daylight too, but mainly I go through the night.

INTERVIEWER: How does this affect your interaction with the rest of society?

OZICK: It's terrible. Most social life begins in the evening, when I'm just starting. So when I do go out at night, it means I lose a whole day's work.

INTERVIEWER: You don't just start at midnight or whenever you get home?

OZICK: I almost never get home at midnight. I'm always the last to leave a party.

INTERVIEWER: What are your regular working hours?

OZICK: You're talking as if there's some sort of predictable schedule. I don't have working hours. I wake up late. I read the mail, which sometimes is a very complex procedure. Then I eat breakfast with the *Times*. Then I start priming the pump, which is to read. I answer the letters.

INTERVIEWER: You answer every letter you get?

OZICK: I am compulsive. I take care of everything.

INTERVIEWER: You are also known as a letter writer.

OZICK: No, I don't feel that. I feel that what I'm doing is conscientiously and responsibly replying. Occasionally, though, an urgent spontaneous letter will fly out—love, polemics, passion.

INTERVIEWER: One of the footnotes in your Forster essay mentions a correspondence you had with Lionel Trilling.

OZICK: Lionel Trilling wrote in response to something I had published about Forster a long time ago. It was an astonishing letter. He said that he realized E. M. Forster was homosexual only years after he had completed his book on Forster's work. It wasn't an issue in the society at the time he was writing. The atmosphere didn't lead anyone to think along those lines, and Trilling himself was unaware. I met Leon Edel at the Academy in May and he's doing . . . That thing [the tape recorder] is going! I just realized that. I thought I was just talking. Hmmm. [*turns on typewriter, starts typing*] Leon Edel is doing a one-volume reissue of his magnificent biography and he said he's putting in a lot of new matter about James and the issue of his possible homosexuality because when he was writing that part of the biography it was the fifties and one didn't talk about such things.

INTERVIEWER: I take it that you're reading even when you're working on a piece of fiction.

OZICK: I read in order to write. I read out of obsession with writing.

INTERVIEWER: So, for example, does what you're reading influence what you write?

OZICK: Not precisely. I read in order to find out what I need to know: to illuminate the riddle.

INTERVIEWER: When you were writing *The Cannibal Galaxy*, what were you reading then?

OZICK: For that? Nothing at all. Oh, yes, street maps of Paris. Guidebooks about Paris. Anything I could find on the Marais, on the rue des Rosiers, for instance: the Jewish quarter.

INTERVIEWER: What are you reading now, for the novella you're working on?

OZICK: Swedish stuff! A book with pictures of the Swedish landscape, a book about the Swedish royal family; a Swedish-English dictionary. But the dictionary is dangerous. Looking up how to say a simple (and immaculate) "Goddamn," I came up (some Swedish friends later wrote me) with a super-four-letter-stinger. The novella will be called, I think, "The Messiah of Stockholm." It takes place in Stockholm. I'd better say no more, or the Muse will wipe it out.

INTERVIEWER: Do you really believe that? Has that happened before?

OZICK: I have lost stories and many starts of novels before. Not always as punishment for "telling," but more often as a result of something having gone cold and dead because of a hiatus. Telling, you see, is the same as a hiatus. It means you're not *doing* it.

INTERVIEWER: When you first graduated from college you undertook a long novel.

OZICK: Immediately after graduate school . . . ah, here I should stop to explain that there was a very short period in the early fifties when would-be writers were ASHAMED to go on to get a Ph.D. A very short period! But that was when one tried out teaching for a while after college—as a teaching assistant on a stipend—and then fled homeward to begin the Novel. Mine, typically, was immensely ambitious. I thought of it as a "philosophical" novel, and was going to pit the Liberal-Modernists against the Neo-Thomists. I wrote about 300,000 words of it.

INTERVIEWER: What possessed you to want to write a novel at all?

OZICK: I never conceived of not writing a novel. I believed—oh, God, I "believed," it was an article of Faith!—I was born to write a novel.

INTERVIEWER: You believed that since childhood.

OZICK: Yes, since my first moments of sentience.

INTERVIEWER: Is deciding to be a writer a question of "personality" or of "content," of what the person has to say?

OZICK: That's an interesting question. I think it's a condition, a given; content comes later. You're born into the condition of being an amphora; whether it's wine or water that fills it afterward belongs to afterward. Lately I think of this given condition as a kind of curse, because there is no way out of it. What a relief it would be to have the freedom of other people! Any inborn condition of this sort is, after all, a kind of slavery. There is no choice. Nor can one choose to stop: although now that I'm no longer young, I talk to writers of my own age about this. About the relief of being allowed to stop. But I know I will never stop until the lip of limitation: that is, disability or the grave. But you ask about the beginning. The beginning was almost physiological in its ecstatic pursuits. I'm embarrassed as I say this—"ecstatic pursuits"!—but I am thinking back to the delectable excitement, the *waiting-to-be-born* excitement, of longing to write. I suppose it is a kind of parallel Eros.

INTERVIEWER: But to return to after graduate school—you took the plunge into a long novel.

OZICK: Yes. I was working on the novel I called, from Blake, *Mercy, Pity, Peace, and Love.* I abbreviated it: Mippel, I called it, deriving that from MPPL. And I developed a little self-mocking joke about that. I referred to it as the Mippel on which I sucked for so long. Somewhere in the middle of it, I read of a paperback company that was doing collections of novellas—a sort of "contest." The editor, I seem to recall, was named Oscar De Liso. I thought I would polish off a novella in, say, six weeks, and then return to Mippel. As it turned out, the novella grew longer and longer and took nearly seven years, and became *Trust.* I had already spent about seven years with Mippel. This is a part of my life that pains me desperately to recall. Such waste, so many eggs in one basket, such life-error, such foolish concentration, such goddamned stupid "purity"! In the middle of *Trust,* as it happened, I stopped to write a shorter novel, which I *did* write in six sustained nonstop weeks. It was called *The Conversion of John Andersmall.* I conceived of it as a relief, a kind of virtuoso joke: a comic novel. It was turned down by, among others, the agent Candida Donadio, and by E. L. Doctorow, then an editor at Dial. I believe there is a carbon of it somewhere up in the attic. It was finally lost somewhere in a London publisher's office.

INTERVIEWER: Were you writing full-time then?

OZICK: Yes. Full-time.

INTERVIEWER: And how were you supporting yourself?

OZICK: I had gotten married and my husband, Bernard Hallote, supported me. I used to say that I was on a "Hallote"; some people are on a Guggenheim, I was on a Hallote.

INTERVIEWER: What sustained you without publication during that period?

OZICK: Belief. Not precisely self-belief, because that faltered profoundly again and again. Belief in Art, in Literature: I was a worshiper of Literature. I had a youthful arrogance about my "powers," and at the same time a terrible feeling of humiliation, of total shame and defeat. When I think about that time—and I've spent each decade as it comes regretting the decade before, it seems—I wish I had done what I see the current generation doing: I wish I had scurried around for reviews to do, for articles to write. I wish I had written short stories. I wish I had not been sunk in an immense dream of immense achievement. For most of this time, I was living at home in my parents' house, already married. But my outer life was unchanged from childhood. And my inner life was also unchanged. I was fixed, transfixed. It was Literature every breathing moment. I had no "ordinary" life. I despised ordinary life; I had contempt for it. What a *meshuggas!*

INTERVIEWER: Can you describe the feeling of first publication?

OZICK: I was thirty-seven years old. I had the baby and the galleys together, and I sat at my desk—the same desk I use now, the same desk I inherited from my brother when I was eight years old—correcting the galleys with my right hand, and rocking the baby carriage with my left. I felt stung when the review in *Time*, which had a big feature on first novels that season, got my age wrong and added a year. I hated being so old; beginning when I thought I'd be so far along. I've had age-sorrow all my life. I had it on publication, but for the next ten years or so the child was so distracting that I hardly noticed what publication "felt" like.

INTERVIEWER: How did you go about getting *Trust* published?

OZICK: Oh! What a story. I mustn't defame the dead. It was a long, hopeless process. I finished it on the day John Kennedy was assassinated, in November, 1963. Publication wasn't until three years later. Those were three hellish years. It began when an agent, Theron Raines, wrote me a letter after a poem of mine had appeared in the *Virginia Quarterly Review*: in those days I was writing poems all the time. The biographical note at the back of the magazine said I was writing a novel, and this interested Raines, who got in touch. He has been my representative ever since. At first an option was taken on the novel by the late Hal Scharlatt, who procrastinated over a year, and just let the manuscript sit there. He was busy, he told me, with the big long manuscript of someone called Henry Kissinger. An unknown name. A political writer of some kind. Scharlatt asked for revisions and said he would tell me what they ought to be; but he never called me in to talk about this. Finally, after a year and a half, I appealed to him to see me. He was sitting at his desk in his office at New American Library with a yellow sheet in the typewriter; he was just making his first notes on the famous "revisions." I saw he was making them up on the spot. And he had kept me dangling and suffering, for a year and a half, over nothing at all! The important editorial ideas he had promised me and for which I'd waited so long turned out not to exist. Vapor. The manuscript was finally taken over by his colleague, David Segal, a remarkable editor who became my friend. His wife, Lore Segal, the novelist, is one of my closest friends now. David Segal sent me a hundred pages with red-pencil marks all over them, and asked for cuts. I had known all along that I would never have accepted any cuts from Scharlatt; and I could not bring myself to accept any from David, whom I respected. I had a dilemma: accept the cuts, and be published; refuse, and languish forever unpublished. I declined David Segal's cuts. He, amazing man, went ahead and published the novel anyhow.

INTERVIEWER: You then turned to shorter fiction.

OZICK: I was afraid of ever again falling into hugeness. It had been a time of extended darkness, and I was afraid.

INTERVIEWER: Now, so much time after that, more than twenty years, almost thirty years later, are you still consciously avoiding length? Avoiding, or in fear of, the large novel?

OZICK: [*starts typing—stops suddenly*] Is it usually part of your interview technique that your subjects end up delivering long confessions? I have a truth-telling syndrome and I wish to God I didn't. . . .

INTERVIEWER: Why?

OZICK: We're strangers and it leaves me utterly unprotected— I don't know what I need protection from, but I can't believe that when you interviewed Isaac Bashevis Singer he told you all about his life-hurts—he didn't. Jerzy Kosinski, whom you also interviewed, is certainly a protected person. Have you ever run into the completely unprotected—or as the psychoanalysts say—undefended?

INTERVIEWER: It's true that Kosinski is very adept at press interaction. But I was conscious of that and . . .

OZICK: You can never second-guess him. You can never penetrate beyond his penetration of you. It's impossible. He's—he's a genius. Your question was about avoiding the longer forms.

INTERVIEWER: The large novel.

OZICK: [*Resumes typing*] The Modernist Dream. I recently did a review of William Gaddis and talked about his ambition—his coming on the scene when it was already too late to be ambitious in that huge way with a vast modernist novel. But I was ambitious that way too. I no longer believe in Literature, capital-L, with the same fervor I used to. I've learned to respect living, perhaps. I think I have gotten over my fear of largeness as well, because I have gotten over my awe—my idolatrous awe. Literature is not all there is in the world, I now recognize. It is, I admit, still my All, but it isn't *the* All. And that is a difference I can finally see.

INTERVIEWER: But what about your literary ambitions in terms of subject matter and length?

OZICK: I see it as a simple matter of choosing a subject, or having the subject choose itself, and letting the subject dictate the length. It's not my "ambition" that dictates the size of the enterprise. I am not interested in ego, if that's what this question is about. "The Pagan Rabbi," for instance, a short story written so long ago, touches on a large theme: the aesthetic versus the moral commitment. Profound subject matter can be encompassed in small space—for proof, look at any sonnet by Shakespeare! *Multum in parvo.* I am not avoiding length these days—not consciously. But perhaps there's some truth in the speculation that I may be living my life backwards! Doing the short forms now, having begun with a "Great Work," a long ambitious "modernist" novel of the old swollen kind.

INTERVIEWER: Can one write and avoid ambition?

OZICK: One *must* avoid ambition *in order to* write. Otherwise something else is the goal: some kind of power beyond the power of language. And the power of language, it seems to me, is the only kind of power a writer is entitled to.

INTERVIEWER: But is writing idolatry?

OZICK: Until quite recently I held a rather conventional view about all this. I thought of the imagination as what its name suggests, as image-making, and I thought of the writer's undertaking as a sovereignty set up in competition with the sovereignty of—well, the Creator of the Universe. I thought of imagination as that which sets up idols, as a rival of monotheism. I've since reconsidered this view. I now see that the idol-making capacity of imagination is its lower form, and that one *cannot* be a monotheist without putting the imagination under the greatest pressure of all. To imagine the unimaginable is the highest use of the imagination. I no longer think of imagination as a thing to be dreaded. Once you come to regard imagination as ineluctably linked with monotheism, you can no longer think of imagination as competing with monotheism. Only a very strong imagination can rise to the idea of a noncorporeal God. The lower imagination, the weaker, falls into the proliferation of images. My hope is someday to be able to figure out a connection between the work of monotheism-imagining and the work of story-imagining. Until now I have thought of these as enemies.

INTERVIEWER: What do you attribute your change of mind to?

OZICK: Somebody gave me this idea. I had a conversation with a good thinker.

INTERVIEWER: Who's that?

OZICK: [*Stops typing*] I don't want to give him the attribution here, because I did once before in print and he was embarrassed by it. So the alternative is to plagiarize. Either embarrass or plagiarize. He's put me in that position.

INTERVIEWER: But in any case, you're still in the storytelling business.

OZICK: I'm in the storytelling business, but I no longer feel I'm making idols. The insight that the largest, deepest, widest imaginative faculty of all is what you need to be a monotheist teaches me that you simply cannot be a Jew if you repudiate the imagination. This is a major shift for me.

INTERVIEWER: And now you feel better about it. But neither of the two positions . . .

OZICK: . . . will stop me from doing it. Exactly. I can't stop. Right, that's true. I'd better write that down. [*Starts typing again*] In any case, whether I were ultimately to regard story-telling as idol-making or not, whether I might some day discover the living tissue that connects the capacity for imagery with the capacity to drive beyond imagery—whatever my theoretical condition, I would go on writing fiction.

INTERVIEWER: How come?

OZICK: Because I will do it. Whether it is God's work or Satan's work, I will do it.

INTERVIEWER: Why?

OZICK: Willfulness.

INTERVIEWER: In your critical articles on the Edith Wharton and Virginia Woolf biographies, you say "the writer is missing."

OZICK: That's true. It's quite true.

INTERVIEWER: What is "the writer" that is missing?

OZICK: Quentin Bell's biography told the story of his aunt, who happened to be the famous writer Virginia Woolf. But it was a family story really, about a woman with psychotic episodes, her husband's coping with this, her sister's distress. It had, as I said, the smell of a household. It was not about the sentences in Virginia Woolf's books. The Wharton biography, though more a "literary" biography, dealt with status, not with the writer's private heart. What do I mean by "private heart"? It's probably impossible to define, but it's not what the writer does—breakfast, schedule, social outings—but what the writer *is*. The secret contemplative self. An inner recess wherein insights occur. This writer's self is perhaps coextensive with one of the writer's sentences. It seems to me that more can be found about a writer in any single sentence in a work of fiction, say, than in five or ten full-scale biographies. Or interviews!

INTERVIEWER: So which sentence of yours shall we take? Shall I pick one out? (*begins rummaging through books*)

OZICK: [*Stops typing*] Oh my God!

INTERVIEWER: I'm calling you on this one.

OZICK: Yes, you are. Good God. Okay. Let's see where this takes us.

INTERVIEWER: We can start with the opening sentence of *The Cannibal Galaxy*: "The Principal of the Edmond Fleg Primary School was originally (in a manner of speaking) a Frenchman, Paris-born—but whenever he quoted his long-dead father and mother, he quoted them in Yiddish."

OZICK: There is a piece of autobiography in that sentence. It may need a parenthetical explanation. I was taking a course with Lionel Trilling and wrote a paper for him with an opening sentence that contained a parenthesis. He returned the paper with a wounding reprimand: "Never, never begin an essay with a parenthesis in the first sentence." Ever since then, I've made a point of starting out with a parenthesis in the first sentence. Years later, Trilling was cordial and very kind to me, and I felt redeemed, though it took two decades to earn his approval. But you can see how the sentence you've chosen for this crafty experiment may not be to the purpose—there's too much secret mischief in it.

INTERVIEWER: What else does it reveal?

OZICK: Nothing.

INTERVIEWER: Shall we turn to *Puttermesser*? "Puttermesser, an unmarried lawyer and civil servant of forty-six, felt attacked on all sides."

OZICK: Cadence. Cadence is the fingerprint, isn't it? Suppose *you* were going to write that sentence with that precise content. How would it come out? It's short enough for you to give it a try just like that, on the spot.

INTERVIEWER: I might just write "Puttermesser felt attacked on all sides."

OZICK: Yes. That's interesting. It's minimalizing, paring away. You are a Hemingwayesque writer, then?

INTERVIEWER: A Hemingwayesque rewriter. But to get back to my question: is the heart of Ozick, the writer, cadence?

OZICK: It's one element, not the only one. Idea counts too.

INTERVIEWER: But you must have a notion of what a writer is. You have criticized the biographies of Wharton and Woolf as "missing the writer," and you have written about the writer as being genderless and living in the world of "as if" rather than being restrained by her own biographical . . .

OZICK: Parochial temporary commitments.

INTERVIEWER: So then how would you define this writer? And how would you define the "Ozick" writer that stems from your written work and stands independent of your biographical data and which otherwise might be missing from this interview?

OZICK: But I worry about any Platonic notion of "a writer." I now *must* (perhaps in defiance of my own old record) believe that a writer is simply another citizen with a profession. I don't want to cling to any pretensions of the writer as that inspired mystical Byronic shaman or special select ideal holy person. I don't want to live in the world with such mystical figures; I don't like self-appointed gurus, and even less the kind that's divinely appointed. A writer is someone born with a gift. An athlete can run. A painter can paint. A writer has a facility with words. A good writer can also think. Isn't that enough to define a writer by? The rest is idiosyncrasy—what I meant earlier when I spoke of the cadence of any single sentence. And what is idiosyncrasy except minute individual difference? In the human species, individual differences *are* minute. Think how we all come equipped with all the parts that make up a face, and how every face is different from every other face, even as, simultaneously, every face is equal to every other face.

INTERVIEWER: How does your Jewishness fit in here? Don't we have to speak about that?

OZICK: To be Jewish is to be a member of a civilization—a civilization with a long, long history, a history that is, in one way of viewing it, a procession of ideas. Jewish history is intellectual history. And all this can become the content of a writer's mind; but it isn't equal to a writer's mind. To be a writer is one thing; to be a Jew is another thing. To combine them is a third thing.

INTERVIEWER: In those writers' classes where one is always told, "Write about what you know."

OZICK: Ah! When I've taught those classes, I always say, "Forget about 'Write about what you know.' Write about what you don't know." The point is that the self is limiting. The self—subjectivity—is narrow and bound to be repetitive. We are, after all, a species. When you write about what you don't know, this means you begin to think about the world at large. You begin to think beyond the home-thoughts. You enter dream and imagination.

INTERVIEWER: Where is the vanishing point? What do you mean by these limits of subjectivity? The limits of our gray cells?

OZICK: Our gray cells aren't our limitations. It's our will to enter the world: by the world I mean history, including the history of thought, which is the history of human experience. This isn't an intellectual viewpoint. In fact, it asks for the widening of the senses and of all experience.

INTERVIEWER: But how far do you intend to go?

OZICK: As far as I can. As far as is necessary.

INTERVIEWER: In the kingdom of As-If, there are some writers who never leave the house, and some writers who are explorers of the Universe.

OZICK: And some who do both at the same time. Emily Dickinson.

INTERVIEWER: Philip Roth stays close to home, Doris Lessing goes out. In terms of content, some are homebodies, some are astronauts, some are chameleons. Which are you?

OZICK: None of the above. An archaeologist, maybe. I stay home, but I'm not a homebody. I go out, but only to dig down. I don't try to take on the coloration of the environment; I'm not an assimilationist. I say "archaeologist," because I like to think about civilizations. They are illuminated in comparison. Stories are splinters of larger ideas about culture. I'm aware that there are writers who deny idea completely, who begin from what happens, from pure experience. But for me ideas are emotions.

INTERVIEWER: Have you ever rejected a story, or character, or idea, because you've felt you couldn't "do" it, or didn't know it?

OZICK: Yes, once. I began a novel meant to trap Freud. I read the Jones biography, read *Civilization and Its Discontents* and some other things, and then quit. I saw it would take a lifetime of study.

INTERVIEWER: Do you have a notion of having created a writer

"Cynthia Ozick" whose nose might be *Levitation*, eyes *Cannibal Galaxy*, and mouth *Bloodshed*?

OZICK: I once was asked to draw a self-portrait. [*starts drawing*] It came out something like this:

What is the true import of this metaphorical question?

INTERVIEWER: Again, I'm trying to get you to define the writer "Ozick."

OZICK: I honest-to-God don't know. Can one say what one *is*? How does one define one's own sense of being alive? I think it is this hum, or buzz, blablablablabla, that keeps on talking inside one's head. A stream of babble. The inner voice that never, never, never shuts up. Never. What is it saying? One can't listen; if one listened, it would be, I think, the moment just before death.

INTERVIEWER: Again this points out how difficult it is for any biographer to seize the inner self of a writer.

OZICK: You've really backed me to the wall—you're saying I was unfair, unreasonable, in criticizing those biographers.

INTERVIEWER: It's not where I started out at—I imagined that if you found something lacking you might yourself have a sense of what belongs there.

OZICK: I've never tried to write a biography and I have no idea if it's doable. But . . . [*starts typing*] I have kept a diary since 1953. Maybe the self-definition of a writer is there, cumulatively, and not on purpose. Maybe the only biography is the writer's diary. And yet that too is partial; mine is a bloodletting, and moans more than feels elation.

INTERVIEWER: On a lighter note . . . I wanted to ask you about the pictures that appear on the back covers of the paperback editions of your works. The pictures on the back . . . three different pictures have been used on the paperbacks. One for *Trust* and *The Pagan Rabbi* and *Levitation*, another for *Bloodshed*, a third for *Art & Ardor* and *The Cannibal Galaxy*.

OZICK: They get older!

INTERVIEWER: It's not that they get older. It's that—when you buy and read a book, you spend a lot of time looking at that picture of the writer. It's what you have of them.

OZICK: I look at photographs of writers very closely too.

INTERVIEWER: Did you have any say in all this: that your pictures are the entire back cover, and did you have any say over which pictures they chose? In the picture on the back of *Art & Ardor* you look like you're scowling.

OZICK: Using photographs was the publisher's idea. But I like the photographer and I like where I was standing and I like the bleak day. Bleak days are introspective, evocative. They smell of childhood reading.

INTERVIEWER: What is it you like about the place? Why do you feel it represents you?

OZICK: Well, it's up the shore a way from Pelham Bay Park where I grew up. I felt at home, inside my own landscape, on my own ground. My sense of that photo is a kind of pensiveness. Anxiety at worst but not a scowl. I hope not a scowl! Especially since after a certain number of years our faces become our biographies. We get to be responsible for our faces. I do the same—draw conclusions about writers from their photos. But when I see you doing that with my photograph I think: it's only a snapshot, it's not a soul. If it *were* soul, you would read tremble rather than scowl. Or so I imagine.

INTERVIEWER: You have dedicated many of your books to your editors. What part have they played in your life?

OZICK: Norman Podhoretz was the first cause of my getting invited to Jerusalem for the first time. That is a large thing to owe someone. He published my short story "Envy; or, Yiddish in America," and that led to a conference in Israel, for which I composed an essay called "Toward a New Yiddish." Gordon Lish was fiction editor at *Esquire* and wrote me out of the blue asking for a story. I took "An Education" out of a drawer and sent it to him along with the letter of rejection I thought he would write back to me. To my amazement, he published that story—which was the first thing I wrote after *Trust*, "in the manner of" Frank O'Connor, and even borrowing one of O'Connor's names for his heroines: Una. My editor at Knopf for many years has been Robert Gottlieb. The day he telephoned me—just after the tragic early death of David Segal—to tell me he would keep me on at Knopf, and publish *The Pagan Rabbi and Other Stories*, which had been accepted by David Segal, was also the day his little daughter was born; he telephoned from the hospital. About once every half-decade I go to see him for two or more hours. I live on what happens in those two hours all the rest of the time. Editors are parental figures, even when they are much younger than oneself; or else they are a kind of Muse. Frances Kiernan at *The New Yorker* is another one of my distant Muses.

INTERVIEWER: In "Envy" you portray a character who many see as I. B. Singer. In "Usurpation" some see Shmuel Agnon and Bernard Malamud. Kosinski is seen in "A Mercenary." Why do you do that?

OZICK: Infatuation perhaps. But I don't do it anymore, and never will again. Even when one invents, invents absolutely, one is blamed for stealing real people. You remind me of something I haven't thought of for a long, long time. One of my first short stories, written for a creative writing class in college, was about plagiarism. Apparently the idea of "usurpation" has intrigued me for most of my life. When I was a small child I remember upsetting my father; I had recently learned, from a fairy tale, the word "impostor" and I made him prove he wasn't an impostor by demanding that he open the pharmacy safe, which had a combination lock. Since only my real father, the pharmacist, knew the combination, his opening it would prove he was my father. I felt both theatrical and anxious at the same time; both real and unreal. I envied orphans; they were romantic. One of my favorite childhood books was called *Nobody's Boy*, and there was a companion volume called *Nobody's Girl.* These were, I believe, translated from the French; who reads them now? I don't know the origin of these fascinations; fairy tales, perhaps, and their extreme sadnesses. Princesses and princes trapped in the bodies of beasts, human souls looking for release.

INTERVIEWER: What about the chutzpah involved?

OZICK: Chutzpah? I never thought of that. I think of the imagination as a place of utter freedom. There one can do whatever one wants.

INTERVIEWER: Aren't you tossing stones at literary houses of glass, bringing these writers to the mat . . . ?

OZICK: No. Such a thought never occurred to me. On the contrary, it was their great fame I was playing with—an act of homage, in fact.

INTERVIEWER: Did "Envy" create an uproar?

OZICK: There was a vast brouhaha over this story. A meeting was called by the Yiddish writers, I learned later. The question was whether or not to condemn me publicly. Privately, they all furiously condemned me. Simon Weber, editor of the *Forward,* wrote an article—he's since apologized—in which he compared me to the "commissars of Warsaw and Moscow," anti-Semites of the first order. I was astonished and unbelievably hurt. I wrote a letter exclaiming that I felt my mother and father had broken my skull. What I had intended was a great lamentation for the murder of Yiddish, the mother-tongue of a thousand years, by the Nazis. Instead, here were all these writers angry at me.

INTERVIEWER: More recently, my far-flung sources informed me, you gave a reading at the Yale Medical School.

OZICK: Oh God. What sources?

INTERVIEWER: I never reveal sources. But I understand you read "The Sewing Harems" there and they didn't get it.

OZICK: No, but out of that, out of their not "getting it," out of this resistance to parable and metaphor, came an essay called "Metaphor and Memory," which I delivered at Harvard recently as the Phi Beta Kappa oration. The incident with the Yale doctors—it was hard on me—inspired whole discoveries about the nature and meaning of metaphor. I owe all this to the Yale doctors' impatience with me. They wanted plain language. Is that what you heard?

INTERVIEWER: I heard you read; they didn't get it. And then you told them that they didn't get it.

OZICK: Yes. I made a mistake. It was I who was obtuse. I was taken by surprise. I was embarrassed at Yale—but also considerably educated. It is possible to profit from being misunderstood.

INTERVIEWER: What about being misunderstood in general? What about audience?

OZICK: I don't want to be the Platonic cow in the forest—if you remember the opening of E. M. Forster's *The Longest Journey*. Or the tree that may or may not fall, depending on if there are any human ears around to hear its thud. Like any writer, I want to be read. I know I can't be "popular," and I regard this as a major failing. There *are* writers who are artists of language—everyone knows who they are!—who can also be read by large numbers of readers, who are accessible. In our own time, Nabokov and Updike, intricate embroiderers.

INTERVIEWER: Major failing?

OZICK: Yes. There is the first consummation, and then there is the second consummation. One can't live without the first; luckily one can live without the second. The first is getting into print. The second is getting read. I have been writing for years and years, without ever being read.

INTERVIEWER: Do you really believe that?

OZICK: It's not a matter of belief. It's a matter of knowing.

INTERVIEWER: Of knowing that very few people who read you are getting it?

OZICK: [*Stops typing*] Very few people read me.

INTERVIEWER: Very few people read you? You're in paperback.

OZICK: That's a small miracle. I have no idea whether any of those paperbacks are finding readers. I'm sure not. I'm sure *Trust* isn't. Those paperbacks represent an act of philanthropy on the part of one person, Bill Whitehead, who originated Obelisk. A publisher willing to lose money.

INTERVIEWER: Really? I don't think that Obelisk or anyone is in the business of publishing to lose money. There are people being read less than you, as well.

OZICK: Given the literary situation in our country, there are always people being read less. Not only young newcomers. I know an established writer with three unpublished novels going the rounds. Finding people who are read less is no trick. Finding out that one is read at all *is* a trick. For a long time I didn't feel I could honorably call myself a writer because I didn't have any of the accoutrements. Readers, mainly.

INTERVIEWER: When did you start feeling you could say you were a writer?

OZICK: Pretty recently.

INTERVIEWER: Things like the Harold and Mildred Strauss Living Award must help.

OZICK: That certainly was a validation. But I always need validation. A major, marvelous, unbelievable event. I was in Italy when the letter arrived and my husband opened it because he had a sense it was important. I came home from the airport and he put the letter in front of me on the kitchen table and said open it. And I did and I simply wept and wept and said I cannot possibly accept this. Why me? There are so many others with the same track record who could use this just as much as I. And I had such a wallow of guilt. I think it took more than a year before I felt that I could receive it with pure—I should say purified—joy without the guilt of having won a lottery and feeling undeserving and unmerited. That's why I don't see that photo as a scowl, I see it as expressing all these things about someone who feels unsure, unvalidated, un-, un-, un-, any word that begins with *un-*.

INTERVIEWER: Do you have a certain amount of bitterness about that?

OZICK: No, not at all. That picture must strike you as a bitter scowl. No, I'm not bitter.

INTERVIEWER: I used the word bitter because I thought *The Cannibal Galaxy* had an edge of bitterness to it.

OZICK: I am still hurt by P.S. 71. The effect of childhood hurt continues to the grave. I had teachers who hurt me, who made me believe I was stupid and inferior.

INTERVIEWER: Yes. You've written about that. Is your validation your revenge?

OZICK: I've discussed "revenge" with other writers, and discovered I'm not alone in facing the Medusalike truth that one reason writers write—the pressure toward language aside; and language is always the first reason, and most of the time the only reason—one reason writers write is out of revenge. Life hurts; certain ideas and experiences hurt; one wants to clarify, to set out illuminations, to replay the old bad scenes and get the *Treppenworte* said—the words one didn't have the strength or the ripeness to say when those words were necessary for one's dignity or survival.

INTERVIEWER: Have you achieved it?

OZICK: Revenge? On P.S. 71? Who knows? Where now are the snows of yesteryear? Where is Mrs. Florence O'Brien? Where is Mr. Dougherty? Alas, I think not. In the end, there *is* no revenge to be had. "Too late" is the same as not-at-all. And that's a good thing, isn't it? So that in the end one is left with a story instead of with spite. Any story is worth any amount of vindictiveness.

INTERVIEWER: "Too late." Is there really such a thing as too late?

OZICK: I am ashamed to confess this. It's ungrateful and wrong. But I am one—how full of shame I feel as I confess this—who expected to achieve—can I dare to get this out of my throat?—something like—impossible to say the words—Literary Fame by the age of twenty-five. By the age of twenty-seven I saw that Holy and Anointed Youth was over, and even then it was already too late. The decades passed. I'm afraid I think—deeply think—that if it didn't come at the right time, at the burnished crest of youth, then it doesn't matter. And I am not even sure what you or I mean by "it." I will not now know how to say what "it" is. So I have put all that away. It is now completely, completely beside the point. One does what one needs to do; that's all there is. It's wrong, bad, stupid, senseless to think about anything else. I think *only* of what it is I want to write about, and then about the problems in the doing of it. I don't think of anything else at all.

INTERVIEWER: The Holocaust figures in many of your stories. Is the Holocaust a subject you feel you must confront in your writing?

OZICK: I write about it. I can't not. But I don't think I ought to. I have powerful feelings about this. In our generation, it seems to me, we ought to absorb the documents, the endless, endless data, the endless, endless what-happened. Inevitably it will spiral into forms of history that are myth, legend: other kinds of truth. For instance, I believed in my childhood—I got it straight from my grandmother—that since the Inquisition there has been a *cherem* around Spain: a ban, a Jewish ban that prohibits Jews from entering Spain ever again. Of course this is pure myth; and yet it tells a great truth about the inheritance of the Inquisition in the hearts of Jews. Probably this sort of thing, in new forms, will happen concerning the destruction of European Jews and their civilization. It *is* inevitable, and it's not going to be a historical mistake. But for now? Now we, each one of us, Jew and Gentile, born during or after that time, we, all of us, forever after are witnesses to it. We know it happened: we are the generations that come after. I *want* the documents to be enough; I don't want to tamper or invent or imagine. And yet I have done it. I can't not do it. It comes, it invades.

INTERVIEWER: I read that you have formed a writer's group. Can you tell me about it?

OZICK: Nothing so official as a "group." Writers who are friends—three novelists, one critic, who meet not very often to talk informally. We meet in a Manhattan restaurant, or sometimes in New Rochelle; one of us lives in the midwest. Lore Segal and Norma Rosen and Helen Weinberg; Helen is the only Ph.D.—the critic.

INTERVIEWER: Are these meetings related in any way to "validation" of oneself as a writer?

OZICK: No! A thousand times no. We talk about our lives. We are very amusing. We are amusing even about our sadnesses. We are amusing about being "smart," and we enjoy one another's minds. We learn from each other in subtle and indirect ways.

Nothing is validated except the sense of being fully and beautifully human.

INTERVIEWER: Would this meeting be in existence if you weren't all writers of a certain level of success?

OZICK: We talk about the children. It's no coincidence, though, that we like to be together because we are writers. I believe unashamedly that writers are the most (maybe the only) interesting people.

INTERVIEWER: You began your literary career by writing poetry. What happened to the poetry in your life?

OZICK: Well, I still do it in a sort of indirect and undercover way: through the infinite bliss of translation. But there the initial work is done! Still, the pleasure of fashioning a new poem in English . . . but I stopped writing my own poetry at around age thirty-six. This fits exactly the dictum—whose? was it T. S. Eliot's?—that all writers write poetry in their youth, but that it's only the real poets who continue writing poetry after the middle thirties. But also, you know, I got discouraged. I sent my manuscript—a book—of poetry to the Yale Younger Poets series year after year, and finally I turned forty, and wasn't eligible any more. So I stopped. But nowadays when I read Amy Clampitt, I think: ah, *she* is myself continued! I hope this admission is not entirely outrageous. It's something I imagine.

INTERVIEWER: I wanted, for the record, to ask you how you've felt about our use of the typewriter.

OZICK: Replying to your questions by typewriter has been an experiment for both of us. It was your idea, and I thought it was wonderful and just right. It has not interfered one iota with spontaneity, because I have been typing extremely fast. It has been a form of speech. The difference is that the sentences are somewhat more coherent than speech allows. At least I can put the punctuation in! At least I can be responsible for the *sound*, in the way I can't be responsible for the looseness and even wildness of talk. Not that this way of talking has been without its wildness! In fact, there may be something excessively open here: a sinister kind of telling-too-much. One thing I've learned. Speech is far more guarded than talking through one's fingers.

INTERVIEWER: You said earlier that you envy my being thirty and having published articles. What I envy in your personal history is your Hallote fellowship.

OZICK: I was waiting for your comment on my being a woman. Is this it? A wife can support a husband quite as capably as the reverse.

INTERVIEWER: That may well be your reaction to my comment, but what I had in mind is more an envy of the financial freedom to write, of having someone willing to support you.

OZICK: Then let me be a kind of sibyl for you, or Cassandra, and with a not-so-bony finger warn you away from what you most desire. You know the old fairy-tale theme: don't wish for something, or you may get it. And then what? Youth is for running around in the great world, not for sitting in a hollow cell, turning into an unnatural writing-beast. There one sits, reading and writing, month after month, year after year. There one sits, envying other young writers who have achieved a grain more than oneself. Without the rush and brush and crush of the world, one becomes hollowed out. The cavity fills with envy. A wasting disease that takes years and years to recover from. Youth-envy, on the other hand, one can never recover from. Or at least I haven't so far. I suffered from it at seventeen. I suffered from it at five, when on a certain midsummer midafternoon I looked at an infant asleep in its pram and felt a terrible and unforgettable pang.

INTERVIEWER: But isn't there anything to be said about what seems to be a luxury—the ability to write full-time?

OZICK: Time to write isn't a luxury, that goes without saying. It's what a writer needs to write. But to have it coextensive with one's whole youth isn't absolutely a good thing. It's unnatural to do anything too much. "Nothing in excess," especially when everything else in the case *must* be in excess: the reading-hunger, language-hunger, all the high literary fevers and seizures. That kind of "excess" is what defines a writer. An image of the writer came to me the other day: a beast howling inside a coal-furnace, heaping the coals on itself to increase the fire. The only thing more tormenting than writing is not writing. If I could do it again, I would step out of the furnace now and then. I'd run around and find reviews to write, articles, I'd scurry and scrounge. I'd try to build a little platform from which to send out a voice. I'd do, in short, what I see so many writers of your generation doing: chasing a bit of work here, a bit there, publishing, getting acquainted. What *you* do, in fact. Churning around in the New York magazine world. What *I* did, a child crazed by literature, was to go like an eremite into a cavern and spin; I imagined that I would emerge with a masterpiece. Instead I emerged as an unnatural writing-beast, sooty with coal dust, my fingers burned and my heart burning up. Have you read *Lost Illusions*?

INTERVIEWER: Oh my God, yes!

OZICK: Eve Ottenberg, a young writer in New York who lives the kind of life I've described—an admirable life, I think—put me on to it.

INTERVIEWER: When you talk about the pain of having read Henry James at too early an age—well, that is nothing compared to reading *Lost Illusions* at the right age.

OZICK: It's understandable. I read *Lost Illusions* only recently. It was so painful it lasted me a whole year, and I never got to the very end. I intend to finish it. But I take it not so much for a warning as for a model and a marvel. Not a model for myself—it's too late for that. What's necessary above all is to publish while young. All those roilings happening at once, the speed, the trajectory! All that activity, all that being-in-the-world, all those plots and devisings, all that early variation, a spoon in every pot! Interchange, intercourse, inter-inter-. You know. If only someone had given me *Lost Illusions* in my cradle! Would I have been saved? There I was, at twenty-five, reading eighteen hours a day, novels, philosophy, criticism, poetry, Jewish history, Gibbon. . . . I read and read and it made me into some kind of monster. I'm still that monster.

INTERVIEWER: But you got some work done then . . .

OZICK: Nothing came of it. Great tracts of words without consummation. All the years I gave to *Mercy, Pity, Peace, and Love*, and nothing left of it but the title, and the title all Blake. Remorse and vacuum.

INTERVIEWER: You don't think your writing is richer for that, and for what you learned from your reading?

OZICK: So what? I still have plenty of gaps in my reading. I'm not Faust, and never was.

INTERVIEWER: But isn't your writing—aren't the ideas in your writing—richer?

OZICK: How can I tell? Living in one's own time is an obligation, isn't it? The isolation and profound apartness of my twenties and early thirties probably crazed me for life. And yet even as I declare my remorse, I'm not certain I believe what I say. Even as I tell you how I would do it otherwise if I had it to do over, I'm feeling the flanks of these words all up and down to see if I detect the lump of a lie in them. I was too fixed, too single-minded, too much drawn by some strange huge Illumination, too saturated in some arcane passion of Ideal Purity . . . Am I normal now? I don't feel so. But I am absolutely on the side of normality. I believe in citizenship.

—TOM TEICHOLZ
1985

13. Joan Didion

Joan Didion, author of novels, essays, and screenplays, was born in Sacramento, California, on December 5, 1934. She majored in English literature at the University of California at Berkeley and edited its literary magazine. In 1956 her article on the architect William Wilson Wurster won *Vogue* magazine's Prix de Paris award for college seniors; as part of the prize she was invited to join *Vogue*'s editorial staff. Didion also contributed on a freelance basis to *Mademoiselle* and the *National Review* before taking a leave of absence to complete her first novel.

The publication in 1963 of that novel, *Run River*, earned her an immediate reputation. The next year she married the novelist John Gregory Dunne, with whom she has written such screenplays as *Panic in Needle Park* (1971) and *A Star Is Born* (1976), in addition to the "Points West" column for the *Saturday Evening Post* (1967–69). She has also been a columnist for *Life* and *Esquire*.

Her other works include two collections of essays, *Slouching Toward Bethlehem* (1968) and the best-selling *The White Album* (1979). She is the author of *Salvador* (1983), a book of reportage on the plight of El Salvador, as well as the novels *Play It As It Lays* (1970), which was nominated for a National Book Award, *A Book of Common Prayer* (1977), and *Democracy* (1984). Her most recent work is *Miami* (1987), a book of non-fiction.

Didion and her husband live in Los Angeles, California, with their teenage daughter, Quintana.

∅ You were both wrong but it's all the same in the end.

As a matter of fact Charlotte had told me that she and Marin once modeled matching tennis dresses in a fashion show at the Burlingame Country Club and that because she did not play tennis she had needed to ask Marin how to hold the racquet correctly.

"I'm quite sure your mother didn't play tennis," I said.

"She always wore a tennis dress," Marin Bogart said.

"More than once?"

"Always."

"Didn't you play tennis?"

"Tennis," Marin Bogart said, "is ∧ mode of teaching an elitest strategy. If you subject it to a revolutionary analysis you'll see that. Not that I think you will." *just one more*

We sat facing each other in the bleak room.

We all remember what we need to remember.

Marin remembered Charlotte in a tennis dress and Charlotte remembered Marin in a straw hat for Easter. I remembered Edgar~~,~~ ~~very clearly, but nothing I remembered would accommodate a~~ ~~meeting with Leonard Douglas in Bogotá.~~ Charlotte remembered she bled. I remembered the light in Boca Grande. I sat in this *Edgar as*

~~"Why did you bother agreeing to see me," I said finally.~~

I did not remember the man who financed the Tupamaros.

room in Buffalo where I had no business being and I talked to this child who was not mine and I remembered the light in Boca Grande.

Another place I ~~had~~ *have* no business being.

~~In the end I had dreamed my life as Charlotte had.~~

∅ It seems to me now.

Mary Lloyd Estrin

Joan Didion

It is usual for the interviewer to write this paragraph about the circumstances in which the interview was conducted, but the interviewer in this case, Linda Kuehl, died not long after the tapes were transcribed. Linda and I talked on August 18 and August 24, 1977, from about ten in the morning until early afternoon. Both interviews took place in the living room of my husband's and my house on the sea north of Los Angeles, a house we no longer own. The walls in that room were white. The floors were of terra cotta tile, very highly polished. The glare off the sea was so pronounced in that room that corners of it seemed, by contrast, extremely dark, and everyone who sat in the room tended to gravitate toward these dark corners. Over the years the room had in fact evolved to the point where the only comfortable chairs were in the dark, away from the windows. I mention this because I remember my fears about being interviewed, one of which was that I would be construed as the kind of loon who had maybe 300 degrees of

sea view and kept all the chairs in a kind of sooty nook behind
the fireplace. Linda's intelligence dispelled these fears immediately.
Her interest in and acuity about the technical act of writing made
me relaxed and even enthusiastic about talking, which I rarely
am. As a matter of fact this enthusiasm for talking technically
makes me seem to myself, as I read over the transcript, a kind of
apprentice plumber of fiction, a Cluny Brown at the writer's trade,
but there we were.

—J.D.

INTERVIEWER: You have said that writing is a hostile act; I have
always wanted to ask you why.

DIDION: It's hostile in that you're trying to make somebody see
something the way you see it, trying to impose your idea, your
picture. It's hostile to try to wrench around someone else's mind
that way. Quite often you want to tell somebody your dream,
your nightmare. Well, nobody wants to hear about someone else's
dream, good or bad; nobody wants to walk around with it. The
writer is always tricking the reader into listening to the dream.

INTERVIEWER: Are you conscious of the reader as you write?
Do you write listening to the reader listening to you?

DIDION: Obviously I listen to a reader, but the only reader I
hear is me. I am always writing to myself. So very possibly I'm
committing an aggressive and hostile act toward myself.

INTERVIEWER: So when you ask, as you do in many nonfiction
pieces, "Do you get the point?" you are really asking if you *yourself*
get the point.

DIDION: Yes. Once in a while, when I first started to write
pieces, I would try to write to a reader other than myself. I always
failed. I would freeze up.

INTERVIEWER: When did you know you wanted to write?

DIDION: I wrote stories from the time I was a little girl, but I
didn't want to be a writer. I wanted to be an actress. I didn't
realize then that it's the same impulse. It's make-believe. It's
performance. The only difference being that a writer can do it
all alone. I was struck a few years ago when a friend of ours—
an actress—was having dinner here with us and a couple of other

writers. It suddenly occurred to me that she was the only person in the room who couldn't plan what she was going to do. She had to wait for someone to ask her, which is a strange way to live.

INTERVIEWER: Did you ever have a writing teacher?

DIDION: Mark Schorer was teaching at Berkeley when I was an undergraduate there, and he helped me. I don't mean he helped me with sentences, or paragraphs—nobody has time for that with student papers; I mean that he gave me a sense of what writing was about, what it was for.

INTERVIEWER: Did any writer influence you more than others?

DIDION: I always say Hemingway, because he taught me how sentences worked. When I was fifteen or sixteen I would type out his stories to learn how the sentences worked. I taught myself to type at the same time. A few years ago when I was teaching a course at Berkeley I reread *A Farewell to Arms* and fell right back into those sentences. I mean they're perfect sentences. Very direct sentences, smooth rivers, clear water over granite, no sinkholes.

INTERVIEWER: You've called Henry James an influence.

DIDION: He wrote perfect sentences too, but very indirect, very complicated. Sentences *with* sinkholes. You could drown in them. I wouldn't dare to write one. I'm not even sure I'd dare to read James again. I loved those novels so much that I was paralyzed by them for a long time. All those possibilities. All that perfectly reconciled style. It made me afraid to put words down.

INTERVIEWER: I wonder if some of your nonfiction pieces aren't shaped as a single Jamesian sentence.

DIDION: That would be the ideal, wouldn't it. An entire piece— eight, ten, twenty pages—strung on a single sentence. Actually, the sentences in my nonfiction are far more complicated than the sentences in my fiction. More clauses. More semicolons. I don't seem to hear that many clauses when I'm writing a novel.

INTERVIEWER: You have said that once you have your first sentence you've got your piece. That's what Hemingway said. All he needed was his first sentence and he had his short story.

DIDION: What's so hard about that first sentence is that you're stuck with it. Everything else is going to flow out of that sentence.

And by the time you've laid down the first *two* sentences, your options are all gone.

INTERVIEWER: The first is the gesture, the second is the commitment.

DIDION: Yes, and the last sentence in a piece is another adventure. It should open the piece up. It should make you go back and start reading from page one. That's how it *should* be, but it doesn't always work. I think of writing anything at all as a kind of high-wire act. The minute you start putting words on paper you're eliminating possibilities. Unless you're Henry James.

INTERVIEWER: I wonder if your ethic—what you call your "harsh Protestant ethic"—doesn't close things up for you, doesn't hinder your struggle to keep all the possibilities open.

DIDION: I suppose that's part of the dynamic. I start a book and I want to make it perfect, want it to turn every color, want it to *be the world*. Ten pages in, I've already blown it, limited it, made it less, marred it. That's very discouraging. I hate the book at that point. After a while I arrive at an accommodation: well, it's not the ideal, it's not the perfect object I wanted to make, but maybe— if I go ahead and finish it anyway—I can get it right next time. Maybe I can have another chance.

INTERVIEWER: Have any women writers been strong influences?

DIDION: I think only in the sense of being models for a life, not for a style. I think that the Brontës probably encouraged my own delusions of theatricality. Something about George Eliot attracted me a great deal. I think I was not temperamentally attuned to either Jane Austen or Virginia Woolf.

INTERVIEWER: What are the disadvantages, if any, of being a woman writer?

DIDION: When I was starting to write—in the late fifties, early sixties—there was a kind of social tradition in which male novelists could operate. Hard drinkers, bad livers. Wives, wars, big fish, Africa, Paris, no second acts. A man who wrote novels had a role in the world, and he could play that role and do whatever he wanted behind it. A woman who wrote novels had no particular role. Women who wrote novels were quite often perceived as invalids. Carson McCullers, Jane Bowles. Flannery O'Connor of course. Novels by women tended to be described, even by their publishers, as sensitive. I'm not sure this is so true anymore, but it certainly was at the time, and I didn't much like it. I dealt with it the same way I deal with everything. I just tended my own garden, didn't pay much attention, behaved—I suppose—deviously. I mean I didn't actually let too many people know what I was doing.

INTERVIEWER: Advantages?

DIDION: The advantages would probably be precisely the same as the disadvantages. A certain amount of resistance is good for anybody. It keeps you awake.

INTERVIEWER: Can you tell simply from the style of writing, or the sensibility, if the author is a woman?

DIDION: Well, if style is character—and I believe it is—then obviously your sexual identity is going to show up in your style. I don't want to differentiate between style and sensibility, by the way. Again, your style *is* your sensibility. But this whole question of sexual identity is very tricky. If I were to read, cold, something by Anaïs Nin, I would probably say that it was written by a man trying to write as a woman. I feel the same way about Colette, and yet both those women are generally regarded as intensely "feminine" writers. I don't seem to recognize "feminine." On the other hand, *Victory* seems to me a profoundly female novel. So does *Nostromo*, so does *The Secret Agent*.

INTERVIEWER: Do you find it easy to write in depth about the opposite sex?

DIDION: *Run River* was partly from a man's point of view. Everett McClellan. I don't remember those parts as being any harder than the other parts. A lot of people thought Everett was "shadowy," though. He's the most distinct person in the book to me. I loved him. I loved Lily and Martha but I loved Everett more.

INTERVIEWER: Was *Run River* your first novel? It seems so finished for a first that I thought you might have shelved earlier ones.

DIDION: I've put away nonfiction things, but I've never put away a novel. I might throw out forty pages and write forty new ones, but it's all part of the same novel. I wrote the first half of *Run River* at night over a period of years. I was working at *Vogue* during the day, and at night I would work on these scenes for a novel. In no particular sequence. When I finished a scene I would tape the pages together and pin the long strips of pages on the wall of my apartment. Maybe I wouldn't touch it for a month or two, then I'd pick a scene off the wall and rewrite it. When I had about a hundred and fifty pages done I showed them to twelve publishers, all of whom passed. The thirteenth, Ivan Obolensky, gave me an advance, and with that thousand dollars or whatever it was I took a two-month leave of absence and wrote the last half of the book. That's why the last half is better than the first half. I kept trying to run the first half through again, but it was intractable. It was set. I'd worked on it for too many years in too many moods. Not that the last half is perfect. It's smoother, it moves faster, but there are a great many unresolved problems. I didn't know how to do anything at all. I had wanted *Run River* to be very complicated chronologically, to somehow have the past and present operating simultaneously, but I wasn't accomplished enough to do that with any clarity. Everybody who read it said it wasn't working. So I straightened it out. Present time to flashback to present time. Very straight. I had no option, because I didn't know how to do it the other way. I just wasn't good enough.

INTERVIEWER: Did you or Jonathan Cape put the comma in the title of the English edition?

DIDION: It comes back to me that Cape put the comma in and Obolensky left the comma out, but it wasn't of very much interest to me because I hated it both ways. The working title was *In the Night Season*, which Obolensky didn't like. Actually, the working title during the first half was *Harvest Home*, which everybody dismissed out of hand as uncommercial, although later there was a big commercial book by Thomas Tryon called exactly that. Again, I was not very sure of myself then, or I never would have changed the title.

INTERVIEWER: Was the book autobiographical? I ask this for the obvious reason that first novels often are.

DIDION: It wasn't except that it took place in Sacramento. A lot of people there seemed to think that I had somehow maligned them and their families, but it was just a made-up story. The central incident came from a little one-inch story in *The New York Times* about a trial in the Carolinas. Someone was on trial for killing the foreman on his farm, that's all there was. I think I really put the novel in Sacramento because I was homesick. I wanted to remember the weather and the rivers.

INTERVIEWER: The heat on the rivers?

DIDION: The heat. I think that's the way the whole thing began. There's a lot of landscape which I never would have described if I hadn't been homesick. If I hadn't wanted to remember. The impulse was nostalgia. It's not an uncommon impulse among writers. I noticed it when I was reading *From Here to Eternity* in Honolulu just after James Jones died. I could see exactly that kind of nostalgia, that yearning for a place, overriding all narrative considerations. The incredible amount of description. When Prewitt tries to get from the part of town where he's been wounded out to Alma's house, every street is named. Every street is described. You could take that passage and draw a map of Honolulu. None of those descriptions have any narrative meaning. They're just remembering. Obsessive remembering. I could see the impulse.

INTERVIEWER: But doesn't the impulse of nostalgia produce the eloquence in *Run River*?

DIDION: It's got a lot of sloppy stuff. Extraneous stuff. Words that don't work. Awkwardnesses. Scenes that should have been brought up, scenes that should have been played down. But then *Play It As It Lays* has a lot of sloppy stuff. I haven't reread *Common Prayer*, but I'm sure that does too.

INTERVIEWER: How did you come to terms with point of view in *Play It As It Lays*? Did you ever question your authority to do it in both first and third person?

DIDION: I wanted to make it all first person, but I wasn't good enough to maintain a first. There were tricks I didn't know. So I began playing with a close third person, just to get something down. By a "close third" I mean not an omniscient third but a third very close to the mind of the character. Suddenly one night

I realized that I had some first person and some third person and that I was going to have to go with both, or just not write a book at all. I was scared. Actually, I don't mind the way it worked out. The juxtaposition of first and third turned out to be very useful toward the ending, when I wanted to accelerate the whole thing. I don't think I'd do it again, but it was a solution to that particular set of problems. There's a point when you go with what you've got. Or you don't go.

INTERVIEWER: How long, in all, did *Play It As It Lays* take to write?

DIDION: I made notes and wrote pages over several years, but the actual physical writing—sitting down at the typewriter and working every day until it was finished—took me from January until November 1969. Then of course I had to run it through again—I never know quite what I'm doing when I'm writing a novel, and the actual line of it doesn't emerge until I'm finishing. Before I ran it through again I showed it to John and then I sent it to Henry Robbins, who was my editor then at Farrar, Straus. It was quite rough, with places marked "chapter to come." Henry was unalarmed by my working that way, and he and John and I sat down one night in New York and talked, for about an hour before dinner, about what it needed doing. We all knew what it needed. We all agreed. After that I took a couple of weeks and ran it through. It was just typing and pulling the line through.

INTERVIEWER: What do you mean exactly by "pulling through"?

DIDION: For example, I didn't know that BZ was an important character in *Play It As It Lays* until the last few weeks I was working on it. So those places I marked "chapter to come" were largely places where I was going to go back and pull BZ through, hit him harder, prepare for the way it finally went.

INTERVIEWER: How did you feel about BZ's suicide at the end?

DIDION: I didn't realize until after I'd written it that it was essentially the same ending as *Run River*. The women let the men commit suicide.

INTERVIEWER: I read that *Play It As It Lays* crystallized for you when you were sitting in the lobby of the Riviera Hotel in Las Vegas and saw a girl walk through.

DIDION: I had thought Maria lived in New York. Maybe she was a model. Anyway, she was getting a divorce, going through grief. When I saw this actress in the Riviera Hotel, it occurred to me that Maria could be an actress. In California.

INTERVIEWER: Was she always Maria Wyeth?

DIDION: She didn't even have a name. Sometimes I'll be fifty, sixty pages into something and I'll still be calling a character "X." I don't have a very clear idea of who the characters are until they start talking. Then I start to love them. By the time I finish the book, I love them so much that I want to stay with them. I don't want to leave them ever.

INTERVIEWER: Do your characters talk to you?

DIDION: After a while. In a way. When I started *Common Prayer* all I knew about Charlotte was that she was a nervous talker and told pointless stories. A distracted kind of voice. Then one day I was writing the Christmas party at the American Embassy, and I had Charlotte telling these bizarre anecdotes with no point while Victor Strasser-Mendana keeps trying to find out who she is, what she's doing in Boca Grande, who her husband is, what her husband does. And suddenly Charlotte says, "He runs guns. I wish they had caviar." Well, when I heard Charlotte say this, I had a very clear fix on who she was. I went back and rewrote some early stuff.

INTERVIEWER: Did you reshuffle a lot and, if so, how? Did you use pins or tape or what?

DIDION: Toward the beginning of a novel I'll write a lot of sections that lead me nowhere. So I'll abandon them, pin them on a board with the idea of picking them up later. Quite early in *Common Prayer* I wrote a part about Charlotte Douglas going to airports, a couple of pages that I liked but couldn't seem to find a place for. I kept picking this part up and putting it in different places, but it kept stopping the narrative; it was wrong everywhere, but I was determined to use it. Finally I think I put it in the middle of the book. Sometimes you can get away with things in the middle of a book. The first hundred pages are very tricky, the first forty pages especially. You have to make sure you have the characters you want. That's really the most complicated part.

INTERVIEWER: Strategy would seem to be far more complicated in *Common Prayer* than in *Play It As It Lays* because it had so much more plot.

DIDION: *Common Prayer* had a lot of plot and an awful lot of places and weather. I wanted a dense texture, and so I kept throwing stuff into it, making promises. For example, I promised a revolution. Finally, when I got within twenty pages of the end, I realized I still hadn't delivered this revolution. I had a lot of threads, and I'd overlooked this one. So then I had to go back and lay in the preparation for the revolution. Putting in that revolution was like setting in a sleeve. Do you know what I mean? Do you sew? I mean I had to work that revolution in on the bias, had to ease out the wrinkles with my fingers.

INTERVIEWER: So the process of writing the novel is for you the process of discovering the precise novel that you want to write.

DIDION: Exactly. At the beginning I don't have anything at all, don't have any people, any weather, any story. All I have is a technical sense of what I want to do. For example, I want sometime to write a very long novel, eight-hundred pages. I want to write an eight-hundred page novel precisely *because* I think a novel should be read at one sitting. If you read a novel over a period of days or weeks the threads get lost, the suspension breaks. So the problem is to write an eight-hundred-page novel in which all the filaments are so strong that nothing breaks or gets forgotten ever. I wonder if García Márquez didn't do that in *The Autumn of the Patriarch*. I don't want to read it because I'm afraid he might have done it, but I did look at it, and it seems to be written in a single paragraph. *One paragraph*. The whole novel. I love that idea.

INTERVIEWER: Do you have any writing rituals?

DIDION: The most important is that I need an hour alone before dinner, with a drink, to go over what I've done that day. I can't do it late in the afternoon because I'm too close to it. Also, the drink helps. It removes me from the pages. So I spend this hour taking things out and putting other things in. Then I start the next day by redoing all of what I did the day before, following these evening notes. When I'm really working I don't like to go out or have anybody to dinner, because then I lose the hour. If I don't have the hour, and start the next day with just some bad pages and nowhere to go, I'm in low spirits. Another thing I need to do, when I'm near the end of the book, is sleep in the same room with it. That's one reason I go home to Sacramento to finish things. Somehow the book doesn't leave you when you're asleep right next to it. In Sacramento nobody cares if I appear or not. I can just get up and start typing.

INTERVIEWER: What's the main difference between the process of fiction and the process of nonfiction?

DIDION: The element of discovery takes place, in nonfiction, not during the writing but during the research. This makes writing a piece very tedious. You already know what it's about.

INTERVIEWER: Are the subject of pieces determined by editors or are you free to go your own way?

DIDION: I make them up. They reflect what I want to do at the time, where I want to be. When I worked for *Life* I did a great many Honolulu pieces—probably more than *Life* might have wanted—because that's where I wanted to be then. Last night I finished a piece for *Esquire* about the California Water Project. I had always wanted to see the room where they control the water, where they turn it on and off all over the state, and I also wanted to see my mother and father. The water and my mother and father were all in Sacramento, so I went to Sacramento. I like to do pieces because it forces me to make appointments and see people, but I never wanted to be a journalist or reporter. If I were doing a story and it turned into a big breaking story, all kinds of teams flying in from papers and magazines and the networks, I'd probably think of something else to do.

INTERVIEWER: You've said that when you were an editor at *Vogue*, Allene Talmey showed you how verbs worked.

DIDION: Every day I would go into her office with eight lines of copy or a caption or something. She would sit there and mark it up with a pencil and get very angry about extra words, about verbs not working. Nobody has time to do that except on a magazine like *Vogue*. Nobody, no teacher. I've taught and I've tried to do it, but I didn't have that much time and neither did the students. In an eight-line caption everything had to work, every word, every comma. It would end up being a *Vogue* caption, but on its own terms it had to work perfectly.

INTERVIEWER: You say you treasure privacy, that "being left alone and leaving others alone is regarded by members of my family as the highest form of human endeavor." How does this mesh with writing personal essays, particularly the first column you did for *Life* where you felt it imperative to inform the reader that you were at the Royal Hawaiian Hotel in lieu of getting a divorce?

DIDION: I don't know. I could say that I was writing to myself, and of course I was, but it's a little more complicated than that. I mean the fact that eleven million people were going to see that page didn't exactly escape my attention. There's a lot of mystery to me about writing and performing and showing off in general. I know a singer who throws up every time she has to go onstage. But she still goes on.

INTERVIEWER: How did the "fragility of Joan Didion" myth start?

DIDION: Because I'm small, I suppose, and because I don't talk a great deal to people I don't know. Most of my sentences drift off, don't end. It's a habit I've fallen into. I don't deal well with people. I would think that this appearance of not being very much in touch was probably one of the reasons I started writing.

INTERVIEWER: Do you think some reviewers and readers have mistaken you for your characters?

DIDION: There was a certain tendency to read *Play It As It Lays* as an autobiographical novel, I suppose because I lived out here and looked skinny in photographs and nobody knew anything else about me. Actually, the only thing Maria and I have in common is an occasional inflection, which I picked up from her—not vice versa—when I was writing the book. I like Maria a lot. Maria was very strong, very tough.

INTERVIEWER: That's where I have difficulty with what so many critics have said about your women. Your women hardly seem fragile to me.

DIDION: Did you read Diane Johnson's review of *Common*

Prayer in *The New York Review of Books*? She suggested that the women were strong to the point of being figures in a romance, that they were romantic heroines rather than actual women in actual situations. I think that's probably true. I think I write romances.

INTERVIEWER: I'd like to ask you about things that recur in your work. There's the line about "dirty tulips" on Park Avenue in a short story and in a piece. Or how about the large, square emerald ring that Lily wears in *Run River* and Charlotte wears in *Common Prayer*?

DIDION: Does Lily wear one too? Maybe she does. I've always wanted one, but I'd never buy one. For one thing emeralds—when you look at them closely—are always disappointing. The green is never blue enough. Ideally, if the green were blue enough you could look into an emerald for the rest of your life. Sometimes I think about Katherine Anne Porter's emeralds, sometimes I wonder if they're blue enough. I hadn't planned that emerald in *Common Prayer* to recur the way it does. It was just something I thought Charlotte might have, but as I went along the emerald got very useful. I kept taking that emerald one step further. By the end of the novel the emerald is almost the narrative. I had a good time with that emerald.

INTERVIEWER: What about the death of a parent, which seems to recur as a motif?

DIDION: You know how doctors who work with children get the children to tell stories? And they figure out from the stories what's frightening the child, what's worrying the child, what the child thinks? Well, a novel is just a story. You work things out in the stories you tell.

INTERVIEWER: And the abortion or loss of a child?

DIDION: The death of children worries me all the time. It's on my mind. Even *I* know that, and I usually don't know what's on my mind. On the whole, I don't want to think too much about why I write what I write. If I know what I'm doing I don't do it, I can't do it. The abortion in *Play It As It Lays* didn't occur to me until I'd written quite a bit of the book. The book needed an active moment, a moment at which things changed for Maria, a moment in which—this was very, very important—Maria was center stage for a number of pages. Not at a party reacting to somebody else. Not just thinking about her lot in life, either. A long section in which she was the main player. The abortion was a narrative strategy.

INTERVIEWER: Was it a narrative strategy in *Run River*?

DIDION: Actually, it was the excuse for a digression, into landscape. Lily has an abortion in San Francisco and then she comes home on the Greyhound bus. I always think of the Greyhound bus and not the abortion. The bus part is very detailed about the look of the towns. It's something I wrote in New York; you can tell I was homesick.

INTERVIEWER: How about the freeways that reappear?

DIDION: Actually, I don't drive on the freeway. I'm afraid to. I freeze at the top of the entrance, at the instant when you have to let go and join it. Occasionally I *do* get on the freeway—usually because I'm shamed into it—and it's such an extraordinary experience that it sticks in my mind. So I use it.

INTERVIEWER: And the white space at the corner of Sunset and La Brea in Hollywood? You mention it in some piece and then in *Play It As It Lays*.

DIDION: I've never analyzed it, but one line of poetry I always have in mind is the line from *Four Quartets*: "at the still point of the turning world." I tend to move toward still points. I think of the equator as a still point. I suppose that's why I put Boca Grande on the equator.

INTERVIEWER: A narrative strategy.

DIDION: Well, this whole question of how you work out the narrative is very mysterious. It's a good deal more arbitrary than most people who don't do it would ever believe. When I started *Play It As It Lays* I gave Maria a child, a daughter, Kate, who was in kindergarten. I remember writing a passage in which Kate came home from school and showed Maria a lot of drawings, orange and blue crayon drawings, and when Maria asked her what they were, Kate said, "Pools on fire." You can see I wasn't having too much success writing this child. So I put her in a hospital. You never meet her. Now, it turned out to have a great deal of importance—Kate's being in the hospital is a very large element in *Play It As It Lays*—but it began because I couldn't write a child, no other reason. Again, in *Common Prayer*, Marin bombs the Transamerica Building because I *needed* her to. I needed a crisis in Charlotte's life. Well, at this very moment, right now, I can't think of the Transamerica Building without thinking of Marin and her pipe bomb and her gold bracelet, but it was all very arbitrary in the beginning.

INTERVIEWER: What misapprehensions, illusions and so forth have you had to struggle against in your life? In a commencement address you once said there were many.

DIDION: All kinds. I was one of those children who tended to perceive the world in terms of things read about it. I began with a literary idea of experience, and I still don't know where all the lies are. For example, it may not be true that people who try to fly always burst into flames and fall. That may not be true at all. In fact people do *fly*, and land safely. But I don't really believe that. I still see Icarus. I don't seem to have a set of physical facts at my disposal, don't seem to understand how things really work. I just have an *idea* of how they work, which is always trouble. As Henry James told us.

INTERVIEWER: You seem to live your life on the edge, or, at least, on the literary idea of the edge.

DIDION: Again, it's a literary idea, and it derives from what engaged me imaginatively as a child. I can recall disapproving of the golden mean, always thinking there was more to be learned from the dark journey. The dark journey engaged me more. I once had in mind a very light novel, all surface, all conversations and memories and recollections of some people in Honolulu who were getting along fine, one or two misapprehensions about the past notwithstanding. Well, I'm working on that book now, but it's not running that way at all. Not at all.

INTERVIEWER: It always turns into danger and apocalypse.

DIDION: Well, I grew up in a dangerous landscape. I think people are more affected than they know by landscapes and weather. Sacramento was a very extreme place. It was very flat, flatter than most people can imagine, and I still favor flat horizons.

The weather in Sacramento was as extreme as the landscape. There were two rivers, and these rivers would flood in the winter and run dry in the summer. Winter was cold rain and tulle fog. Summer was 100 degrees, 105 degrees, 110 degrees. Those extremes affect the way you deal with the world. It so happens that if you're a writer the extremes show up. They don't if you sell insurance.

—LINDA KUEHL

1978

14. Edna O'Brien

Edna O'Brien was born in the west of Ireland in a small village she describes as "enclosed, fervid and bigoted." After finishing primary school in her hometown, she was sent to convent school in Galway, and later to Dublin, where she studied at the Pharmaceutical College. She moved to London with her husband and two sons in 1960, and began to write.

Her first novel, *The Country Girls*, appeared in 1961. Her other works of fiction are *The Lonely Girl* (1962), *Girls in Their Married Bliss* (1964), *August Is a Wicked Month* (1965), *Casualties of Peace* (1966), *A Pagan Place* (1970), a play *Night* (1972), *Johnny I Hardly Knew You* (1977), *Virginia* (1980), a play, *Returning* (1982), *A Fanatic Heart* (1984), a collected edition of her short stories, *The County Girl's Trilogy and Epilogue* (1986), and most recently, *The High Road* (1988), a novel. Her nonfiction includes *Mother Ireland* (1976), *Arabian Days* (1977), and *James and Nora: A Portrait of Joyce's Marriage* (1981). She received the Kingsley Amis Award for fiction in 1962 and the Yorkshire Post Novel Award in 1971.

O'Brien lives in the Little Venice section of London.

Memos For MRS. R. ①

Walking by the rough sea &
frigs → to work the telescope. The
man of course comes to her
rescue, hats it & Joan her
Pov are the ris[?]y waves &
he says "It ds wh-t you
wanted…" and as she continues
to look she sees her dreams
under etc. in the [?] & foam
as she comes back to reality
he as still there …"

Cut to very sedate Tea-Room
Gateau Basque   Cakes.
Choc.   He is reading the
                 menu out
        Mrs L. No. No… No.

Last Lines. And what do you want new
        Mrs R I want you to make love
              to me as if the first time
        Mr R which in a sense it is.
                        Their faces on the glass.

A page from one of Edna O'Brien's manuscripts.

Photo: March Gerger

Edna O'Brien

Edna O'Brien resembles one of her own heroines: beautiful in a subtle, wistful way, with reddish-blond hair, green eyes, and a savage sense of humor. She lives alone in an airy, spacious apartment in Little Venice, London, near the Canal. From her balcony, wrought-iron steps lead down to a vast tree-filled park, where O'Brien often can be found strolling during breaks from her work. The following interview took place in her writing room—a large, comfortable study cluttered with books; notebooks, records, and periodicals. The day I was there, the room was warmed by a log fire burning in the fireplace, and even more so by O'Brien's rich, softly accented Irish voice.

INTERVIEWER: You once said that as far back as you can remember you have been a writer. At what point did you actually start writing literature?

O'BRIEN: When I say I have written from the beginning, I mean that all real writers write from the beginning, that the vocation, the obsession, is already there, and that the obsession derives from an intensity of feeling which normal life cannot accommodate. I started writing snippets when I was eight or nine, but I wrote my first novel when I left Ireland and came to live in London. I had never been outside Ireland and it was November when I arrived in England. I found everything so different, so *alien*. Waterloo Station was full of people who were nameless, faceless. There were wreaths on the Cenotaph for Remembrance Sunday, and I felt bewildered and lost—an outsider. So in a sense *The Country Girls*, which I wrote in those first few weeks after my arrival, was my experience of Ireland and my farewell to it. But something happened to my style which I will tell you about. I had been trying to write short bits, and these were always flowery and overlyrical. Shortly after I arrived in London I saw an advertisement for a lecture given by Arthur Mizener [author of a book on F. Scott Fitzgerald, *The Far Side of Paradise*] on Hemingway and Fitzgerald. You must remember that I had no literary education, but a fervid religious one. So I went to the lecture and it was like a thunderbolt—Saul of Tarsus on his horse! Mizener read out the first paragraph of A *Farewell to Arms* and I couldn't believe it—this totally uncluttered, precise, true prose, which was *also* very moving and lyrical. I can say that the two things came together then: my being ready for the revelation and my urgency to write. The novel *wrote itself*, so to speak, in a few weeks. All the time I was writing it I couldn't stop crying, although it is a fairly buoyant, funny book. But it was the separation from Ireland which brought me to the point where I *had* to write, though I had always been in love with literature.

INTERVIEWER: If you had always loved literature, why did you study chemistry at university rather than English?

O'BRIEN: The usual reason, family. My family was radically opposed to anything to do with literature. Although Ireland has produced so many great writers, there is a deep suspicion about writing there. Somehow they know that writing is dangerous, seditious, as if "In the beginning was the Word and the Word was with God and the Word *was* God." I was an obedient little girl—though I hate to admit it now!—and went along with my family's wishes. I worked in a chemist's shop and then studied at the Pharmaceutical College at night.

INTERVIEWER: The protagonist of *The Country Girls* also works in a shop. Is the novel autobiographical?

O'BRIEN: The novel is autobiographical insofar as I was born and bred in the west of Ireland, educated at a convent, and was full of romantic yearnings, coupled with a sense of outrage. But any book that is any good must be, to some extent, autobiographical, because one cannot and should not fabricate emotions; and although style and narrative are crucial, the bulwark, emotion, is what finally matters. With luck, talent, and studiousness, one manages to make a little pearl, or egg, or something. . . . But what gives birth to it is what happens inside the soul and the mind, and that has almost always to do with *conflict*. And loss— an innate sense of tragedy.

INTERVIEWER: What Thomas Hardy called "the sadness of things," and Unamuno *"el sentimiento trágico de la vida"*?

O'BRIEN: Precisely. Not just subjective sadness, though you have to experience it in order to know it, but also objective. And the more I read about writers, their letters—say Flaubert's—the more I realize it. Flaubert was in a way like a *woman*. There he was, in Rouen, yearning for the bright lights of Paris and hectic affairs, yet deliberately keeping away from all that, isolating himself, in order to burn and luxuriate in the affliction of his own emotions. So writing, I think, is an interestingly perverse occupation. It is quite sick in the sense of normal human enjoyment of life, be- cause the writer is always *removed*, the way an actor never is. An actor is with the audience, a writer is not with his readers, and by the time the work appears, he or she is again incarcerated in the next book—or in barrenness. So for both men and women writers, writing is an eminently masochistic exercise—though I wonder what Norman Mailer would say to that!

INTERVIEWER: Doesn't the theory of masochism apply to all artists, whatever the art form?

O'BRIEN: To some extent. I was reading van Gogh's letters. My God! I'm surprised he cut off only *one* ear, that he wasn't alto-

gether shredded in pieces! But a woman writer has a double dose
of masochism: the masochism of the woman and that of the artist.
No way to dodge it or escape from it. Men are better at escaping
their psyches and their consciences. But there is a certain dogged
strength in realizing that you can make those delirious journeys
and come through.

INTERVIEWER: Some don't. There is a high rate of suicide,
alcoholism, madness among writers.

O'BRIEN: It is only by the grace of God, and perhaps willpower,
that one comes through each time. Many wonderful writers write
one or two books and then kill themselves. Sylvia Plath for instance. She was much younger than Virginia Woolf when she
committed suicide, but if she had survived that terrible crisis, I
feel she would have written better books. I have this theory that
Woolf feared that the flame of her talent was extinguished or
dwindling because her last book, *Between the Acts*, lacked the
soaring genius of the others. When a writer, or an artist, has the
feeling that he can't do it anymore, he descends into hell. So
you must keep in mind that although it may stop, it can come
back. When I was a child in Ireland, a spring would suddenly
appear and yield forth buckets of beautiful clear water, then just
as suddenly it would dry up. The water-diviners would come with
their rods and sometimes another spring would be found. One
has to be one's own water-diviner. It is hard, especially as writers
are always anxious, always on the run—from the telephone, from
people, from responsibilities, from the distractions of this world.
The other thing that can destroy talent is too much grief. Yeats
said, "Too much sorrow can make a stone of the heart." I often
wonder, if Emily Brontë had lived to be fifty, what kind of books
would she have written? Her life was so penalizing—and Charlotte's too—utterly without sex. Emily was thirty when she wrote
Wuthering Heights. I think the grinding suffering might have
killed her talent later. It is not that you have to be happy—that
would be asking too much—but if it gets too painful that sense
of wonderment, or joy, dies, and with it the generosity so necessary to create.

INTERVIEWER: So the catalyst for your own work was that lecture on Fitzgerald and Hemingway. Before that you said that you read a great deal in Ireland, partly to escape. What sort of books did you read? And which ones influenced you most?

O'BRIEN: Looking back on it, it was not so much escape as nourishment. Of course there is an element of escape as well, that entering temporarily into a different world. But I think literature is food for the soul and the heart. There are books that are pure escapism: thrillers, detective and spy novels, but I can't read them, because they don't *deliver* to me. Whereas from one page of Dostoyevsky I feel renewed, however depressing the subject. The first book I ever *bought*—I've still got it—was called *Introducing James Joyce*, by T. S. Eliot. It contained a short story, a piece from *Portrait of the Artist*, some other pieces, and an introduction by Eliot. I read a scene from *Portrait* which is the Christmas dinner when everything begins pleasantly: a fire, largesse, the blue flame of light on the dark plum pudding, the revelry before the flare-up ensues between people who were for Parnell and those who were against him. Parnell had been dead for a long time, but the Irish, being Irish, persist with history. Reading that book made me realize that I wanted literature for the rest of my life.

INTERVIEWER: And you became a ferocious reader, first of Joyce, then of others. Who else did you read in those early days?

O'BRIEN: I am a slow reader, because I want to savor and recall what I read. The excitement and sense of discovery is not the same as in those days when I would get thoroughly wrapped up in *Vanity Fair* or *War and Peace*. Now I set myself a task of reading one great book each year. Last year I read *Bleak House*, which I think is the greatest English novel—I read a few pages a day. But one's taste changes so much. I mentioned Scott Fitzgerald, whom I read, oh, so lovingly and thoroughly! I loved *Tender Is the Night* and *The Great Gatsby*, which is a flawless novel. So I can say that he was one of my early influences. But now I know that fundamentally I respond to European literature in all its dark ramifications. I think the Russians are unsurpassable. Of course Joyce did something extraordinary: he threw out the entire heritage of English literature—language, story, structure, everything—and created a new and stupendous work. But for emotional gravity, no one can compare with the Russians. When I first read Chekhov's short stories, before I saw his plays, I knew I had heard the *voice* that I loved most in the whole world. I wrote to my sister, "Read Chekhov—he does not write, he *breathes* life off the page." And he was, and still is, my greatest influence, especially in short-story writing.

INTERVIEWER: Later on, when you tried your hand at drama, did Chekhov come to your rescue there as well?

O'BRIEN: I think so, though it is very dangerous to take Chekhov as a model. His dramatic genius is so mysterious; he does what seems to be the impossible, in that he makes dramatic something that is desultory. And of course it is not desultory—indeed, it is as tightly knit as that Persian carpet. Shakespeare is God. He knows everything and expresses it with such a density of poetry and humor and power that the mind boggles. But then he had *great* themes—*Othello*, *Hamlet*, the history plays. Chekhov, on the other hand, tells you, or seems to tell you, of a profligate family that is losing an orchard, or some sisters who yearn for Moscow, and inside it is a whole web of life and love and failure. I think that despite his emphasis on wanting to be funny, he was a tragic man. In a letter to his wife, actress Olga Knipper, he says, "It is nine o'clock in the evening, you are going to play act three of my play, and I am as lonely as a coffin!"

INTERVIEWER: The greatness of the Russian classics must be due in part to the vastness and variety of their country, the harshness of climate, and the cruelty and roughness of their society (which hasn't really changed) and which enhances the intensity of the emotions and the extremes of behavior.

O'BRIEN: Certainly. It makes for endurance—those long, savage winters. Also being throttled as they have always been. The more you strangle a man, the deeper he screams. Boris Pasternak put his pain to immortal use in *Dr. Zhivago*.

INTERVIEWER: Did that first book on Joyce send you to read the whole of Joyce?

O'BRIEN: Yes, but I was too young then. Later I read *Ulysses*, and at one point I thought of writing a book on Joyce, *comme tout le monde*! I read a lot of books about Joyce and wrote a monograph. Then I realized that there were already too many books on him and that the best thing you could read about Joyce was Joyce himself.

INTERVIEWER: How do you assess him now, and how is he regarded in Ireland?

O'BRIEN: He is beyond assessment—gigantic. I sometimes read bits of *Finnegans Wake* and feel my brain begin to sizzle. Joyce went mad with genius. When you read *Dubliners* and *Finnegans Wake* you feel that the man underwent a metamorphosis between twenty-five and sixty. H. G. Wells said that *Finnegans Wake* was an immense riddle, and people find it too difficult to read. I have yet to meet anyone who has read and digested the whole of it—except perhaps my friend Richard Ellmann. Joyce killed himself with exertion. He went beyond us into a labyrinth of language, and I don't know whether that was a loss or a gain.

INTERVIEWER: The generation before you in Ireland had an important literary scene: Yeats and Lady Gregory and the Abbey Theatre group, and all the people around them, which ran parallel to London's Bloomsbury group and Eliot's circle. Did you have anything similar in Ireland when you started?

O'BRIEN: Nothing on that level. There was a sort of Irish literary scene but I wasn't part of it. One reason was poverty, another that I didn't have an *entrée*; I was just a chemistry student in a bed-sit. I heard of people like Sean O'Faolain, Frank O'Connor. Samuel Beckett had left and vowed never to return, Sean O'Casey was in England. But it was good for me not to be part of any scene because it meant that I had to do my apprenticeship alone. Sweet are the uses of adversity, are they not?

INTERVIEWER: What about women writers? You haven't mentioned any as a major influence so far.

O'BRIEN: Every woman novelist has been influenced by the Brontës. *Wuthering Heights* and *Jane Eyre*. The poetry of Emily Dickinson, the early books of Elizabeth Bowen—especially the one she wrote about her home in Ireland, *Bowen's Court*. My admiration for Jane Austen came much later, and I also love the Russian poet Anna Akhmatova. Nowadays there are too many writers, and I think one of the reasons for the deterioration of language and literature in the last forty years has been the spawning of inferior novels. Everybody writes novels—journalists, broadcasters, TV announcers . . . it is a free-for-all! But writing is a vocation, like being a nun or a priest. I work at my writing as an athlete does at his training, taking it very seriously. Whether a novel is autobiographical or not does not matter. What is important is the truth in it and the way that truth is expressed. I think a casual or frivolous attitude is pernicious.

INTERVIEWER: Is there any area of fiction that you find women are better equipped to explore?

O'BRIEN: Yes. Women are better at emotions and the havoc those emotions wreak. But it must be said that Anna Karenina is the most believable heroine. The last scene where she goes to the station and looks down at the rails and thinks of Vronski's rejection is terrible in its depiction of despair. Women, on the whole, are better at plumbing the depths. A woman artist can produce a perfect gem, as opposed to a huge piece of rock carving a man might produce. It is not a limitation of talent or intelligence, it is just a different way of looking at the world.

INTERVIEWER: So you don't believe in the feminist argument that the differences between men and women are a question of nurture and not of nature; that women look at the world differently because they have been conditioned to do so?

O'BRIEN: Not in the least! I believe that we are fundamentally, biologically, and therefore psychologically different. I am not like any man I have met, ever, and that divide is what both interests me and baffles me. A lot of things have been said by feminists about equality, about liberation, but not all of these things are gospel truth. They are opinions the way my books are opinions, nothing more. Of course I would like women to have a better time but I don't see it happening, and for a very simple and primal reason: people are pretty savage towards each other, be they men or women.

INTERVIEWER: Yet your own success is, to a certain degree, due to the fact that your writing coincided with the rise of the feminist movement, because invariably it portrayed loving, sensitive, good women, being victimized by hard, callous men, and it hit the right note at the right time. Would you agree with that?

O'BRIEN: I would think so. However, I am not the darling of the feminists. They think I am too preoccupied with old-fashioned themes like love and longing. Though one woman in *Ms.* magazine pointed out that I send bulletins from battle fronts where other women do not go. I think I do. The reason why I resent being lectured at is that my psyche is so weighed down with its own paraphernalia! No man or woman from outside could prescribe to me what to do. I have enough trouble keeping madness at bay.

INTERVIEWER: Your description of small towns and their enclosed communities reminds me of some of America's Southern writers, like Faulkner. Did they influence you?

O'BRIEN: Faulkner is an important writer though an imperfect one. I did go through a stage when I read a lot of Southern writers: Carson McCullers, Eudora Welty, Flannery O'Connor. . . . Any small, claustrophobic, ingrown community resembles another. The passion and ignorance in the Deep South of America and the west of Ireland are the same.

INTERVIEWER: This is the opposite of the high society and the aristocratic world of Proust's *Remembrance of Things Past,* which has also been a major source of inspiration to you.

O'BRIEN: Proust's influence on me, along with his genius, was his preoccupation with memory and his obsession with the past. His concentration on even the simplest detail—like one petal of a flower, or the design on a dinner plate—has unique, manic intensity. Also, when I read his biography by George Painter I felt the tenderness of his soul and wished I could have met him as a human being. You see, Joyce and Proust, although very different, broke the old mold by recognizing the importance of the rambling, disjointed nature of what goes on in the head, the interior monologue. I wonder how they would fare now. These are more careless times. Literature is no longer sacred, it is a business. There is an invisible umbilical cord between the writer and his potential reader, and I fear that the time has gone when readers could sink into a book the way they did in the past, for the *pace* of life is fast and frenetic. The world is cynical: the dwelling on emotions, the perfection of style, the intensity of a Flaubert is wasted on modern sensibility. I have a feeling that there is a *dying*, if not a *death*, of great literature. Some blame the television for it. Perhaps. There is hardly any distinction between a writer and a journalist—indeed, most writers *are* journalists. Nothing wrong with journalism any more than with dentistry, but they are worlds apart! Whenever I read the English Sunday papers I notice that the standard of literacy is high—all very clever and hollow—but no dues to literature. They care about their own egos. They synopsize the book, tell the plot. Well, fuck the plot! That is for precocious schoolboys. What matters is the imaginative *truth*, and the perfection and care with which it has been rendered. After all, you don't say of a ballet dancer, "He jumped in the air, then he twirled around, etc. . . ." You are just *carried away* by his dancing. The nicest readers are—and I know by the letters I receive—youngish people who are still eager and uncontaminated, who approach a book without hostility. But when I read Anita Brookner's novel *Look at Me*, I feel I am in the grip of a most wonderful, imaginative writer. The same is true of Margaret Atwood. Also, great literature is dying because young people, although they don't talk about it much, feel and fear a holocaust.

INTERVIEWER: What about your own relationship with critics? Do you feel misunderstood and neglected by them, or have they been kind to you? Have you ever been savaged by them?

O'BRIEN: Oh yes! I have been savaged all right! I believe one reviewer lost her job on the *New Statesman* because her review of my book *A Pagan Place* was too personal. She went on and on about my illiterate background. On the whole I have had more serious consideration in the United States than in Britain or Ireland. Perhaps because I am not known there as a "personality"! I do not despair though, for the real test of writing is not in the reading but in the rereading. I am not ashamed of my books being reread. The misunderstanding may be due just to geography, and to race. The Irish and the English are poles apart in thought and disposition.

INTERVIEWER: It may also be due to a certain—and very un-British—*démesure* in your writing; I mean they find you too sentimental.

O'BRIEN: I am glad to say that Dickens was accused of sentimentality and, by God, he lives on!

INTERVIEWER: You were brought up as a devout Catholic and had a convent education. At one point you even contemplated becoming a nun. What made you give up religion?

O'BRIEN: I married a divorcé, and that was my first "Fall." Add to that the hounding nature of Irish Catholicism and you can dimly understand. We had a daily admonition which went:

> *You have but one soul to save*
> *One God to love and serve*
> *One Eternity to prepare for*
> *Death will come soon*
> *Judgment will follow, and then*
> *Heaven—or Hell—For Ever!*

INTERVIEWER: In your novel *A Pagan Place*, the heroine does become a nun. Was that a vicarious fulfillment of a subconscious wish?

O'BRIEN: Perhaps. I did think of becoming a nun when I was very young, but it went out of my mind later, chased away by sexual desire!

INTERVIEWER: Another interesting aspect of that novel is that it is written in the second person singular, like a soliloquy. It is somewhat reminiscent of Molly Bloom's soliloquy in *Ulysses*; were you conscious of the influence?

O'BRIEN: I didn't take Molly's as a model. The reason was psychological. As a child you are both your secret self and the "you" that your parents think you are. So the use of the second person was a way of combining the two identities. But I tend not to examine these things too closely—they just happen.

INTERVIEWER: Religion has played such a crucial part in your life and evolution, yet you have not dealt with it on any philosophical or moral level, as have Graham Greene or Georges

Bernanos; you haven't made religion the central theme of any of your novels. Why?

O'BRIEN: That is perhaps one of the differences between men and women who go through the same experiences. I flee from my persecutors. I have not confronted religion.

INTERVIEWER: Do you think you ever will?

O'BRIEN: I hope so—when I have got rid of the terror and the anxiety. Or perhaps when I know exactly what I believe or don't believe.

INTERVIEWER: Let's talk about the subjects that are dealt with in your work, its central themes, which are romantic love and Ireland. Some people—and not only feminists!—think that your preoccupation with romance verges at times on the sentimental and the "Romantic Novel" formula. You quoted Aragon in answer: "Love is your last chance, there is really nothing else to keep you there."

O'BRIEN: Other people have said it too, even the Beatles! Emily Dickinson wrote, "And is there more than love and death, then tell me its name?" But my work is concerned with *loss* as much as with love. Loss is every child's theme because by necessity the child loses its mother and its bearings. And writers, however mature and wise and eminent, are children at heart. So my central theme is loss—loss of love, loss of self, loss of God. I have just finished a play, my third, which is about my family. In it for the first time I have allowed my father, who is always the ogre figure in my work, to weep for the loss of *his* child. Therefore, I might, if the gods are good to me, find that my understanding of love has become richer and stronger than my dread of loss. You see, my own father was what you might call the "archetypal" Irishman—a gambler, drinker, a man totally unequipped to be a husband or a father. And of course that colored my views, distorted them, and made me seek out demons.

INTERVIEWER: Is that why, in nearly all your novels, women are longing to establish a simple, loving, harmonious relationship with men, but are unable to do so?

O'BRIEN: My experience was pretty extreme, so that it is hard for me to imagine harmony, or even affinity, between men and women. I would need to be reborn.

INTERVIEWER: The other central theme of your work is Ireland. It seems to me that you have the same love-hate relationship with Ireland that most exiles have with their native country: on the one hand an incurable nostalgia and longing, and on the other the fact that one cannot go back, because the reasons that made one leave in the first place are still there. There is a constant conflict in the soul.

O'BRIEN: My relationship with Ireland is very complex. I could not live there for a variety of reasons. I felt oppressed and strangulated from an early age. That was partly to do with my parents, who were themselves products and victims of their history and culture. That is to say, alas, they were superstitious, fanatical, engulfing. At the same time they were bursting with talent—I know this from my mother's letters, as she wrote to me almost every day. So I have to thank them for a heritage that includes talent, despair, and permanent fury. When I was a student in Dublin my mother found a book of Sean O'Casey in my suitcase and wanted to *burn* it! *But without reading it!* So they hated literature without knowing it. We know that the effect of our parents is indelible, because we internalize as a child and it remains inside us forever. Even when the parents die, you dream of them as if they were still there. Everything was an occasion for fear, religion was force-fed the way they feed the geese of Strasbourg for pâté! I feel I am a cripple with a craving for wings. So much for the personal aspect. As for the country itself, it is no accident that almost all Irish writers leave the country. You know why? Ireland, as Joyce said, eats her writers the way a sow eats her farrow. He also called it a warren of "prelates and kinechites." Of course there's the beauty of the landscape, the poetry, the fairy tales, the vividness. I have shown my love and my entanglement with the place as much as I have shown my hatred. But they think that I have shown only my hatred.

INTERVIEWER: Is that why they had an auto-da-fé of your first novel in your native village?

O'BRIEN: It was a humble event, as befits a backward place. Two or three people had gone to Limerick and bought *The Country Girls*. The parish priest asked them to hand in the books, which they did, and he burnt them on the grounds of the church. Nevertheless, a lot of people read it. My mother was very harsh about it; she thought I was a disgrace. That is the sadness—it takes you half a life to get out of the pits of darkness and stupidity. It fills me with anger, and with pity.

INTERVIEWER: Do you think that after all these years and through your books you have exorcised the demon and can let it rest?

O'BRIEN: I hope not, because one needs one's demons to create.

INTERVIEWER: After that small auto-da-fé, did anything else of that kind happen?

O'BRIEN: They used to ban my books, but now when I go there, people are courteous to my face, though rather slanderous behind my back. Then again, Ireland has changed. There are a lot of young people who are irreligious, or less religious. Ironically, they wouldn't be interested in my early books—they would think them gauche. They are aping English and American mores. If I went to a dance hall in Dublin now I would feel as alien as in a disco in Oklahoma.

INTERVIEWER: You are not a political writer because, as you say, politics are concerned with the social and the external, while your preoccupations are with the inner, psychological life. Nonetheless, considering your emotional involvement with Ireland, how have you kept away from the situation in Northern Ireland—terrorism, the IRA, etc. . . .?

O'BRIEN: I have written one long piece on Northern Ireland for the German magazine *Stern*. My feelings about it are so manifold. I think it is mad, a so-called religious war, in this day and age. At the same time, I can't bear the rhetoric of the Unionists; I mean Ireland is *one small* island, and those six counties do not belong to Britain. Equally I abhor terrorism, whoever does it, the IRA, the Arabs, the Israelis. But when I stayed in Northern Ireland to research and write the article, I realized that the Catholics are second-class citizens. They live in terrible slums, in poverty, and know no way of improving their conditions. I have not set a novel in Northern Ireland simply because I do not know enough about it. I dislike cant—you get that from politicians. Writers have to dig deep for experience. I might go and live there for a while, in order to discover and later write about it. But so far I have refrained from bringing the topic into a book merely as a voyeur.

INTERVIEWER: Let's get back to Virginia Woolf. . . . Why and when did she become an obsession for you? After all, you are very different as writers and as people.

O'BRIEN: I first read her critical essays, *The Common Reader*, and I saw a woman who loved literature, unlike many critics who just *use* it. The essays are on Hazlitt, Wordsworth, Hardy, everyone. I was overwhelmed first by the generosity of her mind and its perspicacity. Later I read *To the Lighthouse* and my favorite, *Mrs. Dalloway*, which is very spry and sprightly. Then I was asked to write a play about her and I began to read everything she had written—diaries, letters, etc. . . . I realized that she gave of herself so utterly, so *shamelessly*. Her photographs show her as aloof, which she was in some ways. But in the diaries and letters, she tells *everything*! If she buys a pair of gloves she has to commit it to paper. So I came to know her and to love her.

INTERVIEWER: Some critics pointed to the play's neglect of her intellectual vigor and her bitchiness. Do you think her bitchiness was due to lack of sexual gratification?

O'BRIEN: She did have a bitchy side, but alongside it a childlike need for affection. She called people pet names, waited for her husband to come home, adored her sister Vanessa and wanted her approval. I saw Woolf as a troubled, *needful* creature. Her bitchiness was diminishing, certainly, and she would have been a grander figure without it. I selected those parts of her that chart her dilemma, her march towards suicide. Another writer, say an English homosexual, could write a very waspish, very witty play about her. I hope that mine was valid.

INTERVIEWER: Having been successful at novels and short stories, you tried your hand at drama—plays and screenplays. How did that come about?

O'BRIEN: I was asked to adapt my own novel A *Pagan Place* for the stage and it opened a new vista for me. Then with some experience I tackled Woolf. Now I have written a third play, which for the time being is called *Home Sweet Home*, or *Family Butchers*. I feel drama is more direct, more suitable for expressing passions. Confrontation is the stuff of drama. It happens rather than is described. The play starts in the early morning, the voice of an Irish tenor comes over the gramophone—John McCormack is singing "Bless This House, Oh Lord We Pray," then he's interrupted by a gunshot followed by another gunshot. The lights come on, a man and a woman appear, and you know that this is a play about passion and violence. You go straight for the jugular.

INTERVIEWER: When you start a play, or a novel, or a short story, do you have a basic idea? Or a sentence? Something that triggers off the process of creating the work?

O'BRIEN: I always have the first line. Even with my very first book, *The Country Girls*, I went around with this first sentence in my head long before I sat down to write it.*

INTERVIEWER: Once you have started, do you have the whole scheme in your mind or do characters and plot take their own course and lead you, as some novelists say they do? I mean, Balzac was so surprised and moved by Old Goriot's death that he opened his window and shouted, *"Le Père Goriot est mort! Le Père Goriot est mort!"*

O'BRIEN: I know more or less, but I don't discuss it with myself. It is like sleepwalking; I don't know exactly where I am going but I know I will get there. When I am writing, I am so glad to be doing it that whatever form it takes—play, novel, etc.—I am thankful to the Fates. I keep dozens of pens by me, and exercise books.

INTERVIEWER: When success came and you began to be famous and lionized, did it affect your life, work, and outlook in any way? Is success good for an artist, or does it limit his field of experience?

* "I wakened quickly and sat up in bed abruptly."

O'BRIEN: It depends on the degree of success and on the disposition of the artist. It was very nice for me to be published, as I had longed for it. But my success has been rather modest. It hasn't been meteoric. Nor was it financially shattering—just enough to carry me along.

INTERVIEWER: But you have had a great deal of social success: fame, publicity, so on . . .

O'BRIEN: I am not conscious of it. I go to functions more as a duty than for pleasure, and I am always *outside* looking in, not the other way round. But I am grateful to have had enough success not to feel a disaster—it has allayed my hopelessness. Undoubtedly success contributed to the breakup of my marriage. I had married very young. My husband was an attractive father figure—a Professor Higgins. When my book was published and well received, it altered things between us. The break would have come anyway, but my success sped it up. Then began a hard life; but when you are young, you have boundless energy—you run the house, mind the children, *and* write your despair. I don't know if I could do it all now. Looking back I realize that I am one of the luckiest people in the world, since no matter how down I go something brings me back. Is it God's grace or just peasant resilience?

INTERVIEWER: Perhaps it is the creative act of writing. John Updike once said that the minute he puts an unhappiness down on paper, it metamorphoses into a lump of sugar!

O'BRIEN: I think he was simplifying. The original pain that prompted the writing does not lessen, but it is gratifying to give it form and shape.

INTERVIEWER: Did money ever act as a spur? You were very prolific in the sixties, and still are.

O'BRIEN: I have never written anything in order to make money. A story comes to me, is given me, as it were, and I write it. But perhaps the need to earn a living and my need to write coincided. I know that I would still write if tomorrow I was given a huge legacy, and I will always be profligate.

INTERVIEWER: How do you organize your time? Do you write

regularly, every day? Philip Roth has said that he writes eight hours a day three hundred and sixty-five days a year. Do you work as compulsively?

O'BRIEN: He is a man, you see. Women have the glorious excuse of having to shop, cook, clean! When I am working I write in a kind of trance, longhand, in these several copybooks. I meant to tidy up before you came! I write in the morning because one is nearer to the unconscious, the source of inspiration. I never work at night because by then the shackles of the day are around me, what James Stephens (author of *The Crock of Gold*) called "That flat, dull catalogue of dreary things that fasten themselves to my wings," and I don't sit down three hundred and sixty-five days a year because I'm not that kind of writer. I wish I were! Perhaps I don't take myself that seriously. Another reason why I don't write constantly is that I feel I have written all I had wanted to say about love and loss and loneliness and being a victim and all that. I have finished with that territory. And I have not yet embraced another one. It may be that I'm going towards it—I hope and pray that this is the case.

INTERVIEWER: When you are writing, are you disciplined? Do you keep regular hours, turn down invitations, and hibernate?

O'BRIEN: Yes, but discipline doesn't come into it. It is what one has to do. The impulse is stronger than anything. I don't like too much social life anyway. It is gossip and bad white wine. It's a waste. Writing is like carrying a fetus. I get up in the morning, have a cup of tea, and come into this room to work. I never go out to lunch, never, but I stop around one or two and spend the rest of the afternoon attending to mundane things. In the evening I might read or go out to a play or a film, or see my sons. Did I tell you that I spend a lot of time moping? Did Philip Roth say that he moped?

INTERVIEWER: Don't you feel restless and lonely if you have worked all day and have to spend the evening alone?

O'BRIEN: Less lonely than if I were bored at a dinner party. If I get restless I might ring up one of a handful of friends who are close enough to come to the rescue. Rilke said, "Loneliness is a very good practice for eternity." Loneliness is not intolerable—depression is.

INTERVIEWER: Before the film script on Joan of Arc that you are writing now, you wrote another two. One of them, *Zee & Co.*, starring Elizabeth Taylor, was a big-budget, Hollywood film. How did you enjoy that experience?

O'BRIEN: The film world is inhabited by gangsters. I have met many producers and very few of them could I accuse of being sensitive, or interested in writing. They are businesspeople whose material is other people's imagination, and that invariably leads to trouble. People in the clothing industry or the motor business are dealing with merchandise, but the producer's raw material is first and foremost the writer. So I can't say that I had a happy experience. But it *is* possible; low-budget films like *Gregory's Girl* or *The Country Girls* do get made. I had a marvelous time with the latter; they didn't have *four* writers all rewriting my script. It restored my faith. I do believe that cinema and the television are the media of the future, more than books, simply because people are too restive. I put as much into a film script as into anything I write—it is, I believe, an art form, and great directors like Bergman, Buñuel, Hitchcock, and Fassbinder have made it so. What happened with *Zee & Co.*—and what happens generally when you get involved with Hollywood—is that you give them the script and then the director or leading actress proceeds to write their own stuff. They are often as capable of writing as I am of brain surgery! So they just disembowel it. And they do it for two reasons: one is ego and the other is ignorance. They know nothing about writing and therefore think they can bring their own *ideas* to it. Now, in the theater when actors want something changed they ask the author.

INTERVIEWER: If someone had time to read only one of your books, which one would you recommend?

O'BRIEN: *A Pagan Place.*

INTERVIEWER: Do you feel that your best book, the one that every writer aspires to, is yet to come?

O'BRIEN: It had better be! I need to develop, to enlarge my spheres of experience.

INTERVIEWER: When you say you are changing your life, do you also mean that the subject matter of your fiction will change with it?

O'BRIEN: I think so. I am giving a lecture in Boston next month about women in literature. I had to come to the forlorn conclusion that all the great heroines have been created by men. I had an anthology of women's writing called *Bold New Women* in which the editor, Barbara Alson, very wisely says that all women writers have written about sex, because sex is their biological life, their environment, and that for a woman a sexual encounter is not just the mechanical thing it can be for a man but—and she uses this wonderful phrase—"a clutch on the universe." I have written quite a lot of love stories; I don't think I want to write those anymore. I even find them hard to read! It doesn't mean that I am not interested in love anymore—that goes on as long as there is breath. I mean I am not going to *write* about it in the same way.

INTERVIEWER: Could it have something to do with age?

O'BRIEN: *Bound* to have something to do with age. The attitude toward sex changes in two ways. Sexual love becomes deeper and one realizes how fundamental it is and how rich. At the same time, one sees that it is a sort of mutual game and that attraction makes one resort to all sorts of ruses and strategies. To an outsider it is all patent, even laughable. Shakespeare saw through this glorious delusion better than anyone and *As You Like It* is the funniest play about love, yet it is steeped in love.

INTERVIEWER: What about the new cult of chastity? Germaine Greer's new book advocates restraint—a backlash against a decade or so of permissiveness. Have you been influenced by the changing mood?

O'BRIEN: I have always espoused chastity except when one can no longer resist the temptation. I know promiscuity is boring, much more than fish and chips, which is comforting.

INTERVIEWER: Do you find sex scenes difficult to write, considering your puritanical background?

O'BRIEN: Not really. When you are writing you are not conscious of the reader, so that you don't feel embarrassed. I'm sure Joyce had a most heady and wonderful time writing the last fifty pages of *Ulysses*—glorious Molly Bloom. He must have written it in one bout, thinking: I'll show the women of the world that I am omniscient!

INTERVIEWER: What do you think the future has in store for literature? You have been very pessimistic so far. For example, last year nearly three hundred novels were published in France, and few except the ones that won the big prizes were read. Will we go on endlessly writing novels with so few making a mark?

O'BRIEN: As you know the future itself is perilous. But as regards books, there is first the financial aspect of publishing. Already books are very expensive, so that a first novel of quality will have less of a chance of being picked up. Say a new Djuna Barnes, or indeed Nathalie Sarraute, might not get published. If Woolf's *The Waves* were to be published today it would have pitiful sales. Of course, "how-to" books, spy stories, thrillers, and science fiction all sell by the millions. What would be wonderful—what we *need* just now—is some astonishing fairy tale. I read somewhere the other day that the cavemen did not paint what they saw, but what they *wished* they had seen. We need that, in these lonely, lunatic times.

INTERVIEWER: So if we manage to save the planet, is there hope for literature as well?

O'BRIEN: Oh yes! At this very moment, some imagination is spawning something wonderful that might make us tremble. Let's say there will always be literature because the imagination is boundless. We just need to care more for the imagination than for the trivia and the commerce of life. Literature is the next best thing to God. Joyce would disagree. He would say literature *is*, in essence, God.

—SHUSHA GUPPY
1984

15. Joyce Carol Oates

Joyce Carol Oates was born in Lockport, New York, on June 16, 1938. Interested in writing since childhood, she recalled later that her first stories were told through pictures. She attended Syracuse University, where she was elected to Phi Beta Kappa, and in 1960 was graduated first in her class; during her senior year she also won a *Mademoiselle* magazine college fiction award. Oates received her M.A. under a Knapp Fellowship at the University of Wisconsin in 1961 before accompanying her husband, Raymond J. Smith, a college professor, to Texas. There she abandoned her plans to pursue a doctorate in order to concentrate on her fiction. Oates produced several impressive early works, publishing her first collection of short stories, *By the North Gate* in 1963; her first novel, *With Shuddering Fall*, the following year; and a second collection of stories, *Upon the Sweeping Flood*, in 1965.

Since then Oates has maintained an astonishing literary pace, publishing at least one book per year, including the 1970 winner of the National Book Award in fiction, *them*, and two National Book Award nominees, *A Garden of Earthly Delights* (1970) and *Expensive People* (1969). Other works of fiction include *Raven's Wing* (1986), *You Must Remember This* (1987), and *American Appetites* (1989). She is the recipient of a Guggenheim Foundation Award, and the O. Henry Special Award for Continuing Achievement.

Oates, who since 1978 has served as Writer-in-Residence at Princeton University, has also taught at the University of Windsor (Canada) and New York University, and was recently inducted into the American Academy of Arts and Letters and the National Institute of Arts and Letters. She lives with her husband in Princeton, New Jersey.

ax other customers in <u>Rinaldi's</u> to overhear. Voice shrill,
laughter shrill. Must guard against excitement. ...A true
gift, such women possess; "artistic arrangement of life" a
phrase I think I read somewhere. Can't remember. She wants
to understand me but will not invade me like the others.
Sunshine: her hair. (Though it is brown, not very unusual.
But always clean.) Sunshine: dispelling of demons. Intimacy
always a danger. Intimacy/hell/intimacy/hell. Could possibly
make love to her thinking of XXXNXXXNXXX or (say) the boy with
the kinky reddish hair on the bicycle...but sickening to think
of. What if. What if an attack of laughter. Hysterical gig-
gling. And. Afterward. Such shame, disgust. She would not
laugh of course but might be wounded for life: cannot exaggerate
the dangers of intimacy, on my side or hers. The Secret between
us. My secret, not hers. Our friendship--nearly a year now--
on my footing, never hers. Can't deny what others have known
before me, the pleasure of secrecy, taking of risks.

--With XXXNXXXXXX etc. last night, unable to wake this morning
till after ten; already at work; sick headache, dryness of
mouth, throat. But no fever. Temperature normal. XXXXXXXXXXXXX
so bitter, speaks of having been blackmailed by some idiot,
but (in my opinion) it all happened years ago, not connected
with his position here in town. Teaches juniors, seniors.
Advises Drama Club. Tenure. I'm envious of him & impatient
with his continual bitterness. Rehashing of past. What's the
point of it? Of course, he is over forty (how much over forty
is his secret) and I am a decade younger, ■ maybe fifteen years
younger. Will never turn into that. Hag's face, lines around
mouth, eyes. Grotesque moustache: trying to be 25 years old
& misses by a ■ mile.... Yet my pen-and-ink portrait of him
is endearing. Delighted, that it should please even him. &
did not mind the CA$H. Of course I am talented & of course
misused at the agency but refuse to be bitter like the others.
XXXXXXXXXXX lavish, flattery and money. I deserve both but
don't expect everyone to recognize me...in no hurry...can't
demand fame overnight. Would I want fame anyway???? Maybe not.
With XXXXXXXXXXXXX's hundred dollars bought her that $35 book of
Toulouse-Lautrec's work, dear Henri, perhaps should not have
risked ■ it with her but genuinely thought she would like it.
Did not think, as usual. She seemed grateful enough, thanking
me, surprised, said she'd received only a few cards from home
& a predictable present from her mother, certainly did not
expect anything from me--"but aren't you saving for a trip to
Europe"--remembers so much about me, amazing--so sweet--unlike
XXXXXXXXXXXX who calls me by the names of strangers and is
vile. His image with me till early afternoon, tried to vomit
in the first-floor lavatory where no one from the office might
drop in, dry heaving gasps, not so easy to do on an empty ~~stomach.~~ _stomach._
Mind over matter?????? Not with "Farrell van Buren"!

--A complete day **waxx** wasted. Idiotic trendy "collage" for
Mackenzie's Diary, if you please. Cherubs, grinning teenagers,
trophies. An "avant-garde" look to it. Haha. Looking forward
to lay-out for the Hilton & Trader Vic's, at least some precedent
to work from <u>and resist</u>. ...Could send out my Invisible Soldiers
to hack up a few of these bastards, smart-assed paunchy hags
bossing me around. Someday things will be different. (Of course

Joyce Carol Oates

Joyce Carol Oates is the rarest of commodities, an author modest about her work, though there is such a quantity of it that she has three publishers—one for fiction, one for poetry, and a "small press" for more experimental work, limited editions, and books her other publishers simply cannot schedule. And despite the added demands of teaching, she continues to devote much energy to The Ontario Review, a literary quarterly which her husband edits and for which she serves as a contributing editor.

Ms. Oates is striking-looking and slender, with dark hair and large, inquiring eyes. A highly attractive woman, she is not photogenic; no photo has ever done justice to her appearance, which conveys grace and high intelligence. If her manner is taken for aloofness—as it sometimes has been—it is, in fact, a shyness which the publication of thirty-three books, the production of three plays, and the winning of the National Book Award has not displaced.

This interview began at her Windsor home in the summer of

1976 before she and her husband moved to Princeton. When interviewed, her speaking voice was, as always, soft and reflective. One receives the impression that she never speaks in anything but perfectly formed sentences. Ms. Oates answered all questions openly while curled with her Persian cats upon a sofa. (She is a confirmed cat lover and recently took in two more kittens at the Princeton house.) Talk continued during a stroll by the banks of the Detroit River where she confessed to having sat for hours, watching the horizon and the boats, and dreaming her characters into existence. She sets these dreams physically onto paper on a writing table in her study, which faces the river.

Additional questions were asked in New York during the 1976 Christmas season, when Ms. Oates and her husband attended a seminar on her work which was part of that year's Modern Language Association convention. Many of the questions in this interview were answered via correspondence. She felt only by writing out her replies could she say precisely what she wished to, without possibility of misunderstanding or misquotation.

INTERVIEWER: We may as well get this one over with first: you're frequently charged with producing too much.

OATES: Productivity is a relative matter. And it's really insignificant: what is ultimately important is a writer's strongest books. It may be the case that we all must write many books in order to achieve a few lasting ones—just as a young writer or poet might have to write hundreds of poems before writing his first significant one. Each book as it is written, however, is a completely absorbing experience, and feels always as if it were *the* work I was born to write. Afterward, of course, as the years pass, it's possible to become more detached, more critical.

I really don't know what to say. I note and can to some extent sympathize with the objurgatory tone of certain critics, who feel that I write too much because, quite wrongly, they believe they ought to have read most of my books before attempting to criticize a recently published one. (At least I *think* that's why they react a bit irritably.) Yet each book is a world unto itself and must stand alone, and it should not matter whether a book is a writer's first, or tenth, or fiftieth.

INTERVIEWER: About your critics—do you read them, usually? Have you ever learned anything from a book review or an essay on your work?

OATES: Sometimes I read reviews, and without exception I will read critical essays that are sent to me. The critical essays are interesting on their own terms. Of course, it's a pleasure simply to discover that someone has read and responded to one's work; being understood, and being praised, is beyond expectation most of the time. . . . The average review is a quickly written piece not meant to be definitive. So it would be misguided for a writer to read such reviews attentively. All writers without exception find themselves clapperclawed from time to time; I think the experience (provided one survives it) is wonderfully liberating: after the first death there is no other. . . . A writer who has published as many books as I have has developed, of necessity, a hide like a rhino's, while inside there dwells a frail, hopeful butterfly of a spirit.

INTERVIEWER: Returning to the matter of your "productivity": have you ever dictated into a machine?

OATES: No, oddly enough I've written my last several novels in longhand first. I had an enormous, rather frightening stack of pages and notes for *The Assassins*, probably eight hundred pages— or was it closer to a thousand? It alarms me to remember. *Childwold* needed to be written in longhand, of course. And now everything finds its initial expression in longhand and the typewriter has become a rather alien thing—a thing of formality and impersonality. My first novels were all written on a typewriter: first draft straight through, then revisions, then final draft. But I can't do that any longer.

The thought of dictating into a machine doesn't appeal to me at all. Henry James's later works would have been better had he resisted that curious sort of self-indulgence, dictating to a secretary. The roaming garrulousness of ordinary speech is usually corrected when it's transcribed into written prose.

INTERVIEWER: Do you ever worry—considering the vast body of your work—if you haven't written a particular scene before, or had characters say the same lines?

OATES: Evidently, there are writers (John Cheever, Mavis Gallant come immediately to mind) who never reread their work, and there are others who reread constantly. I suspect I am somewhere in the middle. If I thought I *had* written a scene before, or written the same lines before, I would simply look it up.

INTERVIEWER: What kind of work schedule do you follow?

OATES: I haven't any formal schedule, but I love to write in the morning, before breakfast. Sometimes the writing goes so smoothly that I don't take a break for many hours—and consequently have breakfast at two or three in the afternoon on good days. On school days, days that I teach, I usually write for an hour or forty-five minutes in the morning, before my first class. But I don't have any formal schedule, and at the moment I am feeling rather melancholy, or derailed, or simply lost, because I completed a novel some weeks ago and haven't begun another . . . except in scattered, stray notes.

INTERVIEWER: Do you find emotional stability is necessary in order to write? Or can you get to work whatever your state of mind? Is your mood reflected in what you write? How do you describe that perfect state in which you can write from early morning into the afternoon?

OATES: One must be pitiless about this matter of "mood." In a sense, the writing will *create* the mood. If art is, as I believe it to be, a genuinely transcendental function—a means by which we rise out of limited, parochial states of mind—then it should not matter very much what states of mind or emotion we are in. Generally I've found this to be true: I have forced myself to begin writing when I've been utterly exhausted, when I've felt my soul as thin as a playing card, when nothing has seemed worth enduring for another five minutes . . . and somehow the activity of writing changes everything. Or appears to do so. Joyce said of the underlying structure of *Ulysses*—the Odyssean parallel and parody—that he really didn't care whether it was plausible so long as it served as a bridge to get his "soldiers" across. Once they were across, what does it matter if the bridge collapses? One might say the same thing about the use of one's self as a means for the writing to get written. Once the soldiers are across the stream . . .

INTERVIEWER: What does happen when you finish a novel? Is the next project one that has been waiting in line? Or is the choice more spontaneous?

OATES: When I complete a novel I set it aside, and begin work on short stories, and eventually another long work. When I complete *that* novel I return to the earlier novel and rewrite much of it. In the meantime the second novel lies in a desk drawer. Sometimes I work on two novels simultaneously, though one usually forces the other into the background. The rhythm of writing, revising, writing, revising, etcetera, seems to suit me. I am inclined to think that as I grow older I will come to be infatuated with the art of revision, and there may come a time when I will dread giving up a novel at all. My next novel, *Unholy Loves*, was written around the time of *Childwold*, for instance, and revised after the completion of that novel, and again revised this past spring and summer. My reputation for writing quickly and effortlessly notwithstanding, I am strongly in favor of intelligent, even fastidious revision, which is, or certainly should be, an art in itself.

INTERVIEWER: Do you keep a diary?

OATES: I began keeping a formal journal several years ago. It resembles a sort of ongoing letter to myself, mainly about literary matters. What interests me in the process of my own experience is the wide range of my feelings. For instance, after I finish a novel I tend to think of the experience of having written it as being largely pleasant and challenging. But in fact (for I keep careful records) the experience is various: I do suffer temporary bouts of frustration and inertia and depression. There are pages in recent novels that I've rewritten as many as seventeen times, and a story, "The Widows," which I revised both before and after publication in *The Hudson Review*, and then revised slightly again before I included it in my next collection of stories—a fastidiousness that could go on into infinity.

Afterward, however, I simply forget. My feelings crystallize (or are mythologized) into something much less complex. All of us who keep journals do so for different reasons, I suppose, but we must have in common a fascination with the surprising patterns that emerge over the years—a sort of arabesque in which certain elements appear and reappear, like the designs in a well-wrought novel. The voice of my journal is very much like the one I find myself using in these replies to you: the voice in which I think or meditate when I'm not writing fiction.

INTERVIEWER: Besides writing and teaching, what daily special activities are important to you? Travel, jogging, music? I hear you're an excellent pianist?

OATES: We travel a great deal, usually by car. We've driven slowly across the continent several times, and we've explored the South and New England and of course New York State with loving thoroughness. As a pianist I've defined myself as an "enthusiastic amateur," which is about the most merciful thing that can be said. I like to draw, I like to listen to music, and I spend an inordinate amount of time doing nothing. I don't even think it can be called daydreaming.

I also enjoy that much-maligned occupation of housewifery, but hardly dare say so, things being what they are today. I like to cook, to tend plants, to garden (minimally), to do simple domestic things, to stroll around shopping malls and observe the qualities of people, overhearing snatches of conversations, noting people's appearances, their clothes, and so forth. Walking and driving a car are part of my life as a writer, really. I can't imagine myself apart from these activities.

INTERVIEWER: Despite critical and financial success, you continue to teach. Why?

OATES: I teach a full load at the University of Windsor, which means three courses. One is creative writing, one is the graduate seminar (in the Modern Period), the third is an oversized (115 students) undergraduate course that is lively and stimulating but really too swollen to be satisfying to me. There is, generally, a closeness between students and faculty at Windsor that is very rewarding, however. Anyone who teaches knows that you don't *really* experience a text until you've taught it, in loving detail, with an intelligent and responsive class. At the present time I'm going through Joyce's work with nine graduate students and each seminar meeting is very exciting (and draining) and I can't think, frankly, of anything else I would rather do.

INTERVIEWER: It is a sometimes publicized fact that your professor-husband does not read most of your work. Is there any practical reason for this?

OATES: Ray has such a busy life of his own, preparing classes, editing *The Ontario Review* and so forth, that he really hasn't time to read my work. I do, occasionally, show him reviews, and he makes brief comments on them. I would have liked, I think, to have established an easygoing relationship with some other writers, but somehow that never came about. Two or three of us at Windsor do read one another's poems, but criticism as such is minimal. I've never been able to respond very fully to criticism, frankly, because I've usually been absorbed in another work by the time the criticism is available to me. Also, critics sometimes appear to be addressing themselves to works other than those I remember writing.

INTERVIEWER: Do you feel in any way an expatriate or an exile, living in Canada?

OATES: We are certainly exiles of a sort. But we would be, I think, exiles if we lived in Detroit as well. Fortunately, Windsor is really an international, cosmopolitan community, and our Canadian colleagues are not intensely and narrowly nationalistic.

But I wonder—doesn't everyone feel rather exiled? When I return home to Millerport, New York, and visit nearby Lockport, the extraordinary changes that have taken place make me feel like a stranger; the mere passage of time makes us all exiles. The situation is a comic one, perhaps, since it affirms the power of the evolving community over the individual, but I think we tend to feel it as tragic. Windsor is a relatively stable community, and my husband and I have come to feel, oddly, more at home here than we probably would anywhere else.

INTERVIEWER: Have you ever consciously changed your lifestyle to help your work as a writer?

OATES: Not really. My nature is orderly and observant and

scrupulous, and deeply introverted, so life wherever I attempt it turns out to be claustral. Live like the bourgeois, Flaubert suggested, but I was living like that long before I came across Flaubert's remark.

INTERVIEWER: You wrote *Do With Me What You Will* during your year living in London. While there you met many writers such as Doris Lessing, Margaret Drabble, Colin Wilson, Iris Murdoch—writers you respect, as your reviews of their work indicate. Would you make any observations on the role of the writer in society in England versus that which you experience here?

OATES: The English novelist is almost without exception an observer of society. (I suppose I mean "society" in its most immediate, limited sense.) Apart from writers like Lawrence (who doesn't seem altogether *English*, in fact) there hasn't been an intense interest in subjectivity, in the psychology of living, breathing human beings. Of course, there have been marvelous novels. And there *is* Doris Lessing, who writes books that can no longer be categorized: fictional parable, autobiography, allegory . . . ? And John Fowles. And Iris Murdoch.

But there is a feel to the American novel that is radically different. We are willing to risk being called "formless" by people whose ideas of form are rigidly limited, and we are wilder, more exploratory, more ambitious, perhaps less easily shamed, less easily discouraged. The intellectual life as such we tend to keep out of our novels, fearing the sort of highly readable but ultimately disappointing cerebral quality of Huxley's work . . . or, on a somewhat lower level, C. P. Snow's.

INTERVIEWER: The English edition of *Wonderland* has a different ending from the American. Why? Do you often rewrite published work?

OATES: I was forced to rewrite the ending of that particular novel because it struck me that the first ending was not the correct one. I have not rewritten any other published work (except of course for short stories, which sometimes get rewritten before inclusion in a book) and don't intend to if I can possibly help it.

INTERVIEWER: You've written novels on highly specialized

fields, such as brain surgery. How do you research such backgrounds?

OATES: A great deal of reading, mainly. Some years ago I developed a few odd symptoms that necessitated my seeing a doctor, and since there was for a time talk of my being sent to a neurologist, I nervously and superstitiously began reading the relevant journals. What I came upon so chilled me that I must have gotten well as a result. . . .

INTERVIEWER: In addition to the novel about medicine, you've written one each on law, politics, religion, spectator sports: Are you consciously filling out a "program" of novels about American life?

OATES: Not really consciously. The great concern with "medicine" really grew out of an experience of some duration that brought me into contact with certain thoughts of mortality: of hospitals, illnesses, doctors, the world of death and dying and our human defenses against such phenomena. (A member of my family to whom I was very close died rather slowly of cancer.) I attempted to deal with my own very inchoate feelings about these matters by dramatizing what I saw to be contemporary responses to "mortality." My effort to wed myself with a fictional character and our synthesis in turn with a larger, almost allegorical condition resulted in a novel that was difficult to write and also, I suspect, difficult to read.

A concern with law seemed to spring naturally out of the thinking many of us were doing in the sixties: What is the relationship between "law" and civilization, what hope has civilization without "law," and yet what hope has civilization *with* law as it has developed in our tradition? More personal matters blended with the larger issues of "crime" and "guilt," so that I felt I was able to transcend a purely private and purely local drama that might have had emotional significance for me, but very little beyond that; quite by accident I found myself writing about a woman conditioned to be unnaturally "passive" in a world of hearty masculine combat—an issue that became topical even as the novel *Do With Me What You Will* was published, and is topical still, to some extent.

The "political" novel, *The Assassins*, grew out of two experiences I had some years ago, at high-level conferences involving politicians, academic specialists, lawyers, and a scattering—no, hardly that—of literary people. (I won't be more specific at the moment.) A certain vertiginous fascination with work which I noted in my own nature I was able to objectify (and, I think, exaggerate) in terms of the various characters' fanaticism involving their own "work"—most obviously in Andrew Petrie's obsession with "transforming the consciousness of America." *The Assassins* is about megalomania and its inevitable consequences, and it seemed necessary that the assassins be involved in politics, given the peculiar conditions of our era.

The new "religious" novel, *Son of the Morning*, is rather painfully autobiographical, in part; but only in part. The religion it explores is not institutional but rather subjective, intensely personal, so as a novel it is perhaps not like the earlier three I have mentioned, or the racing novel, *With Shuddering Fall*. Rather, *Son of the Morning* is a novel that begins with wide ambitions and ends very, very humbly.

INTERVIEWER: Somewhere in print you called *The Assassins* the favorite of your novels. It received very mixed reviews. I've often thought that book was misread. For instance, I think the "martyr" in that novel arranged for his own assassination, true? And that his wife was never really attacked outside the country house; she never left it. Her maiming was all confined within her head.

OATES: What a fine surprise! You read the scene exactly as it was meant to be read. Even well-intentioned reviewers missed the point; so far as I know, only two or three people read Yvonne's scene as I had intended it to be read. Yet the hallucinatory nature of the "dismemberment" scene is explicit. And Andrew Petrie did, of course, arrange for his own assassination, as the novel makes clear in its concluding pages.

The novel has been misread, of course, partly because it's rather long and I think reviewers, who are usually pressed for time, simply treated it in a perfunctory way. I'm not certain that it is my favorite novel. But it is, or was, my most ambitious. It involved a great deal of effort, the collating of passages (and memories) that differ from or contradict one another. One becomes attached to such perverse, maddening ugly ducklings, but I can't really blame reviewers for being impatient with the novel. As my novels grow in complexity they please me more and please the "literary world" hardly at all—a sad situation, but not a paralyzing one.

INTERVIEWER: It's not merely a matter of complexity. One feels that your fiction has become more and more urgent, more subjective and less concerned with the outward details of this world—especially in *Childwold*. Was that novel a deliberate attempt to write a "poetic novel"? Or is it a long poem?

OATES: I don't see that *Childwold* is not concerned with the outward details of the world. In fact, it's made up almost entirely of visual details—of the natural world, of the farm the Bartletts own, and of the small city they gravitate to. But you are right, certainly, in suggesting that it is a "poetic novel." I had wanted to create a prose poem in the form of a novel, or a novel in the form of a prose poem: the exciting thing for me was to deal with the tension that arose between the image-centered structure of poetry and the narrative-centered and linear structure of the interplay of persons that constitutes a novel. In other words, poetry focuses upon the image, the particular thing, or emotion, or feeling, while prose fiction focuses upon motion through time and space. The one impulse is toward stasis, the other toward movement. Between the two impulses there arose a certain tension that made the writing of the novel quite challenging. I suppose it is an experimental work, but I shy away from thinking of my work in those terms: it seems to me there is a certain self-consciousness about anyone who sets himself up as an "experimental" writer. All writing is experimental.

But experimentation for its own sake doesn't much interest me; it seems to belong to the early sixties, when Dadaism was being rediscovered. In a sense we are all post-*Wake* writers and it's Joyce, and only Joyce, who casts a long terrifying shadow. . . . The problem is that virtuoso writing appeals to the intellect and tends to leave one's emotions untouched. When I read aloud to my students the last few pages of *Finnegans Wake*, and come to that glorious, and heartbreaking, final section ("But you're changing, acoolsha, you're changing from me, I can feel"), I think I'm able to communicate the almost overwhelmingly beautiful emotion behind it, and the experience certainly leaves *me* shaken, but it would be foolish to think that the average reader, even the average intelligent reader, would be willing to labor at the *Wake*, through those hundreds of dense pages, in order to attain an emotional and spiritual sense of the work's wholeness, as well as its genius. Joyce's *Ulysses* appeals to me more: that graceful synthesis of the "naturalistic" and the "symbolic" suits my temperament also. . . . I try to write books that can be read in one way by a literal-minded reader, and in quite another way by a reader alert to symbolic abbreviation and parodistic elements. And yet, it's the same book—or nearly. A trompe l'oeil, a work of "as if."

INTERVIEWER: Very little has been made of the humor in your work, the parody. Some of your books, like *Expensive People*, *The Hungry Ghosts*, and parts of *Wonderland*, seem almost Pinteresque in their absurd humor. Is Pinter an influence? Do you consider yourself a comedic writer?

OATES: There's been humor of a sort in my writing from the first; but it's understated, or deadpan. Pinter has never struck me as very funny. Doesn't he really write tragedy?

I liked Ionesco at one time. And Kafka. And Dickens (from whom Kafka learned certain effects, though he uses them, of course, for different ends). I respond to English satire, as I mentioned earlier. Absurdist or "dark" or "black" or whatever: what isn't tragic belongs to the comic spirit. The novel is nourished by both and swallows both up greedily.

INTERVIEWER: What have you learned from Kafka?

OATES: To make a jest of the horror. To take myself less seriously.

INTERVIEWER: John Updike has been accused of a lack of violence in his work. You're often accused of portraying too much. What is the function of violence in your work?

OATES: Given the number of pages I have written, and the "violent" incidents dispersed throughout them, I rather doubt that I am a violent writer in any meaningful sense of the word. Certainly, the violence is minimal in a novel like *them*, which purported to be a naturalistic work set in Detroit in the sixties; real life is much more chaotic.

INTERVIEWER: Which of your books gave you the greatest trouble to write? And which gave the greatest pleasure or pride?

OATES: Both *Wonderland* and *The Assassins* were difficult to write. *Expensive People* was the least difficult. I am personally very fond of *Childwold*, since it represents, in a kind of diffracted way, a complete world made of memory and imagination, a blending together of different times. It always surprises me that other people find that novel admirable because, to me, it seems very private . . . the sort of thing a writer can do only once.

Aside from that, *Do With Me What You Will* gives me a fair amount of pleasure, and of course, I am closest to the novel I finished most recently, *Son of the Morning*. (In general, I think we are always fondest of the books we've just completed, aren't we? For obvious reasons.) But then I think of Jules and Maureen and Loretta of *them* and I wonder if perhaps that isn't my favorite novel, after all.

INTERVIEWER: For whom do you write—yourself, your friends, your "public"? Do you imagine an ideal reader for your work?

OATES: Well, there are certain stories, like those in *The Hungry Ghosts*, which I have written for an academic community and, in some cases, for specific people. But in general the writing writes itself—I mean a character determines his or her "voice" and I must follow along. Had I my own way the first section of *The Assassins* would be much abbreviated. But it was impossible to shut Hugh Petrie up once he got going and, long and painful and unwieldy as his section is, it's nevertheless been shortened. The problem with creating such highly conscious and intuitive characters is that they tend to perceive the contours of the literary landscape in which they dwell and, like Kasch of *Childwold*, try to guide or even to take over the direction of the narrative. Hugh did not want to die, and so his section went on and on, and it isn't an exaggeration to say that I felt real dismay in dealing with him.

Son of the Morning is a first-person narration by a man who is addressing himself throughout to God. Hence the whole novel is a prayer. Hence the ideal reader is, then, God. Everyone else, myself included, is secondary.

INTERVIEWER: Do you consider yourself religious? Do you feel there is a firm religious basis to your work?

OATES: I wish I knew how to answer this. Having completed a novel that is saturated with what Jung calls the God-experience, I find that I know less than ever about myself and my own beliefs. I have beliefs, of course, like everyone—but I don't always believe in them. Faith comes and goes. God diffracts into a bewildering plenitude of elements—the environment, love, friends and family, career, profession, "fate," biochemical harmony or disharmony, whether the sky is slate-gray or a bright mesmerizing blue. These elements then coalesce again into something seemingly unified. But it's a human predilection, isn't it?—our tendency to see, and to wish to see, what we've projected outward upon the universe from our own souls? I hope to continue to write about religious experience, but at the moment I feel quite drained, quite depleted. And as baffled as ever.

INTERVIEWER: You mention Jung. Is Freud also an influence? Laing?

OATES: Freud I have always found rather limited and biased; Jung and Laing I've read only in recent years. As an undergraduate at Syracuse University I discovered Nietzsche and it may be the Nietzschean influence (which is certainly far more provocative than Freud's) that characterizes some of my work. I don't really know, consciously. For me, stories usually begin—or began, since I write so few of them now—out of some magical association between characters and their settings. There are some stories (I won't say which ones) which evolved almost entirely out of their settings, usually rural.

INTERVIEWER: Your earliest stories and novels seem influenced by Faulkner and by Flannery O'Connor. Are these influences you acknowledge? Are there others?

OATES: I've been reading for so many years, and my influences must be so vast—it would be very difficult to answer. An influence I rarely mention is Thoreau, whom I read at a very impressionable age (my early teens), and Henry James, O'Connor and Faulkner certainly, Katherine Anne Porter, and Dostoyevsky. An odd mixture.

INTERVIEWER: The title *Wonderland*, and frequent other allusions in your work, point toward a knowledge of, if not an affinity for, Lewis Carroll. What is the connection, and is it an important one?

OATES: Lewis Carroll's *Alice in Wonderland* and *Through the Looking Glass* were my very first books. Carroll's wonderful blend of illogic and humor and horror and justice has always appealed to me, and I had a marvelous time teaching the books last year in my undergraduate course.

INTERVIEWER: Was there anything you were particularly afraid of as a child?

OATES: Like most children, I was probably afraid of a variety of things. The unknown? The possibility of those queer fortuitous metamorphoses that seem to overtake certain of Carroll's characters? Physical pain? Getting lost? . . . My proclivity for the irreverent and the nonsensical was either inspired by Carroll or confirmed by him. I was always, and continue to be, an essentially mischievous child. This is one of my best-kept secrets.

INTERVIEWER: You began writing at a very early age. Was it encouraged by your family? Was yours a family of artistic ambitions?

OATES: In later years my parents have become "artistic," but when they were younger, and their children were younger, they had no time for anything much except work. I was always encouraged by my parents, my grandmother, and my teachers to be creative. I can't remember when I first began to tell stories—by drawing, it was then—but I must have been very young. It was an instinct I followed quite naturally.

INTERVIEWER: Much of your work is set in the 1930s, a period during which you were merely an infant at best. Why is that decade so important to your work or vision?

OATES: Since I was born in 1938, the decade is of great significance to me. This was the world of my parents, who were young adults at the time, the world I was born into. The thirties seem in an odd way still "living" to me, partly in terms of my parents' and grandparents' memories, and partly in terms of its treatment in books and films. But the twenties are too remote— lost to me entirely! I simply haven't had the imaginative power to get that far back.

I identify very closely with my parents in ways I can't satisfactorily explain. The lives they lived before I was born seem somehow accessible to me. Not directly, of course, but imaginatively. A memory belonging to my mother or father seems almost to "belong" to me. In studying old photographs I am struck sometimes by a sense of my being contemporary with my parents—as if I'd known them when they were, let's say, only teenagers. Is this odd? I wonder. I rather suspect others share in their family's experiences and memories without knowing quite how.

INTERVIEWER: When we were undergraduates together at Syracuse, you already were something of a legend. It was rumored you'd finish a novel, turn it over, and immediately begin writing another on the back side. When both sides were covered, you'd throw it all out, and reach for clean paper. Was it at Syracuse you first became aware you were going to be a writer?

OATES: I began writing in high school, consciously training myself by writing novel after novel and always throwing them out when I completed them. I remember a three-hundred-page book of interrelated stories that must have been modeled on Hemingway's *In Our Time* (I hadn't yet read *Dubliners*) though the subject matter was much more romantic than Hemingway's. I remember a bloated, trifurcated novel that had as its vague model *The Sound and the Fury*. . . . Fortunately, these experiments were thrown away and I haven't remembered them until this moment.

Syracuse was a very exciting place academically and intellectually for me. I doubt that I missed more than half a dozen classes in my four years there, and none of them in English.

INTERVIEWER: I remember you were in a sorority. It is incredible to contemplate you as "a sorority girl."

OATES: My experience in a sorority wasn't disastrous, but merely despairing. (I tried to resign but found out that upon joining I had signed some sort of legal contract.) However, I did make some close friends in the sorority, so the experience wasn't a total loss. I would never do it again, certainly. In fact, it's one of the three or four things in my entire life I would never do again.

INTERVIEWER: Why was life in a Syracuse sorority so despairing? Have you written about it?

OATES: The racial and religious bigotry; the asininity of "secret ceremonies"; the moronic emphasis upon "activities" totally unrelated to—in fact antithetical to—intellectual exploration; the bullying of the presumably weak by the presumably strong; the deliberate pursuit of an attractive "image" for the group as a whole, no matter how cynical the individuals might have been; the aping of the worst American traits—boosterism, God-fearingism, smug ignorance, a craven worship of conformity; the sheer *mess* of the place once one got beyond the down-stairs. . . . I tried to escape in my junior year, but a connection between sororities and the Dean of Women and the university-housing office made escape all but impossible, and it seemed that, in my freshman naïveté, I had actually signed some sort of contract that had "legal" status . . . all of which quite cowed me. I remember a powdered and perfumed alum explaining the so-rority's exclusion of Jews and blacks: "You see, we have confer-ences at the Lake Placid Club, and wouldn't it be a shame if *all* our members couldn't attend. . . . Why, it would be embarrassing for them, wouldn't it?"

I was valedictorian of my class, the class of 1960. I fantasized beginning my address by saying, "I managed to do well academ-ically at Syracuse despite the concerted efforts of my sorority to prevent me. . . ."

I haven't written about it, and never will. It's simply too stupid and trivial a subject. To even *care* about such adolescent nonsense one would have to have the sensitivity of a John O'Hara, who seems to have taken it all seriously.

INTERVIEWER: I recall you won the poetry contest at Syracuse in your senior year. But your books of poetry appeared relatively later than your fiction. Were you always writing poetry?

OATES: No, I really began to write poetry later. The poetry still comes with difficulty, I must admit. Tiny lyric asides, droll wry enigmatic statements: They aren't easy, are they? I'm assembling a book which I think will be my last—of poems, I mean. No one wants to read a novelist's poetry. It's enough—too much, in fact—to deal with the novels. Strangely enough, my fellow poets have been magnanimous indeed in accepting me as a poet. I would not have been surprised had they ignored me, but, in fact, they've been wonderfully supportive and encouraging. Which contradicts the general notion that poets are highly competitive and jealous of one another's accomplishments. . . .

INTERVIEWER: You say no one wants to read a novelist's poetry. What about Robert Penn Warren? John Updike? Erica Jong? I suppose Allen Tate and James Dickey are poets who happened to write novels. . . .

OATES: I suppose I was thinking only of hypothetical reactions to my own poetry. Robert Penn Warren aside, however, there *is* a tendency on the part of critics to want very much to categorize writers. Hence one is either a writer of prose or of poetry. If Lawrence hadn't written those novels he would have been far more readily acclaimed as one of the greatest poets in the language. As it is, however, his poetry has been neglected. (At least until recently.)

INTERVIEWER: *By the North Gate*, your first book, is a collection of short stories, and you continue to publish them. Is the short story your greatest love? Do you hold with the old adage that it is more difficult to write a good story than a novel?

OATES: Brief subjects require brief treatments. There is *nothing* so difficult as a novel, as anyone knows who has attempted one; a short story is bliss to write set beside a novel of even ordinary proportions.

But in recent years I haven't been writing much short fiction. I don't quite know why. All my energies seem to be drawn into longer works. It's probably the case that my period of greatest productivity is behind me, and I'm becoming more interested in focusing upon a single work, usually a novel, and trying to "perfect" it section by section and page by page.

INTERVIEWER: Nevertheless, you've published more short stories, perhaps, than any other serious writer in America today. I remember that when you chose the twenty-one stories to compose

The Wheel of Love, you picked from some ninety which had been in magazines the two years since your previous collection. What will become of the seventy or so stories you didn't include in that collection? Were some added to later collections? Will you ever get back and pick up uncollected work?

OATES: If I'm serious about a story, I preserve it in book form; otherwise I intend it to be forgotten. This is true of course for poems and reviews and essays as well. I went back and selected a number of stories that for thematic reasons were not included in *The Wheel of Love*, and put them into a collection called *The Seduction And Other Stories*. Each of the story collections is organized around a central theme and is meant to be read as a whole—the arrangement of the stories being a rigorous one, not at all haphazard.

INTERVIEWER: You don't drink. Have you tried any consciousness-expanding drugs?

OATES: No. Even tea (because of caffeine) is too strong for me. I must have been born with a rather sensitive constitution.

INTERVIEWER: Earlier you mentioned Hugh Petrie in *The Assassins*. He is but one of many deranged characters in your books. Have you known any genuine madmen?

OATES: Unfortunately, I have been acquainted with a small number of persons who might be considered mentally disturbed. And others, strangers, are sometimes drawn my way; I don't know why.

Last week when I went to the university, I wasn't allowed to teach my large lecture class because, during the night, one of my graduate students had received a telephone call from a very angry, distraught man who announced that he intended to kill me. So I had to spend several hours sequestered away with the head of our department and the head of security at the university and two special investigators from the Windsor City Police. The situation was more embarrassing than disturbing. It's the first time anyone has so explicitly and publicly threatened my life—there have been sly, indirect threats made in the past, which I've known enough not to take seriously.

(The man who called my student is a stranger to us all, not

even a resident of Windsor. I have no idea why he's so angry with me. But does a disturbed person really need a reason . . .?)

INTERVIEWER: How about the less threatening, but nonetheless hurtful, reactions of friends and relatives—any reactions to conscious or unconscious portraits in your work?

OATES: My parents (and I, as a child) appear very briefly in *Wonderland*, glimpsed by the harassed young hero on his way to, or from, Buffalo. Otherwise there are no portraits of family or relatives in my writing. My mother and father both respond (rather touchingly at times) to the setting of my stories and novels, which they recognize. But since there is nothing of a personal nature in the writing, I have not experienced any difficulties along those lines.

INTERVIEWER: Aside from the singular incident at the university, what are the disadvantages of being famous?

OATES: I'm not aware of being famous, especially here in Windsor, where the two major bookstores, Coles', don't even stock my books. The number of people who are "aware" of me, let alone who read my writing, is very small. Consequently I enjoy a certain degree of invisibility and anonymity at the university, which I might not have at an American university—which is one of the reasons I am so much at home here.

INTERVIEWER: Are you aware of any personal limitations?

OATES: Shyness has prevented me from doing many things; also the amount of work and responsibility here at Windsor.

INTERVIEWER: Do you feel you have any conspicuous or secret flaw as a writer?

OATES: My most conspicuous flaw is . . . well, it's so conspicuous that anyone could discern it. And my secret flaw is happily secret.

INTERVIEWER: What are the advantages of being a woman writer?

OATES: Advantages! Too many to enumerate, probably. Since, being a woman, I can't be taken altogether *seriously* by the sort of male critics who rank writers 1, 2, 3 in the public press, I am free, I suppose, to do as I like. I haven't much sense of, or interest in, competition; I can't even grasp what Hemingway and the epigonic Mailer mean by battling it out with the other talent in the ring. A work of art has never, to my knowledge, displaced another work of art. The living are no more in competition with the dead than they are with the living. . . . Being a woman allows me a certain invisibility. Like Ellison's *Invisible Man*. (My long journal, which must be several hundred pages by now, has the title *Invisible Woman*. Because a woman, being so mechanically judged by her appearance, has the advantage of hiding within it—of being absolutely whatever she knows herself to be, in contrast with what others imagine her to be. I feel no connection at all with my physical appearance and have often wondered whether this was a freedom any man—writer or not—might enjoy.)

INTERVIEWER: Do you find it difficult to write from the point of view of the male?

OATES: Absolutely not. I am as sympathetic with any of my male characters as I am with any of my female characters. In many respects I am closest in temperament to certain of my male characters—Nathan Vickery of *Son of the Morning*, for instance—and feel an absolute kinship with them. The Kingdom of God *is* within.

INTERVIEWER: Can you tell the sex of a writer from the prose?

OATES: Never.

INTERVIEWER: What male writers have been especially effective, do you think, in their depiction of women?

OATES: Tolstoy, Lawrence, Shakespeare, Flaubert . . . Very few, really. But then very few women have been effective in their depiction of men.

INTERVIEWER: Do you enjoy writing?

OATES: I do enjoy writing, yes. A great deal. And I feel somewhat at a loss, aimless and foolishly sentimental, and disconnected, when I've finished one work and haven't yet become absorbed in another. All of us who write work out of a conviction that we are participating in some sort of communal activity. Whether my role is writing, or reading and responding, might not be very important. I take seriously Flaubert's statement that we must love one another in our art as the mystics love one another in God. By honoring one another's creation we honor something that deeply connects us all, and goes beyond us.

Of course, writing is only one activity out of a vast number of activities that constitute our lives. It seems to be the one that some of us have concentrated on, as if we were fated for it. Since I have a great deal of faith in the processes and the wisdom of the unconscious, and have learned from experience to take lightly the judgments of the ego and its inevitable doubts, I never find myself constrained to answer such questions. Life is energy, and energy is creativity. And even when we as individuals pass on, the energy is retained in the work of art, locked in it and awaiting release if only someone will take the time and the care to unlock it. . . .

—ROBERT PHILLIPS
1978

Notes on the Contributors

MARION CAPRON (*Interview with Dorothy Parker*) was a member of the editorial staff of *The Paris Review* and worked for the Public Relations Office of Barnard College in New York City.

SHUSHA GUPPY (*Interview with Edna O'Brien*) is the London Editor of *The Paris Review*, and a regular contributor to the *Daily Telegraph, British Vogue*, and other periodicals. *The Blindfold Horse*, an autobiographical work, will be published by Beacon Press in 1989.

DONALD HALL (*Interview with Marianne Moore*) was for nine years Poetry Editor of *The Paris Review*. His most recent work includes *The One Day*, a book-length poem, and a collection of short stories, *The Ideal Bakery* (1987).

ANNE HOLLANDER (*Interview with Lillian Hellman*) designed costumes, painted, and did translation work.

JANNIKA HURWITT (*Interview with Nadine Gordimer*) is a freelance writer. Her work has been published in *The Paris Review*, the *Village Voice, Soho Weekly News*, and *Yankee Magazine*.

BARBARA KEVLES (*Interview with Anne Sexton*) is a charter Contributing Editor to *Working Woman* and a past Contributing Editor to *American Health*, and has written for leading national publications including *The Atlantic, Esquire, New York, The New York Times, Mademoiselle, Glamour, Cosmopolitan, Good Housekeeping, Redbook, Ladies' Home Journal, People, Harper's Bazaar*, and *The Village Voice*. Barbara Kevles authored the Book-of-the-Month Club and Quality Paperback Book Club choice *Basic Magazine Writing* (WDB, '86) and the introduction, "Occupation: Writer," for the 1981 *Writer's Market*. She has taught at New York University/SCE as an Assistant Adjunct Professor of Creative Writing and at The New School (NYC) and held the rank of Adjunct, New York, in Writing and Criticism at Empire State College, S.U.N.Y. She co-edited an essay collection on traditional curricular theories and practices *In Opposition to Core Curriculum* (Greenwood Press, '82).

LINDA KUEHL (*Interviews with Eudora Welty and Joan Didion*), an authority on jazz, published book reviews and interviews in the *New York Times Book Review, Saturday Review* and *Playboy*. She was at work on a biography of Billie Holiday when she died in 1977 at the age of 38.

JOHN PHILLIPS (*Interview with Lillian Hellman*) is a novelist and is an Advisory Editor of *The Paris Review*.

ROBERT PHILLIPS (*Interview with Joyce Carol Oates*) is the author of sixteen books, including a short-story collection and four books of poetry. His most recent works are *Personal Accounts: New and Selected Poems 1966–1986* and the volume *The Letters of Delmore Schwartz*, which he edited. His work has appeared in a variety of publications, including *The New Yorker, The Hudson Review*, and *Partisan Review*. He is a contributing editor of *The Paris Review*, in which his interviews with William Goyen, Phillip Larkin, and Karl Shapiro were published.

DARRYL PINCKNEY (*Interview with Elizabeth Hardwick*) is on the staff of *The New York Review of Books*.

ELIZABETH SIFTON (*Interview with Mary McCarthy*) is the executive vice president and editor at Alfred A. Knopf, Inc.

TOM TEICHOLZ (*Interview with Cynthia Ozick*) is a writer and attorney in New York. His work has appeared in *New York Woman, Channels, The Forward,* and *Interview.* He is currently at work on a book about the John Demjanjuk trial for St. Martin's Press.

BARBARA THOMPSON's (*Interview with Katherine Anne Porter*) short stories have been published in the *Pushcart Prize* anthologies VII and IX, and the *Shenandoah Anthology: From the First 35 Years.* Her interview with Peter Taylor appeared recently in *The Paris Review.*

EUGENE WALTER (*Interview with Isak Dinesen*) has received the Lippincott Prize for his first novel *The Untidy Pilgrims,* an O. Henry citation for his story "Troubador" which appeared in the first issue of *The Paris Review,* a Sewanee-Rockefeller Fellowship for his *Monkey Poems,* and a Prix Guilloux for his translations of French poetry. His new novel, *Adam's Housecat* and his book of stories, *The Byzantine Riddle* will appear shortly, as will a special issue of *Negative Capability* called "The Polyfarious Eugene Walter," containing much of his new work. He is an Advisory Editor of *The Paris Review.*

MARINA WARNER (*Interview with Rebecca West*) is a British journalist, novelist, and biographer. Her most recent work, *Monuments and Maidens,* is a study of the use of the female form in history.

FOR THE BEST IN PAPERBACKS, LOOK FOR THE

In every corner of the world, on every subject under the sun, Penguin represents quality and variety—the very best in publishing today.

For complete information about books available from Penguin—including Pelicans, Puffins, Peregrines, and Penguin Classics—and how to order them, write to us at the appropriate address below. Please note that for copyright reasons the selection of books varies from country to country.

In the United Kingdom: For a complete list of books available from Penguin in the U.K., please write to *Dept E.P., Penguin Books Ltd, Harmondsworth, Middlesex, UB7 0DA.*

In the United States: For a complete list of books available from Penguin in the U.S., please write to *Dept BA, Penguin*, Box 120, Bergenfield, New Jersey 07621-0120.

In Canada: For a complete list of books available from Penguin in Canada, please write to *Penguin Books Ltd, 2801 John Street, Markham, Ontario L3R 1B4.*

In Australia: For a complete list of books available from Penguin in Australia, please write to the *Marketing Department, Penguin Books Ltd, P.O. Box 257, Ringwood, Victoria 3134.*

In New Zealand: For a complete list of books available from Penguin in New Zealand, please write to the *Marketing Department, Penguin Books (NZ) Ltd, Private Bag, Takapuna, Auckland 9.*

In India: For a complete list of books available from Penguin, please write to *Penguin Overseas Ltd, 706 Eros Apartments, 56 Nehru Place, New Delhi, 110019.*

In Holland: For a complete list of books available from Penguin in Holland, please write to *Penguin Books Nederland B.V., Postbus 195, NL-1380AD Weesp, Netherlands.*

In Germany: For a complete list of books available from Penguin, please write to *Penguin Books Ltd, Friedrichstrasse 10-12, D-6000 Frankfurt Main I, Federal Republic of Germany.*

In Spain: For a complete list of books available from Penguin in Spain, please write to *Longman, Penguin España, Calle San Nicolas 15, E-28013 Madrid, Spain.*

In Japan: For a complete list of books available from Penguin in Japan, please write to *Longman Penguin Japan Co Ltd, Yamaguchi Building, 2-12-9 Kanda Jimbocho, Chiyoda-Ku, Tokyo 101, Japan.*

☐ **WRITERS AT WORK**
The *Paris Review* Interviews: Eighth Series
Edited by George Plimpton

These thirteen interviews of Elie Wiesel, John Irving, E. B. White, and translator
Robert Fitzgerald, among others, reveal definitively that all writers are, in fact,
creative writers.

"Long may this splendid series thrive."—*People*
446 pages   ISBN: 0-14-010761-4   **$8.95**

☐ **THE SECRET MUSEUM**
Pornography in Modern Culture
Walter Kendrick

From the secret museums where the obscene frescoes of Pompeii were kept to the
Meese Commission's report, Walter Kendrick drolly explores society's changing
conceptions of pornography.

"Highly illuminating . . . Kendrick writes crisply and amusingly."
—*The New York Times*
288 pages   ISBN: 0-14-010947-1   **$7.95**

☐ **THE FLOWER AND THE LEAF**
A Contemporary Record of American Writing Since 1941
Malcolm Cowley

Since the early 1920s, Malcolm Cowley has been reading, writing, and reflecting
on literature; this collection of his work presents a fascinating portrait of our times
and our literature.

"The creative logic of his connections make him a writer's writer and a reader's
critic."—*Saturday Review*   390 pages   ISBN: 0-14-007733-2   **$7.95**

☐ **THE WAY OF THE STORYTELLER**
Ruth Sawyer

In this unique volume, a great storyteller reveals the secrets of her art—then goes
on to tell eleven of her best stories.

"As invigorating as a wind blowing over the Spring meadows"
—*The New York Times Book Review*
356 pages   ISBN: 0-14-004436-1   **$6.95**

FOR THE BEST IN WOMEN'S STUDIES, LOOK FOR THE

☐ **SEVEN WOMEN**
Portraits from the American Radical Tradition
Judith Nies

Profiling the lives and careers of Harriet Tubman, Mother Jones, Elizabeth Cady Stanton, and four others, Judith Nies demonstrates the remarkable courage of these women and the radical changes they brought about in our society.

"Buy Nies's book and read it aloud faithfully."—*Los Angeles Times*
236 pages   ISBN: 0-14-004792-1   **$6.95**

☐ **WOMAN'S BODY, WOMAN'S RIGHT**
(REVISED EDITION)
A Social History of Birth Control in America
Linda Gordon

Arguing that birth control remains a matter of social and political acceptability rather than of medicine and technology, Linda Gordon traces the history of the controversy with an emphasis on its importance in today's women's movement.

"A major contribution to the history that feminists *must* know if we are not to repeat it"—*Adrienne Rich*
512 pages   ISBN: 0-14-004683-6   **$9.95**

FOR THE BEST IN PAPERBACKS, LOOK FOR THE

☐ **WRITERS AT WORK**
The *Paris Review* Interviews: Third Series
Edited by George Plimpton

Evelyn Waugh, Allen Ginsberg, Arthur Miller, Norman Mailer, and ten others are the subjects of what Alfred Kazin terms, in his introduction, "the biographical art of the profile."

"[The authors] respond not only with candor but also with gratitude for a medium so sympathetic and intelligent."— *Saturday Review*
368 pages   ISBN: 0-14-004542-2   **$9.95**

☐ **WRITERS AT WORK**
The *Paris Review* Interviews: Fourth Series
Edited by George Plimpton

Among the sixteen writers interviewed in this collection are Eudora Welty, W. H. Auden, John Steinbeck, Anne Sexton, and Vladimir Nabokov.

"Enchanting and instructive"—*Washington Post*
460 pages   ISBN: 0-14-004543-0   **$9.95**

☐ **WRITERS AT WORK**
The *Paris Review* Interviews: Fifth Series
Edited by George Plimpton

In these fifteen profiles, such masters as Joyce Carol Oates, John Cheever, Jerzy Kosinski and Archibald MacLeish, in the words of Van Wyck Brooks, "draw portraits of themselves."

"Richly informative and fascinating"—*Christian Science Monitor*
388 pages   ISBN: 0-14-005818-4   **$9.95**

☐ **WRITERS AT WORK**
The *Paris Review* Interviews: Sixth Series
Edited by George Plimpton

In this collection of twelve character studies, the *Paris Review* interviewers talk with, among others, Tennessee Williams, Bernard Malamud, Kurt Vonnegut, Jr., Nadine Gordimer, and James Merrill.

"The very model of the modern literary interview . . . intimate and engaging"
—*Time*   414 pages   ISBN: 0-14-007736-7   **$9.95**

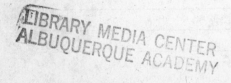